SHAWANGUNKS

TRAIL COMPANION

A Complete Guide to Hiking,

Mountain Biking, Cross-Country

Skiing, and More Only 90 Miles

from New York City

JEFFREY PERLS

BACK COUNTRY

Backcountry Guides
Woodstock, Vermont

Library of Congress Cataloging-in-Publication Data

Perls, Jeffrey, 1954–

    Shawangunks trail companion : a complete guide to hiking, mountain biking, cross-country skiing, and more only 90 miles from New York City / Jeffrey Perls.--

      1st ed. p. cm.

    Includes index.

    ISBN 0-88150-563-3

    1. Outdoor recreation—New York (State)—Shawangunk Mountains—Guidebooks. 2. Trails—New York (State)—Shawangunk Mountain—Guidebooks. 3. Shawangunk Mountains (N.Y.)--Guidebooks. I. Title

GV191.42.N712S527 2003

974.7'3--dc21

                        2003041760

Book design by Black Trout Design

Maps by Mapping Specialists Ltd., Madison, WI; © The Countryman Press

Interior photographs by the author unless otherwise specified

Photograph of Millbrook Mountain on cover and on page 7 © G. Steve Jordan/mohonkimages.com. *Mohonk Image Galleries*: Downtown Gallery, 5 North Front St., New Paltz, NY, 12561 845-256-0323; Water Street Market Gallery, 10 Main St., New Paltz, NY 12561, 845-255-6800

Published by Backcountry Guides

A division of The Countryman Press, P.O. Box 748, Woodstock, Vermont 05091

Distributed by W. W. Norton & Company, 500 Fifth Avenue, New York, NY 10110

Printed in the United States of America

10 9 8 7 6 5 4 3 2 1

SHAWANGUNKS

TRAIL COMPANION

Dedicated to my precious lovely daughter,

Viviana Lee Perls, who accompanied me on many

of the field research trips for this book.

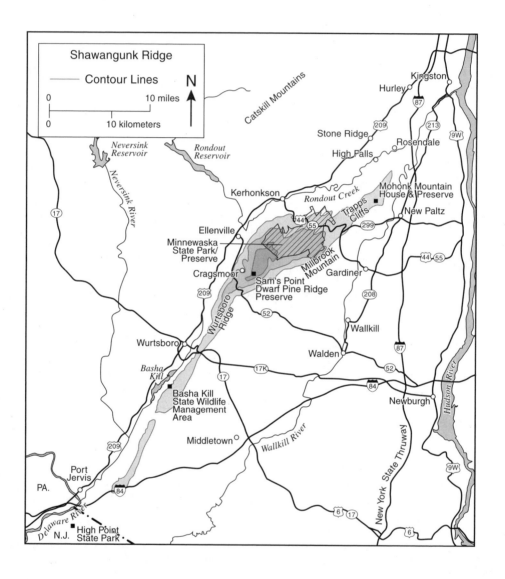

Shawangunk Ridge

Contour Lines

N

0   10 miles

0   10 kilometers

Catskill Mountains

Kingston

Hurley

87

209

213

9W

Stone Ridge

Rosendale

High Falls

Neversink
Reservoir

Rondout
Reservoir

Kerhonkson

Rondout Creek

Mohonk Mountain
House & Preserve

Trapps
Cliffs

New Paltz

17

Neversink River

44

55

299

Ellenville

Minnewaska
State Park/
Preserve

Millbrook
Mountain

44 55

Cragsmoor

Sam's Point
Dwarf Pine Ridge
Preserve

Gardiner

208

209

Wurtsboro Ridge

52

Wallkill

87

Wurtsboro

Walden

52

Basha
Kill

17K

84

17

Newburgh

Basha Kill
State Wildlife
Management
Area

Hudson River

209

Middletown

Wallkill River

Port
Jervis

PA.

84

New York State Thruway

9W

Delaware River

N.J.

High Point
State Park

6   17

6

CONTENTS

ACKNOWLEDGMENTS

A monumental project such as this could not have been completed without the generous help of others. I would like to thank Kermit Hummel, Jennifer Thompson, Ann Kraybill, and the rest of the staff at The Countryman Press for their interest in producing a guidebook on the Shawangunks and their tremendous effort in making it a reality.

I would like to thank Steve Jordan for his magnificent cover photograph.

A number of people and organizations were extremely helpful with the research this project demanded. I wish to thank Gary Hoagland, executive director of the Mohonk Preserve; Hank Alicandri, director of land stewardship and head ranger; Paul Huth, director of research; John Thompson and Bob Larsen of the Dan Smiley Research Center; Tom Cobb, park manager, and Hattie Langsford, park interpreter, of the Minnewaska State Park Preserve; Cara Lee, director of The Nature Conservancy's Shawangunks office; Heidi Wagner, park manager of the Sam's Point Dwarf Pine Ridge Preserve; Bob Anderberg from the Open Space Institute; Pat Vissering, biologist with the New York State Department of Conservation; Eric Roth with the Huguenot Historical Society; Chris Duncan of the Wallkill Valley Land Trust; John Gebhards, executive director of the Orange County land Trust; Keith Labudde, president of the Friends of the Shawangunks; Nina Smiley, director of marketing, and Heidi Jewitt, director of recreation, at the Mohonk Mountain House; Sally Matz, president of the

Cragsmoor Historical Association; Jennifer Dodd, director of education for D&H Canal Museum in High Falls; and Howard Dash with the New York/New Jersey Trail Conference.

I'd also like to thank the following individuals: Marc Fried, Jack Fagan, Al Wegener, Joseph Diamond, Wendy Harris, Maureen Radl, Emily Russell, Evan Pritchard, and Vincent R. Clephas.

In addition I would like to thank the staffs of the Town of Esopus, village of New Paltz, Woodstock, and Ellenville libraries for assisting me in accessing their wonderful archives.

I would also like to bestow a special thanks to the late Pete Howell, with the Adirondack Mountain Club, for introducing me to the Cragsmoor community.

I would also like to thank Mike Sadowy and Marie Caruso with the Mid-Hudson Sierra Club, and Fran Dunwell, for their friendship and guidance.

I wish to thank Jack and Karin Roberts; Seth and Elijah McKee; Douglas Roberts; Damien Kinsella; Kate Folkers; Steve, Olivia, and Isabelle Kasdin; Nancy Ebel; Francesca Tanksley; Fiona Byrne; and Eric and Rowan Oberman for accompanying me on field research trips.

Lastly I would like to express a very special thanks to my beautiful wife, Robin, whose love, patience, kindness, understanding, support, and inspiration helped sustain me through the lengthy and arduous work.

INTRODUCTION

The Shawangunk Ridge (pronounced *Shon-gum*, and often referred to as the Gunks) rises suddenly like a tidal wave above the pastoral scenery of southeastern New York State. With its gleaming white cliffs towering over forested slopes, the mountain ridge presents a striking image to those who encounter it. In terms of size and elevation, it is unremarkable. In fact, it is dwarfed by its northern neighbor, the Catskills Range, which is nearly twice as tall. But in terms of grandeur, scenic vistas, and diversity, it is exceptional: a magnificent wonderland where stark and dramatic features usually associated with western landscapes are found in juxtaposition with the more lush and familiar kind normally found in the Northeast. The combination of turbulent and sublime elements create a landscape of narrative and poetry. There are thousands of acres of nearly undisturbed forestland, plus the largest concentration of sheer cliffs east of the Mississippi. Deep crevices, some which contain ice throughout the year, fields of giant talus boulders, and high plateaus with exposed bare rock and sparse, stunted vegetation are also present. There are glacially formed lakes with beautiful, nearly transparent waters and sparkling clear streams that tumble over rocks, forming pools, cascades, and waterfalls. Home to unique habitats and rare species, the Shawangunk Ridge has been listed by The Nature Conservancy as one of the world's "Last Great Places."

Another defining characteristic is accessibility. Located less than 90 miles from New York City, access has always played a key role in its use by human beings. The first Paleo-Indian hunter-gatherers arrived 12,000 years ago and found the Shawangunk Ridge one of the few places in the region not covered by an immense glacier. Later, Lenape Indians who inhabited and farmed the fertile valleys nearby used the Shawangunk Ridge as a travel route and for hunting game and foraging for edible berries, nuts, and herbs. Early European settlers also hunted and trapped here, later using timber from the forests for fuel and building materials, and the already cleared land to graze cattle and sheep. By the late 19th century, the Shawangunks were only a day's travel from New York City by train and stagecoach. The Smiley brothers built wonderful resort hotels surrounded by an ideal romantic landscape, and created an infrastructure of trails, carriage roads, and summerhouses (rustic gazebos), which made direct experiences with nature possible for wealthy and upper-class urban visitors.

Automobiles and highways have made the Shawangunks even more accessible today, less than two hours from New York City by car or bus. In fact, the mountain ridge has become part of the expanding New York metropolitan area. Today, it's home to commuters and weekend residents and, according to a recent article in the *New York Times*, a chic getaway for those in the fashion and film industries who appreciate the blend of nature and upscale restaurants and shops.

Hiking, mountain bicycling, and cross-country skiing are healthy, rewarding ways to explore the Shawangunk Ridge. These activities can be safely and enjoyably practiced by most people, regardless of physical aptitude or skill level, and they tend to have a lighter impact on the environment than other more intensive uses. I'm pleased to report that the trail and carriage road network built by the Smileys still flourishes and has grown into one of the finest trail systems in the Northeast. This book is a guide to these trails and historic roadways. It describes all of the public access trails located in the Shawangunks as well as the neighboring valleys that flank the ridge. Some are well known. Many are not. In addition, a number of informal routes and trails are purposefully left out to protect these areas from unwanted use and to protect users from wandering into places where they don't belong.

This book is intended as much for the experienced visitor or resident as it is for the newcomer. I thought I was an expert until I started researching this project and found I was actually a novice. Research and exploration introduced me to many wonderful places and experiences I might not have visited otherwise. Keep in mind that the Shawangunk Ridge is an evolving landscape. New trails are created. Others are rerouted or closed. The rules governing access are subject to change. I've tried to include the most up-to-date information possible, but I recommend approaching this material in a tentative manner; when making plans, contact the place where you're going to see if any recent changes have taken place.

In addition to telling you where to go and how to get there, I've also included information about the region's history, natural history, and ecology. I hope this will increase your knowledge of and appreciation for the places you visit, thus enhancing your experience as it did for me. It should also raise your awareness that this is a fragile environment that cannot tolerate misuse and should be treated with the utmost respect. As a guidebook author, I want to encourage responsible use of this resource. With that in mind, happy adventuring.

THE NATURAL LANDSCAPE

PHYSICAL DESCRIPTION

From the New York–New Jersey state line, south of Port Jervis, the Shawangunk Mountain Ridge extends northeast approximately 50 miles. It covers an area of 150,000 acres, with parts located in Orange, Sullivan, and Ulster Counties. The Shawangunks are part of a 245-mile-long mountain ridge that includes the Blue Mountain Ridge in Pennsylvania and the Kittatinnies in New Jersey. More than half the range, the southern part, is a narrow spine, a mile or so in width. However, the northern part widens into a broad, undulating plateau up to 6 miles across. Near Maratanza Lake, it attains its greatest height: 2,289 feet. Just east of Ellenville and west of New Paltz are some of the Shawangunks' most prominent and familiar landmarks: the sky lakes, the Trapps, and Sky Top. As the ridge continues north, it slowly recedes into the surrounding landscape, finally disappearing in a church parking lot just shy of Rondout Creek in Rosendale.

Awosting Falls in Minnewaska State Park Preserve

To the west and northwest is a long, narrow valley. The southern part of this valley is drained by the Neversink River, which empties into the Delaware. The northern part is drained by Rondout Creek, which empties into the Hudson. To the east and southeast is a broad valley drained mostly by the Wallkill River and its tributaries. Both valleys are considered part of the larger Hudson Valley and have average elevations of roughly 250 feet.

One of the chief features of the Shawangunk Ridge is the bedrock—in most places a kind of quartzite conglomerate that is extremely hard and resistant to erosion. In fact, it is one of the hardest rocks known. The Shawangunk conglomerate is also quite brittle. This causes joint cracks to form in the rock as the earth's crust moves or shifts. The softer shale that underlies the conglomerate erodes more quickly, creating open pockets beneath the cliffs. The presence of these open pockets puts added stress on the conglomerate rock above. The cracks that inevitably form may become filled with water, which eventually freezes. As water freezes it expands, thus widening the cracks, creating fissures and crevices in the rock. Sometimes whole huge blocks give way, forming very deep crevices that contain ice year-round and are referred to as ice caves. Ice caves are a fairly unique feature of the Shawangunk Ridge. The largest and most famous are located at Sam's Point Dwarf Pine Ridge Preserve (see chapter 6).

Another key feature of the Shawangunk Ridge are the tall, sheer cliffs, many with dramatic overhanging ledges. At the base of some cliffs are aprons of talus—fields of rock slabs of varying sizes, from tiny pebbles to giant boulders as big as SUVs (some beneath Millbrook Mountain are 40 feet in length). All of these have presumably fallen from the cliffs above. Most of these rockfalls date back thousands of years, but some are of more recent origin.

Prominent on the ridge are broad, elevated plateaus with many barren or nearly barren areas that have little or no soil, plenty of exposed rock, and only sparse vegetation. Again, this is largely due to the conglomerate rock and its resistance to erosion. The slowness of the weathering process means that very little soil created. The glaciers that covered the region thousands of years ago also played a role in scraping away an enormous amount of rock as well as soil from the top of the ridge. In contrast, in areas where softer sedimentary rocks such as shale form the bedrock, soils are thicker and less acidic and thus more favorable for plants.

Another prime feature of the ridge are the five sky lakes: Awosting Lake, Maratanza Lake, Minnewaska Lake, Mohonk Lake, and Mud Pond. Awosting Lake, Minnewaska Lake, and Mud Pond are located in Minnewaska State Park Preserve. Maratanza Lake is located at Sam's Point Dwarf Pine Ridge Preserve, and Mohonk Lake is part of the Mohonk Mountain House property.

In addition to the lakes, a number of picturesque streams drain from the ridge, eventually descending to the neighboring valleys. Some descend gradually to the northeast, including the Peters Kill, Sanders Kill, and Coxing Kill. Others plunge abruptly off the sides of the ridge, like the Verkeerderkill and Palmaghattkill. The portions of streams that flow over conglomerate surfaces tend to have transparent, acidic water; rocky beds often smoothed by the actions of the water; steep narrow ravines; numerous cascades and waterfalls; and occasional deep pools.

The Shawangunk Ridge was created by geologic forces, climate, and natural disturbances such as fire. The cliffs, sky lakes, ice caves, waterfalls, and pitch pine barrens stand as monuments

Bonticou Crag at Mohonk Preserve

to time and the forces of change. Humans also played a huge role shaping the landscape we see today. The impact of humans on the Shawangunk Ridge will be covered partly in this chapter as well as in the next.

GEOLOGIC HISTORY

What we see today in the Shawangunk Ridge are the cumulative effects of hundreds of millions of years of geologic forces, including deposition of sediment, mountain building, and erosion. Landforms, rocks, and soils tell us part of the long story about how the natural physical features we associate with the ridge came to be. The Shawangunks are considered part of the Ridge and Valley Province of the Folded Appalachians. This area stretches from Alabama to Newfoundland and is characterized by long ridges of ancient layered rocks.

The story begins in the early Paleozoic era, during the late Ordovician period, approximately 465 million years ago. What was once the landmass that is today Europe, Africa, and Asia began to push west toward North America. In the area where the Shawangunk Ridge is presently located was a large inland sea called the Iapetus Ocean, bounded on either side by the two landmasses. As the land-masses approached one another, the bottom of the sea was pushed downward, creating a deep trough. Mud slowly accumulated at the bottom of this trough at an average rate of 1 foot every 1,000 years. This mud eventually hardened into dark gray shales more than 10,000 feet thick in places. Today these shale deposits, called the Martinsburg Formation, are characterized by their very thin bedding and rock that is relatively soft and cracks and crumbles easily. Martinsburg shale may be observed in numerous road cuts, in quarries, and as the soft surfacing material for the many old carriage roads throughout the area. Life was probably sparse in the oxygen-poor, highly acidic conditions. However, imprints of bra-chiopods—marine shellfish that once were extremely plentiful, but are uncom-mon today—are sometimes found in the shale layers, as are graptolites, an extinct jellyfishlike animal that floated on the surface of the ocean. The leaf-shaped car-bonized remains of these creatures look like pencil marks on the shale.

Toward the end of the Ordovician period, approximately 450 million years ago, a string of volcanic islands in advance of the Eurasian-African landmass collided with North America. The force of the collision created great pressure, causing the Taconic Mountains to rise in the area that's now the border between New York State and New England. This mountain-building event, which took millions of years, is called the Taconian Orogeny. The Taconic Mountains may have risen as high as 10,000 feet. The rise of this mountain range uplifted and folded the older shale deposits.

For the next 10 to 30 million years, there's a gap in the rock record. In other words, no rocks from that age have been found in the area. It's believed that during this time, the Shawangunk region as well as all of eastern New York State was above sea level. It's also surmised that erosion was taking place as the Taconic Mountains stopped growing and began to weather down. By the middle of the Silurian period, approximately 420 million years ago, sands and gravels washed westward from the eroding mountains were deposited in braided streams. These layers of sand and stream-rounded quartzite pebbles and stones were later buried under younger rocks. Heat and pressure compressed and fused together the pebbles with quartz, a natural cement. The rock hardened and eventually became the Shawangunk conglomerate, a quartz-rich, white-colored sedimentary rock formation. No one knows for sure how thick these beds were, since millions of years of erosion probably removed hundreds of feet of rock. What remains is approximately 500 feet thick in places. The conglomerate sometimes contains lead and zinc ores, which were mined in the 18th and 19th centuries.

You may wonder whether life-forms were present during this time. It's likely that conditions in the region were not favorable to support prolific animal or plant life. The granular deposits were certainly not favorable for their preservation, and the pressure that the rock later endured probably erased all traces. However, an important fossil locale was discovered in a small quarry 0.3 mile west of the village of Otisville. In thin beds of black shale interspersed between thicker layers of the conglomerate, numerous well-preserved fossil eurypterid remains were found. Eurypterids, often called sea scorpions, are an extinct marine arthropod that inhabited shallow inland seas during the Silurian period. They may have been the dominant animal, some reaching up to 7 feet in length. These distinct-looking creatures have been designated the official New York State fossil. More eurypterid remains have been found in New York than anyplace else.

Most eurypterid remains have been found in the central and western parts of the state. Otisville is the easternmost Silurian eurypterid locality in New York. The site is also unique in that most of the remains recovered are of young eurypterids in all stages of development, from larvae up to adults. The area was probably once a sandy tidal flat where shallow, protected water served as a nursery for the young.

Eventually the land began to sink and another shallow sea, southwest of the region, gradually expanded north and east, slowly inundating the land, finally reaching the area of the Shawangunks. For the next 12 to 13 million years, during the late Silurian period, more sediments were deposited in mudflats and shallow-water conditions in an arm of the sea that now covered the entire region. The once high Taconic Mountains had by then completely eroded away. Rocks from this period can be found in the hills and lowlands north of the Shawangunk Ridge and in a narrow band along the west side. They include shales, sandstones, and dolomites (calcium carbonate that's been partially replaced by magnesium carbonate) of the High Falls and Binnewater Formations, and the dark gray dolomites and thinly bedded limestones of the Rondout Formation. The rocks of the Rondout Formation were deposited in conditions of poor circulation and high salinity and are famous as a rich source of natural cement, heavily mined during the 19th century in the vicinity of Rosendale and High Falls. A fine sequence of middle and late Silurian rocks can be observed along Rondout Creek in High Falls.

The presence of shallow seas continued into the Lower Devonian period. These shallow seas had better circulation and lower salinity and supported a wide variety of ancient sea life, including brachiopods, corals, crinoids (sea lilies), pelecypods (ancient clams and mussels), and trilobites, extinct marine arthropods that superficially resemble the horseshoe crab. Abundant fossils of these creatures may be found in the limestones, sandstones, and shale that were deposited. These rocks later eroded to form the floor of the valley west of the Shawangunk Ridge. By the middle of this period, approximately 350 million years ago, another continental collision caused the Acadian Mountains to rise in the east in what's now New England and the Canadian Maritime Provinces. The intense pressure of this mountain-building activity caused the Shawangunk conglomerate and the Martinsburg shale to fold, as well as the younger rocks that had been deposited on top of them. Folds in rock take the form of anticlines (upperward facing) and synclines (downward facing). In the shale, which has been folded many times, the folds are tight and steeply angled. There are many examples of tilted beds of Shawangunk conglomerate, some dramatically so. Examples of anticlines are the ridges on which Minnewaska and Mohonk Lakes are located. A good example of a syncline is Coxing Clove. A series of complete anticlines and synclines can be observed in the northern Shawangunks, but south of Sam's Point to the New Jersey border, only the upward-facing slope of a single anticline forms the narrow spine of the ridge.

As the mountains of the Acadian Orogeny began to weather away, rivers deposited the sediment in large deltas in the area that's now the Catskills Mountains. From the time of the Acadian Orogeny, the Shawangunk region would never again be underwater, and no new rocks would be deposited.

At the beginning of the Permian period (toward the end of the Paleozoic era), approximately 285 million years ago, large-scale disturbances called the Alleghenian Orogeny took place along the eastern half of North America, forming the Appalachian mountain range. What effect these disturbances had on the Shawangunks is largely unknown, although we can surmise that the rock beds of the Shawangunk Ridge were raised and tilted into their present position. In addition to folding and general uplift, faulting (when the rock beds crack and move) also occurred. This activity resulted in the extraordinary high cliff faces we see today.

But the story doesn't end there. For hundreds of millions of years, natural forces such as water, wind, and ice continued to remove the softer rocks deposited on top of the Shawangunk conglomerate. Once these were eliminated, the harder, more resistant conglomerate was exposed—and it, too, slowly began to erode away. In some places, such as the flat shale-based meadow where the Peter's Kill parking area is located, the conglomerate was entirely removed.

Much of what we see on the ridge today has been shaped by glaciation. During the Pleistocene period, approximately 2 million years ago, worldwide temperatures were much colder, and at least four separate ice sheets invaded the region in succession. The last, the Wisconsin Ice Sheet, began about 75,000 years ago, advancing southward at approximately a foot a day. About 21,750 years ago, it reached its farthest extent. During this time, most of eastern North America, including parts of New Jersey and Pennsylvania and all of the Shawangunk Ridge, was covered by a tremendous ice sheet thousands of feet thick. The ice sheets sliced away sections of rock, exposing the dramatic cliff faces, and scooped out the basins that later filled with water to create the sky lakes. The glaciers scraped huge amounts of rock and soil from the top of the ridge.

There is no way of knowing for sure how much rock was removed, but pieces of Shawangunk conglomerate have been found as far away as Long Island.

The glaciers also dragged stones and other smaller debris along their bottoms, scratching, scraping, and polishing open surfaces of bedrock as the glaciers inched their way across. Today, smooth rock surfaces with grooves and scratches called striations are common in areas where bedrock is exposed. Sometimes stones and debris, carried by the glaciers, were left behind. Smaller debris deposited by the glaciers is called glacial till. Larger debris—rocks or boulders transported by the glacier—are known as glacial erratics. Some from the Catskills and other distant places have been found here.

As the climate began to warm again, the ice melted, and the Wisconsin Ice Sheet began a long retreat northward. Some scientists believe that the Shawangunk Ridge was free of ice 2,000 years before the neighboring valleys. According to them, the lingering presence of ice in the neighboring valleys caused frequent freezing and thawing, which pried large masses of rock from cliff faces. These rocks landed on top of the ice sheet, but as the ice melted, they slid downhill, forming huge talus fields beneath cliffs such as Millbrook Mountain.

The postglacial climate was mostly cool and damp. Melted snow and ice filled the lakes, ponds, and wetland areas. Areas free of snow and ice were recolonized by hardy plants like algae, lichens, mosses, and later the herbaceous plants and small shrubs that today inhabit treeless tundra areas of northern Canada and Alaska. A few of these fragile tundra plants survived and can still be seen on the ridge, including a species of mountain sandwort that's also native to Greenland, and the broom crowberry, which is native to Labrador. As the climate continued to warm, plants and animals that had retreated south during the glacial period returned. Eventually coniferous forests of spruce, balsam fir, willows, and birch became prevalent. A relic of these ancient boreal forests is the red spruce that today can be found in Spruce Glen in Minnewaska State Park Preserve. Extinct mastodons and mammoths, woolly members of the elephant family, roamed the neighboring valleys. Remains of caribou and horses, animals now extinct in the region, have also been found.

CLIMATE

Another factor that profoundly affects the type of plants and animals that live on the ridge is climate. The climate of the Shawangunk Ridge and surrounding lowlands may be categorized as temperate, which means the area has well-defined seasons: moderately cold winters and warm, humid summers. At the Mohonk Lake Cooperative Weather Station (NW5), long-term records indicate the average annual temperature is 48 degrees. In January, the average is 25 degrees; in July, it's 70. The lowest recorded temperature was 24 degrees below zero; the highest was 98. Latitude—distance from the poles and the equator—and position of the earth in relation to the sun are two important factors affecting average temperatures. Basically, the farther north you go, the colder average temperatures become. Another major factor affecting climate is elevation. Generally, the higher up you go, the thinner and colder the air gets, a phenomenon that explains the presence of snow on mountaintops long after it has melted in the valleys and lowlands. While the Shawangunk Ridge isn't that high, relatively speaking, a difference of even a few hundred feet in elevation can affect an area's climate and the kinds of animals and plants that live there. Ridgetops and other areas of higher elevation can sometimes support species of animals and plants south of their normal ranges. Areas of dramatic relief such as tall cliffs create a variety of climatic conditions.

The Shawangunk Ridge and neighboring Catskills also act like a barrier, blocking the passage of air, forcing it to rise, which cools it and causes condensation and the formation of clouds and precipitation. Thus the Shawangunk Ridge receives more precipitation than the neighboring valleys. The average annual precipitation is 47 inches, although periods of heavy or little to no precipitation are fairly typical. Annual snowfall varies year to year from 16 inches to more than 123 inches. Other factors may affect climates in very small areas. For example, open areas of higher elevation, such as ridgetops that have more sun and wind exposure, tend to experience more extreme maximum and minimum temperatures and lower relative humidity. Meanwhile, a sheltered ravine may experience damper, more even conditions with fewer fluctuations. Deep crevices that receive little sunlight and contain ice that persists well into summer may act as natural iceboxes, cooling the immediate vicinity.

In addition, human beings also have an impact on climate. One area of concern is the phenomenon of global warming. According to some theories, large-scale emissions of greenhouse gases such as carbon dioxide and ozone (primarily from the burning of fossil fuels) are slowly causing the earth's atmosphere to warm. This warming effect may eventually induce parts of the polar ice caps to melt, which could, in turn, cause the oceans to rise, flooding large sections of coastal plain. More extreme weather and the greater frequency of catastrophic storms are also sometimes blamed on global warming, as are drought conditions known to have a negative impact on chestnut oaks. When these changes might take place and whether they are already happening are subjects of hot debate, but such questions have raised awareness of the effects of human activity on climate and other natural phenomena.

SEASONS

Weather conditions can be quite variable from day to day, but in a temperate climate, overall variation depends primarily on season. Seasonal changes in conditions present a huge challenge for plant and animal life, which must adapt to the changes in order to survive. The effects of these changes are among the most fascinating aspects of this region's natural history and ecology. Springtime brings warmer temperatures and melting snow, which turns tiny streams into torrents, prompting waterfalls to gush and spray, and sometimes causes creeks and rivers like the Neversink, Rondout, and Wallkill to overflow their banks, flooding lowlands and depositing fresh new soil. Spring also brings green buds to the area's forests. Many species of trees flower before their leaves emerge in order to take full advantage of wind for pollination and seed dispersal. Spring is prime time for most woodland flowers, which bloom while sunlight can still penetrate to the forest floor.

Spring is when many animals emerge from months of wintertime hibernation. It is also the time of the great bird migration north. The Shawangunk Ridge is part of a major bird migration route. The presence of abundant insect food, less competition, fewer predators, and longer days are some of the theoretical reasons scientists believe birds migrate up from the Tropics. In March, amphibians migrate to swamps and vernal pools—shallow, temporary bodies of water, the result of spring rains and snowmelt—to mate and reproduce. Newly hatched juveniles (including frog and toad larvae, or tadpoles) live in the water and breathe through gills, switching to lungs when they become adults. Vernal pools usually dry up during summer, so the young must reach maturity before this happens or perish.

In early summer, plants in old fields begin producing brilliant displays of mostly nonnative flowers. This takes place when insect activity is at its peak and competition for pollinators is greatest. Often the biggest and brightest flowers will attract the most insects. The insects help spread the pollen, which enables these plants to reproduce. In early to mid-June forests feature the wonderful spectacle of mountain laurel bursting with large clusters of white and pink blossoms. By midsummer, blueberries and huckleberries appear on the ridgetops. Birds and other creatures consume the ripe fruits, then later defecate the indigestible seeds, spreading them around.

Fall brings shorter days and cooler, drier weather. The most spectacular event in fall is, of course, the annual change of colors, which peaks in mid October. This occurs at roughly the same time every year regardless of climatic conditions. Anticipating shorter days and less sunlight and to conserve moisture for winter, plants cease photosynthesizing and transpiring water through their leaves. Trees and shrubs withdraw their sap reserves into the trunk and roots. No longer a part of the plant's life activity, the leaves slowly die. Shedding leaves also helps protect the plant from damage from snow and ice: If snow or ice sticks to leaves, the resulting accumulation can weigh down the branches, causing them to break or sometimes even toppling a whole tree. The dramatic color changes are the result of the deterioration of green chlorophyll pigments, a process that reveals the other pigments present in the leaf. These also decay, and the leaf eventually turns brown and falls off. Temperature seems to have little effect on this process.

In fall, many species of birds migrate south, as do monarch butterflies, to avoid the rigors and reduced food supply of winter. The shortening day length appears to be the signal that it's time to migrate. Migration over hundreds or thousands of miles is extremely arduous and requires tremendous energy and effort. To prepare for the journey or for the hardships of winter, many birds will fatten up on a diet of fruit. The availability of insect prey declines in fall at the same time that many trees are bearing fruit. Mammals also build up their fat reserves in fall.

Winter days in the Gunks are short, and temperatures are generally cold. The ground may be covered by snow. These conditions pose a serious challenge for plants and animals. Despite the apparent calm of the winter landscape, however, life processes go on. Snow can provide some insulation from exposure to cold air, thus protecting the animals that live and forage beneath it. Birds have high body temperatures and thick coverings of feathers, which provide effective insulation from the cold. Many also roost in tree cavities protected from windchill. In the worst weather they become inactive, conserving precious energy to stay warm. Birds use shivering as a primary means of maintaining their body temperature. Mammals are afforded similar protection by their coats of fur and layers of fat, enabling some, like deer, squirrels, and snowshoe hares, to remain active throughout the winter. Normally solitary mice and voles will huddle in nests with other individuals to share precious body warmth, curling their bodies to help protect extremities. Deer depend heavily on their stored fat reserves to get them through the winter. They will also reduce their level of activity, bedding at night in the protection of hemlock groves and during the day in the open to absorb the heat of sunlight.

Many plants and animals of the region have evolved dormancy mechanisms to adapt to the winter's cold and extreme fluctuations in conditions. Because such animals as reptiles, amphibians, and insects are endothermic and cannot generate their own heat, they must hibernate in winter. Hibernating animals decrease their respiration rates, heart rates, and body temperature, expending as little energy as possible. For all intents and purposes, they exist in a state of suspended animation. Still, hibernating animals can tolerate only so much cold.

Many depend on the protection of an insulating cover of snow, or the safety of deep burrows or den sites. Frogs, turtles, and some aquatic insects will bury themselves in the mud at the bottom of ponds. Certain mammals, like chipmunks and bears, will become temporarily inactive and survive on stored body fat. They do not decrease their body temperature much and are easily aroused, becoming active again during warm spells.

During winter, most moisture is frozen and unavailable for life-sustaining activity. This presents another serious challenge for plants and animals to face. Though broad-leafed hardwoods shed their leaves prior to the onset of winter, evergreens have reduced water loss because their tiny needles have a hard waxy coating and a relatively small surface area. They also shed enough snow so that it doesn't build up and weigh down the branches. Evergreen needles are filled with a resin that protects them from freezing. The leaves of evergreen shrubs such as rhododendron and mountain laurel curl up and point downward, reducing their surface areas, thus conserving moisture. Mosses and lichens become active during intermittent warm spells, drawing moisture from the thin layers of soil that have temporarily thawed.

FIRE AND OTHER NATURAL DISTURBANCES

Changes that take place as a result of geology or climate tend to be quite slow and subtle. These are rarely observable during the course of a human lifetime. However, natural disturbances such as forest fires, floods, droughts, storms, wind, insects, and disease can produce changes that are swift and dramatic. A heavy snowfall or ice storm, for example, can break branches and even topple trees, creating openings in the canopy. Hemlocks, because of their brittle wood and shallow root systems, tend to be especially susceptible. Human beings, psychologically dependent on sameness and continuity, tend to overreact emotionally to these disturbances, but they are an entirely normal and necessary part of the ecosystem's life. Openings in the forest allow sunlight to reach a forest floor that was previously shaded, creating an excellent opportunity for species of plants that require sunlight for growth. They also provide an opportunity for colonizing species to gain a foothold in the forest. Seeds of colonizing plants may sit dormant in the soil for years, waiting for conditions suitable for germination. Thus, when growth opportunities arise as the result of disturbances, colonizing species have to be fast growing and fast reproducing to take advantage.

Forest fires are a natural phenomenon that have always played a significant role in the ecology of the Shawangunk Ridge. Of course, humans accidentally or intentionally also set fires, a subject that will be dealt with more in the next chapter. Pitch pine, scrub oak, chestnut oak, blueberries, and other plant species that inhabit dry, exposed places are specially adapted to survive fires. These species have either thick bark that protects them from fire, or deep root systems that survive and resprout after fires occur. Vegetation fires in the Shawangunks are most often ground fires that burn leaf litter, dead twigs and branches, dry herbaceous plants, small live trees, and larger fire-sensitive species. Removal of fire-sensitive competition permits the fire-resistant trees and shrubs to survive and thrive. Thus natural communities dominated by fire-resistant species remain common throughout the Shawangunks.

NATURAL COMMUNITIES

The great variety of landforms present in the Shawangunks creates a number of diverse habitats called natural communities. A *community* is defined as an assemblage of interacting plant and animal populations that share a common environment. A vegetation survey of the northern Shawangunk area by The Nature Conservancy, published in 1996, identified 36 natural communities and eight human-made ones. Please note that most natural communities have seen major human impacts. Some biological communities are rare, and some are unique to the Shawangunk Ridge. Some support a number of rare plants and animals. Always keep in mind that these habitats are often quite fragile and highly sensitive to human interference.

Sky Lakes and Ponds

The five sky lakes—Minnewaska, Awosting, Mohonk, Maratanza, and Mud Pond—are the most prominent and unique aquatic environment of the Shawangunk Ridge. Because of their relatively small drainage basins, the conglomerate rock that surrounds them, and the infertility of the ridgetop soils, the waters of these sky lakes have very low nutrient levels, high acidity, and extreme clarity. While the clear waters of the lakes are quite stunning, their use by aquatic organisms is limited, and to the casual visitor they may appear largely devoid of life. However, life does exist. The pure waters permit penetration of light all the way to the bottom of the deepest lakes. Therefore, bladderworts and green algae carpets the bottoms. Water lobelia, a vascular plant with a stem and blue flowers, can be found in shallow waters; sphagnum moss, a type of peat moss, is seen along shorelines. There are no fish in any of the lakes except Mohonk (its partly shale bottom and resulting lower acidity might explain how fish can survive there). The absence of fish predators in Minnewaska Lake permits organisms that tolerate high acidity, such as two-lined salamanders and certain insect larvae, to thrive. This is the only known instance of two-lined salamanders using lakes for breeding.

Ponds are bodies of water that tend to be smaller than lakes and certainly more shallow. Ponds and lakes have a natural cycle whereby they gradually accumulate leaves and other organic matter, slowly filling, at which point they may turn into marshes or swamps, and eventually into dry land. Rhododendron Swamp, Spruce Glen, and Sleepy Hollow are swamps that were once small glacial ponds. Many ponds, especially those located in the valleys, are human made.

Streams and Rivers

Clear streams located in areas of conglomerate bedrock, like the lakes, tend to have high acidity and be nutrient poor, making them unsuitable habitats for the majority of aquatic organisms. No fish are found in the upper reaches of any of the streams whose origin is in conglomerate bedrock areas. Certain small plants and animals are known to thrive in the cool, nutrient-poor waters of the Shawangunks. One example is diatoms—microscopic algae that can be found in areas of standing water. The absence of fish predators also creates ideal conditions for certain insect larvae to thrive.

Larger streams and rivers are associated with the neighboring valleys. Examples include the Wallkill, Rondout, Shawangunk Kill, and Neversink. These support a variety of plant and animal life-forms and are often bordered by areas of wetlands and floodplain forests, which are temporarily submerged during certain high-water times of the year like spring.

Wetlands

There are numerous wetlands both on the Shawangunk Ridge itself and in the neighboring valleys. A number of large wetland areas are associated with the valleys' larger streams and rivers and their tributaries. The largest of these is the Basha Kill, located in the watershed of the Neversink. It is the largest area of wetlands in eastern New York State.

The region has different types of wetlands. Bogs are small wetlands that occur in depressions in the nonporous conglomerate bedrock, often scooped out by glaciers thousands of years ago. These areas tend to feature high acidity, have no inlets or outlets, and depend on rainwater for moisture. Rainwater, unlike groundwater, tends to be low in nutrients. The lack of nutrients and high acidity create an environment inhospitable to most plants. Bogs are usually populated with sphagnum moss, which can soak up many times its weight in moisture, live without soil, and grow upon the remains of dead moss. As decomposing moss accumulates over thousands of years, it is compressed into peat. Due to lack of competition, certain unusual or rare plants—including those that are carnivorous—often thrive in bogs.

Marshes are areas of shallow water and thick muck, a good portion of which is decomposing plant material. Thin grasslike vegetation such as bulrushes, rice cut-grass, sedges, cattails, and common reeds (phragmites) inhabit marshes, as does the nonnative purple loosestrife. Numerous animal species including muskrats, beavers, and otters inhabit marshlands, along with a number of fish species, insects, amphibians, reptiles, and birds. (Indeed, the region's best area for bird-watching is around the Basha Kill wetlands.) Swamps are similar to marshes, but are populated by shrubs such as swamp azalea, spicebush, winterberry, black chokeberry, arrowwood, and mountain laurel, and herbs such as ferns, sedges, and jewelweed. A wide variety of trees like red maple, black gum or tupelo, swamp white oak, American elm, pin oak, and black ash can also be found in swamps. Marshes and swamps that are isolated from larger streams, lakes, or rivers tend to slowly fill with leaves and other organic matter, eventually turning into dry land.

In upland forest areas, a number of small (less than 1 acre), isolated (no inlets nor outlets), shallow (less than 3 feet deep) bodies of water are temporary, deriving moisture from spring rains and snowmelt. These tend to dry by mid- to late summer and are referred to as vernal pools. Vernal pools are an important habitat for certain vascular plants, and also serve as breeding areas for amphibians including the wood frog and the rare spotted and Jefferson salamanders.

Wetlands, especially those in the valleys, may have been formed or significantly altered by human development such as road or residential construction, which sometimes blocks drainage and creates wetlands. Nonnative and/or pest species like purple loosestrife and common reeds (phragmites) are often prevalent in these areas.

Forests

Forests are the dominant natural community of the Shawangunk Ridge. The moist climate and soils on slopes and in the valleys are favorable for the development of forests. More than 60 percent of the northern Shawangunk study area is forestland. Since practically all forests on the ridge and neighboring lowlands were cleared at one time or another, the age of particular sections may vary. Older mature areas of forest are characterized by trees with wide trunks. These areas have clearly discernible layers. The crowns of the tallest trees form the canopy. Trees compete for sunlight; during summer, when trees have their full complement of leaves, the canopy of a mature forest captures up to 99 percent of the sun, leaving the area below dark and shaded. In many cases, there is an understory of shade-tolerant smaller or immature trees. Below the understory is the shrub layer, and beneath that a layer of ferns and herbaceous plants. Fallen trees provide shelter and habitat for slugs (shell-less gastropods), spiders and other arachnids, salamanders, toads, and snakes. Mosses become established on rotting logs. Atop the soil itself is a litter of decomposing leaves and wood. The litter provides habitat for bacteria and fungi, which consume up to

90 percent of the decaying matter on the forest floor. They, in turn, provide food for insects, roundworms, and protozoans. The forest floor is also home to numerous arachnids, such as spiders, daddy longlegs, millepedes, and centipedes. Isopods (also called pill bugs, these are a form of land crustacean), beetles, ants, termites, other insects, and earthworms are other inhabitants of the forest floor.

The current suppression of forest fires and prohibitions against clear-cutting in protected areas have resulted in mature forests becoming more widespread on the ridge. However, old-growth (never-cut) forests are rare in the eastern United States and practically nonexistent in the Shawangunks. Scattered trees more than 300 years old have been found in a number of remote or difficult-to-access locations such as talus slopes and pitch pine barrens. Most of these are pitch pines, white pines, chestnut oaks, or hemlocks, and most are small and stunted. Crustose and foliose lichen communities found on Shawangunk rocks are truly old growth. Some are estimated to be 400 to 500 years old.

Much of the forest in the region is young: second-, third-, or fourth-generation growth. In most cases, young forests have a higher diversity of trees of varying heights; forest layers are therefore not as discernible. The trunks of younger trees usually average less than a foot in diameter. In areas that were once fields, there may also be large old trees—usually white oaks or red oaks that once provided shade and thus were spared the ax. Young forests tend to feature thick layers of shrubs and herbaceous plants, because sunlight is more plentiful and the litter layer tends to be thinner than it is in mature forests.

Sited on the edge of the Atlantic Coastal Plain, the Shawangunk Ridge and surrounding lowlands lie in the transition zone between the mixed deciduous forests of the South and northern hardwood forests. Both northern- and southern-ranging species are found in the chestnut oak forest—by far the most common type of woodland community in the Shawangunks, covering approximately 30,000 acres and probably the largest continuous chestnut oak forest in New York State. The dominant trees in this forest are the chestnut oak and red oak. Chestnut oak leaves superficially resemble those of the once common American chestnut and are oval in shape. Red oak leaves are angular with many points. Other trees in this type of forest include red maple, gray birch, and white oak. Oaks tend to be fire resistant. They also recover quickly from cutting, sprouting from stumps and even burned logs. Oak seedlings can survive with little sunlight. Oaks produce nuts called acorns, which serve as a food source for deer, turkeys, chipmunks, mice, and squirrels. By burying acorns and sometimes forgetting where, squirrels play a primary role as dispersal agents for these trees. Chestnut oaks are vulnerable to a combination of gypsy moth consumption and drought (chestnut oaks are the preferred target of gypsy moths, a nonnative species accidentally released in Massachusetts around the turn of the 20th century), and deer grazing on acorns and seedlings. The absence of former predators like the wolf and mountain lion, the return of forests, as well as the large number of abandoned farms and new developments where old fields and clearings with edges provide an ideal source of food and shelter, has resulted in a dramatic upsurge in the region's deer population.

White oak and American chestnut once shared dominance with chestnut oak on the upper elevations of the ridge. The white oaks, however, were prized for the dense and durable quality of their wood, and most were removed in the 18th and 19th centuries by selective cutting. In 1904, a shipment of Asian chestnut trees to the Bronx Zoo was found to be carrying the fungus *Cryphonectria parasitica*. The fungus quickly spread; by 1913, it had reached the Shawangunk Ridge, wiping out the entire population of mature chestnut trees within 10 years. However, some chestnut crowns still survive and sprout young trees, which can form an important part of the forest understory in places. These young trees always succumb to the blight before reaching maturity. Mountain laurel, blueberry, and huckleberry, members of the heath family, are common shrubs in chestnut oak forests. Mountain laurel thrives in soils that are highly acidic. Pennsylvania sedge, wild sarsparilla, wintergreen, and pincushion moss are characteristic ground-layer species.

The second most common forest type is Appalachian oak-hickory forest. The dominant trees are red oak, white oak, and black oak. Pignut and shagbark hickories (also fire-resistant, nut-producing trees), American elm, white ash, and red maple can also be found. Flowering dogwood is a typical understory tree. Shadbush, witch hazel, and hop hornbeam are common tall shrubs. A typical low shrub is the maple-leaved viburnum. Speedwell, tufted sedge, and hog peanut are common ground cover.

Less common, but fairly prevalent are forest habitats dominated by northern hardwoods. These are the northernmost ranging of the deciduous forests. Beech, red maple, sugar maple, yellow birch, and black birch are the dominant trees; white ash, white pine, and oaks are also common in some areas. On land that was previously cleared for farming, sugar maple is often the dominant tree and in some places is dominant in the canopy, understory, and shrub layer. Shrubs such as witch hazel, striped maple, hop hornbeam, and Japanese barberry are found in these northern hardwood forests. Typical herbs include cutgrass, Christmas fern, hay-scented fern, jack-in-the-pulpit, Canada mayflower, partridgeberry, and club mosses.

Along streams such as the Palmaghatt Kill, Peter's Kill, and Coxing Kill are forests dominated by hemlock, though white pine, sugar maple, red maple, yellow birch, black birch, and black cherry may also occur. The dark shade of hemlocks and their extensive root systems make it difficult for other types of trees to establish themselves nearby. (Common tall shrubs in these areas include witch hazel, rhododendron, and mountain laurel. Due to deep shade and high acidity in the soil, the ground layer is usually sparsely populated.) Hemlock seedlings can tolerate very deep shade. They grow slowly and have been known to survive for hundreds of years, though they're very sensitive to wind and fire. Another threat is the woolly adelgid, a tiny, aphid-like insect that first arrived from Japan 20 years ago. Woolly adelgid form a white woolly mass on the base of hemlock needles and slowly suck juice from the tree until it dies. Today three quarters of the hemlocks on the ridge are infested.

Forest Succession

Land once cleared by natural causes such as fire or by humans for cultivation, pasture, timber, or even for aesthetic reasons, if left alone, will over a period of decades return to forest through a process called succession. Some old fields in the Mohonk Preserve are purposefully maintained by infrequent mowing in order to maintain the historic legacy and promote diversity.

Many of the first plants to populate old fields are broad-leafed herbs such as ragweeds, asters, and goldenrods, as well as grasses. Nonnative species tend to thrive in these conditions. Some of the herbs are annuals, which complete their entire life cycle in a single season, sprouting in spring, growing to maturity, flowering by late summer, and dropping seeds in fall. Since reproduction is essential, annuals often have bright colorful flowers to attract insect pollinators.

Annuals can tolerate conditions of strong direct sunlight. However, they do not compete well with biennials and perennials, plants whose life cycles are longer. Grasses and herbs are followed by vines and brambles like Virginia creeper, wild grapes, bittersweet, blackberries, and poison ivy. Some vines, such as cow vetch and bindweed, utilize the stalks of taller upright plants. Lacking their own strong supporting trunks, vines need fewer nutrients and mineral resources, and most of their energy is devoted to leaf production and rapid growth. Vines and brambles are succeeded by shrubs like hybrid honeysuckle, multiflora rose, shadbush, sumac (a relative of poison ivy), and blackberries.

Shrubs are followed by small fast-growing, sun-loving "pioneer" trees like aspen, black cherry, red cedar, black locust, red maple, white ash, and gray birch. Red cedars, members of the pine family, depend on birds to eat their seeds and defecate them, thus dispersing them. Other pioneer trees depend on wind for seed dispersal. As the trees grow larger and produce more shade, only shade-tolerant seedlings such as oaks, hickories, birches, and maples can survive. These eventually replace the species that require sunlight to reproduce. The process of succession rarely follows a precise course. All sorts of new disturbances, both natural and human made, can alter the pattern.

It is in the early stages of succession that species diversity is greatest, and many of the herbs and shrubs are an ideal food source for deer and other animals. Insects like the cecropia moth, monarch butterfly, and bumblebee are attracted to the colorful flowers that decorate old fields. Other inhabitants include cicadas, spiders, ants, and grasshoppers. The American toad, box turtle, and eastern garter snake also are found here, along with numerous small mammals like mice, voles, and rabbits. Red and gray foxes, striped skunks, woodchucks, coyotes, and deer comprise some of the larger animals that inhabit old fields. Twenty-five of the species of birds that nest in the Shawangunks nest exclusively in old fields. These include bobolinks, eastern meadowlarks, savannah vespers, song and field sparrows, and American goldfinches. Wild turkeys and ruffed grouse are also frequent inhabitants of old fields. American kestrels, northern harriers, and red-tailed hawks find old fields ideal grounds for hunting small mammals.

Transition areas between forests and old fields include species from both habitats, and thus may support a greater diversity of species than either one. Milk snakes, black racers, box turtles, deer, foxes, woodchucks, and rabbits are regularly found in these areas.

Fissures and Crevices

Deep fissures and crevices in the conglomerate rock are cool, sunless environments. Some of the deepest ones even contain ice year-round. The cooling caused by the ice creates environments distinct from others found on the ridge. Northern and alpine plants (vascular plants, mosses, and lichens) such as mountain club moss, creeping snowberry, and goldthread have been found in the vicinity of ice caves. These plants are either very rare or absent in the rest of the Hudson Valley. In addition, certain small mammals like the star-nosed mole, brown bat, hoary bat, and the endangered Indiana bat have been reported from Shawangunk fissures.

Cliff Faces and Talus Slopes

Vertical cliff faces are quite prevalent in the Shawangunks. Lack of soil and the difficulties of attaching to sheer surfaces pose an extreme challenge for plants and animals in these types of environments. Therefore, vegetation is often sparse. Ledges, some of them extremely narrow, may permit the accumulation of soil and the growth of trees such as hemlock, shrubs like mountain laurel, and herbs. Species of lichens and bryophytes may be found attached directly to rock surfaces. Common ravens and peregrine falcons are known to nest on cliff faces.

Talus slopes also are usually lacking in soil and pose similar attachment problems for plants as cliffs. In some places, the absence of trees can create a harsh environment of little shade and too-intense sunlight. Some talus slopes are also unstable, and the frequent shifting of blocks prevents the growth of larger vegetation that requires a more settled base. Deep, moist crevices between the rocks may receive little or no sunlight.

Plants that inhabit these environments include a number of species of lichens, mosses, rock tripes (which resemble small scorched pancakes), ferns, herbs, and woody plants like white pine and hemlock. Some white pines found on talus slopes are known to be more than 300 years old. Talus slopes also shelter many animals, including millipedes, spiders, beetles, black snakes, copperheads, five-lined skinks (a lizard), raccoons, and porcupines.

Exposed Ridgetop Environments

As mentioned previously, glaciers scraped much soil and rock off the ridgetops and rocky summits of the Shawangunk Ridge thousands of years ago. The conglomerate, because it weathers very slowly, creates little new soil; thus areas along the ridgetop remain bare, or nearly devoid of soil and vegetation. Without soil or plants to absorb it, rainwater tends to run off. Soils in these areas occur in cracks in the rock, or shallow depressions. Where soils do exist, they are generally thin, finely textured, dry, nutrient deficient, and acidic, and thus relatively poor for plant growth. Usually they are composed of glacial till (a mix

Bare rock and pitch pine at Minnewaska State Park Preserve

of rock fragments) and organic matter (dead leaves and the like) dropped by plants or blown in. These are harsh environments with a lot of sun and wind exposure. Fires are also common and may burn off vegetation and soil, reexposing the mineral soil and bedrock. Conglomerate surfaces tend to reflect a lot of sunlight and heat because of their whiteness. Plants and animals that can tolerate poor conditions—but not competition from other organisms—may thrive in these challenging places. Small shrubs like blueberry and chokeberry and small patches of scrub oak and pitch pine exist in pockets where soil gathers. Lichens and mosses may be found directly on exposed bedrock.

Forests, where they do exist, tend to be stunted. Pitch pines, at most 20 to 30 feet high, are the dominant trees in these environments, called pitch pine barrens. Pitch pine, which is generally a southern-ranging tree, is common in ridgetop environments in the Shawangunks. These trees grow very slowly. Their tough, thick bark makes them extremely resistant to fire. Fires help eliminate competition from fire-sensitive species. Vegetation in these forests tend to be sparser, and trees are usually widely spaced apart among areas of dense vegetation as well as exposed slabs of bedrock. Besides pitch pine, chestnut oak, white birch, gray birch, white pine, and sassafras also occur. Shrubs include mountain laurel and scrub oak that can tolerate the high acidity of the soil. Blueberries, huckleberries, sheep laurel, and wintergreen are common on the forest floor.

The most interesting and unique examples of ridgetop habitats on the Shawangunk Ridge are the pitch pine plains, where dwarf pitch pines averaging less than 5 feet tall are the dominant trees. These areas of diminutive pitch pines are referred to as dwarf pine ridge communities. There are approximately 4,000 acres of pitch pine barrens and pine plains in the Shawangunks; they're located primarily in the Sam's Point Dwarf Pine Ridge Preserve and adjacent areas of Minnewaska State Park Preserve. A dwarf pitch pine community on elevated bedrock of this size is reputed to be unique in the world. The New York Natural Heritage Program, a cooperative effort of the New York State Department of Environmental Conservation (DEC) and The Nature Conservancy, has listed the Shawangunk pitch pine barrens and pine plains as globally significant. These areas' uniqueness and significance weren't always fully appreciated, as evidenced by a 1977 evaluation report for the federal government stating that the "general watershed area outside of the Ice Caves has no special ecological value." Other pitch pine barrens are located in sandy coastal plains and glacial outwash plains. The most famous such area is, of course, the New Jersey Pine Barrens.

RARE AND ENDANGERED PLANT SPECIES

The Shawankgunks host at least 23 species of plants known to be rare. Probably the best known are the fernlike mountain spleenwort, the triffid rush, and the small broom crowberry, a relic of glacial times that is normally found at scattered localities along the Atlantic Coastal Plain north to Labrador. Its surprising occurrence on the Shawangunk Ridge represents its only known habitat in New York State. The rhodora, considered rare in New York State, is a member of the heath family and a cousin of the mountain laurel. It's found in the pitch pine area around Maratanza Lake. Swedish shield lichens, Iceland moss, and reindeer moss are rare nonvascular plants found in the Shawangunks.

FAUNA

Fauna species diversity may be low in certain areas of the Shawangunks due to unfavorable conditions—lack of soil, harsh conditions, and so forth—but overall it is very high because of the presence of numerous diverse habitats and the combination of both northern- and southern-ranging species. The following information is applicable to the northern Shawangunks between the Rondout and Wallkill Rivers and Route 52 in the south.

There are 19 species of amphibians, including frogs, toads, and salamanders. Of them, the Jefferson salamander, spotted salamander, spring salamander, and the southern leopard frog are state-designated species of special concern.

There are 18 species of reptiles. The colorful five-lined skink is the region's only lizard. It inhabits talus slopes and rugged cliff areas. The northern Shawangunks probably represent its most northerly range limit. Skinks enjoy sunning on open rocks and feed on insects.

Eleven species of snakes are found in the area. Black rat and northern black racers are among the more common. The two are very similar in appearance and easily confused. The black racer has smoother scales and feeds on a greater variety of prey, including small mammals, amphibians, and even other snakes. It's reputed to be the area's fastest snake, especially on rough terrain. The black rat snake is thinner and longer; it's the longest snake in the United States, sometimes up to 6 feet. Unlike the racer, it is an expert tree climber and can scale the rough bark of vertical trees. It can often be seen hanging from limbs very high up.

There are two species of poisonous snakes in the region. Both are pit vipers, with diamond-shaped heads and an ability to sense heat that makes them more effective when striking warm-blooded prey. Northern copperheads are 3 to 4 feet long and common throughout the Northeast. Their shyness, protective coloration (similar to dead leaves), and tendency to hide in talus and stone walls mean that casual visitors are unlikely to see one. They feed exclusively on small mammals. They're often confused with the eastern milk snake, a harmless species of similar size and brown markings.

The timber rattlesnake is the region's other poisonous snake. It has been listed as a Threatened Species in New York. It requires rocky areas such as talus slopes for winter den sites. The population of rattlesnakes has suffered from habitat loss and also deliberate killing and collecting by humans. They are most vulnerable when they gather in large numbers near their den sites just before and after winter. Like the copperhead, they feed on small mammals.

There are five species of native turtles. The colorful eastern painted turtle is common in ponds and other permanent wetlands. The snapping turtle is amazingly adaptive. It inhabits all types of wetlands in both highland and lowland areas and feeds on a wide assortment of fish, amphibians, small mammals, and vegetation. The box turtle is entirely terrestrial and primarily herbivorous. It is well adapted for defense since its dome-shaped shell closes completely. The wood turtle is an inhabitant of forests and wetlands. The spotted turtle is exclusively a wetland turtle. Both are uncommon in the Hudson Valley and are state-listed Species of Special Concern.

At least 219 species of birds have been reported in the northern Shawangunks; 110 are known to breed in the region. Birds occur in virtually all habitats and are likely the most common creatures you will see. Many birds, especially small ones or those that frequent forest canopies, may be difficult to spot. If you can discern their different calls, you may have more success spotting them.

There are nine species of hawks known from the Shawangunk Ridge. One of the most common is the red-tailed hawk, which has a distinctive, fan-shaped orange-colored tail. It is often seen circling high above fields searching for small mammal prey, which it spots with its keen eyesight. Red-shouldered and Cooper's hawks—both Species of Special Concern that have been in decline throughout the Hudson Valley, probably due to pesticides and habitat loss—have begun making a comeback in the Shawangunks. The Shawangunks are among the southernmost locations where goshawks are known to nest. Another rare hawk occasionally found in the Shawangunks is the northern harrier.

The peregrine falcon is a state-designated Endangered Species. It feeds primarily on other birds that it strikes from the air. Peregrines can dive at speeds of up to 180 miles per hour, the world's fastest-known creature. Up until 1956, peregrines nested on the Shawangunk cliffs. Use of DDT, a cheap and powerful pesticide, caused the raptors to disappear from southeastern New York State and decline throughout the United States. Insects sprayed with the DDT were consumed by birds, which in turn were eaten by peregrines. The DDT reduced the birds' calcium uptake, which resulted in eggs laid with thinner shells. Because these shells were easily crushed, the number of surviving peregrine chicks plummeted. After the threat became known, DDT was banned in 1971.

As part of a program to reintroduce the peregrine, juvenile birds raised in captivity were released in 1977 from Sky Top. Ironically, some of the peregrines migrated to New York City, where they built nests on tall bridges and skyscrapers and fed on the abundant pigeon population. By 1998, a single nesting pair was reported in the Shawangunks, the first in 42 years. In 1999, the first fledgling was reported from the Shawangunk nest; another was spotted the following year. This nest is carefully monitored and studied. Peregrines are extremely sensitive to visual disturbances above their nesting sites and roosting ledges. It is therefore vital that all human activity be restricted in areas where peregrines are known to nest.

Among the more striking birds you might observe are vultures. Circling high above the ridge or the neighboring lowlands, they're almost a trademark for the region. Adult turkey vultures have a distinct reddish-colored head that is devoid of feathers, along with a wingspan of up to 6 feet. They launch themselves from cliffs and glide at high altitudes using thermal currents. Vultures feed exclusively on carrion. They have the keenest sense of smell of all birds, which enables them to locate a carcass miles away. Primarily in fall and to a lesser degree in spring, large numbers of hawks and other raptors use the updrafts and tailwinds that occur along the ridges of the Appalachian Chain, including the Shawangunks, as a major migration route. These enable the birds to soar long distances while expending less energy. There are a number of sites atop the cliffs where people can observe these raptors as they drift by.

Woodpeckers are heard more than they're seen. They use their strong claws to hang on to bark while their long chisel-like bills drill holes in the trunks of trees in search of ants and other insects. The crow-sized pileated woodpecker is the largest of the seven species, but the sparrow-sized downy woodpecker is the most common. Crows are probably more abundant these days than ever before. The prevalence of roadkill along the highways provides a rich food source for these carrion consumers. Their larger, less common relative the raven makes its nests of twigs on ledges of cliffs and is highly sensitive to human presence. Ruffed grouse, wild turkeys, and bobolinks are among the birds that nest on the ground. Some will actively defend their nests and even act as decoys to ward off predators. Once extirpated from the area, wild turkeys are now quite plentiful thanks largely to the return of mature forests. Ruffed grouse will shock the unwary hiker when their rapidly beating wings suddenly explode into flight. They depend on open areas, young forests, and the vegetation that borders fields. Therefore, the return of mature forests has not been so favorable to them. Chickadees and nuthatches are year-round residents, commonly seen in winter. Other common birds in the Shawangunks include flycatchers, wrens, wood thrushes, vireos, the blue jay, swallows, the northern oriole, finches, the cedar waxwing, the brilliant scarlet tanager and northern cardinal, 12 species of sparrows, and 30 species of wood warblers.

There are 41 species of mammals reported from the northern Shawangunks. The most commonly observed are those that are diurnal, active in the daytime. These include squirrels, chipmunks, and deer. The fissures and crevices of the Shawangunk Ridge make ideal habitats for a number of bat species, including some rare and endangered ones like the Indiana bat, a federally listed Endangered Species that hibernates in caves and mines, and the eastern pipistrelle and hoary bat, both of which are considered regionally rare. Bats feed primarily on insects that they locate with radar. They are best observed just after sunset.

The forest floor is often alive at night with the scurrying of small mammals such as mice, voles, moles, and shrews. The long-tailed shrew is a regionally rare species ranging from New Brunswick, Canada, to Georgia. It is found almost exclusively on talus slopes. The Allegheny woodrat was a common inhabitant of caves and talus slopes at Mohonk between 1930 and 1967, but the species hasn't been reported there since 1980.

The coyote, a native of the West, has migrated eastward and was first reported in the Shawangunks in 1980. They are now quite prevalent and feed primarily on small mammals, carrion, and occasionally fawns.

The fisher is a medium-sized member of the weasel family, valued for its fur and as a natural predator of porcupines. Once extirpated from southeastern New York, it was reintroduced to the Shawangunks and Catskills in the late 1970s by the state DEC from specimens collected in the Adirondacks. Since then, the population has become established.

While they are more abundant in the neighboring Catskills, sightings of bobcats are not uncommon despite the fact they are primarily nocturnal. The numbers of black bears also seem to be on the rise. Black bears were once considered transient visitors on the ridge, but in the last two to three years, they have become year-round residents. They may be migrating here because the mature forests of the ridge now offer a plentiful supply of the vegetation that is their primary food, especially blueberries.

THE HISTORICAL LANDSCAPE

W hile much of the Shawangunk Ridge appears pristine and natural, what we are really seeing is a delicate balance of natural and human forces. The truth is, no area of the Shawangunks hasn't been affected by humans. Human impact on the ridge started out relatively minor, because early human inhabitants and visitors were small in number and their economies, technologies, and culture demanded little from the environment. The level of human impact has grown over time, especially since the arrival of European settlers. Today, humans play a huge role in shaping the physical and biological landscape of the Shawangunk Ridge. To study the ridge is to learn about these forces and changes over time.

NATIVE LAND

For thousands of years before the arrival of the first European colonists, the Shawangunk Ridge and surrounding lowlands were home to Native peoples. Unlike their counterparts in other regions of the Americas, the indigenous peoples of this region did not build monuments or permanent dwellings. They did, however, alter the landscape with their hunting and agriculture, though these impacts seem relatively small compared to those of later European settlers. Study of the area's prehistoric peoples presents a challenge for archaeologists. The Native inhabitants of the region left no written record, they rarely dwelled in one site for long periods, and many of their important objects, such as clothing, don't preserve well. Widespread development—agricultural, commercial, and residential—has destroyed many potential archaeological sites, and amateur collecting has damaged or ruined a host of others. Therefore, much of the legacy of these early inhabitants has been lost.

Most impact by Native Americans took place in the valleys that border the Shawangunk Ridge. These were sites for habitation and cultivation as well as hunting and gathering. Excavations in the New Paltz area by James Burggraf in the 1950s revealed projectile points, scrapers, fishing sinkers, and other tools, along with pottery and food storage pits. More recent yearly excavations (1998 to the present) on Huguenot Street in New Paltz by Professor Joseph Diamond and students from SUNY New Paltz uncovered a ceremonial dog burial, pottery, food remains, carved stone pieces, and a ceramic face. The discovery of a range of artifacts at the above sites of different ages and cultures shows that they were used repeatedly over a span of thousands of years.

Use of the Shawangunk Ridge by Native Americans was primarily restricted to hunting, gathering, and travel. In 1918–19, Max Schrabisch, an amateur who helped pioneer prehistoric archaeology in the northeastern United States, surveyed two large tracts of land on the ridge itself and identified at least 35 rockshelter sites as well as a number of open-air sites. A rockshelter was a temporary seasonal dwelling that made use of overhanging rock ledges to provide shelter from the elements. When draped with animal skins and heated with campfires, these overhangs were a highly effective means of protection. Such overhangs are plentiful in the northern Shawangunks. Rockshelters were used by individuals as well as large extended families. They range in size from 18 to 300 square feet. Shelter sites had to be easily accessible and close to water sources.

The Mohonk Rock Shelter was first reported by Schrabisch. It was excavated in 1931 by Dan Smiley with the help of Boy Scouts. In 1982–83, Leonard Eisenberg, with the help of archaeology students from SUNY New Paltz, conducted a major excavation that yielded 1,024 stone tools, 130 potsherds, innumerable pieces of debris, and evidence of four fire pits. These artifacts cover all major periods of human habitation, including ones as early as 8,200 BCE and possibly 11,500 BCE. The shelter was a campsite for up to six or eight individuals who hunted in the vicinity and butchered game. From the types of tools present, we can guess they also processed nonedible animal material: bone, antler, hides, and sinew. It's also likely they crafted tools at the site.

Archaeologists have divided the span of pre-European Native habitation into three basic periods: the Paleo-Indian stage, the Archaic stage, and the Woodland stage.

Paleo-Indian Stage

As far as we know, the Native peoples of the region were descendants of emigrants from Asia who crossed the Bering Strait on a temporary land bridge more than 20,000 years ago. They arrived in the region probably as the Wisconsin Ice Sheet retreated, between 12,000 and 11,000 years ago. The Shawangunk Ridge was a likely route of migration northward from the Appalachians. It may have been free of ice 2,000 years before the neighboring valleys. Once the glacier melted and retreated, it left much of the neighboring valleys submerged beneath meltwater and the land, which would have been treeless tundra, wet and marshy. Thus Paleo-Indian artifacts are normally restricted to higher ground.

Paleo-Indians were nomads who traveled in bands of 20 to 75 individuals in pursuit of large migratory game—primarily caribou and possibly mammoths and mastodons. Depending on the season, they ranged widely, covering areas of up to 1,000 square miles. The locations of Paleo-Indian sites suggest that they preferred open areas with high animal populations. These ancient hunters may have used clifftop vantage points on the ridge for spotting herds in the lowlands below.

Paleo-Indian hunters used large "fluted," pressure-flaked spearheads known as Clovis points, similar to ones used throughout North America at the time. Evidence elsewhere indicates that they already could use fire for warmth and cooking, and they fashioned clothing made of skins to protect themselves from the harsh, cold climate. They probably lived in simple shelters made of willow branches draped with animal skins and moss. In addition to hunting, Paleo-Indians likely gathered berries and other plant foods, which made up a significant part of their diet. Evidence of their presence is sparse. By 8000 BCE, Paleo-Indians had vacated the area, probably because of climatic changes and the departure or extinction of their principal food sources.

Archaic Stage

This stage lasted from 8000 to 1300 BCE, at a time when deciduous forests slowly replaced the postglacial tundra and boreal forests of Paleo-Indian times, and the climate and conditions became similar to those of the present. Archaic peoples had not yet developed the use of pottery or agriculture; they were primarily forest dwellers who were skillful at exploiting the resources of their habitat. They were hunters and gatherers and fished the rivers and streams in the lowlands using nets and spears. Unlike their Paleo-Indian predecessors, they did not need to wander such great distances. They used sophisticated tools, made jewelry of copper and bone, could grind and polish stones, and felled trees, shaping the wood into useful objects. Canoes fashioned from hollowed-out logs were an important means of transport. Their chief weapon was the atlatl, a 2-foot-long flat piece of wood used as a spear thrower. Acorns, which were pounded into a coarse flour, made up a significant part of Natives' diet.

By the late Archaic stage, they were using light dwellings constructed of bark and saplings. During the warmer months, Archaic peoples settled in the lowlands near larger water bodies to fish and hunt waterfowl. The onset of winter led to a general dispersal of the population into smaller bands, probably based on family groupings. They spent the winter deep in the forest or in the mountains, living in temporary camps such as rockshelters and hunting bigger game such as deer and bear.

Evidence of early and early-middle Archaic presence in the region is sparse. However, the recent discovery of 55 Neville age projectile points from the Mohonk Rock Shelter (see above), dating back roughly to 6,000 to 8,000 BCE, is by far the largest such find in New York State and provides strong evidence of a much larger presence than previously thought during this period.

Woodland Stage

The period from 1300 BCE until the arrival of the first Europeans is referred to as the Woodland stage. During the beginning of this stage, often referred to as the Transitional Period, stone pots were introduced into the Northeast, later to be replaced by ceramic ones. As time passed, styles of pottery and decoration became more ornate and varied. Other technological developments during this period include the use of the bow and arrow. Later in this stage, agriculture was developed; by 1300 to 1400, it had become widespread in the region. Produce from agriculture provided a larger and more stable food source than was available to Natives who had previously relied solely on hunting, fishing, and gathering. This encouraged an overall increase in the Native population in the area and more stable settlements.

NATIVE LIFE AT THE TIME OF
THE FIRST EUROPEAN EXPLORERS

What we know about Native Americans during this period is largely the product of observations by the European explorers and colonists, as well as archaeological investigations. At this time, the Wallkill and Rondout Valleys were inhabited by Native Americans of the Delaware or Lenape, a loose confederation of many tribes located between the Hudson and Susquehanna Rivers that shared a common language (Algonquin) and culture. The Lenape who lived in the area of New York between the Delaware and Hudson are referred to as the Munsee (people of the stony country); they spoke their own distinct variation of Algonquin. The Munsee consisted of several tribes. Tribes included a number of clans, based on matrilineal descent. They were led by sachems, leaders responsible for promoting the welfare of the tribe and maintaining friendly relationships and alliances with other tribes. For the most part, tribes acted independently of one another, although at times the sachem would convene a general council to make collective decisions and sometimes form cooperative alliances. The Minisink tribe inhabited the Upper Delaware, including the area around Port Jervis. The four northernmost Munsee tribes are often collectively referred to as the Esopus. They included the Warwarsinks, who inhabited the area in the Rondout Valley that's now the town of Wawarsing (Ellenville); the Mamekotings, who lived in what's now the town of Mamakating in Sullivan County (Wurtsboro); and the Warrenawonkongs, who lived in the area along the Hudson from Newburgh north to Saugerties.

The Esopus primarily inhabited the valleys that bordered the northern Shawangunk Ridge. Areas in close proximity to floodplains along rivers and streams such as the Wallkill were preferred. Seasonal flooding deposited fresh soil in these areas, helping maintain their fertility. These lands were also better drained and more easily worked. Agricultural produce made up a large portion of the Esopus Natives' diet. Most of agricultural work was probably performed by women, who cultivated the fields for an assortment of corn, beans, squash, and tobacco. Crops were mixed to help preserve the fertility of the soil, inhibit weed growth, reduce maintenance, sustain the soil's moisture, and produce higher yields. Food was often stored in pits.

Fields were cleared by burning: Fire obviously reduces the need for labor in cutting and clearing a forest, and it also releases minerals in the soil, which act as fertilizers and decrease acidity. In addition to agriculture, the Esopus fished the area's larger streams, even traveling as far as the Hudson to catch sturgeon and other fish. They also practiced hunting and gathering within a large territorial radius that included the Shawangunk Ridge. A variety of herbs, nuts such as chestnuts and various acorns, berries (extremely plentiful on the ridge), and tubers, as well as medicinal plants, were obtained. Native Americans would hunt and eat just about any animal they could get, including waterfowl, deer, elk, opossums, squirrels, rabbits, and turtles. Muskrats, otters, and beavers were trapped.

When game was scarce in the valleys, Native men would go on extended trips up the ridge. In wintertime, hunters would pursue larger game, following tracks in the snow. Bears, which were a rich source of meat and fat and especially vulnerable during the wintertime hibernation period, would be favored game at this time of the year. Well-established trails across the Shawangunks connected tribes to their brethren in valleys on either side of the ridge as well as to lands favored for hunting or gathering. The sparser vegetation and absence of rivers and large streams on the ridge also provided an easier route for those traveling between the Appalachian Mountains in the south and the Hudson Valley in the north—hence the name *Shawangunk*, which in Algonquin translates to "near and high place where you go south."

Before the Europeans arrived, the Esopus lived in seasonal settlements—smaller residences located on the floodplains amid neighboring crop fields, easily evacuated in the event of high water—and larger longhouse residences on higher ground, up to 107 feet long and 30 feet wide, which could house up to 30 or 40 individuals. These were probably winter residences for extended families. Evidence shows that these large residences were partitioned for nuclear families. There may have been five or six of these residences in a typical community spread out within a 10-acre area with a total population of 150 to 200. These shelters were constructed from a frame of bent hickory poles covered with tree bark.

Village sites were frequently abandoned due to a depletion of local resources such as firewood and game. Shelters were constructed so they could be dismantled quickly, easily moved, and reassembled. Similarly, tools, weapons, and supplies had to be light and easily transportable. Moving allowed old village sites to replenish themselves, permitting future exploitation. The Native Americans had no concept of landownership, but each family had rights to certain lands for hunting.

The Native inhabitants practiced a subsistence lifestyle, producing only enough for immediate needs and to guarantee survival. Their transience discouraged the accumulation of personal possessions. In this class society, status was communicated through clothing decorated with shell ornaments, porcupine quills, feather mantles, and copper jewelry. These were usually acquired through trade with other clans and tribes. Trade held a special significance for Native Americans, who used it as a primary means of communication and exposure to the world outside their immediate community. Trade also dispersed knowledge of technological innovations. Canoe travel on the Wallkill River, which extends south into New Jersey, was an important trade and communication link with Lenape tribes in that region.

Native Americans were very aware of their dependence on the land and nature for what they needed—an awareness that was reflected in their beliefs and spiritual practices. For them, there was little separation between the activities of daily living and the rituals of the spirit. They saw themselves as an integral part of the natural world. Fishing, farming, and hunting were, in part, spiritual enterprises. The size of the harvest or the bounty of the hunt was seen to be as much a reflection of their relationship to the higher powers as it was a measure of skill or effort. According to Robert C. Kraft, the Lenape believed that each object in nature contained a spirit (manetu). These spirits/objects were treated with respect since some were capable of causing great mischief and evil, especially when slighted or offended. Each hunter had a moral obligation to kill no more than was absolutely necessary for meat and skins, and to release the spirit of the slaughtered animal so that it might return to the spirit world and be reborn again at some future date. No important journey, no special project commenced without consulting the spirits first. Dancing, singing, and the sacrifice of meat or tobacco were used to curry favor or allay malevolent effects. Ceremonies in late fall gave thanks for a good harvest and bring fortune to hunters.

EXPLORATION AND SETTLEMENT

In 1609, the English navigator Henry Hudson, sailing for the Dutch East India Company, explored the region along the great river named for him and claimed the territory for the Netherlands. The Dutch named their colony New Netherland and settled outposts along the river, trading with the Native Americans primarily for furs, which were very much in demand back in Europe. The Natives obtained copper pots, steel knives, and other tools, cloth, and alcohol. Wampum—long strands of shell beads—were an important status symbol and especially desired. The Dutch obtained wampum from Native tribes that lived along the coast, which they then used to barter pelts. In 1652, a group of European settlers established a small farming community called Esopus (now the city of Kingston). Trade and exposure to European culture ultimately proved destructive to the Native Americans, and to the Esopus tribe in particular. Trade fostered a growing dependence on European trade goods. It also introduced European diseases such as smallpox, which decimated the Native population, and alcohol abuse. During this period, the Esopus moved from more dispersed settlements into tightly clustered villages of 10 or more dwellings. These were protected by rows of sharpened timbers, called palisades, a style of fortification the Natives probably copied from the Dutch. The spread of Dutch settlement led to conflicts with the Esopus who lived nearby.

In 1659, these tensions erupted in violence in which both European settlers and Natives were killed. For protection from Native attacks, Esopus was fortified and renamed Wiltwyck (wild wood). In 1663, the Esopus Natives attacked Wiltwyck and the neighboring satellite community of Nieuw Dorp (New Town), killing a number of settlers and taking many of the women and children hostage. In order to rescue hostages and avenge the massacre, the Dutch militia counter attacked and on July 27 destroyed a recently vacated Native American fortress near Kerhonkson, also burning crop fields and demolishing food storage pits. On September 5, the Dutch militia destroyed another partially fortified Esopus village on the Shawangunk Kill, near the present-day community of Gardiner, killing warriors as well as women and children. Twenty-three of the hostages were rescued. Mohawk Natives were enlisted by the Dutch, and their combined brutal efforts led to the eventual defeat of the Esopus tribes. Following theses defeats and later capitulation, the Esopus dispersed into smaller settlements in or near the mountains, away from the Europeans. They ended up selling most of their land and relocating farther west with their Minisink brethren in the valley of the Delaware, and later to the Upper Susquehanna. Those who remained saw their numbers dwindle due to disease, alcoholism, and loss of land for hunting and planting, which destroyed their livelihood. However, parties of Esopus Natives continued to travel from their new refuges to their old lands to hunt and trade.

During the hostilities, Louis Dubois, a French Huguenot, took part in efforts to rescue his wife and other hostages. Pursuing the Esopus captors and their hostages took them through the valley of the Wallkill River with its rich alluvial plains. After rescuing the hostages, Dubois, accompanied by 11 of his Huguenot associates, returned and in 1677 purchased a 39,683-acre plot from the Esopus Natives, called the Paltz Patent. (A patent is a very large plot of land.) The patent covered the area between what's now Mohonk and the Hudson River.

In 1664, the British had seized the colony from the Dutch and renamed it New York. Following the signing of the Paltz Patent, Dubois and his Huguenot associates settled there. The Huguenots were French Protestants who suffered persecution and warfare in their largely Catholic home country. Establishing their own community separate from the Dutch, the Huguenots hoped to maintain their distinct culture, language, and religion. The population of Dutch New Netherland, and later the English colony of New York, was quite diverse and included many such refugee groups.

Once established, the new settlers built sturdy homes of stone in the style of the early Dutch pioneers. There are many such homes throughout the Hudson Valley—especially in Ulster County, where more than 300 still stand. These homes took months to build. Stone was plentiful locally. Stone walls were warmer in winter and cooler in summer and were considered both more fire resistant and more impervious to Native American attack. The permanence of these dwellings helped tie families to the land. They became storehouses of family histories. The homes had steeply sloping roofs that could effectively shed snow in winter. Glass was imported, so windows were usually tiny. Ceilings were low to conserve precious heat, and large timbers were fashioned into beams to support attic floors that were utilized for storage of grain and as slave or servant quarters. The stone residences were surrounded by numerous wooden structures: barns, corncribs, sheds, and animal pens.

The primary crop was wheat. During the 18th century, the Hudson Valley was the primary wheat-growing region in the Western Hemisphere, and much of it was exported to other colonies dependent on nonedible cash crops. Gristmills were constructed on many of the area's streams to grind the grain for flour. Another important crop was flax for spinning thread. Settlers also planted fruit trees imported from their homelands as well as grass seed, since native varieties were poor for grazing and haying. Clearing land, planting crops, and building homes and other structures gave settlers a sense that they possessed the land. The settlers also brought in cattle, sheep, and swine as additional sources of food and other necessities. Large predators such as bears, mountain lions, and wolves that threatened humans and livestock were killed whenever possible.

Because there was so much land to clear and farm and only so many Dutch or Huguenots to do the work, many families owned slaves to help with the labor. Slave ownership was widespread in the region. During the 18th century, 15 percent of the population of Ulster County consisted of slaves. Unlike the South, where large plantations with hundreds of slaves were often the rule, in this region most families owned relatively small homesteads and just a few slaves, although some of the Huguenot settlers owned six or seven, and one landowner in Marbletown owned eight. These slaves usually lived in the same household with the owners, though usually in the attic or basement, and worked beside them in the fields and/or performed the more onerous household duties. It's assumed they were usually better fed and treated than their southern counterparts. Still, physical and sexual abuse and forced cohabitation for procreation were fairly common practices even among those with more enlightened owners. Slaves were considered property on the same level as farm animals. Slaves in the region were generally isolated from other slaves and thus never able to participate in the kind of shared slave culture that was a part of the South. Also, slave families were often broken up because owners could not afford too many slaves. Sojourner Truth (1797–1883) was born a slave in Rifton on the Wallkill. Her last owner mistreated her, and in 1826 she escaped. The following year, slavery was outlawed in New York State, though it continued to be practiced in the area until 1848. In 1828, with the help of Quakers, Truth won the freedom of her son, whom her master had sold illegally. She went on to become a famous evangelist and abolitionist, traveled widely, and was acquainted with William Lloyd Garrison and Abraham Lincoln.

CLEARING THE FOREST

To the early European settlers, the Shawangunk region appeared to be a vast wilderness of endless untapped resources. As newcomers moved into the region, they initially settled in small cluster communities such as New Paltz and practiced a cooperative form of agriculture on nearby lands already cleared by the Native Americans. Living in relatively close quarters provided protection from the threat of Native raids, as well as social opportunities and a community life. As population grew due to a high birthrate (according to the 1703 New Paltz census, half the population was under 16) and the arrival of new settlers, more land was needed, and so many acquired farmsteads away from the core settlements.

Clearing played a huge role in the evolution of the visual landscape. It was regarded as the first step in the process of "improvement." Initially, only enough land was cleared to raise food for the settler's family; for most new settlers, the goal was self-sufficiency. As population expanded, however, merchants and artisans in nearby communities became markets for surplus food and timber. The area's new arrivals needed food supplies to survive until they could become established. Selling or bartering these products became an important source of income for farmers, who expanded their fields to make more money. Once prosperous, the desire for more material comforts and status symbols prompted farmers to raise more crops and expand their fields even farther. The use of horses or oxen for plowing and pulling carts, as well as the introduction of technological improvements, permitted the cultivation of larger fields and more forest clearing. Many of the new settlers also grazed livestock, which required that more tracts of forestland be cleared. Often livestock, especially swine, were allowed to graze neighboring forest areas, foraging for chestnuts, acorns, roots, and shoots (collectively known as mast).

Clearing the forest with an ax required time and tremendous effort. Many settlers hired neighboring farmers or itinerant laborers to help clear the land. Cut timber was set aside for fuel, for building material, or for sale. Indeed, without such cut timber to heat settlers' homes, especially in winter, the area would have been uninhabitable. Sometimes excess timber was burned on the ground and the ashes used as a nutrient for the soil.

Trees weren't the only things that needed to be cleared from the land. Most fields in the area were covered with stones. Removing them was extremely arduous work. Sometimes they were left in piles, but more often they were stacked in fences 3 to 4 feet high topped with one or two split rails. These were used to separate fields and keep foraging livestock from damaging cultivated areas. Many stone fences survive today in areas that have since returned to forest.

Not all of the forest in the neighboring valleys was cleared. Remnants left on steeper slopes, on rockier and less fertile ground, and in the farther reaches of the settlers' property, called woodlots, were used for grazing, as a barrier from cold winds and the sun's heat, and as a source of timber.

At first, timber was plentiful in the region and very much in demand for fuel and as a building material. Rural industries such as blacksmith shops, tanneries, and ironworks also provided a big market for surplus timber. Processing timber was one of the primary commercial activites in the region. In fact, it was one of the leading industries in America through the 18th and much of the 19th centuries. Sawmills were an indispensable accompaniment to frontier settlement. Most were small, part-time, seasonal operations (wood cuts best in the cold, and logs are easier to haul on sleds in the snow) run by individual farmers or families. They were located along the area's streams, as close as possible to the source of the timber to minimize haulage. In a typical mill of the time, power from a stream was used to turn a circular waterwheel, which moved a wooden frame holding a single vertical saw. This would cut a log that was thrust against it. Processed timber was easier to transport to markets via wagon or boat.

European settlers, believing the resources of the region were unlimited, tended to be very wasteful in their use. Early fireplaces burned very inefficiently, losing about 80 percent of their heat through the chimney. They consumed huge quantities of wood for cooking and to keep homes warm. As the region's farms grew more prosperous, farmers built larger homes, using clapboard wood built around timber frames, or brick, in the more fashionable English style rather than the stone structures of the earlier Dutch and Huguenot settlers. These larger homes used a considerable amount of wood in their construction and required more wood to heat. The use of brick meant large amounts of wood were needed to fire the bricks.

Pioneers in the region who were dependent on nature for their survival and livelihood, and who suffered enormous hardships in the process of subduing it, usually held the utilitarian view that the land existed primarily for humans to exploit for economic gain. Many took the Puritan view that wild nature was unruly, dangerous, and profane. For many Europeans, therefore, the challenge of taming and transplanting their refined vision of civilization to the region's wild landscape was seen as a noble mission—a moral crusade.

The expansion of human population and the loss of forest had profound effects on the ecology of the region. Sawdust from sawmills polluted streams. Hunting and loss of habitat caused wolves, mountain lions, elk, and beavers (victims of the fur trade) to vanish from the area. Other creatures such as deer, bears, and wild turkeys were greatly reduced in numbers. Loss of the forest canopy, which shaded the soil from direct sunlight, resulted in an increase in evaporation, drying the soil, decomposing its organic matter, and reducing its capacity to hold water. The indiscriminate clearing of steep slopes also increased precipitation runoff. Soil erosion and flooding became more widespread. Roads into the mountains acted as channels when it rained, contributing to rapid runoff. In areas that had been cleared, erosion resulted in steeper, narrower ravines. Loss of soil through erosion made land no longer suitable for agriculture; many farms were eventually abandoned.

The reduction of forest and the decline or elimination of certain predators created an ideal habitat for certain opportunistic and adaptable native and nonnative species to thrive. Domestic animals and plants as well as numerous nonnative species of wild plants and animals were introduced by accident or on purpose. These took up a sizable niche in the region's altered human environment.

WAR ON THE FRONTIER

The area of the Shawangunks would for many years see conflict, violence, and bloodshed. During the French and Indian Wars, Native American tribes including the Lenape staged a series of violent raids against the English colonists in the region. The Lenape sided with the French because they felt threatened by English settlers' incursions on their land and hoped that with the help of the French, they could regain what they'd lost. A number of settlers were killed in these raids. Many left, and settlers west of the Wallkill were evacuated to more protected lands. The small number of Native Americans who still inhabited the region were often blamed for the raids, and in 1736 almost 200 were relocated to the Schoharie Valley in the company of the Mohawks. Eventually the British erected a number of small fortifications to defend this vulnerable frontier.

In the long conflict between the British and Americans seeking independence (1775–82), the area of the Shawangunks was contested by both sides. By this time, the population of the region included refugees from other areas fleeing the British or the conflict in general. The land west of the Shawangunk Ridge was still thinly populated frontier largely isolated from more settled areas east of the ridge, and was frequently exposed to the threat of raids by Native American warriors. In the Revolution, Native Americans often sided with the British, partly because of their long-standing relationship, promises of support and weapons if they did, and also increasing incursions by colonial settlers on their land (which posed for them the greatest threat). The Natives were often joined by Tories—colonists who out of loyalty to the Crown, fear of change, or hopes for personal gain sided with the British cause against the American side.

On May 4, 1779, Colonel Joseph Brant, a Mohawk chief educated by the colonists and actively courted by the British, led a force of Iroquois warriors and Tories disguised as Natives (to hide their true identities from their neighbors), which attacked three families of settlers along the Fantine Kill, just north of present-day Ellenville. Eleven were massacred and their farms set ablaze. Among the dead were direct descendants of Louis Bevier, one of the original New Paltz patentees. On July 20 of that same year, Brant, commanding a force of 65 Iroquois warriors and 29 Tories, attacked the small frontier community of Minisink (later renamed Port Jervis), destroying crops, slaughtering livestock, killing a disputed number of inhabitants, burning their houses, and taking hostages. Some settlers in fortified homes managed to successfully defend themselves from their attackers. A contingent of Orange County militia sent to apprehend Colonel Brant's party was ambushed and slaughtered.

On August 12, 1781, the largest raid in the area took place. A force of approximately 400 to 500 Natives and Tories surprise-attacked the Americans at Wawarsing. Five or six homes and seven barns were plundered and burned, and cattle and horses were driven off. Only one settler was killed. A brave and stubborn defense by the local inhabitants, as well as the arrival of New York's 2nd Regiment, prevented greater loss of life and saved some farms from destruction. A number of Native warriors were killed in the engagement.

The American victory in the war led to the pacification and removal of Native Americans who posed a threat to the region's settlers. With the area now secure, more settlers migrated to the region, population increased, and more forest clearing took place.

THE D&H CANAL

The Shawangunk region remained largely agricultural into the 19th century, but it would soon see a major transformation. Philadelphia businessmen and brothers William and Maurice Wurts acquired land in northeast Pennsylvania, an area rich in anthracite coal. Anthracite was less popular than bituminous coal, which was considerably softer and easier to light. Once lit, though, anthracite burned much more cleanly and efficiently than bituminous coal. When technologies for using anthracite were improved, the demand for it grew. There were four beds of anthracite coal in eastern Pennsylvania, but the largest bed, the Wyoming Field, lay far to the north and was nearly inaccessible. This was where the Wurts brothers owned land.

Because of the great distance and high cost of overland transport, the Wurts brothers were unable to compete with anthracite mines in southeastern Pennsylvania that marketed their coal in Philadelphia. New York City, however, was growing rapidly and was seen as a potentially lucrative market for anthracite. Hoping to access this market with their coal, the Wurts brothers decided in 1823 to build a canal. Planning and constructing a canal through rugged and unsettled terrain required very specialized skill and knowledge, so the brothers hired Benjamin Wright—principal engineer of the Erie Canal, which was still under construction—to survey a potential route from their mines in Pennsylvania to the Hudson River and the port of New York. Wright hired a young engineer, John B. Jervis, to do most of the detailed fieldwork (by 1827, Jervis would replace Wright as the chief engineer). In a region where all prior construction was the product of apprenticeship, tradition, and trial and error, the canal was the area's first major design project. Wright's proposed route followed the valleys of the Rondout and Neversink just west of the Shawangunk Ridge.

In 1825, the year the Erie Canal was completed, the Delaware & Hudson Canal Company was created—at the time America's largest and first million-dollar private corporation. Phillip Hone, then mayor of New York City, was elected president of the new company, and construction began in July of that year.

The canal took three years and $1.2 million to finish. The 60-mile-long New York section was completed in only 18 months! At the height of construction, 2,500 workers in 200 teams, most of them Irish immigrants, labored on the canal. Much of the work was done by hand. Completed, it stretched 108 miles from Honesdale, Pennsylvania, to Rondout (Kingston), New York, on the Hudson River. From there, coal and other goods were transferred to bigger barges and steamships and transported down river to New York City. The D&H was the first canal in this country to be build by private enterprise. It was originally 32 feet wide and 4½ feet deep; there were exactly 108 hydraulic locks that could lift or lower boats an average of 10 feet, depending on which direction they were headed. Canal boats were pulled by mules at 1 to 3 miles per hour and could travel the length of the canal in 7 to 10 days. In addition to coal, farm products, timber, Rosendale cement, and other building materials were transported on the canal.

In a time when most roads were little more than dirt paths, the canal became the region's chief transportation artery. Indeed, it became so popular that it soon was overcrowded. In the 1840s and 1850s, the canal was enlarged to 6 feet deep to improve efficiency by handling bigger boats with cargoes up to 130 tons. New wire suspension bridges were built to carry the canal over the Neversink and Rondout. These were designed by famed engineer John A. Roebling, a German immigrant who later designed the Brooklyn Bridge.

The canal had a profound effect on the region. It opened new areas for exploitation and settlement. Prior to the canal, the primarily rural population was largely isolated by a poor road system, limited to trips to the nearest village for church-going, shopping, social visits, and special events. Most rarely left the township where they lived. The canal helped decrease the area's social and economic isolation. By flooding the region's shops with imported goods, it also encouraged specialization and market agriculture, which in turn decreased self-sufficiency. Growing communities located along the canal became big markets for locally produced farm products. Farmers also discovered that the canal was a cheap, dependable means for shipping their goods to faraway markets like New York City.

The canal resulted in dramatic population growth and a large new influx of people into the region, including Irish and German immigrants. Towns along the canal such as Rosendale, High Falls, Ellenville, and Port Jervis prospered and grew. As many of the region's farms suffered from gradual soil depletion and competition from farms in the west, farmers moved to these new boom-towns along the canal in search of jobs in the factories or work on the boats as canawlers. Economic growth in the valley west of the Shawangunks encouraged the construction of toll roads called turnpikes across the ridge. The canal also brought the Industrial Revolution to the area, with such new industries as boatbuilding and repair, glassworks, and foundries located in the vicinity of the canal. Timber, building stone, charcoal, and other products harvested from the Shawangunk Ridge found new markets in canalside communities. These products could also be transported more easily to distant markets, which in turn increased the demand for them and resulted in more exploitation.

MOUNTAIN COMMUNITIES

With the successful conclusion of the American Revolution, the elimination of the threat of raids by Native Americans, and the completion of the D&H Canal, the population of the region grew rapidly. Up to this point, the Shawangunk Ridge had remained wild forest used primarily for hunting game, trapping, and

The ruins of an 18th century farmhouse are visible from
Cedar Drive in the Mohonk Preserve.

gathering berries, herbs, and chestnuts. As forestland in the valleys disappeared, the region's settlers gradually turned to the forests on the mountain ridge, which eventually became a major supplier of timber. Much was used locally for firewood and building, but some was exported to growing urban centers like New York. The growing population, rising affluence and expectations concerning housing and furnishings, expansion of industry, and spread of transportation systems like canals and railroads all increased the demand for timber. In the 1840s, New York State led the nation in timber production; by the 1870s it was importing a million tons annually.

At the beginning of the 19th century, much of the Shawangunk Ridge—like the neighboring Catskills—was covered with hemlock forests. Tannin, present in the bark of hemlocks, was an important ingredient in the processing of leather. By the early 1800s, settlers in Coxing Clove were stripping hemlock bark and hauling it to the McKinstry Tannery in nearby Gardiner. There was also a large tannery located in Ellenville. The tanning industry decimated the population of hemlock trees, often only taking the bark and leaving the trunks to rot. By the 1860s, the supply of hemlocks had dwindled, and the tanning industry disappeared. Hemlock saplings that grew on already logged-over land were a rich source of hoops used in the manufacture of wooden barrels, a key storage component in the 19th century. Barrels were often used locally for shipping Rosendale cement. Practically every mountain homestead had a hoop shed. One manufacturing plant in Ellenville was reported to be the largest producer of barrel hoops in the country at that time.

The hardwood forests of chestnut and oak that sprouted up in the place of the hemlocks were often a good source for charcoal. Charcoal supplied various industries such as glassmaking and metalworking. Wood was cut in 6- to 10-foot lengths, then piled into a cone- or dome-shaped structure called a pit and covered with damp leaves and turf, with an open chimney on top where the fire was lit. Usually 10 to 12 cords of wood were used at a time. After 10 days, the fire was extinguished, the earth removed, and the charcoal excavated. Generally, the longer and slower the burn, the better the charcoal. A cord of wood produced between 20 and 40 bushels of charcoal. Charcoal burning required constant attention in order to keep the fire lit and contained. Piles of slash waste left in areas cleared for timber or charcoal were highly flammable, and thus forest fires became more prevalent during this period of forest clearing.

As the population in the neighboring valleys swelled, land available for farming became scarce. New settlers then came to the mountains in search of farmland and by the late 1700s had settled in Coxing Clove. They used areas already cleared of timber for grazing cattle and sheep and for subsistence farming, producing small crops of corn, buckwheat, rye, potatoes, and oats. Many worked at least part time cutting timber, stripping hemlocks, picking berries, producing barrel hoops and charcoal, or quarrying millstones. Products were sold, but more often bartered for supplies and essential items. The population of Coxing Clove expanded, and by the middle of the 19th century a recognizable community—Trapps Hamlet—had been established in the area where present-day Route 44/55 and Clove Road meet. Trapps Hamlet was one of a number of small mountain communities located in the Shawangunks.

By 1856, the Wawarsing–New Paltz Turnpike had connected the community to the valleys on either side of the ridge. By 1880, there were 50 homes in this community with approximately 200 residents, a hotel, a school, a store, and, by 1881, a chapel. By this time, however, the hemlocks were gone and the tanneries closed. The reduction of forest meant that less timber was available for use or for export, and the thin soil made agriculture difficult. The population began a slow decline. After the Civil War, many farmers were anxious to sell their land and move west. As farmland was abandoned and people departed, the Smileys (see below) purchased large tracts of this land at very low prices to add to their resorts. The forest gradually returned to these formerly cleared lands. Many of the remaining Trapps residents found employment working for the neighboring resorts. The men were often employed cutting cordwood for the resorts or in projects such as the construction of carriage roads. Even into the 20th century, Trapps Hamlet remained poor and isolated. Homes still lacked telephones, electricity, and indoor plumbing. The population of the hamlet continued to decline; by 1956, Irv Van Leuven, the last Trapps resident, had died. Today, Trapps Hamlet is a designated National Historic District.

STONES

Though secondary to timber, mining and quarrying operations played a role in the economy of the Shawangunks. Lead and zinc may have been mined from the Shawangunk Ridge as early as the 17th century, though mining activity certainly peaked in the 19th century. There were three principal mines: the Ellenville Mine near Ellenville, which operated from 1852 to 1854, 1860 to 1866, and finally from 1902 to 1907; the Shawangunk Mine near Summitville, open from 1830 to 1840 and intermittently thereafter; and the Guymard Mine near Godfrey, which operated from 1863 to 1870. There were also a number of other smaller mining operations at various locations along the Shawangunk Ridge. The Ellenville Mine was the largest. It included a chamber more than four stories tall.

The ore was found in fissures and bedding planes in the Shawangunk conglomerate, fractured by the mountain-building activity that took place near the end of the Paleozoic era. These fissures and cracks were penetrated by mineral-bearing solutions that left vein deposits ranging in width from a few inches up to 5 feet of zinc, lead, and other minerals (including copper and silver, though these occurred in quantities too small to mine profitably). The Ellenville Mine was reported to have the finest pockets of galena ore ever found. The largest-known chunk of pure zinc ore—more than 2 tons—was found there and later exhibited at the World's Fair in New York.

Though initially profitable, the mines' best ores were found near the surface, and the veins proved to be small and scattered. Many of the deeper veins also contained large deposits of sulfur, which had to be smelted in order to extract the lead and zinc. Smelting operations added to the cost and decreased the profitability of the mines. Ores were mined from the hard bedrock by hand, using picks and shovels. The scanty deposits didn't lend themselves to the more sophisticated mechanized mining developed later in the century and used more profitably in mines out west.

From the late 18th century until the early 20th, the Shawangunk Ridge was the primary source of millstones for the northeast United States. Prior to the Revolutionary War, millstones were imported to the colonies from Europe. During the British blockade, however, a new source was needed, and the fine-grained Shawangunk conglomerate, because of its hardness and durability, proved to be ideal. Much of the northern Shawangunk Ridge was quarried for millstones, though the most extensive quarries were located on Rock Hill, now part of the Mohonk Preserve. Most of the laborers were local farmers who cut millstones

A millstone at High Falls

part time to supplement their income from farming. Laborers could earn from $5 to $100 per stone, depending on its size and the quality. Millstones ranged in size from 15 inches to 7 feet in diameter, though 3 to 4 feet was average. The stones were generally 6 to 8 inches thick. The whiter the color of the stone, the better the quality.

Quarrying millstones was extremely arduous work. A seam 20 inches thick would be split by drilling holes with chisels and sledgehammers and filling the holes with black powder. The powder was then ignited, and (hopefully) the rock would split along the seam. Once removed, the rock was rounded into a circle by hammering in holes and then inserting iron wedges (called feathers) to force the holes apart. If a stone cracked in the process, it was discarded. Besides carving out the edge, one side of the stone was always polished. Finishing a stone in this manner took, on average, three to four weeks. Workers operated in small teams of three or four. Sometimes, temporary shelters of canvas and tarpaper were used to protect the workers from the elements.

Once quarried, a millstone was placed on a horse-drawn sled and carried down the ridge to boats waiting along the Delaware & Hudson Canal. From there, they were shipped to New York City and elsewhere. Shawangunk millstones, popularly referred to as Esopus Stones, were first used primarily for grinding grain. Later, they were used for grinding cement and other industrial applications. Today, remnants of millstone quarry operations are still apparent at many sites along the ridge. Discarded millstones—some still intact in varying stages of completion, but inexplicably never finished—can be found in a number of places.

ROMANCE WITH NATURE

By the 19th century, a change had taken place in Americans' attitudes toward nature. The romantic movement, which started in Europe in the 18th century, had spread to America's shores. Romantics viewed nature as innocent, pure, mysterious, and sublime—evidence of God's handiwork. Knickerbocker writers such as William Cullen Bryant, Washington Irving, and James Fenimore Cooper described and celebrated the American frontier experience. Hudson River painters like Thomas Cole and Frederic Church glorified America's natural landscapes, and Americans were urged to rediscover the natural splendors of this country. Wealthy tourists flocked to luxury resorts in magnificent natural settings like the Catskill Mountain House.

Not everyone viewed the technological "progress" of the 19th century with favor. Some intellectuals (most of them urban dwellers) felt that America was becoming overcivilized. They were concerned about the artificiality and materialism of modern industrial society. They were also distressed by the wanton destruction of the nation's forests and wilderness areas. For writer-philosopher Henry David Thoreau, the freedom and solitude of nature offered a respite from the stress and demands of society and an opportunity to discover one's natural self. John Muir, an environmentalist, explorer, and writer, helped promote the idea of protecting unspoiled natural areas from development, as refuges where people could experience nature firsthand.

By the late 19th century, hiking, bird-watching, and other forms of nature study were becoming popular. The Appalachian Mountain Club (AMC) and Sierra Club promoted preservation of natural areas as well as outdoor activities that increased the public's awareness of them. Avid sportsmen like Theodore Roosevelt and other wealthy outdoors enthusiasts organized exclusive clubs that promoted conservation to protect game and establish reserves for their own private use. The nature writings of the popular Hudson Valley poet-naturalist John Burroughs also increased the public's appreciation of nature and the environment.

THE SMILEYS

Identical twin brothers Albert and Alfred Smiley were born in Maine in 1828 and raised as Quakers. They grew to appreciate a good education, nature and the outdoors, and the importance of aesthetic values in everyday life. For Alfred, leisure time was often spent on long walks and picnics. On one such outing in 1869,

Alfred and his family visited Paltz Point (Sky Top). Impressed with the view, Alfred, using his brother's money, purchased the land around the neighboring glacial lake (then the site of a tavern). There the Smileys built the popular resort later known as the Mohonk Mountain House. By 1870, the Wallkill Valley Railroad had extended service to the village of New Paltz, making the resort only a day's travel from New York. In terms of spectacular scenery, the Mohonk Mountain House rivaled other mountain house resorts in the neighboring Catskills.

In 1879, Alfred opened his own resort at Minnewaska Lake. By the late 19th century, many farms, especially those in more marginal areas such as Trapps Hamlet, were sold or abandoned. Through a series of purchases, the Smiley brothers bought these lands very cheaply, expanding both of their resorts eventually to better than 17,000 acres. The same farmers and their families who sold their farms often provided the labor needed to build and operate the resorts. Sometimes neighboring farmland and fields were preserved to keep the resorts supplied with fresh produce, dairy products, and hay.

On land that had been farmed and timbered for more than 100 years, the Smileys tried to create an ideal "natural" romantic landscape by allowing the forests to regenerate, but also adding "improvements." Between 1870 and 1929, more than 200 miles of carriage roads and trails were constructed by hand at a cost of roughly $1 a foot. The carriage roads meandered through the fields and woodlands, taking guests on foot or in horse-drawn carriages in search of

Sky Top from the Wallkill Valley Rail Trail

fabulous vistas. Areas of forest were often cleared to create open views, and hundreds of summerhouses (gazebos) were built for the pleasure of guests. The Smiley brothers created an infrastructure that made direct experiences with nature accessible to the professional urban middle class: bankers, merchants, doctors, lawyers, scholars, executives, managers, and well-to-do clergy. They hoped to provide the best of what nature and civilization had to offer—comfortable accommodations in a beautiful, rustic setting.

A REVOLUTION IN TRANSPORTATION

Many people in the 19th century viewed the development of the railroad as a great sign of technological progress. Ralph Waldo Emerson wrote, "Railroad iron is a magician's rod, in its power to evoke the sleeping energies of land and water." However, those who owned and operated canals viewed this new technology with suspicion and rightfully saw the railroad as a threat to their business and often used their influence and political power to stop rail development. The success of the D&H Canal certainly retarded rail development in this region. Over time, though, railroads proved both their reliability and that they could transport goods and people more rapidly than canals could. They also could operate in winter when canals that froze over were forced to close.

Many others began to embrace this new technology and view canals as a slow, old-fashioned form of transport. The rail network gradually expanded. In 1851, the Erie Railroad passed through Port Jervis. By 1871, the Ontario & Western (O&W) Railroad began operating a line from Port Jervis to Ellenville; in 1872, it opened the 3,857-foot-long Highview Tunnel through the Shawangunk Ridge west of Bloomingburg, creating a continuous rail line from the Hudson River to Lake Ontario. The Wallkill Valley Railway also began service in 1872. These new rail lines created cost-effective routes for bringing Pennsylvania anthracite to the New York market. They also provided a swifter means for transporting raw materials harvested from Shawangunks, primarily timber. Urban centers like New York City became big markets for perishable farm goods such as fruit and dairy products. Using the rail network, these products could now be shipped rapidly to market and sold fresh. Many farms in the region began to specialize in these goods.

The expanding rail network also provided an avenue of escape for the masses of urban dwellers who sought refuge in the country. New York City, like other large urban centers of the 19th century, was a crowded, dirty, unhealthy place. Diseases such as smallpox, typhoid, tuberculosis, cholera, and malaria were rampant, epidemics frequent, and the death toll shockingly high. Fresh air and exposure to country living were greatly desired. The idea of vacationing away from the city at one of many health resorts became popular. There guests came for treatment and exercise, to eat healthy locally produced fresh food, and to breathe clean, unpolluted air. Exposure to nature and the outdoors was also considered good for one's mental health.

Resort areas in the Shawangunks, now only a day's travel from New York, became popular destinations for tourists and health seekers. Providing accommodations and activities became a major component of the local economy. As previously mentioned, the Mohonk Mountain House and the hotels at Minnewaska Lake took advantage of the new means of transport to increase the number of visitors. In addition, many boarding homes, inns, and smaller resorts opened to cater to this flood of summertime guests. In order to increase ridership, the railroads themselves heavily marketed the charm and scenery of this area to potential visitors. Unlike the larger mountain house resorts, which drew a wealthier, more fashionable clientele, many of the new boarding homes, inns, and smaller resorts (most were located in Sullivan County in close proximity to the O&W) primarily catered to middle- or working-class guests, many of whom were immigrants—including the Jews, who were excluded from a number of older resorts.

Unable to compete with the new rail technology, canal traffic rapidly dwindled. The D&H lasted until 1898, when the last boat traversed its length. The canal was officially closed the following year and sold. The section between High Falls and Rondout reopened and remained in operation for another 11 years, until the decline of the natural cement industry made it obsolete. The closing of the canal and collapse of the cement industry had a drastically negative impact on the economy of the region, which lost a considerable amount of its population, especially in the towns along the canal. In 1901, the O&W Railroad purchased a section of the old canal and built a rail line between Kingston and Ellenville, some of which traversed the canal. It began operating in 1902.

By the end of the 19th century, of course, railroads were facing new competition in the form of automobiles, which offered freedom and personal control that other forms of transportation couldn't match. The Shawangunks' antiquated system of country roads, poorly maintained during the canal and railroad period, proved totally inadequate to handle the increased volume of automobile traffic. These roads needed improvements, and new roads and highways needed to be built. In 1917, Route 4—the Liberty Highway, later renumbered as Route 17—was completed, taking the place of the Newburgh–Cochecton Turnpike. New York State Route 44/55, then called the Minnewaska Trail, opened in 1929 to take the place of the old Wawarsing–New Paltz Turnpike.

This new technology was not welcomed by everyone. The owners of Mohonk felt that automobiles conflicted with the peaceful atmosphere of horse-drawn carriages. Indeed, it wasn't until the 1950s that guests were permitted to drive their vehicles to the Mountain House, though speed limits of 10 to 20 miles per hour were, and still are, strictly enforced.

The advent of the automobile had a dramatic effect on the region. More than any of the other transport technologies, the automobile decreased the isolation of the area's residents, providing them opportunities to travel for work and other activities. Rising income and increased leisure time, a result of the Industrial Revolution and improvements in technology, allowed multitudes to take advantage of automobile transport to visit the Shawangunks. Automobiles and buses also enabled many middle-class city and suburban dwellers to travel to resorts in Sullivan County in close proximity to the new Route 17. Catering to a mostly Jewish and Eastern European clientele, these included the Nevele in Ellenville and the Granite in Kerhonkson. This area came to be known as the Borscht Belt. In addition to scenery and fresh air, these resorts offered community, culture, religious observance, and big-name live entertainment to draw guests. As the Borscht Belt grew in importance, the older mountain house resorts declined. Many closed, including those at Minnewaska Lake; even the Mohonk Mountain House struggled to survive.

Jews and Eastern Europeans weren't the only groups to visit the Shawangunks. Urban blacks were attracted to black-owned resorts in the region. Peg Leg Bates, an emcee at the Apollo Theater in Harlem, opened a resort near Accord. (Route 209 has since been named the Peg Leg Bates Highway in his honor.) In the 1930s, followers of Father Devine—a famous black religious cult leader—established a number of communes called Heavens, including one in High Falls. They also settled in Upper Coxing Clove, where there were two black-owned resorts.

Autos contributed substantially to suburban sprawl, and the resulting development pressures have had a major impact on the region. Auto and truck pollution poses a threat as well. Railroads, like their predecessors the canals, were largely unable to compete with the new technology. In 1957, the O&W ceased operating, as did the Wallkill Valley Railroad in 1977.

BLUEBERRY PICKERS

The thin soil and frequent forest fires of the Shawangunk Ridge create ideal conditions for blueberries and huckleberries, which are especially prevalent in the area between Sam's Point and Awosting Lake. As noted, Native Americans were the first to forage the ridge for berries, and European settlers also picked the fruits. By the mid–19th century, new roads had improved access, and railroads provided the means to rapidly ship this perishable crop. The numbers of berry pickers grew. Many hiked up from the neighboring valleys for the day, collected their berries, and returned to their homes in the valleys by nightfall. Some stayed and established seasonal camps used in summer and fall. The primary access was Sam's Point. In 1901, Smiley Road was completed to bring guests arriving by train in Ellenville up to the hotels by Minnewaska Lake. Commercial berry pickers also used the road and erected a number of seasonal camps along the way.

Berry pickers were a fairly diverse group, though most were residents of the neighboring valleys who depended on seasonal work for their livelihood. Residents of the German Camp at Sam's Point were longshoremen from New York City. Others were middle-class residents of the New York metropolitan area who used berry picking as a long summer vacation in the outdoors. Separated from "civilization" in the neighboring valleys, they became a kind of subculture. Many individuals and sometimes whole families would stay in tents or flimsy tarpaper shacks. Small stores kept them supplied with necessary goods, and a strong sense of community often developed among the pickers. Some were colorful characters, and more than a few were heavy drinkers with reputations for rowdiness.

Berry picking had a huge impact on the ecology of the ridge. Pickers deliberately set fires to create conditions conducive for berry growth: Blueberries and huckleberries are resistant to fire, and the ashes served as fertilizer helping the crop to flourish. Fire also removed vegetation that would compete with the berries for sunlight. Thus fires set by berry pickers helped maintain communities dominated by fire-resistant plants such as dwarf pitch pines. Some of these fires got out of control and threatened berry pickers' camps.

Berries were gathered in metal pails or handmade wicker baskets. Up to 20 to 40 quarts could be picked in a day, though many opted to pick just enough to buy the day's food and drink. Shawangunk berries had a cherished reputation for being exceptionally flavorful. They were sold to the resorts at Mohonk and Minnewaska as well as nearby towns, but large quantities were shipped to New York and other centers.

Commercial berry picking on the ridge flourished in the early 20th century but gradually declined; it ended by the early 1960s as access points became impassable for vehicles or were blocked, and one by one the camps were closed. Remains of old roads, trails, and summer dwellings can still be found in the areas where berry picking was prevalent. Anyone interested in the colorful history of berry picking on the ridge should read Marc B. Fried's *The Huckleberry Pickers*.

ENTER THE CLIMBERS

Those who enjoyed the Shawangunk Ridge for outdoor recreation were joined by a new group—rock climbers. The sport of climbing developed in Europe in the 19th century and slowly spread to North America. A world-class mountaineer named Fritz Wiessner came to New York City as an immigrant. During a violent thunderstorm in 1935, on a fateful climb on Breakneck Ridge towering over the Hudson near Cold Spring, the clouds suddenly parted and Fritz saw light shining brilliantly on some "sparkling white cliffs" north on the horizon. The following weekend, he and some friends scouted the cliffs of Sky Top and made the first recorded ascents. Wiessner was soon joined by another renowned German climber, Hans Kraus.

In the early days of climbing in the Gunks, the numbers of practitioners were relatively small. Climbing was primarily practiced as a social activity by members of college clubs or close-knit circles of friends. Rock climbing had yet to establish itself as a sport distinct from mountain climbing. Most climbers were mountaineers (mountain climbers) who practiced their rock climbing skills in the Gunks before heading elsewhere to ascend the big peaks.

For the sport's first 35 years or so—until 1960—climbing activity in the Gunks was dominated by clubs, many connected with different colleges. By far the largest was the Appalachian Mountain Club, whose members called themselves "Appies." The Rock Climbing Committee of the AMC (Hans Kraus was a chairman) provided training and organized weekend outings in which both experienced climbers and novices could participate. Because of liability concerns (even in those days!) and the fear that the area might be closed to climbers if there were accidents or lawsuits (the Palisades Interstate Park Commission had already restricted climbing in the Palisades and Hudson Highlands), the AMC exerted a conservative influence on climbing, stressing safety, insisting that all climbers register with the club, and that only qualified, trained individuals, using approved techniques and equipment, would be permitted to lead climbs. In 1959, the accidental death of a Yale student who wasn't a qualified climber heightened these concerns.

The high level of organization and conservative emphasis caused dissension both inside and outside the ranks of the Appies. Some members began distancing themselves from the main group. Meanwhile, other groups, such as the Connecticut AMC and the Intercollegiate Outings Clubs of America, frequently defied the rules. There were also "bootleggers" who simply climbed without registering.

The most prominent of these outsider groups came to be known as the "Vulgarians." (It's disputed exactly how the Vulgarians got their name.) Initially they were City College students, but later they welcomed anyone who liked to climb and party. Most were urban dwellers looking for an escape from stress and pressure. They were famous for their rebellious and lewd antics, including jalopy racing, nude rock climbing, and wild all-night partying.

To the Vulgarians, climbing represented the ultimate freedom from rules—a chance to be themselves and to act a little crazy. Their resistance to conformity was echoed by other anti-establishment groups of their time, especially the beatniks and, later, the hippies. Animosity between the Appies and Vulgarians grew, and the level of pranks and gags increased to quite ridiculous proportions. Eventually the Appies relinquished their control of the Gunks; today, no single group dominates.

Thanks to the Vulgarians and others, the Gunks were one of the places where technical rock climbing became an end unto itself, where the focus was on the difficulty of particular moves instead of the height of a certain climb. The Vulgarians themselves went on "tour," visiting other famous climbing sites around the country such as the Tetons and Yosemite. Often they managed to distinguish themselves for their skills as climbers as well as their pranks and raucous behavior. Exaggerated stories of impossible sheer cliffs and impregnable overhangs began to circulate. Soon many of the best climbers from across the United States and even abroad—Yvon Chouinard, Layton Kor, Royal Robbins—were visiting the Gunks.

THE RETURN OF FORESTS

Since the late 19th century, agriculture has been in decline in the valleys that flank the Shawangunks. The area's thin, rocky soil (except in the floodplains), as well as erosion, led to declining fertility and productivity. Also, competition from the west caused most farms in the area to be abandoned. Those that survived primarily raised fruit, dairy products, and vegetables. Fruit trees, especially apples, thrive in a moist, temperate climate, and the thin, rocky soil is more than adequate for them. However, rising land values and taxes, the result of increased suburbanization and sprawl, have also led to the sale and abandonment of many farms.

Meanwhile, the process of forest clearing has slowed. The use of coal and then oil reduced the demand for wood fuel, while concrete, brick, and steel largely replaced wood as a building material. Also, forest fires were suppressed for aesthetic reasons and to protect forests and residential development. For the last half century, the number of fires and their size has decreased. This was largely achieved through better fire-fighting equipment and techniques, the use of watchtowers to spot fires, and greater public awareness of fire prevention through media campaigns such as Smokey the Bear. In the Shawangunks, the return of forests received its primary impetus from the Smiley brothers (see above), who purchased land and encouraged forests to regenerate.

Trees have an amazing capacity to grow if left alone. In most cases, abandoned Shawangunk farmland and areas cleared of timber were slowly replaced by forest in the process known as succession (see chapter 1). Such regeneration is part of a general trend affecting much of the area between the Appalachian Mountains and the East Coast, where forests have seen a great resurgence in recent decades. There has been a corresponding increase in the numbers of wild creatures—in particular the white-tailed deer—aided by the absence of large predators. The prevalence of deer has in turn had a huge impact on the region's plant and animal life. Other creatures to return include wild turkeys, porcupines, and bears.

It's worth noting that the new forests are not a carbon copy of what the first European settlers encountered. Some old species like the timber wolf, mountain lion, lynx, elk, and mature chestnut tree are no longer present, while many new immigrant species of plants and animals are. The present mix of plant and animal species reflects more than 300 years of intense human impact. The new forests also contain remnants of previous human settlement and exploitation in the form of old roads, foundations, stone walls, and quarries. The forests are largely fragmented, as well—crisscrossed by roads, power lines, and neighboring areas of human development. Still, some very large tracts of forestland now exist on the Shawangunk Ridge and in neighboring valleys.

METROPOLITAN GROWTH

Following the late 19th century, much of the region experienced a decades-long decline in population and economic activity. As noted above, agriculture—the region's primary economic enterprise—particularly suffered.

While improved access by automobiles and better roads increased the number of visitors to the Shawangunk Ridge, many of these were day visitors who didn't stay, but returned to their home communities at night. The growth of commercial aviation also increased the competition from resort areas outside the region. As a result, many of the older hotels and resorts in the Borscht Belt and Minnewaska Lake eventually closed. During the time of economic contraction, many residents held public-sector jobs. State institutions like the university at New Paltz and huge prisons at Wallkill, Otisville, and Napanoch were leading employers during this period—and still are.

Eventually, however, the situation of decline began to change. Due to a rising population, expanding economy, and improved transport, the New York metropolitan area continued to spread outward into New Jersey, Westchester, and, by the 1980s, the mid-Hudson region: Orange, Dutchess, Ulster, and (later) Sullivan Counties. Many new residents came in search of more privacy and independence, more affordable housing, and a more countrified lifestyle away from crowded urban centers with their crime and pollution. Meanwhile, many urban dwellers sought weekend and summer getaways.

A result of the region's new expansion of population has been an increase in development pressure on those areas of the Shawangunks that currently are not protected. Forest plots with pretty views are now appealing sites for residential and resort development. The two most famous development threats were the controversial 1979–87 plans by the Marriott Corporation to build a resort at Minnewaska Lake and a 1983–86 plan to develop a 1,200-acre wind energy farm near Sam's Point. Due to unfavorable economics and strong opposition from local environmental groups, both of these plans failed.

AN EXPLOSION OF POPULARITY

The decades since the late 1960s have seen growing general interest in the environment and appreciation of nature and the outdoors. This was symbolized by the first Earth Day celebration in 1970. The ecology movement led to increased involvement in environmental protection and programs to "Save the Earth." In 1969, the Woodstock Festival took place in nearby Bethel. Hundreds of thousands of counterculture youth discovered the rural beauty of upstate New York. Many soon swarmed to the Gunks to experience firsthand this natural paradise of woodlands, rocks, and clear streams (often enhanced by ingesting or inhaling hallucinogenic substances)—to meditate and stroll through the forests, shedding clothes and skinny-dipping to cleanse, purify, and liberate themselves from the polluted realm of industrial civilization.

Along with the growing appreciation for nature and the environment came a growing participation in outdoor leisure activities. Part of this stems from the environmental movement and part is a product of the fitness craze that blossomed in the late 1970s and early 1980s. Outdoor education programs like Outward Bound introduced a whole new generation of young people to nature and activities such as hiking, cross-country skiing, and rock climbing. There's also been a technological revolution that has produced new, lighter, more comfortable, and protective garments and better equipment for outdoors enthusiasts, making these activities more accessible. For example, the introduction of mountain bikes in the 1980s provided a popular new means for exploring the area's numerous carriage roads. Youth embraced rock climbing and mountain biking, and the sites where these sports were practiced—like the Shawangunk Ridge—attained the status of hip, cool places. Marketing also played a part in the dramatic surge in popularity. The media has glamorized the adventurous aspects of these sports to promote sales of SUVs, insurance, medicine, and other products.

The publication of new guidebooks and maps also helped make the Gunks accessible. Ironically, efforts to protect the Gunks from developers like Marriott received a lot of media coverage, which publicized the scenic resources of the region. Increased use led to improvements in facilities—new and bigger parking areas, new trails, new visitors centers—and these probably increased usage further still.

In addition to local residents, visitors from all over the metropolitan region are drawn to the Gunks. The Shawangunks are within a day's drive of more than

40 million people, and according to studies done at Minnewaska State Park Preserve, approximately a third of the visitors come from beyond the local mid-Hudson or New York metropolitan region. This large-scale visitation supports the local tourist industry (the number one economic activity in Ulster County), which provides accommodations, shopping, and dining for visitors as well as marketing the region as a tourist destination. The results of this popularity are easily apparent on weekends in many areas of the Gunks like Minnewaska Lake and the Trapps: Parking lots fill early, and there can be long traffic jams. Those coming to the Gunks in search of solitude are often finding anything but—if, that is, they're lucky enough to find an open parking space. So-called low-impact leisure activities can have a detrimental impact on the fragile ecology of the Shawangunk Ridge. Multiplied many times, these uses can be responsible for soil erosion, trampling of vegetation, and disturbing wildlife. Due to the thinness of ridgetop soil, at a number of sites, trampling has removed it entirely.

Some have pointed out that in the past most users appreciated the natural environment, while many current users, especially rock climbers and mountain bicyclists are there primarily to practice their sport and are less appreciative of the environment and thus more likely to act in an insensitive manner.

The effects of recreational use are being carefully studied and efforts are underway to limit the harm done.

3

HITTING THE TRAIL

DIRECTIONS

The primary access to the Shawangunk Ridge is through the village of New Paltz. Those arriving by the New York State Thruway should get off at exit 18 and go left (west) on Route 299, which becomes Main Street. Drive just over 1.5 miles through town, passing through the main intersection of Routes 32 and 208, and continuing downhill to cross the Wallkill River.

Follow Route 299 as it gradually climbs and passes farms, orchards, and wonderful views of the Shawangunk cliffs. At 5.8 miles after crossing the Wall kill, you'll reach a T-intersection with Route 44/55. Go right and continue uphill for 0.6 mile, passing the Mohonk Preserve's Trapps Gateway Visitors Center on the right. At 0.3 mile past the Trapps Gateway Center, Route 44/55 makes a hairpin turn; you'll find parking available here, as well as a refreshment stand open in spring, summer, and fall.

The road continues uphill, passing another parking area on the left 0.5 mile from the hairpin turn. Just beyond the parking area, the road reaches a crest and passes underneath the steel Trapps Bridge. The road descends; 0.4 mile past the bridge, the Mohonk Preserve's West Trapps parking area appears on the right. Another 0.2 mile beyond this, Clove Road appears on the right. A right turn here will take you 1.1 miles to the Mohonk Preserve's Coxing parking area. If you continue straight on Route 44/55, the highway begins a very gradual ascent; 2.1 miles past the steel bridge, the Peters Kill parking area for Minnewaska State Park Preserve appears on the right. Continue another 1.1 miles to the park's main entrance on the left. The Minnewaska Lake parking area is located 0.8 mile up the paved entrance road. Continue 0.3 mile beyond the main entrance to reach, on the left, the Minnewaska State Park Preserve's Lower Awosting parking area.

If you're heading to the Mohonk Mountain House property or the Mohonk Preserve's Spring Farm parking area, make a right turn from Route 299 onto Springtown Road, 0.1 mile west of the bridge over the Wallkill River. The road bends to the left and, after 0.5 mile, reaches a fork with Mountain Rest Road. Turn left onto Mountain Rest Road. After 1.2 miles, Mountain Rest Road reaches a four-way stop. Continue straight, climbing and winding uphill for another 2.3

miles to the Mohonk Mountain House gatehouse entrance on the left. Just beyond the entrance, the road reaches a crest, becomes Mohonk Road, and passes underneath a small bridge. It makes a steep descent for 1 mile, then turns sharply to the left while Upper 27 Knolls Road turns off to the right. Follow this road for 0.2 mile to the Spring Farm parking area.

For directions to Sam's Point Dwarf Pine Ridge Preserve and the southern Shawangunks, please refer to those separate chapters.

TRAILS

Trails may be viewed as a means toward an end—a way to get to a desired destination. Or they can be viewed as their own special entity, a means to new adventures and freedom. The Shawangunk region offers a great diversity of trails, thanks largely to its unique economic and recreational history. Each offers its own variety of landmarks and experiences. Most trails described in this book are marked with signs, colored metal or plastic discs fixed to trees or posts, paint blazes on trees or rocks, or cairns, which are piles of stones. Three markers together in a roughly triangular pattern indicates the beginning of a trail. Two markers together indicate a change in direction, the top marker pointing in the direction the trail is headed. Bushwhacking (hiking off-trail) is not covered in this book and is illegal in most places. Only those with good wilderness skills, especially in map reading and the use of a compass, should attempt to bushwhack.

Trails don't just happen. They are usually the result of arduous efforts of planning, politicking, fund-raising, and implementation. Considering the relatively low material costs of building most trails, it is surprising how difficult the process is, and how long it can take. It usually takes a number of highly motivated individuals and groups to create trails. Most new trail construction is the product of volunteer efforts. Funding for trail construction usually results from grants and private donations. There are also maintenance costs and liability issues, especially if the trails cross private land. Maintaining trails is another area that requires effort, usually from dedicated volunteers.

Carriage Roads and Carriageways

These are referred to as carriage roads at Mohonk and as carriageways at Minnewaska. Carriage trails are generally wide, usually easy-grade roadways with a surface of either dirt or crushed stone, often shale. They were built in the late 19th and early 20th centuries to bring guests to resorts and facilitate enjoyment of the outdoors and scenery. Spectacular vistas were a primary destination for many of these trails, which were designed primarily for use by horse-drawn carriages. While the carriages are mostly gone now, these are still multiple-use trails for hiking, horseback riding, cross-country skiing, and, in some cases, mountain biking. Most are regularly maintained; those that aren't are more like woods roads or trails (see below). Service vehicles sometimes use the carriage roads for maintenance, patrolling, research, and rescue.

Rail-Trails and Canal Towpaths

Rail-trails and canal towpaths are similar to carriage roads in appearance. The rail-trails, of course, were formerly rail lines. After the tracks closed, the rails and ties were removed; what remains are relatively wide, flat surfaces suitable for a number of recreational uses, including hiking, cross-country skiing, mountain biking, and horseback riding. One of the great advantages of rail-trails is their convenient location, often close to population centers. There are rail-trails located in both the Wallkill and Rondout Valleys that border the Shawangunk Ridge. Though they weren't designed to take in views, many fine views and natural areas can be accessed from them. The rail-trails vary in quality, though most described in this book are excellent multiuse trails. The Basha Kill section of the O&W Rail Trail is more like a hiking trail, though bikes and cross-country skiers can use it.

Whereas most of the old D&H Canal has been closed for more than 100 years, some segments of the towpath have been restored as multiuse trails similar to rail-trails. These are located in the valleys west of the Shawangunk Ridge. Besides scenery, these trails also offer a number of historical sites associated with the canal, including old locks, aqueduct abutments, and other structures.

Old Roads

These are old logging, mining, and farm roads, no longer in use and usually not maintained. Often they're not marked on any maps. They are generally rougher than carriage trails and rail-trails, but smoother, wider, and easier than trails or paths. The quality may vary considerably due to the lack of maintenance and other factors. These old roads often cross private land, so be sure you're on a designated trail or on public land. Where permitted, they are suitable for hiking and snowshoeing; in some places, mountain biking and cross-country skiing may be practiced as well.

Trails and Paths

These are much narrower, single-track routes through woods and open areas, suitable for hiking or, in winter, snowshoeing, but generally not mountain biking or cross-country skiing. Official trails are usually marked and maintained. They vary considerably, from surfaces that are nearly level and relatively smooth to ones that are steep, rocky, muddy, or have exposed tree roots. In some places, there may be considerable elevation gain or loss. It also may be occasionally necessary to scramble with your hands and feet to climb over rocks or downed trees.

Routes

These are marked routes through cliffs, talus fields, and crevices. They are always rough and always involve scrambling to climb over rocks. Wooden ladders and other aids may be present to facilitate the climbing. However, there is rarely any exposure (danger of falling), and technical skills or equipment are unnecessary.

Long-Distance Trails

Some people, like myself, hate to reach the end of a trail and realize there's no place else to go. Fortunately, in the Shawangunks that rarely happens. Most of the trails are physically linked to one another and part of the Appalachian Trail System, a linear network of trails more than 2,000 miles long covering the Appalachian mountain chain between Georgia and Maine. Two important segments of this linkage are situated in the Shawangunks: the Long Path and the Shawangunk Ridge Trail (SRT).

The Long Path is a 329-mile-long continuous hiking trail that extends from the New Jersey side of the George Washington Bridge to John Boyd Thatcher State Park, 15 miles west of Albany. There are plans to eventually extend the trail north to the Mohawk River and the Adirondacks. The trail was originally conceived by Vincent Schafer and his brother, Paul, in the early 1930s. The state of Vermont had recently constructed its own Long Trail. Unlike other hiking trails, the Long Path was first envisioned as a bushwhacking route through a 10-mile-wide protected corridor. While the New York–New Jersey Trail Conference tried to popularize the idea, little of the trail was actually built, and the idea was largely forgotten for 25 years. In 1960, it was revived, but suburban development had made the bushwhacking route unfeasible; the plans shifted to development of a marked footpath. In the 1960s and 1970s, volunteers of the New York–New Jersey Trail Conference negotiated rights-of-way and constructed entirely new sections of trail as well as using segments that already existed. Though different markers are used to indicate the Long Path in different areas, the turquoise-colored paint blaze is by far the most common and familiar marker.

The Long Path enters the Shawangunk Ridge 3 miles south of the Summitville–Roosa Gap Road, 2 miles north and east of the village of Wurtsboro. It continues north for 9 miles to the entrance to Sam's Point Dwarf Pine Ridge Preserve. It then continues another 2.8 miles through Sam's Point and 9.6 miles through Minnewaska State Park Preserve. The trail leaves the park at the Jenny Lane parking area, continuing north from the Shawangunk Ridge across the Rondout Valley and into the Catskills.

The Shawangunk Ridge Trail was conceived in the 1980s as an alternate route of the Long Path. Development in Orange County forced most of the trail route there onto roadways. Another route linking the Appalachian Trail to the Long Path via a new trail across the southern Shawangunk Ridge was then proposed, and in 1989 a grant from the National Park Service's Rivers and Trails Conservation Assistance Program funded a feasibility study. In 1992, more than 100 volunteers from the New York–New Jersey Trail Conference (the Shawangunk Ridge Roving Trail Crew, led by Gary Haugland) constructed most of the new trail, beginning at its intersection with the Appalachian Trail in High Point State Park in New Jersey and continuing 28.6 miles north to its intersection with the Long Path just north and east of the village of Wurtsboro. Although it never became the official Long Path route, it is considered to be an alternate route of the Long Path. Like the Long Path, the SRT utilizes roadways, old railroad rights-of-way, and existing trails, as well as new sections on private and public lands.

HIKING

Hiking is the most popular recreational activity on the Shawangunk Ridge. Given the area's amazing scenery and wonderful variety of trails, this should surprise no one. Hiking is an activity most people can do regardless of age or physical condition. It generally helps keep you in optimum shape without putting undue stress on the body. It involves the least expense as far as equipment goes. Hikers have access to many miles of trails and places that mountain bicyclists don't. Hiking's relaxed pace affords observation of things like wildflowers and wildlife that those going faster might miss. In fact, walking is *about* patience: Even when we don't rush, we'll still get where we're going eventually.

By *hiking*, I mean everything from casual strolls on easy well-graded paths to rock scrambling on steep talus slopes that involve the use of hands as well as feet. Hikers should know their preferences and abilities. Be careful not to overextend yourself. Trying to do too much can lead to frustration, muscle pain, blisters, and fatigue. My advice is to start small and gradually work your way up to bigger things. Muscles usually get in shape quickly, and feet toughen up with use. Before you know it, your body and mind are ready for bigger challenges.

One way to plan a hike is to pick a reasonable destination, hike directly there, and return via the same route. However, many people prefer more variety and try to return via a different route. With so many trail options in the Shawangunks, planning a circular or loop hike is usually easy and should make your trip more interesting. In the text, I make a number of suggestions for loop possibilities. Still, some long linear adventures don't lend themselves to loops. In this case, parking or "spotting" cars at both the beginning and the end destination of the hike may be your best option.

PLANNING AND MAPS

Careful planning usually results in a better outing. I don't feel you lose anything in terms of spontaneity when you plan. In the outdoors, no matter how much you plan, most of your experiences will be unanticipated. Good planning puts you in a place where pleasurable and meaningful experiences can happen. Planning means asking yourself what you would like to do, estimating how much you can do, and determining where and how best to do it.

Besides guidebooks like this one, maps provide an idea of what to expect before you actually arrive at a site. They are a key planning tool for any outdoor experience. Before I go on a trip, I always study the map first, trying to familiarize myself with the terrain and the location of significant landmarks and sights. Contour lines on a map can provide a sense of a trail's difficulty—when they are squeezed tightly together, it usually indicates a dramatic change in elevation, either up or down depending on which way you're going. Once on the trail, maps help you stay on track. Given the dense network of trails in the Gunks, maps are an essential guide for preventing wrong turns and getting lost.

The New York–New Jersey Trail Conference publishes an excellent series of maps for the northern Shawangunks, the area where most of the trails and land open to the public are located. These maps are highly accurate, easy to follow, and made of tough, water-repellent, tear-resistant material. They can be purchased at many stores selling outdoor recreation clothes and equipment, as well as some bookstores. They can also be ordered directly from the Trail Conference (see "Resources" at the back of this book).

The Mohonk Preserve, Mohonk Mountain House, Minnewaska State Park Preserve, and Sam's Point Dwarf Pine Ridge Preserve all distribute maps to visitors at their entrance stations. If one isn't offered when you arrive, request it.

BACKPACKING

Camping in remote areas, often miles from the nearest road, is rarely practiced in the Shawangunks. Most of the landowners on the ridge do not permit it. The only exception is the New York State DEC, which does allow camping on its forest preserve lands, located mostly south of Route 52, though not in the Basha Kill Wildlife Management Area. You must be knowledgeable about where these properties are and their boundaries. Therefore, accurate maps are essential. Backpackers will have to carry everything they need—tents, sleeping bags, food, cooking equipment, and clothes—with them, usually in a big backpack. There are no lean-tos or designated camping areas in the Shawangunks. Be forewarned that because of the giardiasis threat, water sources should always be treated. Also, most water sources on the ridge may be dry by mid-summer or fall.

WITH CHILDREN

One of the great pleasures of hiking in the Shawangunks is the opportunity for families to enjoy the activity together. Bringing children can add to the joy, but must be done with care and planning. Infants and toddlers at least six months old can be carried in special backpacks. Most respond favorably to the scenery and motion. Jogging strollers are well suited to the carriage roads in Mohonk and Minnewaska, as well as to the rail-trails and canal towpaths described in this book. Be sure to bring plenty of snacks, juice, and water, and use sunscreen when necessary. Bring extra clothing and items for changing.

For children old enough to walk, plan shorter hikes. Avoid areas with dangerous cliffs. Give the children tasks such as locating trail markers, searching for animals or distinctive plants, or taking photos. Bring along an older friend. Let older children read the maps and help plan the journey. Make it an adventure. Break up the hike into shorter segments with special landmarks that the children can anticipate. Provide a treat at the end of the hike.

DAY PACK PACKING LIST

- ❑ water
- ❑ plastic bags for garbage
- ❑ food
- ❑ sunscreen
- ❑ first aid supplies
- ❑ insect repellent
- ❑ rain jacket or poncho
- ❑ extra socks and sock liners
- ❑ map and guidebook
- ❑ moleskin
- ❑ whistle
- ❑ extra clothes
- ❑ knife
- ❑ flashlight and extra batteries
- ❑ compass
- ❑ matches
- ❑ tissues
- ❑ cell phone (optional)
- ❑ toilet paper
- ❑ binoculars (optional)
- ❑ camera (optional)
- ❑ notebook (optional)

WITH PETS

Many pets love the outdoors, and hiking with an appreciative animal companion can be a wonderful experience. Before you go, however, make certain that your destination allows pets. The Mohonk Mountain House property, for example, does not. Dogs should always be leashed. Again, most properties that permit pets require leashes. Never bring a pet into the forest unless the animal is trained and you're reasonably sure you can control it. Being in the wild can excite a pet's instincts, and the presence of wild animals may make it difficult to control. Also, avoid areas where there are dangerous cliffs or rock scrambling.

HIKING CLUBS

Hiking with organized groups can provide social opportunities, safety, learning, and an introduction to the activity—as well as to new places—for newcomers as well those who are experienced. Minnewaska State Park Preserve and Sam's Point Dwarf Pine Ridge Preserve both offer organized outings, usually with an educational focus. There are also a number of hiking clubs in the region. Besides scheduling outings, hiking clubs often are involved in conservation work, trail maintenance, and building new trails. A few of the clubs that lead outings in the Shawangunks are listed below; contact information for all is provided in "Resources."

- The Mohonk Preserve has a number of organized outings led by volunteers and staff. These include hikes, nature walks, cross-country skiing, and mountain biking, not just in the preserve but also in Minnewaska and other areas. Some are exclusively for singles, while others cater to children and families. These are publicized in the preserve's quarterly newsletter and are free to all members of the preserve. Nonmembers can also participate but must pay a fee. Volunteer members are also involved in trail building, trail maintenance, and policing trails. To find out more, call the preserve headquarters.

- The New York–New Jersey Trail Conference is a nonprofit federation of 9,500 individuals and hiking clubs whose memberships total 106,000. Primarily a volunteer organization, its chief focus is on building and maintaining trails as well as protecting the lands where trails are located. It is also a source of information about trails and hiking and publishes an excellent series of maps and guidebooks for the region. Solely through volunteer efforts, the Trail Conference maintains all hiking trails in Minnewaska State Park Preserve as well as the Long Path and Shawangunk Ridge Trail.

- The Adirondack Mountain Club (ADK), though it focuses on the Adirondacks, has a very active local chapter that offers numerous hikes and mountain bike trips in the Shawangunks. It has also been involved in trail work at Sam's Point Dwarf Pine Ridge Preserve. To get in touch with the local chapter, contact the Lake George office.

THREATS AND DANGERS

The Shawangunks generally harbor fewer risks and dangers than you might encounter in more rugged mountain or desert areas. However, injuries and even deaths can and do occasionally occur, and more minor injuries such as broken ankles, sunburn, blisters, rashes, bumps and scratches, and mosquito and tick bites are fairly common. Probably the greatest danger in the Shawangunks is the prevalence of sheer cliffs and deep crevices. Always act cautiously and respect the environment; it's when you don't that accidents happen. Also, always be prepared for serious injury. In the event of emergencies, contact:

Ben Secours Community Hospital (Port Jervis) 845-858-7000
845-858-5262—emergency department
Kingston Hospital (Kingston) 845-331-3131
845-334-2890—emergency department
Benedictine Hospital (Kingston) 845-338-2500
845-334-4902—emergency department
Ellenville Regional Hospital (Ellenville) 845-647-6400
Vassar Brothers Hospital (Poughkeepsie) 845-451-8500
Saint Francis Hospital (Poughkeepsie) 845-483-5000

GETTING LOST

This is a primary fear, but in relatively small and well-visited areas like the Shawangunks, people rarely get so seriously lost as to require rescue. Wrong turns and ending up in places far from where you intended are fairly commonplace occurrences, however. Confusing trail signs, failure to pay attention, and many people's inability to decipher a map can contribute to getting lost. The Shawangunks have a maze of trails, and making wrong turns or missing intersections is fairly easy. It happens even to experienced people who know the area well. Good planning and skill at map reading greatly reduce your chances of getting lost. Those who are inexperienced should walk only on well-marked trails and stick with the more popular places where they're likely to see other people if they become confused and need to ask directions. Also, if you're a novice it's a good idea not to go alone. Going with a more experienced partner or on an organized outing led by one of the local clubs has many advantages when it comes to getting to know the region. Even if you're with a larger group, however, always bring a map you can follow—there's a danger of getting separated from the group. A compass may be useful if you've lost your bearings, and a whistle or flashlight may allow you to signal for help. A cell phone can also be useful, but be forewarned that in rugged mountain terrain, cell phones often don't work. Telling people where you're going and when you expect to return may alert them to trouble if you don't appear on time.

If you get lost, stay calm and don't panic. Stay put, conserve your energy, and try to stay warm. The longer you survive, the greater the likelihood you'll be rescued.

FIRST AID

Except for insect bites, sunburn, and blisters, most people have very positive experiences in the outdoors. Good planning, common sense, and preparation help. Carry a first-aid kit that includes antiseptic cream, anti-itch medication (antihistamine or cortisone), aspirin or other pain relievers, alcohol, swabs, surgical tape, Band-Aids, gauze, bandages, butterfly closures, scissors or a knife, and, of course, a first-aid handbook. Basic training in simple first-aid techniques would be an excellent idea.

CROSS-COUNTRY SKIING AND SNOWSHOEING

Many feel the Shawangunks are most magnificent in winter. The sparkling beauty of new snow, the crispness of the air, the awesome silence, the chance to beat the crowds, and the incredible views all make the Gunks a rewarding wintertime destination. The most popular way to explore the area in winter is cross-country skiing. The good news is, the wonderful network of Shawangunk trails offers some of the best cross-country skiing anywhere.

Most of the best cross-country ski trails are located on carriage roads at Mohonk and at Minnewaska State Park Preserve. When conditions are suitable, most of these are open for cross-country skiing, and most are groomed (grooves are cut in the snow by machines, providing easy passage for skis). On a number of trails, but not all, the snow has been flattened for ski skating. There are also a number of carriage roads that are not groomed. Unless the trails are well used, skiers will have to cut their own trails, which requires more skill and experience. Both Mohonk and Minnewaska have special maps showing winter ski trails rated for level of difficulty. Mohonk uses signs that indicate national standards of difficulty. On weekends when conditions are good, expect the trails at Mohonk and Minnewaska to be crowded. Cross-country skiing in the Gunks obviously is not limited to these two places. The Williams Lake resort north of Rosendale also has groomed ski trails. Sam's Point, the Basha Kill, rail-trails, canal towpaths, and old woods roads offer skiing on ungroomed trails.

There are three primary types of skiing: classical, which utilizes the diagonal stride (skis move straight ahead and parallel, usually in tracks); skating, in which the skis glide at an angle out of the tracks across packed, groomed snow in a distinctive V-shaped formation similar to ice or in-line skating; and downhill. There's also backcountry skiing on ungroomed trails and off trails. It requires specialized skills and equipment. Cross-country skis and equipment can be rented at Minnewaska State Park Preserve and at shops in New Paltz.

SNOWSHOEING

When snow is too deep for regular boots, snowshoeing is the best option for explor-ing the rugged Shawangunk backcountry. Snowshoeing has always been a utili-tarian way to get around in the snow, but in recent years its popularity for outdoor recreation has grown. Snowshoes open up areas where cross-country skiing is impractical. There are plenty of marked hiking trails and old roads, railroad rights-of-way, and canal towpaths that may be suitable for snowshoeing. Older, tradi-tional snowshoes are made of wood and rawhide; the newer, high-tech versions use aluminum, nylon, and plastic. Ski poles can add stability and thrust. Snow-shoes can be rented at shops in New Paltz. They often feel incredibly awkward at first, but with practice users find them a proficient way to get around in deep snow, even in rough terrain. When snowshoeing in the Shawangunks, please avoid groomed cross-country ski trails, because the shoes ruin the tracks.

MOUNTAIN BIKING

Bicycles are and have historically been primarily a means of transport. At some point, however, they also began to be used for recreation. Mountain bikes started out as old clunkers adapted to off-road use. In 1977, the first true mountain bike was crafted, and by the late 1980s their popularity had exploded. Today, an esti-mated 32 million Americans ride mountain bikes; nearly half of all bikes sold are mountain bikes. Mountain bikes provide access to the wilderness. When biking, you can see more and cover more terrain than you can hiking. The activity is also a great calorie burner, and you don't have to be an athlete or especially skillful to do it. Biking in the Shawangunks is not about speed or skill or facing difficult challenges. It's about moderate exercise and being outdoors and appreciating wonderful scenery in a unique and special environment. Be forewarned that prac-tically all of the biking trails described in this book are on wider tracks: carriage roads, rail-trails, and canal towpaths. There is very little single-track biking in the Shawangunks. Those looking for real challenges or a place to break in that new $3,000 dual-suspension titanium wonder should go elsewhere.

If you're planning on buying a bike and are considering a mountain bike, think about where you plan to use it. I assume that cyclists buying this book are interested in bicycling the carriage roads of Mohonk and Minnewaska, or the rail-trails or canal towpaths. Many, however, will actually use their bikes mostly on paved roads. If that's true, you should know that most mountain bikes are slower and perform less well on pavement than your average 10-speed road bike. Hybrids incorporate features of both road bikes and mountain bikes. As such, they aren't as good as mountain bikes for off-road trails, nor as good as road bikes on pavement. I own a hybrid and have found it perfectly adequate for the carriage roads of Mohonk and Minnewaska as well as the rail-trails and canal towpaths described in this book. However, true mountain bikes perform better in these type of environments.

MOUNTAIN BIKING RULES

Be aware and anticipate. Always wear a helmet. Do not wear earphones. Keep a straight, predictable course. Do not weave. Avoid riding when trails are most likely to be crowded with other users. Always yield to walkers and horseback riders. Slow down and assure a wide enough berth for others to pass without feeling confronted or threatened. Environmental sensitivity should come before athletic challenge. Stay on designated bike trails: Bicycling off-trail is forbidden. The maximum speed for bikes in most areas, including Mohonk and Minnewaska, is 15 miles per hour. Give animals extra time and room to adjust to you. Lower your speed when visibility decreases. Only experienced mountain bicyclists should attempt difficult, steep, or rocky terrain. The Mohonk Preserve has a brochure stating the rules for mountain biking in the Shawangunks. Available at the Trapps Gateway Visitors Center, it includes a map of all trails open to mountain biking in Mohonk and Minnewaska. The nonprofit International Mountain Biking Association (IMBA) has been a strong advocate for mountain bike users as well as promoting responsible use (see "Resources" at the back of this book). Locally, the Gunks Mountain Bike Association (GUMBA) has also been an advocate for trail use when landowners threatened to ban bikes from the ridge. Members perform trail work and maintenance as well as providing training for responsible use. Contact them through the Mohonk Preserve.

ROAD BIKING

Bicycling the roadways that either cross or circle the Shawangunk Ridge is another way to explore and savor the wonderful scenery.

Routes 299 and 44/55 west of New Paltz and Gardiner cross the ridge and thus offer a wide variety of forests, cliffs, and views. So does Route 52 south of Ellenville. Route 209 north of Kerhonkson has lovely views. Mountain Rest Road/Mohonk Road also crosses the ridge, visits a variety of different scenery. Butterville Road between Mountain Rest Road and Route 299 provides ideal pastoral scenery and panoramic views of the ridge and Sky Top. Route 208 between New Paltz and Gardiner is an especially scenic stretch. County Road 7 between Route 44/55 west of Gardiner and Route 52 west of Pine Bush has a number of fine views and rural scenery. Be mindful that these country roads, despite their idyllic appearance, often experience a lot of traffic, and many lack the wide shoulders necessary for safety.

When riding on pavement, ride defensively. Remember that automobiles may have difficulty seeing you—and even if they do, they may not respect your rights to the road. Keep a safe distance between you and other vehicles and riders. Allow plenty of room for braking. Obey all traffic laws. Ride with the traffic. When in a group, always ride in single file. A proposal currently under consideration would list roads that circle or cross the northern Shawangunk Ridge as part of a state-designated Scenic Byway.

PUBLIC TRANSPORT

Most communities in the valleys that border the ridge enjoy daily bus service directly from the Port Authority in New York City. Adirondack Trailways has service to New Paltz. For information about schedules and fares, call 1-800-858-8555. Shortline Bus has service to Port Jervis, Otisville, Wurtsboro, Ellenville, and Kerhonkson; call 1-800-631-8405.

Metro-North offers daily passenger train service to Port Jervis and Otisville on its Port Jervis Line; call 1-800-638-7646. Arriving in the nearby towns, you'll still have to find a means of getting to the trailhead—via cab, or by walking or riding. Bikes can be carried on buses, but you should contact the bus company to find out about packing rules. Bikes can ride on Metro-North trains with a proper permit.

ACCOMMODATIONS

Ulster County Traveler's Information, Orange County Tourism, and the Sullivan County Visitor's Association are excellent sources of information about local accommodations; see "Resources" at the back of this book. New Paltz, Ellenville, and Port Jervis have chambers of commerce worth visiting or contacting. Also check out the web site www.travelhudsonvalley.com. There is an accommodation hot line open 9 AM–9 PM: 845-687-0757 or www.hudsonvalleybandbs.com.

Considering that this is a mountain ridge, the scarcity of camping sites is somewhat of a surprise. Most of the large public-access properties on the ridge—including the Mohonk Mountain House, Mohonk Preserve, Minnewaska State Park Preserve, and Sam's Point Dwarf Pine Preserve—do not have campgrounds; nor do they permit camping of any sort. There are a few private campgrounds located in the neighboring valleys; check out the traveler's resources listed above to find them. The 88-acre Shawangunk Multiple Use Area, a DEC property located on Route 299 (it's 5 miles west of New Paltz and 0.7 mile east of the intersection with Route 44/55), has a number of free campsites, but no facilities such as water or bathrooms. A new campground run by the Appalachian Mountain Club, which will have at least basic facilities, is planned to open soon and will be located near the DEC area.

There is one youth hostel located in the region: The New Paltz Hostel is located at 145 Main Street, right by the bus station. Contact 845-244-6676 or www.newpaltzhostel.com. It is currently affiliated with the American Youth Hostel Association, but you don't have to be an AYH member to stay there.

New Paltz, Kerhonkson, Ellenville, Wurtsboro, and Port Jervis all have motel accommodations; if you're looking for the larger, fancier chains, check out Kingston, Poughkeepsie, or Newburgh. Motels tend to be located where access is convenient, in proximity to major roads. Therefore, the settings tend to be lackluster. For a listing, see the traveler's resources mentioned above.

There are a fair number of bed & breakfast establishments throughout the area. The largest concentration is in the area around Stone Ridge, Accord, and High Falls and in the vicinity of New Paltz and Gardiner. Many offer close proximity to the Shawangunk Ridge, and some are located in historic, charming 18th- and 19th-century residences. Again, see the resources above.

Resorts have been a fixture in this tourist region since the late 19th century. Though most are long gone, a few remain. Among the noteworthy are the Mohonk Mountain House, the Nevele in Ellenville, the Hudson Valley Resort and Spa in Kerhonkson (formerly the Granite Hotel), Williams Lake in Rosendale, and Rocking Horse Ranch in Highland. Besides providing lodging, meals, and lovely settings, they also offer a host of activities that may include hiking, cross-country skiing, biking, golf, swimming, tennis, horseback riding, and entertainment. For a listing, see above.

TOURS AND GUIDE SERVICES

Check out Highland Flings for two- to five-day walking or hiking tours with lodging at local inns. Table Rock Tours & Bicycle Shop in Rosendale offers one- to two-day bike tours. Both are listed in "Resources" at the back of this book.

OTHER ACTIVITIES

While hiking, mountain biking, and cross-country skiing are three of the most popular and least damaging ways of exploring the Shawangunks, there certainly are other options. The Shawangunk cliffs have been attracting rock climbers since the 1930s. Today, the Gunks are considered a world-class rock climbing destination—the most popular such site east of the Mississippi. In fact, rock climbing here is internationally famous and one of the reasons the Gunks are so well known. Easy access from New York City obviously accounts in part for the area's popularity with climbers. Also, the climbs themselves are usually easily accessible, like those along Undercliff Carriage Road in the Mohonk Preserve. In addition, Shawangunk rock is hard and dependable, and the cracks and ledges provide numerous handholds. The many overhanging ledges provide an exciting challenge for climbers. All levels of climbing routes are represented here; more than 1,000 have been described and rated in the Mohonk Preserve alone. Most of the primary climbing areas, such as the Trapps cliffs, are located there. The Peters Kill cliffs, located in Minnewaska State Park Preserve, are also open for climbing. Both areas require special rock climbing permits in addition to regular day-use permits.

If you're interested in climbing in the Gunks, visit or call Rock and Snow, a shop in New Paltz that has specialized in selling rock climbing gear for the past 30 years. The folks there can link you up with reputable climbing schools and local guides. They're located at 44 Main Street; contact 845-255-1311 or www.rocksnow.com. Another possibility is the Eastern Mountain Sports Climbing School, located at the intersection of Route 299 and Route 44/55. Call 845-255-3280 or 1-800-310-4504, or visit www.emsclimb.com. Those interested in climbing might also check out www.gunks.com.

Swimming has traditionally been a popular activity in the cool, clear waters of the Shawangunks. Mohonk Lake offers swimming for guests of the Mountain House. Minnewaska Lake and Awosting Lake, both located in Minnewaska State Park Preserve, have small swimming areas with lifeguards. The swimming area in Minnewaska Lake is far more accessible, but Awosting Lake is larger and finer. However, it is nearly 4 miles (8 miles round trip) from the nearest parking area. The Peters Kill, located in Minnewaska State Park Preserve, and the Coxing Kill in the Mohonk Preserve both have beautiful small pools used for wading and sunbathing. To swim or wade does not require anything beyond the regular day-use permits. And what about scuba diving? If you're thinking, *In the Shawangunks?* the clear waters of Minnewaska Lake are actually considered an ideal place to practice underwater skills. There is even a special access point on the lake for scuba divers, who must be licensed or be accompanied by a licensed instructor.

While the Mohonk Mountain House does rent out boats on Mohonk Lake for its overnight guests, the only place canoeing and kayaking are permitted and can realistically be practiced in the Shawangunks is on Minnewaska Lake. Special boating permits are required there. The rivers and streams in the neighboring valleys offer a host of wonderful opportunities for canoeing, kayaking, and rafting. There is an interesting moderate-level whitewater run on Rondout Creek from Route 209 in Napanoch down to the Route 32 bridge in Rosendale, with one short portage required around the dam in High Falls. The best season is April and May. The Wallkill River also offers whitewater between Walden in the south and the dam at Sturgeon Pool above Rifton, just 0.5 mile shy of where the Wallkill enters the Rondout. The best season is from April to early May. Later, most sections are too shallow and rocky, though some calm, deeper segments, including one that runs right through New Paltz, remain open through the entire year except winter. The 11 miles of the Neversink River from Route 209 in Cuddebackville down to where it runs in to the Delaware in Port Jervis are considered easy whitewater, best in April. The Basha Kill Wildlife Management Area is virtually a paradise for leisurely canoeing or kayaking through the many channels and open water of its enormous wetland. Bird-watching and other wildlife viewing are among the highlights, as is the scenery. The Delaware River—which runs through Port Jervis—is by far the busiest canoeing river in New York State, and probably one of the busiest anywhere. Above Port Jervis there are many exciting and challenging whitewater areas, some requiring competent skills and experience. The whitewater season extends into summer and fall, depending on releases from dams upstream. The Upper Delaware is a federally designated National Recreation Area.

Equestrians will find that the carriage roads in Mohonk and at Minnewaska State Park Preserve provide excellent riding. Special permits and vaccination records are required; expect to share the trail with mountain bicyclists, who may spook your horse. You might also want to check out the various rail-trails and towpaths, which do not require permits. A number of resorts in the area offer guided horseback tours, many of which are suitable for beginners. Mid-Hudson Horse Trails is an organization of horse lovers and owners dedicated to the preservation and creation of horse trails. Contact them at www.mid-hudsonhorsetrails.org.

The tall ridges and deep valleys of the Gunks create thermal conditions ideal for hang gliding. The Mountain Wings Hang Gliding Center is located in Ellenville at 150 Canal Street. Contact 845-647-3377 or www.flightschool.net.

THE MOHONK MOUNTAIN HOUSE AND MOHONK PRESERVE

The 2,200-acre Mohonk Mountain House Resort and 6,400-plus-acre Mohonk Preserve that surrounds it together make up more than 8,600 acres of some of the most picturesque scenery and best opportunities for outdoor recreation on the Shawangunk Ridge. It's a diverse setting of forests, valleys, and ridgetops that includes the Trapps cliffs, Sky Top, Bonticou Crag, the Coxing Kill, Mohonk Lake, and other prominent natural landmarks. Mohonk is also a historical landscape in which the past is both celebrated and preserved and where awareness of and connection to it is part of the experience. Notable human-made landmarks include the magnificent Mountain House, 46 miles of winding carriage roads, and 125 rustic gazebos (known locally as summerhouses). In addition,

Mohonk Mountain House from the Skytop Path

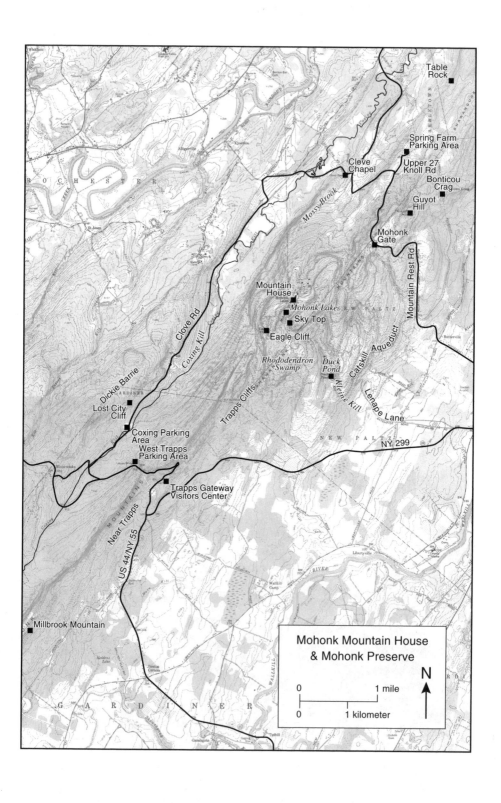

Table
Rock

Spring Farm
Parking Area

Upper 27
Knoll Rd

Clove
Chapel

Bonticou
Crag

Guyot
Hill

Mohonk
Gate

Mossy Brook

Mountain
House

Mohonk Lakes

Sky Top

Eagle Cliff

Clove Rd

Coxing Kill

Rhododendron
Swamp

Duck
Pond

Catskill Aqueduct

Kleine Kill

Lenape Lane

Trapps Cliffs

NEW PALTZ

NY 299

Dickie Barrie

Lost City
Cliff

Coxing Parking
Area

West Trapps
Parking Area

Trapps Gateway
Visitors Center

Near Trapps

US 44/NY 55

Millbrook Mountain

Mountain Rest Rd

Mohonk Mountain House
& Mohonk Preserve

N

0   1 mile

0   1 kilometer

there are 49 miles of hiking trails and scrambling routes, which require days to fully explore. Mohonk—not just the Mountain House, but also 83 other buildings, carriage roads, trails, and the surrounding land—was designated a National Historic Landmark in 1986.

A sign near the gatehouse off Mountain Rest Road reads SLOWLY AND QUIETLY, to emphasize that Mohonk stands apart as a refuge from the loud, hyperdrive world we normally inhabit. Mohonk is about the outdoors and nature appreciation. Hiking the trails, walking, riding, or skiing the carriage roads, and resting in the summerhouses reflect distinctly 19th-century notions of these activities. At Mohonk, you can journey back in time to a romantic "wild" setting where civilization and nature seem balanced.

The Mohonk Mountain House and Mohonk Preserve are two distinct entities. Mountain House property includes the land around the Mountain House and Mohonk Lake, as well as Sky Top and Eagle Cliff. The Mohonk Preserve includes land along the Coxing Kill, Millbrook Ridge, Laurel Ledge, the Trapps, Dickie Barrie, Duck Pond, Spring Farm, and Bonticou Crag. The Mountain House is a private resort; the Mohonk Preserve is the largest private nature preserve in New York State. The Mountain House and the Mohonk Preserve serve different purposes and have different rules—yet the two have much in common. They started out as one entity. They share a common boundary. Activities and stewardship are often coordinated, and visitors travel freely between the two.

Sky Top from Eagle Cliff

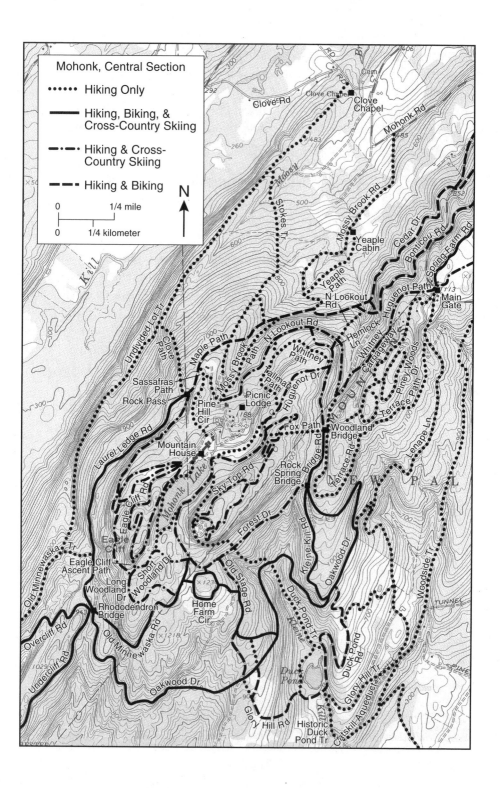

Mohonk, Central Section

Hiking Only

Hiking, Biking, & Cross-Country Skiing

Hiking & Cross-Country Skiing

Hiking & Biking

0   1/4 mile
0   1/4 kilometer

N

HISTORY

The human history of Mohonk probably dates back more than 10,000 years. In the 1980s, excavations of the Mohonk Rock Shelter near Rhododendron Swamp uncovered prehistoric remnants of practically all the Native American cultures that inhabited the region and probably used the Mohonk area for travel, hunting, and foraging for herbs, nuts, and berries. The first European visitors probably also used the area for hunting, trapping, and foraging. As land was cleared in the neighboring valleys, the Mohonk area was increasingly exploited for timber for fuel and construction, and tannin from hemlocks for the tanning industry. Neighboring Coxing Clove was settled in the late 18th century by farmers who used the already cleared lands for grazing sheep and cattle and raising crops. By the mid–19th century, John F. Stokes owned and operated a tavern and 10-room inn at Paltz Pond (later renamed Mohonk Lake) that featured drinking and dancing and catered to mostly local residents. Stokes hoped to someday develop his property as a major resort.

Alfred Smiley (born in 1828 in Maine) first visited Mohonk in 1869 on a leisure outing to Paltz Point (Sky Top). He was impressed with the view and the scenery around Paltz Pond and expressed an interest in purchasing the property. Stokes was having financial difficulties and so was willing to sell his land. Alfred persuaded his twin brother Albert, a school administrator from Providence, Rhode Island, to come up with the money, and the 280-acre property was purchased for $28,000. Alfred managed the resort, which he remodeled in 1870 to accommodate 40 guests. The completion of the Wallkill Valley Railroad to New Paltz improved access to the resort. Carriage roads and paths were constructed, as well as numerous rustic gazebos for relaxing and savoring the lovely vistas. The carriage road system—built over a span of roughly 50 years, between 1870 and 1920—was an innovative means that allowed guests to travel around the property in comfort while enjoying the scenery. It was copied by the Rockefellers and others for use on their own vast estates. Schuyler Colfax, the vice president of the United States, was one of Mohonk's first guests. He compared the magnificent scenery here to Yosemite Valley.

The Smileys were Quakers. This was reflected in the rules governing the operation of their resort. Alcohol was strictly banned. (This ban was finally revoked in 1970, and now alcohol is served at the resort.) Dancing and card playing were also forbidden. There were daily worship services. Recreational activities included nature walks, lectures, evening concerts, hymn singing, bowling, boating, horseback riding, fishing, and, after they became fashionable, tennis and golf. The resort catered to the East Coast's urban elite looking for a getaway, who appreciated nature and scenery but still enjoyed the refined comforts and culture of a luxury resort. Guests included John D. Rockefeller, poet-

The Trapps, Millbrook, and Coxing Clove from Eagle Cliff

naturalist John Burroughs, environmentalist John Muir, William Jennings Bryan, Presidents William Taft, Rutherford B. Hayes, Theodore Roosevelt, and Chester A. Arthur, and Mrs. Ulysses S. Grant.

During the 1870s, the hotel was enlarged to accommodate more guests. Gardens were added and neighboring properties were purchased, creating a buffer to protect and enhance the environment around the resort as well as permitting its expansion and the growth of the carriage road network and trails. The decline of agriculture in the area made much of the land available at low prices. Aesthetic forestry was practiced to enhance the scenery, create views, encourage the proliferation of flowering shrubs like mountain laurel, and provide the resort with timber. A thousand acres of Mohonk land was cultivated or used as pasture to supply fresh milk, vegetables, and meat for the resort's guests.

Much of the resort's advertising was via word of mouth, but brochures containing favorable reviews and comments from prominent guests were circulated door to door in wealthy neighborhoods of Manhattan to attract new guests. It was also heavily marketed by railroads anxious to increase ridership.

In 1876, Alfred Smiley purchased the property around Minnewaska Lake; by 1879, he had resigned as manager of Mohonk in order to operate his new resort. His brother Albert gave up his position as a school administrator and moved to Mohonk to run the resort on a full-time basis. That same year, Albert was offered an appointment by President Rutherford B. Hayes as a member of the U.S. Board of Indian Commissioners. He offered his 23-year-old half brother Daniel, a schoolteacher, a position in the business. In 1881, Daniel moved to Mohonk, and by 1892 was given full charge of the resort's operations. Much of the present-day Mountain House was erected under his supervision.

As a philanthropist and member of the Board of Indian Commissioners, Albert Smiley used Mohonk as the site of the annual Conference of Friends of the Indian (1883–1916) and the annual Lake Mohonk Conferences on International Arbitration (1895–1916) to promote world peace—activities for which he was posthumously nominated for a Nobel Prize. These were attended by many notables. Mohonk is still the site of many important meetings and conferences.

The resort continued to expand and add new facilities. In 1963, the non-profit Mohonk Trust was established to preserve and protect Mohonk lands. Most of the outlying Mountain House property was transferred to its jurisdiction. In 1981, the trust changed its name to the Mohonk Preserve. It continued to purchase new adjoining properties, eventually expanding to become the largest nonprofit privately owned nature sanctuary in New York State. More than 150,000 members and guests visit the Mohonk Preserve annually.

MEMBERSHIP AND PERMITS

The Mohonk Mountain House property and Mohonk Preserve are both open to guests of the hotel. The Mountain House itself and the area immediately adjacent to it are restricted to overnight guests and those who purchase a meal at the Mountain House. Mohonk Preserve members have free access to Mohonk Preserve and Mountain House property except for these restricted areas. Preserve members will also have to pay a parking fee if they park at the Mohonk Gatehouse on Mountain Rest Road.

Day visitors who aren't guests of the Mountain House or members of the Mohonk Preserve have to purchase a day-use permit, available at the Trapps Gateway Visitors Center or any of the designated parking areas. The most expensive access is the Mohonk Gatehouse, where only a limited number of day-use permits are available. All other parking areas charge the same fees. Permits are more expensive on weekends and during holidays. In the backwoods, a ranger may request presentation of your permit or membership card. Please note that mountain biking and rock climbing require special permits for Mohonk Preserve lands.

Yearlong membership to the Mohonk Preserve, a nonprofit organization, may be purchased at the Trapps Gateway Visitors Center on Route 44/55 or through the mail. Membership supports the stewardship of the land. Members receive a monthly newsletter and a membership card that can be used as a day pass. Members can also participate in a number of organized outings, including hikes, ski trips, and educational programs. Please note: Rules governing access to trails and lands are subject to change.

FACILITIES

The primary facility for Mohonk Preserve members is the Trapps Gateway Visitors Center located on Route 44/55 just below the Trapps. Picnic Lodge is the visitors center for day guests who have purchased a Mohonk Mountain House day hiking pass. It is located on the Mountain House property just east of the formal gardens, about 1.75 miles from the Mohonk Gatehouse (see below). You can reach it by walking, biking, or taking a shuttle from the gatehouse (available seasonally on weekends for a small fee). The Picnic Lodge is closed in winter.

ACTIVITIES

Overnight guests of the Mohonk Mountain House can participate in a wide range of activities at the resort. There are daily hikes and walks led by trained guides. During the Hiker Holiday—held midweek in May—there are at least four hikes per day. Boating, fishing, and swimming are available in Mohonk Lake. There are children's activities, tennis, horseback riding, carriage rides, and golf. In winter, there is cross-country skiing, ice skating, snow tubing, and snowshoeing. Overnight hotel guests can sign out equipment for cross-country skiing and snowshoeing from a shop in the Council House. Day-use visitors and members of the Mohonk Preserve can hike, mountain bike on preserve roads designated for bike use (only with a special permit), swim in the Coxing Kill, rock climb in designated areas (only with a special permit and definitely not on Mountain House property!), and cross-country ski and snowshoe. The Mohonk Preserve has its own organized outings for members.

HIKING

When planning hikes at Mohonk, there are a number of factors to consider. The area's carriage roads, narrow footpaths, and scrambling routes vary in difficulty. You should be mindful of distance, elevation changes, and the fact that narrow trails and scrambling routes are much slower and more physically challenging than the carriage roads. Scrambling routes will sometimes require the use of hands as well as feet to navigate through rocks and other obstacles. Practically all carriage roads and trails are marked with signs. Hiking trails in the Mohonk Preserve are also marked with paint blazes, as are scrambling routes. Always exercise caution: There are many cliffs potentially dangerous to those who wander too close to the edges. There have been accidental deaths. Be careful and stay on marked paths and routes. In wintertime, when they're open for skiing, all designated ski routes are closed to hikers.

MOUNTAIN BIKING

Mountain bikers must have a special pass or special membership that permits mountain biking. There is a small extra charge for these passes or memberships. Mountain biking is restricted to those carriage roads specially marked as mountain bike routes. Please note that Mohonk Mountain House grounds are severely restricted for mountain bikes. That includes the area around the Mountain House, Mohonk Lake, Sky Top, and Eagle Cliff. Follow the rules. Do not go on carriage roads or hiking trails that do not permit bike use. Be mindful of pedestrians. Helmets must be worn at all times. The speed limit is 15 miles per hour. A brochure available at the Mohonk Preserve Trapps Gateway Center shows the designated bike routes.

CROSS-COUNTRY SKIING

When snow conditions are right, Mohonk's 35-plus miles of designated, groomed cross-country ski trails make up one of the best such networks in the East. Most ski trails utilize the carriage roads. These are rated using national standards. *Easier* trails, marked with green signs, are for beginners. They generally have little relief, mild grades, and gentle turns. *More difficult* trails are marked with blue signs and are best for those with intermediate-level skills. *Most difficult* trails are marked with black. These are rougher trails with more challenging ascents and descents, and are best left to experienced skiers. Designated ski routes are groomed. Most are groomed with tracks for diagonal skiing. A few are groomed for skate skiing, and some are groomed for both. There are also some carriage roads and backcountry trails left ungroomed for more experienced backcountry skiers. Snowshoeing may be practiced on hiking trails and off-trail in the backcountry. Day visitors seeking to cross-country ski on Mohonk Mountain House trails pay a fee at the Mohonk gate house.

RULES

Please note that while the rules of the Mohonk Preserve and the Mohonk Mountain House are similar, there are a few differences. In particular, pets and rock climbing are not allowed on Mountain House property, and mountain biking there is severely restricted.

1. Access to the Mountain House is limited to overnight guests or those who have a meal reservation only. Day-use visitors are not permitted inside.
2. Swimming or boating in Mohonk Lake is restricted to overnight guests.
3. Rock climbing is not permitted on Mohonk Mountain House grounds. All outdoor activities on Mohonk Mountain house and Mohonk Preserve property is pursued at your own risk.

4. Backcountry camping is not permitted. Fires are not permitted anywhere on the property.

4. Visitors must remain on carriage roads and designated trails.

6. Radios and tape or CD players without earphones are not permitted.

7. Glass containers and alcoholic beverages are not permitted.

8. There's a take-it-in, take-it-out policy. Please leave no refuse in the park.

9. Follow the directives of park rangers and resort personnel.

10. Pets are not allowed on Mohonk Mountain House property.

ACCESS

There are a number of access points to the Mohonk Mountain House property and Mohonk Preserve: the Mohonk Gatehouse located off Mountain Rest Road, which is the primary route to the Mountain House; Spring Farm, with access to the northern Mohonk Preserve; the Mohonk Preserve Trapps Gateway Center off Route 44/55 at the base of the Trapps; the West Trapps parking area; and the Coxing parking area. Guests spending the night at the Mountain House or who have a meal reservation there may enjoy the privilege of driving up to the parking area right by the Mountain House. You can also access Mohonk from Minnewaska State Park Preserve via Trapps Road, the Millbrook Ridge Trail, the Coxing Trail, and the High Peters Kill Trail.

MOHONK GATEHOUSE PARKING AREA

As stated above, this is the most expensive access point to the Mohonk Mountain House and Mohonk Preserve. Preserve members will still have to pay a small parking fee. Day-pass availability for nonmembers is limited, and this parking area tends to be full on busy weekends in fall and spring. On the positive side, this entry point (elevation 1,113 feet) has a number of fine carriage roads and trails in the vicinity. These provide the best access to Mohonk's famed attractions. If you walk or ski the Huguenot Trail and parts of Whitney and North Lookout Roads, it is 1.7 miles from the Mohonk Gatehouse to the Picnic Lodge. There is also access via Spring Farm Road to the northern section of the Mohonk Preserve. There are enough attractions in the immediate vicinity to make exploration worthwhile; the Rock Rift Crevices, for instance, are among Mohonk's best scrambles, and North Lookout is one of the finest north-facing views in the Shawangunks. Definitely take your time passing through.

To get to the Mohonk Gatehouse from New Paltz, drive west on Route 299 (Main Street), crossing the bridge over the Wallkill River, and making the first right turn at Springtown Road. Continue for 0.5 mile to where Mountain Rest Road departs on the left. Turn left and proceed 1.7 miles to a four-way stop. Go straight, continuing on Mountain Rest Road uphill for another 1.8 miles.

An old field near Spring Farm in the Mohonk Preserve

The Mohonk Gatehouse is located on the left side of the road just before the crest of the ridge and a wooden bridge that spans the road.

A signboard with a large trail map of the resort is adjacent to the parking lot. The gatehouse building has rest rooms and vending machines. On most weekends from spring until fall, a shuttle bus will take day visitors from here to the Picnic Lodge. The bus stop is at the top of the wooden stairs leading up from the parking area. The left side of the parking lot is better for shade. Opposite the gatehouse is the Mohonk Golf Course, first laid out in 1897. The rustic clubhouse, built in 1903, is one of the oldest surviving golf houses in the United States. Mountain Rest Road was originally New Paltz–Allgierville Road, constructed in 1825. Mountain Rest, previously known as Whitney's Gap, was once the site of a boardinghouse, opened in 1885, and cottages that provided less expensive accommodations for resort guests.

Multiple-Use Roads and Trails

Huguenot Trail

Length: 0.3 mile. **Markings:** Signs at intersections. **General description:** The Huguenot Trail runs roughly parallel to Huguenot Drive from the Mohonk Gatehouse parking area out to Whitney Road. Mountain biking is not permitted. **Highlights:** For hikers and skiers, this is part of the most direct route to Mohonk's many attractions. **Downside:** Traffic noise. **Difficulties and hazards:** As a cross-country ski route, it is rated more difficult; skiers may find its short ascents and descents challenging, a tough introduction to Mohonk skiing. It is not recommended for beginner skiers. Walkers shouldn't have any difficulty.

From the back of the parking area next to the map, follow the wide unmarked path (there's a sign). The trail bears left. There's a steep slope to the right of the trail with partial views through the trees in winter. Observe numerous white pines in the vicinity. There are a few ascents and descents. The sound of cars on Huguenot Drive overhead echoes through the forest. The trail descends, passing a hemlock grove on the right. The trail bends left and climbs again, then bends to the right and intersects Whitney Road. Veer right in order to continue to the Picnic Lodge, Mountain House, and Mohonk Lake.

Whitney Road

Length: 0.3 mile. **Markings:** Signs at both ends. **General description:** This short carriage road connects Huguenot Drive with North Lookout Road. It is suitable for hiking and cross-country skiing. Mountain biking is not permitted. **Highlights:** For walkers and skiers, it provides an essential link between the Mohonk Gatehouse and the Mohonk Lake area. **Downside:** Traffic noise. **Difficulties and hazards:** As a ski route, it is rated more difficult, primarily because of the short steep section at the end.

Less than 0.5 mile from the gatehouse, Whitney Road departs on the right from the automobile road. Almost immediately, you encounter the Huguenot Trail on the right (see above). A right turn here will return you to the Mohonk Gatehouse.

Whitney Road bends sharply to the left and begins a gradual descent. There are numerous birches and hemlocks off to the right of the road. The road briefly levels and veers to the right. There's a steep slope on the right; Huguenot Drive is above on the left. The road begins another slow descent. A ravine appears on the right. The road descends more steeply just before reaching North Lookout Road (see below). Go left at the intersection to continue to the Mohonk Lake area. Walkers may go straight, using a shortcut that comes out farther up North Lookout Road.

Rock Rift Road

Length: 0.2 mile. **Markings:** Signs at both ends. **General description:** A short carriage road that descends from the three-way intersection with Bonticou and North Lookout Roads and ends intersecting Cedar Drive. Mountain biking is permitted. However, it is not a ski trail. **Highlights:** It passes the impressive Rock Rift Crevices. **Downside:** None. **Difficulties and hazards:** Use caution when descending. Going up, it can be fairly strenuous. Watch for deep crevices just off the road.

From the intersection of North Lookout and Bonticou Roads, turn north and proceed downhill, passing talus boulders and deep crevices on the right side of the road. These are the Rock Rift Crevices. Continue to descend and cross the red-marked Rock Rift Trail (see below). A right turn here will access the Rock Rift Crevices. Be forewarned, though, that this is a very rough path. Pass a number of mature hemlocks and cliffs and talus boulders on the left side of the road. The road soon intersects Cedar Drive (see below). A right turn here leads to Mohonk Road and the Spring Farm parking area. A left will soon bring you to Mossy Brook Road (see below), which leads to the Mountain House and other attractions in the Mohonk Lake area.

North Lookout Road

Length: 1.8 miles. **Markings:** Signs at intersections. **General description:** This carriage road, completed in 1904, begins at the three-way intersection of Bonticou Road and Rock Rift Road and ends at the three-way intersection of Mossy Brook Road and Pine Hill Road. Well graded with only a gradual ascent near the beginning, it is a moderately easy trek. As a ski route, it is rated easiest. Bikes are not permitted. **Highlights:** For the majority of its length, from the intersection with Whitney Road to the end, North Lookout Road is part of the most direct route for walkers and skiers traveling up from the Mohonk Gatehouse to the numerous attractions in the Mohonk Lake area. Besides its obvious advantage as a direct route, North Lookout Road offers one of the finest north-facing views in the Gunks. It also provides access to the Rock Rift Crevices, one of the best rock scrambles in the area. **Downside:** None. **Difficulties and hazards:** Avoid steep slopes off the side of the carriage road.

From the three-way intersection of Bonticou and Rock Rift Roads, go south on North Lookout Road. The road bends to the left and makes a very gradual ascent. Bonticou Road appears below on the left. The road continues to ascend, crossing a stream and bending to the right. A quarter mile from the beginning, arrive at its intersection with Whitney Road, which appears on the left (see above). From here on, North Lookout Road is part of the most direct route from the gatehouse to the Picnic Lodge and the Mohonk Lake area. A shortcut path for hikers departs on the right here and meets up with North Lookout Road a short distance ahead.

The road continues uphill around the aptly named Beech Bend. Admire the emerald glen, where the Glenn Anna Path (see below) departs on the left. Continue uphill. Soon the shortcut path mentioned above appears on the right. A short distance beyond, the red-marked Rock Rift Trail (see below) descends on the right to the Rock Rift Crevices. The road veers slowly to the left. North Lookout appears on the right. Behold a glorious panoramic view that includes all of the most prominent peaks in the Catskills: from Peekamoose to North Point, the Rondout and Hudson Valleys, and the Berkshires to the north. There's a gazebo conveniently located by the side of the road here.

The road continues veering left. Hemlock Lane (see below) enters on the left. A short distance beyond, a trail on the left leads to the Whitney and Tallman Paths (see below). Then a cliff appears on the left, towering above the carriage road. The road bends to the right; a direct route uphill to the Picnic Lodge departs on the left. The road then spans the upper reach of Mossy Brook. Mossy Brook Path (see below) crosses the road here. You'll soon arrive at the intersection of Mossy Brook Road and Pine Hill Road (see below). A left turn here leads to the Mountain House and Mohonk Lake.

Bridge Road

Length: 0.3 mile. **Markings:** Signs at both ends. **General description:** This short carriage road starts at Woodland Bridge and ends at Rock Spring Bridge. It is a multiuse road open for hiking and also a designated route for mountain biking and crosscountry skiing. As a ski route, it is rated more difficult. **Highlights:** Bridge Road links Woodland Bridge with Rock Spring Bridge, significant hubs where a number of carriage roads and trails meet. It is also an important link between the gatehouse and Duck Pond and an alternate route to the Mohonk Lake area. Therefore, Bridge Road is likely to be traveled at some point in your excursion. The forest scenery, which includes the Pinnacle Cliffs, though not spectacular, is pleasing enough. **Downside:** None. **Difficulties and hazards:** None.

Bridge Road starts on the west side of Woodland Bridge. (Note that there is a bridge here but no water.) Follow the road as it slowly descends a shallow ravine. Pinnacle Path, marked on some older maps, used to depart on the right here. It was closed in 1997 after a clifftop section collapsed, sending a hiker to her death. Soon the Pinnacle Cliffs appear on the right. These are the beginning of the same cliffs that farther south and west become the famous white cliffs of Sky Top. There is an impressive array of boulders at the base of the cliffs. A stream appears on the right emerging out of the rocks. Bridge Road ends just beyond at Rock Spring Bridge where Forest Drive and Kleine Kill Road (see below) meet. A right turn on Forest Drive leads to Sky Top and the Mohonk Lake area. A left turn on Forest Drive leads to Oakwood Drive and Lenape Lane. A left turn on Kleine Kill Road leads to Duck Pond.

Lenape Lane

Length: 3.1 miles. **Markings:** Some signs at intersections. **General description:** Lenape Lane is a private farm road whose entry is off Mountain Rest Road just east of the Mohonk Gatehouse. It ends at Butterville Road. Utilizing part of the old stage route, it was constructed in 1925 by Daniel Smiley as the primary automobile access road to the resort. Lenape Road crosses New York City's Catskill Aqueduct. **Highlights:** It provides access to the Duck Pond area (see below). The southern section has wondrous views and a chance to observe a couple of working farms. Be respectful of residents' privacy, stay on the road, and don't interfere with farm operations. **Downside:** More remote than some people would prefer. **Difficulties and hazards:** Occasional vehicular traffic, especially on the lower section of the road. There is a substantial ascent if you're traveling in the opposite direction, though it is fairly gradual in most places.

From the Mohonk Gatehouse, Lenape Lane bends to the left 0.1 mile from the beginning; the Terrace Path (see below) departs on the right. Just beyond, a road on the right leads up to a corral and stables. Lenape Lane bends to the right. Pitch pine and white pine are plentiful along the roadway. The road gradually descends and passes a shale embankment on the right; it then crosses a small drainage and bends to the left, descending more steeply. You'll soon cross a second drainage with a small cascade except when the water's dry or nearly so. The road then bends to the right. Continue to descend. One mile from the beginning, Oakwood Drive (see below) appears on the right with a wire gate.

Lenape Lane continues to descend, crosses a small stream, and bends to the left then right. A private road enters on the left. Just beyond, there's a horse corral on the right. Pass an old field on the left. Kleine Kill Farm Road—which goes to Duck Pond Road—appears on the right. Lenape Lane enters open fields with fine east-facing views of the Wallkilll Valley and Marlboro Hills. Pass a farmhouse on the right. Just past it, another farm road departs on the right. Sheds, barns, and corrals may be seen on both sides of the road. Horses are usually present.

The road continues its descent, bending to the left and crossing New York City's Catskill Aqueduct 2 miles from the beginning. The blue-marked Woodside Trail (see below) is on the left. The 92-mile-long Catskill Aqueduct is the largest of New York City's aqueducts. It transports water from the Ashokan Reservoir to New York and has a capacity of 500 million gallons a day. It was constructed between 1907 and 1915 and was (and still is) considered a major engineering feat. The aqueduct crosses the Shawangunk Ridge, tunneling beneath Bonticou Crag. Due to contamination fears (heightened since September 11, 2001), there is no trespassing on the aqueduct except in the vicinity of designated trails.

Lenape Lane bends sharply to the right and continues to descend. Pine Road soon crosses at a diagonal. A right turn here leads to the Glory Hill Trail (see below) and Duck Pond. Continue downhill. The road makes a sharp bend to the left. As it does, a carriage road departs on the right; you can follow it to the Historic Duck Pond Trail (see below). Lenape Lane makes a sharp right turn at White Oak Bend. Sure enough, the road is flanked by a pair of very old white oaks. Once white oaks were one of the dominant trees in the Shawangunk forest. Prized for their dense, durable wood, they were one of the first species to be cut down. Today, they are uncommon in the Gunks.

The road continues to descend. A field appears on the right. The road levels. Cedar, birch, maple, and oak are some of the trees in the vicinity. Winterberry, a deciduous holly, is also fairly prevalent. The road veers to the right. Pass an old farmhouse to the right and a barn on the left. The road veers to the left, crosses the Kleine Kill, a lovely stream, and enters an open hay field. Continue level a short distance and begin a slow ascent. At this point, turn about-face and look behind you. There is a classic panoramic view of the Shawangunk Ridge, from Bonticou Crag in the north to Gertrude's Nose in the south, with Sky Top's familiar profile dominant in the center. Butterville Road is just beyond.

Old Glenn Anna Road

Length: 0.3 mile. **Markings:** Signs at both ends. **General description:** A carriage road starting from Bonticou Road and ending at Cedar Drive. **Highlights:** Access to Rock Rift Crevices and views of Glenn Anna, a deep ravine. **Downside:** None. **Difficulties and hazards:** Some moderate uphill climbing if you're going in the opposite direction as described.

From Bonticou Road, descend and bend sharply to the left. Bonticou Road is visible above and on the right. There's also a stream on the right, a tributary of Mossy Brook. On the left are rock outcrops. These grow more impressive the farther you descend. Meanwhile, the ravine on your right progressively deepens. Approximately halfway along, the Rock Rift Trail, marked in red (see below), appears on the left.

Old Glenn Anna Road bends to the left again and departs from the cliff area. However, the ravine on your right continues to deepen and impress. Soon you arrive at Cedar Drive (see below). A right turn here leads to the Spring Farm parking area. A left turn leads to Mossy Brook Road and eventually to the Mohonk Lake area.

Hiking Trails, Roads, and Scrambling Routes

Glenn Anna Path

Length: 0.1 mile. **Markings:** Signs at both ends. **General description:** This short trail connects North Lookout Road with Huguenot Drive near Woodland Bridge, where a number of hiking trails and carriage roads converge. This path is closed in wintertime. **Highlights:** For hikers coming up from the Mohonk Gatehouse, the Glenn Anna Path provides a convenient shortcut to the Mohonk Lake area. **Downside:** The roughness of this path will not appeal to everyone. **Difficulties and hazards:** A somewhat rough path, uphill the entire way, but it shouldn't present too much difficulty for most hikers.

From Beech Bend on North Lookout Road (see above), the Glenn Anna Path departs on the left just after fording a small stream. The trail climbs gradually to the right of the stream, soon crossing it again on rocks. Continue uphill through the woods. The trail bends to the right and arrives at a wooden staircase. Ascend the stairs and arrive at the intersection of Garden Road, the automobile road, and, just across the way, Huguenot Drive (see below), a carriage road. A left here will bring you a short distance to Woodland Bridge.

Rock Rift Trail

Length: 0.2 mile. **Markings:** Red blazes, red arrows, and signs. **General description:** This relatively short trail starts on North Lookout Road, crosses Rock Rift Road, and ends on Old Glenn Anna Drive. Between Rock Rift Road and Old Glenn Anna Drive, the trail is primarily a scrambling route through the Rock Rift Crevices—a labyrinth of many crevices, some wide, that slice into the conglomerate, the result of the bedrock cracking over a period of thousands of years. **Highlights:** The Rock Rift Crevices are among the most spectacular in Mohonk. Steep narrow crevices, slanting boulders, and an exciting venture over rocks and through tight holes make this a rewarding excursion for those who are up for the challenge. A flashlight isn't necessary, but may add to the experience. **Downside:** Climbing rocks and squeezing through tight holes isn't everybody's notion of fun. Also, some of the crevices may be flooded in spring, making the bottoms wet or muddy. **Difficulties and hazards:** This trail involves climbing on rocks that may be steep and/or slippery. Footing may be troublesome in spots. You'll also have to squeeze through some pretty tight places too small for a backpack. Large people and small children may have an especially tough time. Those with claustrophobia should avoid this one altogether.

Depart from North Lookout Road (see above) on the red-marked trail, descending a steep rocky path through hemlocks. The trail zigzags down the slope and then crosses Rock Rift Road (see above). Immediately after crossing the road, the trail enters the area of the Rock Rift Crevices. Following the markers, turn right and descend to the bottom of a crevice. Veer right and continue through a very narrow fissure. Squeeze past a hemlock tree growing upward from the bottom of the crevice that nearly blocks the way. Pass a "room" on the right and descend a ladder into a still-narrower crevice. Come out into the open and turn right. Cross an area of jumbled boulders underneath a rock overhang. Turn right and enter a large enclosed crevice. Proceed to the end to a V-shaped room where two crevices intersect like Times Square; climb boulders as you turn into the next crevice.

Descend rocks to the bottom of the second crevice. Turn right, climb, and squeeze through a narrow hole. Pass a slanting crevice on the right. Bend to the right and climb rocks. The trail veers to the left between enormous chunks of conglomerate, then bends left. Follow it and climb out into the open again. Pass a rock wall on the right. Bend right and climb more rocks. The trail veers to the left between more huge conglomerate blocks. It zigs and zags and squeezes through a narrow cleft. Then it turns left through another tiny passage. The trail turns right and left and enters a small crevice. Cross boulders, watching your step. Turn left and follow the narrow passage between rocks. The trail zigzags again into a slanted crevice. Turn left and climb through another hole. Bend right into a wide-open crevice. Then turn left into a narrow, enclosed crevice, crossing rocks. Turn left again and return to the open, leaving the crevice area. Arrive at Old Glenn Anna Road (see above). A right turn here leads to Bonticou Road; a left, to Cedar Drive.

Terrace Path

Length: 0.6 mile. **Markings:** Signs at both ends. **General description:** This pleasing jaunt through the woods starts off Lenape Lane and ends on Piney Woods Drive not far from Woodland Bridge. **Highlights:** A useful way for getting to Sky Top and other attractions in the Mohonk Lake area. It also tends to see less foot traffic so may be preferable to those seeking a quieter walk. **Downside:** Traffic noise may deter from the experience. **Difficulties and hazards:** Be careful crossing Terrace Road.

To get there, turn onto Lenape Lane (see above) just east of the Mohonk Gatehouse. Follow this unpaved road for 0.1 mile. A driveway will appear on the right; just before it, the Terrace Path departs on the right and up the hill (there's a sign). Follow the trail as it skirts stables and a corral on the left. Traffic noise from nearby Terrace Road, an automobile road, can be heard. The trail levels and veers left. The trail then veers right and slowly climbs. Pass through deciduous forest with scattered white pine and hemlock. The trail veers more to the right and comes out on Terrace Road. Use caution crossing the road.

The trail resumes on the other side and runs closely parallel to the roadway on the left. Arrive at an intersection. Going straight takes you a short distance out to the roadway opposite a shale bank and Terrace Road (see below). To stay on the trail, make a sharp right turn and follow briefly, soon intersecting Piney Woods Drive (see below), which appears on the right. A right turn here will return you to the Mohonk Gatehouse. A left will bring you out to Woodland Bridge.

Piney Woods Drive

Length: 1.8 miles. **Markings:** A sign where it intersects the Terrace Path. **General description:** This carriage road starts from Terrace Road right behind the entrance gate, climbs the shale-based ridge (elevation 1,260 feet), does a considerable amount of meandering, and finally descends and concludes at Huguenot Drive near Woodland Bridge. Though there is some climbing involved, it is very gradual. Shortcuts considerably decrease its length. Mountain biking and cross-country skiing are not permitted. **Highlights:** Solitude and a pleasant stroll through the woods. Many partial views when the leaves are down. **Downside:** If you're in a hurry to get somewhere, don't go this way. **Difficulties and hazards:** There are steep slopes next to the road in a few places.

Follow Terrace Road just past the Mohonk Gatehouse. Piney Woods Drive departs on the right as a paved roadway. It climbs the slope and bends left then left again, passing a number of attractive private residences along the way. Please do not disturb! The road bends to the right and left. After a NO TRESPASSING sign, the pavement stops, and it becomes a more traditional carriage road. You'll soon pass ruins on the left, including an upright chimney. The road then bends to the left; there's a steep slope on the right. The road bends left again. A short-cut appears on the right. If you don't take the shortcut, the road bends to the left and then loops to the right and continues to ascend gradually, with a steep slope on the left side of the road.

The road bends right and left, crosses the shortcut again, and follows the spine of the ridge with a steep slope off to the right of the road and partial views of the Rondout Valley and distant Catskills Range. There are shale outcrops on the left side of the road. The road loops left and then bends to the right, passing the shortcut on the left. Descend and intersect the Terrace Path (see above) on the left. Continue straight, now level, a short distance to Huguenot Drive. A left here will bring you a short distance to Woodland Bridge.

Terrace Road

Length: 0.7 mile. **Markings:** A sign at one end. **General description:** This road starts at a shale pit on Terrace Road, the automobile route, and ends at Woodland Bridge. **Highlights:** Using the Terrace Path and/or Piney Woods Drive, this is part of an alternate route to the Mohonk Lake area. Bicycling and cross-country skiing are not permitted on this road. **Downside:** The unsightly shale pit. **Difficulties and hazards:** Crossing Terrace Road, the automobile route, watch out for vehicles.

From Terrace Road, the paved automobile road, enter the shale pit. Across the road is the Terrace Path (see above). Passing through the pit, notice rusty old quarrying machinery on the left. Shale is used as a surfacing material for the carriage roads. The road departs from the shale pit and enters the forest. There's a partial view of the Wallkill Valley on the left through the trees, obviously better when the leaves are down. The road bends to the right. There is a ropes course on the right. Visitors should not trespass. A ravine appears on the left with a partial view of the Pinnacle Cliffs. Bridge Road becomes visible below. Arrive at Woodland Bridge. A sharp left on Bridge Road (see above) leads to Forest Drive and Duck Pond. A right leads to Huguenot Drive (see below), Sky Top, and the Mohonk Lake area.

Length: 0.5 mile. **Markings:** Signs at both ends. **General description:** A footpath through the woods starting from Huguenot Drive and ending at the Tallman Path. **Highlights:** A pleasant, quiet route for walkers traveling from the gatehouse to the Mohonk Lake area. **Downside:** None. **Difficulties and hazards:** Footing on this trail may be somewhat challenging in a few places. Crossing Garden Road with automobile traffic should be done with caution.

From Huguenot Drive (see below), the Whitney Path departs on the right as Huguenot Drive begins a sharp bend to the left. There's a sign at this intersection. Follow the Whitney Path as it makes a very gradual descent through open forest; you'll soon cross paved Garden Road. Watch out for traffic. Continue the gradual descent. The path here is eroded down to solid bedrock in places.

The trail briefly levels then descends more steeply as a rocky path. The Whitney Path then veers to the left and soon reaches an intersection. A right turn here will lead a short distance to North Lookout Road (see above). If you continue straight, the Whitney Path soon bends sharply to the left and becomes the Tallman Path (see below).

MOHONK LAKE AREA

Whether you've parked by the hotel, taken the shuttle bus to the Picnic Lodge Day Visitors Center (for an extra fee), or walked, biked, or skied here from one of the various entry points, you've now arrived at the center of Mohonk. Primary attractions include Mohonk Lake, views of the magnificent Mohonk Mountain House, and Sky Top, as well as a host of others. There's a dense network of trails that realistically would take several days to explore. Please note that bike traffic is extremely restricted in this area; very few of the carriage roads permit bike use. Also, day-use visitors are not permitted in the Mohonk Mountain House.

Located in a magnificent setting, the rambling Mohonk Mountain House, nearly an eighth of a mile long, rises like a castle seven stories from the shore of the lake. It is the largest, most prominent human-made feature of the entire Shawangunk Ridge. In fact, its grandeur, setting, and rustic decor make it one of the most impressive buildings in all New York State. During the late 19th and early 20th centuries, it was one of several opulent mountain houses located in the Shawangunks and neighboring Catskills. Today, it is the sole survivor of that period. The Mountain House features 251 guest rooms, three dining rooms, 150 working fireplaces, 200 balconies, and half a dozen parlors. It takes more than 400 employees to serve its clientele and maintain the structure. Like other grand resorts of the 19th century, the Mountain House combines natural beauty with comfortable Victorian accommodations.

As stated above, the Mountain House began as a simple tavern and 10-room inn; it was then purchased by the Smileys in 1869 and expanded over the years. If what you see standing today looks like a patchwork of architectural styles, it is, because it was constructed over a period of 30 years from 1879 to 1910. The Rock Building, located at the south end, is a wooden structure built over rock. It is the oldest original section of the hotel still standing. In 1887–88, the Central Building, designed by the New York architectural firm of LeBrun and Sons, was added. Four years later, the Grove Building, the dining room, and the kitchen building, designed by the same firm, were constructed. The Stone Building, designed by New York architect James E. Ware, was completed in two sections in 1899 and 1902, as well as the rustic Parlor Building in 1899 that included impressive outside porches with balustrades and millwork of yellow pine. The most recent addition is the circular glass-enclosed Dining Room Extension, with its impressive west-facing views. It was built in 1910.

The Picnic Lodge, first opened in 1907, is reserved especially for day-use visitors, though hotel guests can use it as well. It includes a snack bar, dining room, and rest rooms. It is located northeast of the Mountain House and gardens and served by shuttle bus from the Mohonk Gatehouse.

Another landmark of the Mohonk Lake area is the massive barn and stables, built in 1888 and 1910. It was reputed to be the largest barn in New York State when it was constructed. Inside is the Barn Museum, which opened in 1972. The museum has a large display of antique carriages, sleighs, old cars, farm implements, ice harvesting tools, lithographic fruit labels, and other historical memorabilia including the original hydraulic elevator from the Mountain House. The Barn Museum is open seasonally. At the north end of the lake is the Council House, built in 1876 as a four-alley bowling saloon. In 1960, it was converted to its present use as a meeting place. It is the oldest surviving structure in the vicinity of the lake. Next door is the 18,000-square-foot ice skating pavilion, which opened in 2001. The pavilion is open only for hotel guests and occasionally the general public.

Nearby are the lovely 25-acre formal gardens and greenhouse that were first established by Albert Smiley as a centerpiece of the property. They were started in 1883 and completed in 1888. Numerous glacial boulders had to be removed and hundreds of wagonloads of soil transported from a swamp near the south end of the lake. Some prime features of the gardens are a one-of-a-kind stone summerhouse made of Shawangunk conglomerate and Rosendale cement, completed in 1897, a rose garden, and a maze. Another feature is a scale replica of the solar system. There is a Garden Holiday at the end of August for Mountain

House guests, which includes lectures, demonstrations, and a tea party. The first greenhouse was completed in the 1890s. The present one, which was completed in 1905, with a new section added in 1977, has wonderful displays of plants and flowers both indoors and out. It also offers plants for sale. Hours are posted on the entrance door.

The Albert K. Smiley Memorial Tower is located at the very top of Sky Top. It is one of the most prominent and familiar landmarks of the Shawangunk Ridge and is visible from a long distance away. It was completed in 1923 to serve as both an observation tower and fire tower. It was built of Shawangunk conglomerate quarried near the site and designed by Boston architect Francis Allen. The tower took two years to complete. It was used by the New York State Department of Environmental Conservation as a fire tower until 1971. This is the fourth observation tower erected on Sky Top's summit. The first, a 20-foot-high octagonal wooden tower, was built in 1870. In 1872, a larger three-story, 25-foot-high wooden tower was constructed. It burned down in 1877. A third wooden tower, four stories tall, was erected the following year. The top floor had a covered balcony. In 1909, it burned down.

Carved out by glaciers and lined with sheer white cliffs, the 0.5-mile-long, 60-foot-deep Mohonk Lake is the scenic centerpiece of the resort. Lying at 1,247 feet above sea level, it covers 17 acres and is the fourth largest of the sky lakes. Originally called Paltz Pond, in 1869 it was renamed Lake Mohunk. By 1883, its name was changed to Mohonk Lake. Between 1893 and 1926, the lake supplied all of the Mountain House's water needs. Between 1870 and 1964, ice was harvested from the lake for refrigeration purposes. In 1875, black bass purchased by Alfred Smiley were introduced into the lake; in 1920, it was stocked with trout. Today, a variety of fish are found in Mohonk Lake, the only sky lake that supports such a population. Its partly shale bottom accounts for the lower acidity that allows fish to survive.

Other natural landmarks include Sky Top and Eagle Cliff, two of Mohonk's highest vantage points, with superb views in all directions. Both are accessible via trails and carriage roads. Visible from many miles away, Sky Top is probably the single most distinctive, familiar, and prominent natural landmark in the Shawangunks. There are superb views of Sky Top from Eagle Cliff. A huge crevice on the face of Sky Top—officially named the Crevice, but popularly and erroneously called the "Lemon Squeeze"—is located just below the Smiley Tower. It is accessible via wooden ladders from the Labyrinth Path.

Multiple-Use Roads and Trails (in Alphabetical Order)

Cope's Lookout Path

Length: 0.3 mile. **Markings:** Signs at both ends. **General description:** This short, smooth, well-graded trail connects Eagle Cliff Road with Cope's Lookout Road and Cope's Lookout. Bikes are not permitted, but the trail is open to cross-country skiers in winter, rated easiest. **Highlights:** Cope's Lookout is one of the most famous and magnificent viewpoints in Mohonk. This path can also be utilized for any number of scenic circular hikes or ski trips that take in other worthy points of interest. It is easily accessible from the Mountain House. **Downside:** None. **Difficulties and hazards:** None.

To get there from the Mountain House, go south to the left tennis courts and continue south on Eagle Cliff Road (see below). Just past the tennis courts, the Cope's Lookout Path turns off to the right. It soon passes an athletic field on the right. The trail continues as a wide path through the woods, shortly reaching an intersection with Cope's Lookout Road (see below). You can continue straight for a very short distance to Cope's Lookout and the four-way intersection of Cope's Lookout, Laurel Ledge, and Humpty Dumpty Roads (see below). From Cope's Lookout, you look directly south along the ridge, with the Trapps cliffs and Millbrook Mountain most prominent. Coxing Clove and Dickie Barrie may be observed to the right. There's a gazebo to sit and enjoy this amazing vista. A second cliffside gazebo stands prominently just below off the blue-marked Cathedral Path (see below).

Cope's Lookout Road

Length: 0.5 mile. **Markings:** Signs at both ends. **General description:** Like the Cope's Lookout Path, this carriage road connects the Mohonk Mountain House with Cope's Lookout. Bikes are not permitted, but the carriage road is open to cross-country skiers in-season, rated easiest. **Highlights:** Following this road, it is an easy jaunt from the Mountain House to one of Mohonk's most celebrated views. Returning via the Cope's Lookout Path would make an exceptionally easy circuit hike or ski. **Downside:** None. **Difficulties and hazards:** None.

To get there, begin from the tennis courts by the Mohonk Mountain House. Notice the area off to the right that was once a 16-acre paddock housing a herd of deer from 1904 to 1947. By the time the Smileys purchased the property, wild deer were nearly extirpated from the area, and a display herd was kept here for the enjoyment of hotel guests. They were finally released when it became too difficult to maintain them. Ironically, deer are so plentiful now that they pose a threat to the environment as well as motorists. Go south past the tennis courts on the left. Just past the basketball courts on the right, the Sunset Path (see below) departs on the right. Pass the athletic field on the left. Continue south, through the woods. The road veers to the left. Laurel Ledge Road can be seen below on the right, running parallel. Soon you'll cross the Cope's Lookout Path (see above) and, just beyond, arrive at Cope's Lookout.

Eagle Cliff Road

Length: 1.8 miles. **Markings:** Signs at intersections. **General description:** This carriage road, built in 1872, loops around the top of Eagle Cliff (elevation 1,434 feet). While the road climbs almost 200 feet, the ascent is gentle and not very taxing. Note the presence of many informal paths that provide opportunities to shorten the trip or take in more views. **Highlights:** Accessibility and ease as well as many rewarding vistas in all directions, especially south to the ridge and east to Mohonk Lake and Sky Top, make this one of the best and most popular trails in Mohonk. There are numerous gazebos along the way for resting and enjoying the views. In winter, this road makes an excellent cross-country ski trail, rated easiest. Bikes are not permitted. **Downside:** It isn't the best place to go if you're looking for tranquility. **Difficulties and hazards:** Steep cliffs off the side of the road in a few places.

The carriage road begins to the left of the tennis courts, just south of the Mohonk Mountain House. Pass the shuffleboard and tennis courts on the right. A trail on the left leads to the Granary, an apt name for what was once a shed that stored grain for the deer paddock (see above). In 1965, it was moved to its present location. Today, it is an outdoor refreshment area restricted to overnight guests. Pass a gazebo on the right, the first of many. Just beyond, the Cope's Lookout Path appears on the right (see above). On the left is Lambdin's Path (see below), which descends to the shore of Mohonk Lake. Eagle Cliff Road begins to climb gradually. The road veers to the left. There's a steep slope on the right and a protective fence. A number of mature hemlocks line the road. The road bends to the right and left and continues to ascend.

The road bends to the right (east) and passes a gazebo with a fine south-facing view of the ridge; the Trapps cliffs, Near Trapps, and Millbrook Mountain lie in the distance, and the Rondout Valley is off to the right. The road bends to the left and continues to climb. Pass a gazebo on the left with a fine open view looking north to the Rondout Valley and the Catskills Range in the distance,

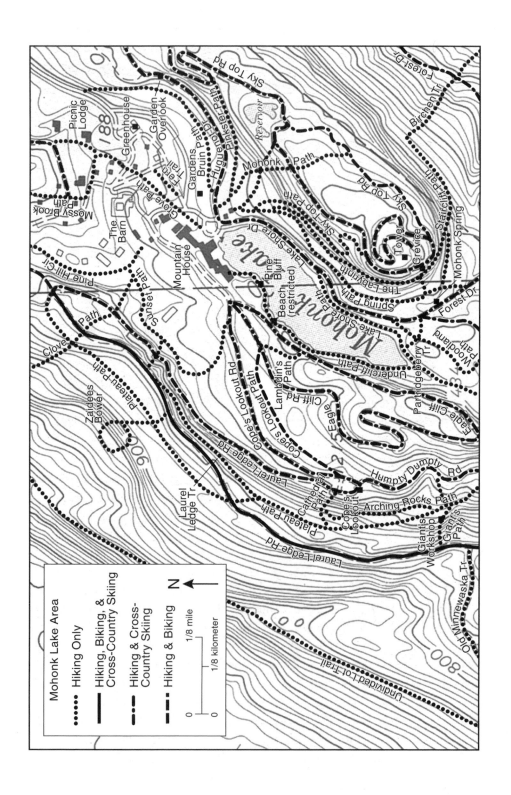

Mohonk Lake Area

∙∙∙∙∙ Hiking Only

━━━━ Hiking, Biking, & Cross-Country Skiing

∙━∙━ Hiking & Cross-Country Skiing

∙∣∙∣ Hiking & Biking

N ←

0   1/8 mile
0   1/8 kilometer

Picnic Lodge

Greenhouse

Garden Overlook

Fern Trail

Gardens

Bruin Path

Huguenot Dr

Pinkster Path

Sky Top Rd

Forest Dr

Birchen Tr

Reservoir

Mohonk Path

Sky Top Rd

Staircliff Path

Mohonk Spring

Tower

Crevice

The Labyrinth

Spring Path

Forest Dr

Woodland Path

Mossy Brook Path

The Barn

Grove Path

Mountain House

Lake Shore Dr

Pine Bluff

Beach (restricted)

Lake Shore Path

Mohonk Lake

Underdiff Path

Partridgeberry Tr

Eagle Cliff

Pine Hill Gtr

Sunset Path

Clove Path

Plateau Path

Zaidees Bower

Cope's Lookout Rd

Lambdin's Path

Cliff Rd

Eagle Cliff Rd

Cope's Lookout Path

Laurel Ledge Rd

Laurel Ledge Tr

Plateau Path

Cathedral Path

Cope's Lookout

Humpty Dumpty Rd

Arching Rocks Path

Giant's Workshop

Giant's Path

Laurel Ledge Rd

Old Minnewaska Tr

Undivided Lot Trail

188

906

800

800

800

including all of the major peaks. Note the cedar tree on the right. The road continues to loop to the right. Pass a branch of Eagle Cliff Road on the left with a shortcut connecting the two sections. The road continues to veer right, ascending gradually. There's a steep slope on the right. Pass the first of three gazebos on the right with open views looking west to Coxing Clove, Dickie Barrie, the Rondout Valley, and the distant Catskills. The road then makes a sharp turn to the left (east). There is an awesome view on the right looking south from the top of Eagle Cliff, a real classic; look for the Trapps, Near Trapps, Millbrook Mountain, and Wallkill Valley, with the Hudson Highlands in the distance. Huntington Lookout, a gazebo on the right, is a perfect spot to enjoy this vista. There's a gazebo perched on top of the rock cliff with a broad open view looking south, and also east and west, with a talus field located just below. Just beyond, the Eagle Cliff Ascent Trail appears on the right. This steep route descends to Short Woodland Drive (see below).

Eagle Cliff Road bends more to the left. An impressive view looking east to Sky Top and the Albert K. Smiley Memorial Tower appears on the right. The road continues to climb. The road turns sharply to the left again and then to the right. Another branch of Eagle Cliff Road appears just below on the left. The road bends to the left (north) and begins to descend. Pass the first of four gazebos on the right. The first has a magnificent view of Mohonk Lake below, with the Mountain House at the far end of the lake and Sky Top across the way, its tower standing prominently. The Wallkill Valley and the village of New Paltz can be seen in the distance.

The Mountain House disappears from view as the road loops left, closely parallel to the other section of Eagle Cliff Road. The road then loops to the right between other sections of road above and below. There's another view on the right of the lake below and Sky Top across the way. The road loops to the left. A shortcut appears on the left that leads to the other section of Eagle Cliff Road, passed earlier. The road then loops to the right and passes another shortcut trail on the right. The Undercliff Path appears below, hugging the lakeshore. The road crosses a wooden bridge over Lambdin's Path (see below). On the opposite side of the bridge, a path descends and joins the trail below. Turning right onto this trail will bring you down to the Undercliff Path and the shore of Mohonk Lake.

A path on the right leads to another gazebo with a fine east-facing view of Sky Top and the lake. A view overlooking the beach area is passed on the right. The road passes the Granary on the left. The Undercliff Path (see below) and beach area entrance appear on the right. This area is restricted to hotel guests. A trail on the right leads up to Pine Bluff, Washington's Profile, and five gazebos with clifftop views of the lake. Continue on the road, which bends to the left. Pass the south end of the Mohonk Mountain House on the right as Eagle Cliff Road joins the automobile road just northeast from where you started.

Forest Drive

Length: 2.1 miles. **Markings:** Signs at intersections . **General description:** This carriage road begins from the four-way intersection of Old Minnewaska Road, Lake Shore Drive, and the Patridgeberry Trail, just southeast of Mohonk Lake, and continues out to Oakwood Drive east of Rock Spring Bridge. There's a long, gradual descent most of the way, with a steeper descent between Rock Spring Bridge and Oakwood Drive. It is an official maintained cross-country ski route rated more difficult, except for the section from Rock Spring Bridge to Oakwood Drive, which is rated most difficult. Bikes are only permitted between Rock Spring Bridge and Oakwood Drive. **Highlights:** For much of its length, Forest Drive follows the base of Sky Top cliff, with fine views of the cliffs and talus slopes when the leaves are down and at least partial views the rest of the year. It is a longer, but pleasant alternate route to get from the Mohonk Gatehouse to the Mohonk Lake area. Scrambling routes up to Sky Top as well as trails to Duck Pond can be accessed from this carriage road. **Downside:** Longer and more remote than some people might prefer. **Difficulties and hazards:** Only the last steep section between Rock Spring Bridge and Oakwood Drive presents any challenges.

From the four-way intersection of Old Minnewaska Road, Lake Shore Drive, and the Patridgeberry Trail (see below), go east on Forest Drive, soon passing Mohonk Spring on the left underneath a quaint stone shelter, dedicated in 1904. A sign warns that the water is untested; drink at your own risk. Continue a short distance and pass the Spring Path on the left (see below). Huge talus boulders appear on the left side of the road. There's a partial view of Sky Top cliff above through the trees. The road bends to the right and descends to cross a small stream, then bends sharply to the left. An unmarked shortcut trail appears on the left. Enter a grove of white pine trees. Home Farm Drive (see below) appears on the right. Forest Drive levels and loops to the left. Old Stage Road (see below) appears on the right. Forest Drive now leaves the white pine area and bends sharply to the right. The unmarked shortcut trail appears again on the left.

The beginning of a deep ravine, part of the Kleine Kill, appears on the right. Pass more talus boulders on the left. Descend and pass the red-marked Birchen Trail on the left, a short scrambling route up to the base of the Sky Top cliff (see below). Opposite, on the right, is the red-marked Duck Pond Trail (see below). There's a gazebo at this juncture. Forest Drive veers left and continues to descend. Pass more views on the left of the cliffs towering above, visible only in winter. Pass the Rock Spring Path on the left, now closed. Just beyond, reach Rock Spring Bridge, the intersection of Bridge Road on the left (see above), which leads to Woodland Bridge and the Mohonk Gatehouse, and, on the right, Kleine Kill Road (see below), which leads to Duck Pond.

Forest Drive, now part of the bike route, turns right at the above intersection. The road immediately climbs and veers to the left amid white pine and hemlock. The road then bends to the left and begins a long descent. It loops to the right, briefly levels, bends to the left, and intersects Oakwood Drive 0.6 mile from Rock Spring Bridge. Going right here will take you out to the Duck Pond area and eventually Rhododendron Bridge. Going left leads to Lenape Lane and the Mohonk Gatehouse.

Hemlock Lane

Length: 0.2 mile. **Markings:** Signs at both ends. **General description:** A carriage road that descends from Huguenot Drive, crosses Garden Road, and ends at North Lookout Road. It is groomed for cross-country skiing and rated more difficult. Bicycling is not permitted. **Highlights:** Part of an alternative route from the gatehouse to Mohonk Lake and Sky Top. Fine north-facing views. **Downside:** Traffic noise. **Difficulties and hazards:** Steep slopes and cliffs just off the trail. Watch out for vehicles when crossing Garden Road.

From Huguenot Drive, Hemlock Lane departs at an angle and slowly descends. Garden Road, the automobile route, appears below on the right. There's a steep slope on the right and a wooden guardrail. Cross Garden Road, passing a gazebo on the left. There's a view looking north into Glenn Anna. The road resumes its descent on the other side, bending left and right. A steep rocky slope drops away on the right. Pass another gazebo with a wonderful north-facing view of the Rondout Valley and distant Catskills Range. Just beyond, North Lookout Road appears below on the right. Hemlocks are plentiful in the vicinity. Pass more north-facing views on the right as the road veers left, soon joining North Lookout Road (see above) and ending.

Huguenot Drive

Length: 1.1 miles. **Markings:** Signs at intersections. **General description:** This carriage road, completed in 1881, links the Mohonk Mountain House with Woodland Bridge. It is a designated cross-country ski trail rated more difficult. Bikes are not permitted. **Highlights:** Huguenot Drive provides access to the formal gardens, Garden Overlook, and the gentlest approach to Sky Top. **Downside:** None. **Difficulties and hazards:** None. Please note that the section of Huguenot Drive from the Mohonk Gatehouse to Woodland Bridge is part of the automobile route and is not recommended for pedestrians.

From the putting green circle just north of Mohonk Lake and just east of the Mountain House, go north on Huguenot Drive, an unpaved carriage road, to the left of the Council House. Pass the formal gardens on the left. The road veers to the right, and the Bruin Path (see below) departs on the left through the gardens. The road ascends gradually, with views of the gardens on the left, as well as the Rondout Valley and distant Catskills to the north and west. The road then veers left and passes the Happel Seat, a gazebo on the left with a view of the gardens and the Mountain House. There's an open, west-facing view of the huge barn. The road continues to climb gradually. Cliffs appear on the right side of the road. The Fox Path crosses the road (see below), descending a wooden staircase on the left.

The road bends to the left. A path on the left descends to the Bruin Path (see below). Arrive at Garden Overlook, with views facing south and west to the formal gardens, barn, Mountain House, and Rondout Valley and Catskills in the distance. There are a number of benches on the hillside above, as well as an unmarked path on the right that leads up to Sky Top Road. Cliffs appear below on the left. The road then bends to the right, and the Tallman Path (see below) departs on the left. Just beyond, Sky Top Road (see below) appears on the right. Huguenot Drive begins to descend very gradually through a stunted deciduous forest of oak and maple, scattered pitch pine, and mountain laurel. The road levels and the Whitney Path departs (see below) on the left. Huguenot Drive then bends sharply to the right and continues its descent. Hemlock Lane appears on the left (see above), descending to the automobile road below. The road veers left and right, descending gradually with the auto road below on the left. The Fox Path appears on the right as the road bends to the left and reaches the auto road just before Woodland Bridge. A wooden staircase on the opposite side of the road leading to the Glenn Anna Path (see above) is the most direct route for hikers to the Mohonk Gatehouse.

Humpty Dumpty Road

Length: 0.4 mile. **Markings:** Signs at intersections. **General description:** This winding carriage road connects Cope's Lookout (at a four-way intersection with the Cope's Lookout Path, Cope's Lookout Road, and Laurel Ledge Road) with Short and Long Woodland Drives. Mountain bikes are not permitted, but in winter this groomed path makes a superb cross-country ski trail, rated more difficult. **Highlights:** The carriage road traverses the base of Eagle Cliff, where there's a talus slope of boulders referred to as Humpty Dumpty, and impressive south-facing vistas of the Shawangunk Ridge. **Downside:** None. **Difficulties and hazards:** There are sharp bends that may challenge skiers. Beware steep cliffs off the side of the road.

From Cope's Lookout (described above), turn south on Humpty Dumpty Road. The blue-marked Cathedral Path (see below) descends a wooden staircase on the right. The road bends right, climbs, then levels. A gazebo on the right has a broad open view of the ridge looking south, with the Trapps cliffs and Millbrook Mountain most prominent. Looking west (on the right), you see the Rondout Valley and the Catskills Range in the distance.

The Giant's Path, marked in blue (see below), appears on the right. The road descends and bends to the right, the left, then the right and starts to climb again. The road bends sharply to the left (skiers may have difficulty negotiating this turn). It then veers left, with nearly continuous views on the right looking south. The road descends, passing talus boulders on both sides of the road. The Humpty Dumpty Path, marked in red (see below), departs on the right. Pass another gazebo on the right with an amazing view looking south across the talus slope: Growing among the boulders of the Humpty Dumpty talus slope are 300-year-old dwarf white pines and hemlocks that are among the oldest ever found in this part of New York State. The Trapps cliffs and Millbrook Mountain can be seen, as well as the Wallkill Valley off to the left and Dickie Barrie, Coxing Clove, the Rondout Valley, and the Catskills off to the right. Pass more magnificent views on the right and continue a short distance south to the three-way intersection of Short and Long Woodland Drives (see below).

Lake Shore Drive

Length: 0.5 mile. **Markings:** Signs at intersections. **General description:** This popular and easy carriage road starts from the putting green circle by the north end of the Mohonk Mountain House, follows the shore of Mohonk Lake, and ends at the four-way intersection of Old Minnewaska Road, Forest Drive, and the Patridgeberry

Trail. It was built by the Smileys in 1870, the very first of what would eventually become an elaborate system of carriage roads. In winter, it is a cross-country ski route, rated easiest. Bicycling is not permitted. **Highlights:** There are fine views of Mohonk Lake and the Mountain House. The road can be utilized for any number of pleasant and or challenging walks around Mohonk Lake and to other points of interest. **Downside:** None. **Difficulties and hazards:** None.

From the putting circle, go south, to the right of the Council House and Conference Center and to the left of Mohonk Lake. The Sky Top Path departs on the left (see below). The road soon reaches the lakeside, with fine views looking south of Mohonk Lake; the Mountain House is to the right. Cross a wooden bridge. On the right, there's a gazebo on an island, connected by a wooden bridge. The Labyrinth Path (see below) departs on the left through a maze of boulders at the base of the cliff. Just beyond, the Spring Path (see below) also departs on the left. Continue south, following the lakeshore, passing a number of gazebos on the right and benches on the left. The Spring Path runs parallel to the road, just above on the left. An unnamed trail departs on the right for Open Camp, a beach area, as the road veers away from the lakeshore. The Lake Shore Path then crosses the road (see below).

Lake Shore Drive bends to the left and climbs moderately. The Lake Shore Path lies below on the right. The Woodland Path (see below) departs on the right. The road continues to veer left and away from the lake. A bench appears on the left with a dramatic view of Sky Top and the Albert K. Smiley Memorial Tower standing directly above. Just beyond, an unnamed path on the left leads to the Spring Path and the Crevice. Lakeshore Drive veers to the right and ends at the four-way intersection of Forest Drive (see above) on the left, the Patridgeberry Trail (see below) on the right, and Old Minnewaska Road (see below) straight ahead.

Laurel Ledge Road

Length: 2.2 miles. **Markings:** Signs at intersections. **General description:** This carriage road goes from Cope's Lookout to Rhododendron Bridge. From Cope's Lookout to where the Old Minnewaska Trail branches off to the right, the road is a nearly continuous gradual descent. The entire road is groomed as a cross-country ski trail in-season, rated very difficult. (I feel that this rating only holds true if you're following this road uphill in the opposite direction from what's described below.) The section from the intersection with the Maple Path by Rock Pass to Rhododendron Bridge is part of a designated bike route. **Highlights:** West-facing views, cliffs, and talus slopes. There are also connections to numerous hiking trails. **Downside:** Bicyclists should note that biking is not permitted on the upper section of this road. **Difficulties and hazards:** Skiers may find the long, steady incline taxing and the turn at Rock Pass challenging. Beware the steep cliffs off the side of the road in a few places.

From Cope's Lookout, turn right and follow this carriage road as it proceeds north, gradually descending. There's a steep slope on the left side of the road. Cope's Lookout Road is visible above to the right. Pass a gazebo on the left with a west-facing view of Coxing Clove and Dickie Barrie. Continue to descend through dense hemlock on both sides of the road. The red-marked Fern Ledge Path (see below) descends a wooden ladder on the left. On the right, a trail climbs up to the Sunset Path (see below). There's a cliff on the right with a gazebo on top: Sunset Rock. Continue north. The red-marked Clove Path (see below) crosses the road. There are more cliffs to the right of the road.

The road makes a sharp U-turn where the blue-marked Maple Path enters on the right at the base of Rock Pass (see below). The Maple Path is part of a designated bike route that enters Laurel Ledge Road at this point and follows it the rest of the way to Rhododendron Bridge. Continue for a short distance. The red-marked Plateau Path (see below) appears on the right. Laurel Ledge Road bends to the left. You soon encounter a wooden bench on the left with a view through an opening in the forest filled with mountain laurel, looking west to the Rondout Valley and Catskills, with Peekamoose Mountain dominating the skyline. There's a steep slope on the right side of the roadway.

The red-marked Clove Path again crosses the carriage road. Cliffs on the left side of Laurel Ledge Road appear, with hemlocks growing out of narrow fissures in the rock. The blue-marked Laurel Ledge Path (see below) climbs a cliff on the left. There are talus slopes at the foot of the cliff. You'll soon cross the yellow-marked Zaidee's Path (see below). A short distance beyond, the red-marked Plateau Path returns, crossing Laurel Ledge Road at an angle and continuing off to the left.

The road passes through a hemlock grove. There are sheer rock cliffs to the left of the roadway and steep slopes off to the right. The forest opens up to oaks and mountain laurel, with partial views of Coxing Clove below on the right. Laurel Ledge Road then passes through an area with enormous boulders on both sides of the road and, just beyond, crosses a talus slope. The blue-marked Giant's Path on the left (see below) leads to Giant's Workshop. The road finally levels. Continue a short distance. On the right, the blue-marked Old Minnewaska Trail enters the roadway (see below).

A short distance beyond and to the left is Rhododendron Swamp, a 6-acre wetland densely populated with rhododendron. There are cliffs on the right side of the road. The swamp used to be a small sky lake that slowly, over thousands of years, filled with sediments. A number of species of rare plants are known to inhabit the swamp. The road bends to the left, skirting the swamp. A shortcut up to Overcliff Road enters on the right. Laurel Ledge Road bends to the right. There's a stream to the left of the road. Soon it arrives at Rhododendron Bridge (elevation 943 feet), a stone bridge over the stream where five carriage roads meet. There's a map of the immediate vicinity located on the bridge. Overcliff Road is on the right, and Undercliff Road is straight ahead (see below). On the opposite side of the bridge lie Oakwood Drive (to the right of the bridge) and Old Minewaska Road (to the left; see below).

Long Woodland Drive

Length: 0.6 mile. **Markings:** Signs at intersections. **General description:** This carriage road climbs from Old Minnewaska Road up to the three-way intersection with Short Woodland and Humpty Dumpty Roads. No bikes are permitted. As a cross-country ski trail, this road is rated more difficult. **Highlights:** South- and west-facing views. Continue north to Humpty Dumpty Road, which has even more views. **Downside:** None. **Difficulties and hazards:** There are a number of curves that may be difficult to negotiate when going downhill on skis.

Long Woodland Drive departs from Old Minnewaska Road (see below). Heading north, it passes a small vernal wetland on the right. It then bends sharply to the left and descends gradually. The road veers right and begins climbing again. Pass another vernal pool on the left. The road bends to the right, then veers left and descends. The road levels, bends to the left, and then loops in a wide circle to the right. There are views on the left through the trees looking south along the ridge, with the Trapps cliffs most prominent. There's a short climb to an open view on the left looking south and west of Coxing Clove and Dickie Barrie.

The road veers to the right, then veers left and descends. It levels once more. Pass an unmarked shortcut to Short Woodland Drive on the right. Long Woodland Drive makes a sharp left and climbs, soon intersecting Short Woodland Drive (see below) and Humpty Dumpty Road (see above). There's a bench with a wonderful vista looking south to Coxing Clove, Dickie Barrie, the Trapps, and Millbrook.

Maple Path

Length: 0.4 mile. **Markings:** Blue blazes; signs at both ends. **General description:** This trail, which connects Mossy Brook Road with Laurel Ledge Road, is part of a continuous bike route. **Highlights:** The thrilling descent through cliff-faced Rock Pass just before it meets Laurel Ledge Road. **Downside:** None. **Difficulties and hazards:** As a bike route, it is somewhat rougher and more challenging than the carriage roads. You need to walk your bike through Rock Pass.

From the right (west) side of Mossy Brook Road, the blue-marked trail (clearly identified as a bike route) departs the carriage road and climbs a relatively steep slope. The trail is somewhat rocky and interrupted with plastic water bars. After a short distance, it reaches a power-line right-of-way and the unmarked Stokes Trail (see below). Make a sharp left on the Stokes Trail and follow it for a short distance. The Maple Path soon departs on the right. The trail bends to the left and right, and then left again, to the right of a small cliff. The trail continues through a thicket of mountain laurel. The Sassafras Trail departs on the left (see below).

The blue-marked Maple Path begins a sharp descent through Rock Pass. (Bicyclists are warned to dismount for the next 250 feet.) Tall, sheer rock cliffs appear on both sides of the trail. There are huge hemlocks at the base of the cliffs, with smaller ones growing from the ledges and out of the sides of the cliff. At the base of the cliff, the trail levels and soon meets Laurel Ledge Road (see above). Going right leads to Rhododendron Bridge. A left leads to Cope's Lookout and the Mohonk Mountain House. The bike route continues to the right.

Mossy Brook Road (Upper Section)

Length: 1.2 miles. **Markings:** Signs at intersections. **General description:** This woodland carriage road starts from the intersection with Cedar Drive and ends at Greenhouse Road by the formal gardens east of Mohonk Lake. Mossy Brook Road is part of the original approach used by John F. Stokes from Chapel Farm to his tavern by the lake. The section from Cedar Drive to the Maple Path is open for bicyclists. However, skiing is not permitted. **Highlights:** This trail provides an excellent and easy route for traveling from the north part of Mohonk to the Mohonk Lake area and vice versa. It is also useful for any number of loop hikes. **Downside:** None. **Difficulties and hazards:** Bicyclists should watch the signs and avoid the sections that do not permit bikes.

From the intersection of Cedar Drive and the lower section of Mossy Brook Road (see below), the road ascends gradually, passing cliffs and talus on the left. Pass Mossy Brook Spring on the left; this is usually gushing water, but may be dry in summer. Since 1926, water pumped from the spring has helped supply the Mountain House. The road bends to the right, and the Mossy Brook Path (see below) departs on the left. The road then bends to the right and continues to ascend gradually. On the right lies a small seasonal stream, the upper reach of Mossy Brook, which the road soon crosses. Pass tilted slabs of conglomerate above on the right. The blue-marked Maple Path (see above) appears on the right. Bicyclists must depart here.

Mossy Brook Road bends to the right and left. The Stokes Trail (see below) appears on the right. Mossy Brook Road soon crosses a gate and becomes asphalt paved as it enters Cottage Grove, a private residential area with late 19th- early 20th-century homes. The road splits. Go right. Soon Pine Hill Drive (see below) enters on the right, while North Lookout Road (see above) enters left. Mossy Brook Road continues straight but soon bends to the left. The huge barn with the museum (see above) appears above on the right. Mossy Brook Path appears again on the left, leading to the Picnic Lodge. Mossy Brook Road then bends to the right and crosses Barn Road, passing a small fire station on the left and returning to an unpaved condition. The road soon crosses Grove Path (see below), which provides direct routes to either the Picnic Lodge (left) or the Mountain House (right). Pass the Fern Trail (see below) on the right. Mossy Brook Road ends at Greenhouse Road across from the formal gardens.

Old Minnewaska Road

Length: 0.9 mile. **Markings:** Signs at intersections. **General description:** Not to be confused with the Old Minnewaska Trail, a hiking trail, this carriage road was built in 1876 to link Mohonk with Alfred Smiley's new resort at Minnewaska Lake. Today, it travels from the intersection of the Patridgeberry Trail, Lake Shore Road, and Forest Drive to Rhododendron Bridge. For most of its length—Home Farm Drive to Rhododendron Bridge—it is a designated bike route. It is also a cross-country ski route, rated very difficult. **Highlights:** An important north–south link that also provides access to a number of destinations and carriage roads. **Downside:** None. **Difficulties and hazards:** Remoteness. Also, for almost a third of its length the road features a steep incline, relatively severe for a carriage road. Whether you're on foot, skis, or a bike, going uphill can seem like a relentless trudge. Going downhill, particularly on skis, can be a thrilling or scary run—the best in the Gunks if you don't lose your balance and fall.

From the intersection of the Patridgeberry Trail (see below), Lake Shore Road, and Forest Drive (see above), near the southeast end of Mohonk Lake, go south and west on the carriage road, passing Short Woodland Road (see below) on the right. Old Minnewaska Road soon bends to the right. Behind you and above through the trees, you can see Sky Top and the Smiley Memorial Tower. A field appears on the left side of the road. Home Farm Drive (see below) departs on the left. From this point, Old Minnewaska Road becomes a bike route. Pass a corral on the left with an open east-facing view across a sloping field to the Wallkill Valley with the Marlboro Hills in the distance and the Hudson Highlands far to the south.

The road bends to the right and intersects Long Woodland Road (see above) on the right (for skiers, this is the last chance to detour before the big hill). Descend briefly and cross a small stream. The road bends to the left. Pass a small wetland on the left. The road bends right. There's a dramatic south-facing open view on the left to the Trapps cliffs. The road then begins a relatively long, 0.25-mile descent with an unforgiving steep slope off to the left. At the bottom of the incline, the road bends sharply to the left (skiers and bicyclists going at high speeds may have difficulty negotiating this turn). The road continues to descend, more gradually now, passing a shale pit on the left and a stream on the right and finally ending at the intersection with Rhododendron Bridge on the right. Straight ahead, veering to the left, is Oakwood Drive (see below). Across the bridge is the three-way intersection of Undercliff and Overcliff Roads (see below) with Laurel Ledge Road (see above).

Short Woodland Drive

Length: 0.4 mile. **Markings:** Signs at both ends. **General description:** This short carriage road connects Old Minnewaska Road with Long Woodland Drive and Humpty Dumpty Road. As a cross-country ski route, it is rated more difficult because of some steep sections. No bikes are allowed. **Highlights:** Although it offers no views until the end, this is a pleasant jaunt through the woods. It connects to other trails and carriage roads and may be useful for any number of worthy circuit hikes or ski ventures. **Downside:** None. **Difficulties and hazards:** Skiers may find this a little challenging.

From Old Minnewaska Road, southeast of Mohonk Lake, go west and climb briefly. Intersect Woodland Path (see below) on the right. There's a ropes course set up in the woods here. Do not disturb. The road descends and turns left. Pass an unmarked shortcut to Long Woodland Drive on the left as the road bends to the right and begins to ascend. Lake Shore Path appears on the right (see below). Short Woodland Drive bends to the left and levels. The road then veers right and continues through a beautiful grove of hemlock, white pine, and mountain laurel. Eagle Cliff Ascent Path appears on the right (see below). The road then veers to the left and descends, passing a talus slope on the right, soon reaching the three-way intersection of Long Woodland Drive and Humpty Dumpty Road (see above). There's a bench and an expansive ridgeline view looking south, with the Trapps cliffs and Millbrook Mountain most prominent.

Sky Top Road

Length: 2.2 miles. **Markings:** Signs at intersections. **General description:** This gentle and popular approach to the Albert K. Smiley Memorial Tower begins at Huguenot Drive just beyond Garden Overlook and continues up to the reservoir. It then loops around the top and the tower. As a cross-country ski route, it is rated more difficult. Bikes are not permitted. **Highlights:** Spectacular views in all directions from Mohonk's most familiar landmark. **Downside:** The top isn't the most serene place. Expect crowds on fair-weather weekends. **Difficulties and hazards:** Dangerous cliffs by the side of the carriage road in a number of places.

From the intersection of Huguenot Road (see above), Sky Top Road climbs and bends right and left, passing Garden Overlook on the right, with a southwest-facing view of the formal gardens and the Mohonk Mountain House. The road ascends gradually, looping sharply to the right and passing Dawn Seat, a gazebo with a north-facing view of Guyot Hill and the Hudson Valley in the distance. The road bends to the left and continues in a southerly direction. There's a gazebo on the right with a southwest view of Garden Overlook below. An informal path on the right leads down to Huguenot Drive. The road then bends to the right. The Fox Path (see below) crosses the road.

The road bends right and left and comes upon another gazebo with a view facing west and south. Just beyond, there's a fine open view looking west and north, with the Rondout Valley and Catskills in the distance. The Pinkster Path (see below) enters on the right. Continue south and west, gradually ascending and passing shortcut paths on the left that lead up to a second loop of Sky Top Road. The road loops sharply left and right, passing more great west-facing views of the Mountain House, the Barn, formal gardens, and other structures, as well as distant views of the Rondout Valley and Catskills Range.

By now you're facing directly south, continuing to ascend, then passing a stone dam on the right. Just beyond is the Big Reservoir. It is an idyllic, romantic spot. The pond displays colorful waterlilies and is surrounded by white pines. There's a croaking din of amphibians. A gazebo on an island in the middle is connected by wooden bridge to the shore. This used to be the main reservoir for the hotel. A carriage road departs on the right and follows the south shore of the reservoir out to Cleveland Seat, a gazebo with a west-facing view, and the Reservoir Path (see below).

Just beyond the pond, Sky Top Road forks again. From this juncture, Sky Top Road loops around the top of Sky Top, so you have the option of going either way. In order to get to the views quicker, we will turn right here. Go a short distance and intersect an unnamed carriage road (see above) that follows the south shore of the Big Reservoir. From this juncture, turn left (south). The Mohonk Path (see below) crosses the road. The road bends to the left and right a couple of times. Pass Dawe's Seat, which provides a classic view looking west and north to Mohonk Lake and the Mountain House way below, with the Rondout Valley and the entire Catskills Range in the distance.

A short distance beyond, the Sky Top Path (see below) crosses the road. Going left here is a shortcut to the tower, which is now visible above and to the left. Continue south, with continuous open views on the right looking west and south. The road bends sharply to the left (east). The Labyrinth Trail departs on the right down through the Crevice. A descent this way is not recommended. Pass benches on the left with fine south-facing views down the spine of the Shawangunk Ridge. Sky Top Road continues to loop to the left (north), passing the tower on the left. The road then circles around what was once a quarry supplying the stone that built the tower. Later, it served as a reservoir to store water in case of fire, connected to the Mountain House by a 12-inch pipe. Pass a picnic area and an information board on the right with a fine map display of trails and carriage roads.

You've arrived at the top (elevation 1,542 feet), the highest point on the Shawangunk Ridge north of Route 44/55. The road passes the back of the tower and circles around to its entrance on the opposite (south-facing) side. If you have the strength, climb the 101 steps to the observation deck and, when it's clear enough, enjoy the panoramic 360-degree vista that includes the Hudson Valley, the Taconics, the Berkshires, the Shawangunk Ridge, the Kittatinnies, the Catskills, the Hudson Highlands, the Rondout Valley, and glimpses of six states: New York, Massachusetts, Connecticut, New Jersey, Vermont, and Pennsylvania.

From the tower, Sky Top Road continues westward briefly, then bends sharply to the right (north). Pass the Sky Top Path on the left and then (on the right) the same information board you saw just a little while ago. There are continuous views looking west and north. The road then bends to the right (east), circling the top as it gradually descends. The road bends to the left (south), then loops sharply to the right and begins to descend in earnest. It bends to the left again, passing an open view on the right looking south and east of the Wallkill and Hudson Valleys with the Marlboro Hills and Hudson Highlands in the distance. Odell Outlook, a gazebo, is on the right. The Staircliff Path on the right is closed for safety reasons.

The road loops back and forth a few times, with more open views looking south and east and the village of New Paltz in the distance. Continue level through the woods, veering to the right. Pass another gazebo on the right with an east-facing view. The road veers left and right, then descends and bends right and left (north). The Mohonk Path appears again on the left. A short distance beyond, the road intersects the other branch of Sky Top Road on the left.

Hiking Trails and Scrambling Routes (in Alphabetical Order)

Arching Rocks Path

Length: 0.2 mile. **Markings:** Red blazes and signs. **General description:** This very short route connects the Giant's and Humpty Dumpty Paths with the Cathedral Path. **Highlights:** Much of the way, this unique route follows the base of tall, spectacular cliffs with magnificent overhanging ledges in a truly primeval forest setting, an experience not to be missed. **Downside:** Tougher hiking than some people might enjoy. **Difficulties and hazards:** Some relatively easy scrambling over rocks is involved. Watch your footing. Also, you have to hike more difficult trails just to get here.

From the three-way intersection of the Giant's and Humpty Dumpty Paths (see below), the red-marked Arching Rocks Path meanders through forest to the base of the cliffs up ahead. Climb rocks, then turn left and descend. Follow red blazes along the base of the cliff wall past fallen slabs, crevices, and cool spots. Very large mature hemlocks stand next to the cliffs. Pass a section of wall on the right in the process of separating from the main cliff. Huge overhanging rock slabs tower above. The red-marked trail turns left and soon joins the blue-marked Cathedral Path (see below).

Birchen Trail

Length: 0.1 mile. **Markings:** Red blazes, arrows, and signs. **General description:** This scrambling route starts at Forest Drive across from the Duck Pond Trail and climbs up to the base of the Sky Top cliff, where it meets the Staircliff Path. **Highlights:** A challenging climb on talus boulders in an area of dramatic topography. **Downside:** Climbing up hill on rocks isn't everyone's idea of pleasure. **Difficulties and hazards:** Follow the blazes carefully, because the route is far from obvious. Footing is poor.

From Forest Drive (see above) across from the Duck Pond Trail (see below), the red-marked Birchen Trail meanders upward through the forest, crosses an area of talus rocks, then turns left, climbing into an area of larger boulders and turning right then left, climbing more steeply. The imposing Sky Top cliff appears above like a castle wall. The route continues to climb toward the base of the cliff. The trail then veers to the left and arrives at an open sun-filled patch beneath the cliff wall. Here meet the Staircliff Path (see below), which turns left and follows the base of the cliff.

Bruin Path

Length: 0.3 mile. **Markings:** Signs at both ends. **General description:** An easy, well-graded footpath from Huguenot Drive by the formal gardens to Garden Road. This is a nature trail with numbered signs. A booklet by Ruth Happel Smiley (illustrations by R. B. Matteson) is available from the Mountain House gift shop that describes the numbered signs. **Highlights:** Easy to access from the Mountain House and Picnic Lodge, this trail provides a fine exposure to the area's ecology and both human-made and natural scenery. **Downside:** None. **Difficulties and hazards:** None.

From Huguenot Drive (see above), just north of the putting green and Mohonk Lake, the Bruin Path departs on the left. There's a sign. The trail skirts the formal rose garden, a delight in summer and fall. Continue to the right of the garden, passing a gazebo on the right. The trail reaches a fork. Turn right and continue to a four-way stop. Turn right again. Leave the lawn area and cross a bridge over a drainage. Climb the slope to the right of the garden. There's a view on the left looking west to the Rondout Valley and distant Catskills Range. The Mountain House is off to the extreme left. There's a bench here for sitting and enjoying the vista.

Just beyond, the Fox Path departs on the right (see below). The Birchen Path veers left and passes an unusual two-story gazebo on the left. Cross a grass field with a view of the greenhouse below on the left and rock cliffs on the right, with gazebos perched along the top. This is the Garden Overlook. A trail on the right with steps leads up to Huguenot Drive. A rock cliff appears on the right with talus boulders below it. The trail S-curves left and right, then passes a second cliff on the right with an overhang ledge that's typical of Shawangunk cliffs. The trail loops to the left, descends and bends to the right, and ends at Garden Road. Just beyond on the right is the Tallman Path (see below). A left turn here returns you to the area by the Mountain House.

Cathedral Path

Length: 0.2 mile. **Markings:** Blue blazes and signs at intersections. **General description:** A steep scrambling route from the Plateau Path up to Cope's Lookout. **Highlights:** A wonderland of towering cliffs, talus boulders, and an amazing south-facing view from the top. Also, access to the Arching Rocks Path. **Downside:** This difficult scrambling route is certainly not for everyone. **Difficulties and hazards:** Climb on rocks practically the whole way, some very steep and slippery when wet. Footing is poor. You must also navigate through some pretty tight spots. Be extra careful around the edges of steep cliffs.

Depart from the red-marked Plateau Path opposite a viewpoint overlooking Coxing Clove. The trail starts out level, then veers left and right and begins climbing up talus boulders. Turn right and continue to climb through rocks, following the markers since the trail isn't obvious. The trail bends to the right and briefly descends. Then it turns left and continues to climb through rocks, approaching a dramatic cliff face with detached hunks of rock wall lying jumbled at its base. From the bottom of the cliff, the blue-marked Cathedral Path intersects the red-marked Arching Rocks Path (see above). Turn left at this juncture and climb on boulders with overhanging ledges suspended overhead.

Scramble up fallen boulders using your hands. The route squeezes between rocks, then hooks to the right and again climbs very steep rocks. It then squirms through a very tight hole contrived of fallen boulders. The trail hooks sharply to the left and climbs another boulder, then on to the next higher boulder, and so on. It finally emerges to an open view overlooking Coxing Clove and the Rondout Valley, with the Catkills Range in the distance. The trail follows the edge of the cliff. Beware the steep precipice on the right. Notice the Arching Rocks Path beneath the cliff. Turn left and follow the base of a small cliff, and then right. Again, beware the dangerous cliffs off to the right. Climb into the open on an exposed rock slab. There's a summerhouse perched there for relaxing and savoring the broad, expansive south- and north-facing vista. The Trapps are off to the left. Millbrook Mountain can be seen on the horizon. Make a sharp left at the summerhouse and climb the wooden stairs up to the intersection where Cope's Lookout Road, Humpty Dumpty Road, and the Cope's Lookout Path all intersect (see above).

Clove Path

Length: 0.7 mile. **Markings:** Red blazes for part of the way. Signs at most intersections. **General description:** A hiking trail that descends from the Sunset Path, crosses two sections of Laurel Ledge Road and the Plateau Path, and ends when it meets the Undivided Lot Trail. **Downside:** Parts of this trail are very remote. **Difficulties and hazards:** A rocky path with some steep stretches and poor footing, though use of hands isn't necessary.

From the Sunset Path (see below), descend steeply. Pass a rock wall on the right. The trail then veers to the left. Don't worry if you lose the trail. Keep descending. It's a very short distance to Laurel Ledge Road (see above). Cross the road at a diagonal. Once across the road, the trail improves. It continues to descend gradually, veering to the left and then right through mountain laurel. The trail bends right and left and descends more steeply. Arrive at Laurel Ledge Road again, having crossed the loop the road makes. Turn left on the road, follow it for a very short distance, then turn right and depart from the road and into the woods again. This section of the trail is marked with red blazes.

The trail veers right and descends, soon crossing the red-marked Plateau Path (see below). Renew your gradual descent. Cross a rocky flood channel. Continue through a hemlock grove. Descend at a steeper pitch through patches of grass and bare stone slabs. The trail continues to veer right as it descends a rocky slope. The Clove Path then veers left and descends a more gentle slope. The incline steepens once more just before arriving at the blue-marked Undivided Lot Trail (see below). A left turn here leads to the Old Minnewaska Trail; a right leads to Clove Chapel.

Eagle Cliff Ascent Path

Length: 0.1 mile. **Markings:** Signs at both ends. Red blazes and arrows. **General description:** This short, moderate scrambling route climbs up from Short Woodland Drive to Eagle Cliff Carriage Road. **Highlights:** Both a shortcut and a challenge. The view from the top is worth the effort for most. **Downside:** The steepness, rock scrambling, and climbing a wooden ladder aren't everyone's idea of a good time. **Difficulties and hazards:** A precipitous trail that involves scrambling on rocks. Some may have difficulty on the wooden ladder.

From Short Woodland Drive (see above), just east of its intersection with Long Woodland Drive, depart from the roadway on the red-marked trail. The trail veers to the left and immediately starts climbing through rocks. Turn right and continue climbing. Note the cool air emanating from deep crevices below. The trail squeezes between two boulders, then climbs over rocks to the right of an enormous boulder. The trail then veers to the left and over a wooden footbridge.

The trail bends to the right and climbs over talus rocks. Arrive at a small rock overhang, turn left, and climb a steep incline. You will need your hands here. There's a south-facing view on the left of the Trapps and Coxing Clove, with Millbrook Mountain on the horizon. The trail turns right. Climb a wooden ladder to the top of a bare rock slab with a grand open view looking south, which includes the Wallkill Valley below and to the left. Turn left once more and climb stone steps up to Eagle Cliff Carriage Road (see above).

Fern Ledge Path

Length: 0.1 mile. **Markings:** Red blazes and signs. **General description:** A very short, steep, but moderate scramble up a rocky slope from the Laurel Ledge Path to Laurel Ledge Road. **Highlights:** A challenging shortcut. **Downside:** May be too challenging for some. **Difficulties and hazards:** Footing is generally poor and worse when wet. The wooden ladder at the end may intimidate some.

From the blue-marked Laurel Ledge Path (see below), the red-marked Fern Ledge Path departs on the left (there's an arrow) just above Laurel Ledge Road. Climb up steep rocks and make a sharp left turn. The trail then veers to the right. The incline steepens and the trail turns right, then left, then right again. The grade levels for a short distance. Laurel Ledge Road appears above on the left. The trail then bends to the left and climbs a steep wooden ladder. The top of the ladder comes out on Laurel Ledge Road (see above). A trail on the opposite side of the road leads up to the Sunset Path (see below).

Fern Trail

Length: 0.1 mile. **Markings:** Signs at both ends. **General description:** A very short, well-graded, easy-to-follow trail, perfect for beginners. It starts from Greenhouse Road and ends on Mossy Brook Road between the Mountain House and the formal gardens. The Fern Trail was established in 1965. **Highlights:** A variety of ferns such as Christmas fern and cinnamon fern, shrubs like spicebush, and wild herbs and flowers such as wood hyacinth and lily-of-the-valley may be observed along this trail, which provides a small illusion of wilderness in the center of landscaped grounds. Easily accessible from the Mountain House and Picnic Lodge. Many of the plants are labeled. **Downside:** None. **Difficulties and hazards:** None.

From Greenhouse Road, turn left and follow the path into a tiny patch of woodland. Pass a number of labeled plants along the trail. Cross a small stream about midway. The trail winds through a field of tall ferns and comes out on Mossy Brook Road (see above). A right turn here leads to the formal gardens and greenhouse.

Fox Path

Length: 0.3 mile. **Markings:** Red arrows on rocks in some places. Signs at intersections. **General description:** This rough trail goes from Huguenot Drive near Woodland Bridge to the Bruin Path near the greenhouse. **Highlights:** Pleasant forest scenery, an impressive rock overhang, and wonderful views looking north and west. This is a great direct route for hiking from the gatehouse to the Mohonk Lake area. **Downside:** This trail is a bit rough for some folks, especially beginners. **Difficulties and hazards:** Some climbing on rocks, stone steps, and a steep wooden staircase, though use of hands is not required.

From Huguenot Drive (see above), the Fox Path departs and climbs, levels briefly, and climbs again, veering to the right. The trail soon approaches a cliff face and turns left at the base. It then makes a steep ascent, passing a large overhanging rock ledge on the right. The trail veers right and makes another steep climb. It then bends to the left and continues to climb steadily. The trail then arrives at a dry plateau of chestnut oak forest. There's a brief ascent over a rock ridge; just beyond, Sky Top Road (see above) appears. A left turn here leads to the Smiley Memorial Tower. There's a clearing and a gazebo on the right with views looking north and west to the Rondout Valley and distant Catskills Range.

After crossing the road, the trail appears to split. Take the left fork into the forest, descending two sets of stone steps and passing small rock ledges on the left. The trail then crosses Huguenot Drive (see above), with more views looking north and west. Descend a steep wooden staircase, which is closed in winter, and continue down stone steps. Finally arrive at the Bruin Path (see above), with a fine view of the Mountain House, the greenhouse below, and, to the right, the Rondout Valley and distant Catskills Range.

Giant's Path

Length: 0.3 mile. **Markings:** Blue. Signs at intersections. **General description:** This short route climbs 200 feet from Laurel Ledge Road up to Humpty Dumpty Road. The trail meanders through Giant's Workshop, a complex of tall cliffs, deep crevices, and massive talus boulders. Warning: Backpacks will have to be removed in order to make it through some tight spots. **Highlights:** An array of intriguing rock formations. For those who appreciate challenges, this one is not to be missed. Also, enjoy deliciously cool crevice temperatures in summer. **Downside:** This hike is definitely not everyone's idea of pleasure. **Difficulties and hazards:** A demanding, tough scramble over rocks and through exceptionally tight spaces that are claustrophobic. Dangerous cliffs and deep crevices in a few spots.

From Laurel Ledge Road (see above), just north of the intersection with the Old Minnewaska Trail, the trailhead is on the right (east) side of the road. The trail proceeds uphill, bends to the left, and comes to the edge of a talus boulder field. The trail enters a crevice on the left between sharply tilting rock walls. The blue-marked route scrambles past a deep "hole" on the left that may be worth exploring with a flashlight. Continue climbing on rocks. The route makes a sharp left, then a U-turn, and continues its ascent. Cross a wooden plank over a crevice, turn left, and squirm through a tight tunnel (backpacks might not make it).

At the end of the tunnel, make another sharp U-turn, this time to the right, and proceed into an open crevice. Climb the last few boulders up to an open rock slab with a fantastic view looking south to the Trapps and Millbrook, and west to Coxing Clove. The trail makes a sharp right here and intersects the red-marked Plateau Path (see below). Just beyond, cross another wooden plank over the same deep boulder-strewn crevice you just scrambled through. The trail turns right and follows the edge of a steep precipice. It then bends left and intersects the Arching Rocks Path on the left (see above) and Humpty Dumpty Path on the right (see below), both marked in red. Continue straight, uphill. Turn right and follow the boulder-strewn path. Turn left, still climbing, and eventually arrive at Humpty Dumpty Road (see above). There's a gazebo on the left, perfect for resting and enjoying the view.

Grove Path

Length: 0.2 mile. **Markings:** Signs at both ends. **General description:** A very short, easy trail connecting Barn Road and Garden Road. **Highlights:** This trail is a direct route between the Picnic Lodge and Mohonk Lake. **Downside:** None. **Difficulties and hazards:** None.

From Barn Road nearly opposite the Mossy Brook Path (see below), follow the well-surfaced path. You'll soon cross Mossy Brook Road. Pass the formal gardens on the left and the Fern Trail (see above). The path ends at Garden Road across from the Mountain House. Mohonk Lake is straight ahead.

Humpty Dumpty Path

Length: 0.2 mile. **Markings:** Red blazes; signs at both ends. **General description:** This short route scrambles over the Humpty Dumpty talus field starting from Humpty Dumpty Road and ending at the three-way intersection of the Giant's and Arching Rocks Paths. **Highlights:** Experience a talus field up close. **Downside:** This kind of hiking may be too rough for some. **Difficulties and hazards:** The route climbs over and around boulders and skirts deep crevices. You have to follow markers, because the route is not obvious.

From Humpty Dumpty Road (see above), descend and follow the red blazes as you scramble over open boulders that are part of the Humpty Dumpty talus field. From the edge of the talus field, dip into a shady spot between rock walls. Emerge into the open, climbing through more talus boulders and bearing right. Pass deep crevices on both sides of the trail. Finally enter a hemlock grove. Descend and soon arrive at the three-way intersection with the blue-marked Giant's Path and red-marked Arching Rocks Path (see above).

Labyrinth Path

Length: 0.4 mile. **Markings:** Red blazes; arrows and signs at intersections. **General description:** This route, first marked in 1871, starts from Lake Shore Drive just south of the Mountain House, scrambles through crevices and talus boulders, and climbs 300 feet to Sky Top Road. It is closed in winter due to ice. **Highlights:** Arguably the most exciting and challenging short hike in the Gunks. The highlight (for some) is a steep climb up a series of tall ladders in a narrow crevice (popularly but erroneously referred to as the Lemon Squeeze). The payoff is the incredible view from Sky Top's summit. **Downside:** Expect your clothes to get soiled. Those who are nervous about heights and tight places should avoid this one. Also, beware rowdy adolescents! **Difficulties and hazards:** Don't let the short distance fool you. It's a tough scramble through rocks and crevices almost the entire way, and you'll have to use your hands and squirm through some pretty tight spots. Predict at least 45 to 60 minutes to complete the trail.

From the Mountain House, proceed south along Lake Shore Drive (see above), following the lake for 0.1 mile to a sign for the Labyrinth Path on the left. You'll immediately enter a jumble of huge talus boulders, crevices, and caves. Red paint blazes on the rocks lead you through this maze that's too complex to describe in detail for this book. Flashlights will help you explore some dark nooks and crannies, but don't stray far from the designated path. Nearly halfway along, there's an exit path up to the Sky Top Path on the left and one down to the Spring Path on the right (see below). After 30 to 60 minutes of scrambling, reach the base of the Sky Top cliff. Here you meet the red-blazed Staircliff Path (see below) and an unnamed red-marked route that descends to the Spring Path and Lake Shore Drive. Above is the Crevice, where a huge, towering hunk of conglomerate separated from the main cliff in glacial times. A system of rustic ladders leads you up through this narrow passage that tapers toward the top—one of the most exhilarating, or terrifying, nontechnical routes in the Shawangunks. At the top of the cliff, cross a narrow wooden plank over the crevice you just climbed and intersect Sky Top Road (see above), which loops around the summit.

Lake Shore Path

Length: 0.4 mile. **Markings:** Signs at both ends. **General description:** This easy, scenic trail runs from the Spring Path out to Short Woodland Drive, passing through a huge boulder field and following the shoreline of Mohonk Lake. **Highlights:** Fine views of the lake and Mountain House. It is useful for any number of circuit hikes in the Mohonk Lake area. **Downside:** None. **Difficulties and hazards:** None.

From the spot where the Spring Path (see below) departs Lake Shore Drive, southeast of the Mohonk Mountain House, go right (there's a sign and a gazebo at the intersection). The trail winds through huge talus boulders fallen from the cliffs above. Descend and cross Lake Shore Drive (see above). Open Camp, a beach area, is to the right. The Lake Shore Path follows the steep southeast bank of Mohonk Lake, with Lake Shore Drive above on the left. Continue south, cross a small wooden bridge, and intersect the Patridgeberry Trail on the left (see below). Just beyond, there's a fine view looking north of the entire lake, with the Mohonk Mountain House standing prominently at the north end. Eagle Cliff can be seen across the way, and there's a gazebo on the opposite shore. The trail reaches the south end of the lake and intersects the Undercliff

Path (see below). Turn left at this intersection. There's a sign indicating TO WOODLAND DRIVE. Climb briefly. The trail then levels. Cross another small wooden bridge over a tiny brook and arrive at Short Woodland Drive (see above).

Lambdin's Path

Length: 0.1 mile. **Markings:** Signs at both ends. **General description:** This very short trail near the south end of the Mohonk Mountain House begins at the Undercliff Path on the shore of Mohonk Lake and ends at Eagle Cliff Road. **Highlights:** It may be utilized for any number of circuit hikes around the lake and to other points of interest. **Downside:** None. **Difficulties and hazards:** You have to climb a tall wooden staircase.

From the Undercliff Path, which follows the lakeshore, Lambdin's Path appears on the right (left if you're going north) as a wooden staircase. Ascend the stairs all the way through the narrow crack in the cliff face. It becomes a footpath at the top, soon crossing underneath a wooden bridge where Eagle Cliff Road spans the trail (see above). A trail on the right ascends the embankment to the road. Lambdin's Path descends briefly and continues through the woods, bends to the right, and comes out on another branch of Eagle Cliff Road, by the tennis courts. Cope's Lookout Path (see above) is just across the road on the right.

Laurel Ledge Path

Length: 0.3 mile. **Markings:** Blue blazes and signs at intersections. **General description:** This woodland trail starts from Laurel Ledge Road and ends at the Plateau Path, running closely parallel to Laurel Ledge Road for much of the way. **Highlights:** Cliffs, talus, forest scenery. **Downside:** At times, the trail runs so close to Laurel Ledge Road that you may wonder what the point is. **Difficulties and hazards:** Some scrambling on rocks with poor footing and climbing or descending a wooden ladder. This trail isn't obvious, so follow the blazes carefully.

From Laurel Ledge Road (see above), the blue-marked trail departs and enters the forest to the right of rock outcrops running parallel to the road. The red-marked Fern Ledge Path soon departs on the left (see above). The blue-marked trail squeezes between rock ledges and boulders. Descend a steep wooden ladder. Turn left and climb beneath cliffs. The trail then veers right and continues parallel to Laurel Ledge Road.

Pass a small rock pinnacle on the left that's separated from the main cliff. Zaidee's Path, marked in yellow, departs on the right (see below). Continue along the base of the cliff, gradually veering away from the roadway. The trail crosses the side of a forested slope and intersects the red-marked Plateau Path (see below).

Mohonk Path

Length: 0.4 mile. **Markings:** Red blazes on rocks and signs at intersections. **General description:** A rough woodland trail that starts from Huguenot Drive and climbs steeply up to Sky Top Road. Please note that the short section between the east loop of Sky Top Road and the former Pinnacle Path is now closed. **Highlights:** A great uphill workout, useful for any number of loop hikes in the Sky Top area. **Downside:** This is a strenuous route, not for everyone. **Difficulties and hazards:** Steep climbing on innumerable stone steps.

To get there from the putting green north of Mohonk Lake, follow Huguenot Drive (see above) for a short distance. Turn right after the Council House, passing the skating pavilion on the right. Arrive at the intersection with the Pinkster Path (see below). From here, the Mohonk Path begins climbing up a steep rocky slope. The trail bends to the left and crosses the Reservoir Path (see below). The trail continues to climb, zigzagging up stone steps, and finally crossing the west loop of Sky Top Road (see above). A right turn here leads to open views and the Albert K. Smiley Memorial Tower. The trail continues through the woods, soon becoming level and veering to the left. The trail descends, eventually reaching the east loop of Sky Top Road and ending. The section of the Mohonk Path that lies beyond is closed.

Mossy Brook Path

Length: 0.5 mile. **Markings:** Signs at both ends. **General description:** A woodland path starting from Mossy Brook Road and ending at Barn Road near the Picnic Lodge. It follows Mossy Brook for much of the way. **Highlights:** A more rustic route to the Mohonk Lake area than some of the alternatives. It also sees fewer hikers and thus has more solitude to offer. Mossy Brook itself is tiny, but scenic. **Downside:** This moderately rough trail isn't for everyone. **Difficulties and hazards:** The trail isn't well trodden, and footing may be challenging in a few places. Also, the trail route may be obscure at times.

From Mossy Brook Road, the trail departs from the road and goes uphill, bending left and right. It continues to ascend gradually. Pass Mossy Brook on the left, sliding through narrow chutes in the rock. The trail stays to the left of the stream and crosses bare rock slabs. Ford the stream on rocks. The stream plunges 4 feet over moss-covered rock slabs on the left. Just beyond, private residences of Cottage Grove appear ahead on the right. Cross paved North Lookout Road (see above). Continue uphill for a short distance to a fork in the trail and turn left. Follow this level path briefly and turn right to continue your ascent. The trail bends to the left. A trail to the Picnic Lodge appears on the left, crossing a small drainage on a wooden bridge. The Mossy Brook Path continues straight to the right of the drainage and passes a short rock wall on the right. A tiny distance beyond, the path reaches Barn Road. To the left are the greenhouse and formal gardens. To the right is the Barn Museum. Straight ahead is the Grove Path (see above), which leads to the Mountain House and Mohonk Lake.

Patridgeberry Trail

Length: 0.1 mile. **Markings:** Signs at both ends. **General description:** This short, easy, well-graded trail connects Lake Shore Drive, Old Minnewaska Road, and Forest Drive with the Lake Shore Path on the shore of Mohonk Lake. **Highlights:** Lovely forest scenery. It can be utilized either as a shortcut or as part of a circuit trip. **Downside:** None. **Difficulties and hazards:** None.

At the four-way intersection southwest of Mohonk Lake where Lake Shore Drive, Old Minnewaska Road, and Forest Drive (see above) all meet, follow the footpath—unmarked, but obvious. The trail winds through a grove of hemlocks and white pines, staying fairly level and closely parallel to Lake Shore Drive on the right. The trail bends to the left and crosses the Woodland Path (see below), then makes a brief descent to the shoreline of Mohonk Lake, where it meets the Lake Shore Path (see above).

Pine Hill Drive

Length: 0.4 mile. **Markings:** Signs at both ends. **General description:** This carriage road built in 1886 starts from the intersection with Mossy Brook and North Lookout Roads and ends by the Fiddler Green parking area. It is open only for hiking; bicycling and skiing are not permitted. **Highlights:** North-facing views. Easy to access from the Mountain House and Picnic Lodge. **Downside:** None. **Difficulties and hazards:** Occasional vehicular traffic.

From the intersection of Mossy Brook and North Lookout Roads (see above), the road begins a slow ascent. Sawmill Road, a residential cul-de-sac and dump site, soon departs on the right. Pine Hill Drive continues to veer to the right for a short distance, then bends sharply to the left, still climbing. Just before a clearing on the right, it begins to level, and the Sassafras Path (see below) departs on the right. Just beyond, the Pine Hill Summerhouse appears on the right, with a fine north-facing view across the Rondout Valley to the Catskills Range in the distance.

Pass a private residence on the left. There's another, similar open view on the right. The road veers to the left and descends. Then it bends more to the left. The Sunset Path (see below) appears on the right. Just beyond is the Fiddler's Green parking area.

Pinkster Path

Length: 0.2 mile. **Markings:** Signs at both ends. **General description:** A short, relatively easy woodland trail that climbs up from the intersection with the Mohonk Path and ends at Sky Top Road. It was named for the flowering wild azaleas that used to bloom along it. Unfortunately, the azaleas have all departed. **Highlights:** A welcome easier alternative to the strenuous Mohonk Path. It is useful for any number of loop hikes in the Sky Top area. **Downside:** None. **Difficulties and hazards:** Though gradual and relatively gentle, it is still an uphill ascent.

From the intersection with the Mohonk Path (see above), the Pinkster Path starts out fairly level and then begins to ascend gradually across the side of a steep slope. As the trail climbs gently through the forest, it veers to the left. It then bends to the right and, in a short while, reaches Sky Top Road (see above). A right turn here leads to the Sky Top summit.

Plateau Path

Length: 0.9 mile. **Markings:** Red blazes and signs at intersections. **General description:** An easy footpath through woodlands starting from Laurel Ledge Road by Rock Pass, crossing Laurel Ledge Road about halfway, and ending at the intersection with the Giant's Path. The trail runs roughly parallel to Laurel Ledge Road the entire way. **Highlights:** For walkers, a quieter alternative to Laurel Ledge Road. There are fine clifftop views looking south and west and access to a number of other trails with a multitude of possibilities for circular hikes. **Downside:** None. **Difficulties and hazards:** Dangerous steep cliffs along the edge of the trail.

From Laurel Ledge Road (see above), make a right turn on the red-marked trail right as Laurel Ledge Road makes a hairpin turn at Rock Pass. The trail bends to the left and passes through an open patch of sweet fern and young mountain laurel. Cross a small seasonal stream on rocks. Then cross the red-marked Clove Path (see above). A right turn here leads to the Undivided Lot Trail (see below). Continue straight through a hemlock grove. Cross the yellow-marked Zaidee's Path (see below). A right turn here will lead to Zaidee's Bower. The Plateau Path continues straight and soon crosses Laurel Ledge Road at a diagonal.

After crossing the road, the Plateau Path starts to climb. Pass the blue-marked Laurel Ledge Path (see above) on the left. Arrive at an open area of bedrock cut by deep fissures. There are views looking west to Coxing Clove, the Rondout Valley, and the distant Catskills. The blue-marked Cathedral Path departs on the left (see above). Continue along the top of the ledge, with more views looking south of Coxing Clove and Dickie Barrie. Note that the cliffs here are high and steep, and the path along the top is narrow. The views are nearly continuous here. Behold a view looking south along the spine of the ridge at least as far as Millbrook Mountain when it's clear. You can also see the Lost City cliffs and the Trapps. Climb steadily. The Giant's Workshop maze of crevices and rocks appears below on the right. The trail turns left and continues to climb. The red-marked path ends at the intersection of the blue-marked Giant's Path (see above). There are fine south-facing views here from the top of a tilted slab of conglomerate.

Reservoir Path

Length: 0.2 mile. **Markings:** Signs at both ends. **General description:** An easy ascent from the Sky Top Path to Sky Top Road. **Highlights:** Pleasant walking. A fairly direct route from Mohonk Lake to a lovely reservoir useful for a number of loop hike possibilities. **Downside:** None. **Difficulties and hazards:** Steep slopes just off the trail in some places.

From the Sky Top Path (see below) just south of the huge skating pavilion, the Reservoir Path departs on the left, turning sharply to the right and then left as it ascends. The skating pavilion is below on the left. About halfway along, the Mohonk Path (see above) crosses the trail. There's a steep slope on the left. The trail continues its slow ascent, crossing the slope at an angle. Finally arrive at Sky Top Road (see above). A right turn brings you to the summit of Sky Top; a left leads to the reservoir.

Sassafras Path

Length: 0.1 mile. **Markings:** Signs at both ends. **General description:** A rough trail that descends from Pine Hill Drive to the Maple Path. **Highlights:** Beautiful hemlocks and rock outcrops. **Downside:** The roughness of this trail will discourage some. **Difficulties and hazards:** A steep and rocky trail with poor footing. Use caution, especially when it's wet. Dangerous cliffs in the vicinity.

From Pine Hill Drive (see above), the trail descends a steep incline, soon bending to the right. The trail continues to veer to the right, descending more slowly through hemlocks. There are dangerous cliffs off to the left, with rock outcrops on the right. The trail finally bends to the left and arrives at the Maple Path (see above). Beware speeding bicycles.

Sky Top Path

Length: 0.4 mile. **Markings:** Signs at intersections. **General description:** This relatively easy and popular route (approximately 30 minutes of walking) ascends 300 feet from Mohonk Lake to Sky Top Road near the Albert K. Smiley Memorial Tower. **Highlights:** This trail provides the most direct access to Sky Top's summit from the Mountain House. It also boasts a number of extraordinary and famous views of Mohonk Lake and the Mountain House. **Downside:** It is uphill, and some may find this too much of an ordeal. **Difficulties and hazards:** Steep cliffs and deep crevices just off the trail. Watch your step and watch your kids.

From the Mountain House, go around the northeast corner of the lake past the putting green, passing the Council House and the Conference Center building on the left. A sign marks the beginning of the Sky Top Path. The trail veers right, with immediate and continuous views of the lake and Mountain House. A pair of gazebos appear on the right, reachable via wooden bridges over deep crevices that separate massive stone blocks from the main cliff. The new skating pavilion appears on the left. Just beyond, the Reservoir Path (see above) departs on the left.

Continue to follow the Sky Top Path as it gradually ascends. An unmarked trail departs on the right, following the cliff edge with many intriguing views peering down into a maze of rocks and crevices. Views grow more expansive as you ascend higher. The trail reenters on the right; there's also a gazebo on the right with a splendid panoramic view of the lake, Mountain House, Rondout

Valley, and distant Catskills Range to the north and west. Below is a jumble of colossal boulders. Ridge Rock Seat, a gazebo, appears on the right, with a view of a precariously tilted hunk of rock perched in front collecting stones and other objects people have tossed there.

A rough path departs on the right down to the Labyrinth (see above). The Sky Top Path climbs up through hemlocks and loops sharply to the left and then right. Arrive at an open area with a gazebo and a classic sweeping view of the lake and the Mountain House, now way below, as well as fine views looking north, west, and south to the Catskills, the Rondout Valley and Coxing Clove, Eagle Cliff, Trapps cliffs, Millbrook Mountain in the distance, and the Wallkill Valley off to the far left. A short trail on the right leads out to Thurston Rock, a gazebo with a similar classic view that also includes the dramatic sheer face of the Sky Top cliff. Below there's a huge talus field at the base of the cliff. Near the top, the trail crosses Sky Top Road (see above), switchbacks to the left, and ends at a second loop of Sky Top Road. To reach the Albert K. Smiley Memorial Tower, go right and follow the road as it bends to the left. Continue to the entrance to the tower.

Spring Path

Length: 0.4 mile. **Markings:** Signs at both ends. **General description:** An easy, well-graded path that starts at Lake Shore Drive across from the Mountain House and ends at Forest Drive. **Highlights:** Views of the lake and hotel, monstrous talus boulders, and Mohonk Spring are just some of the high points of this brief jaunt that's also good for any number of loop excursions. There's access routes to the Labyrinth and the Crevice. **Downside:** None. **Difficulties and hazards:** None.

From Lake Shore Drive (see above), the Spring Path departs on the left. Almost immediately, steps leading to the Labyrinth (see above) depart on the left. The Spring Path continues level past a wall of giant fallen blocks on the left and fine views on the right looking across Mohonk Lake, with the Mountain House standing on the opposite shore. The trail starts to climb gradually and enters the forest. It then splits. The Lake Shore Path (see above) departs on the right.

The Spring Path veers left and continues its gradual ascent, winding through the forest past huge boulders. Just beyond, a ladder route up to the Labyrinth appears on the left (see above). The trail enters a hemlock grove, then levels and veers more to the left. There's a view of the Sky Top cliffs on the left through the trees. The trail continues through a mountain laurel thicket, veering left again. A trail to Lake Shore Drive appears on the right, while a red-marked scrambling route appears on the left, leading up a rocky talus slope to the infamous Crevice. Soon the Spring Path bends sharply to the right and descends. Just as it does, another red-marked scrambling route departs on the left for the Staircliff Path (see below).

The Spring Path continues to descend. It bends to the left and passes the rustic stone structure that shelters the Mohonk Spring on the right. The trail continues for a short distance and ends at Forest Drive (see above). A left turn here leads to Rock Spring Bridge; a right will return you to the lake.

Staircliff Path

Length: 0.2 mile. **Markings:** Red blazes and arrows. **General description:** This very rough scrambling route basically follows the base of the Sky Top cliff from where it meets the Birchen Trail to where it ends at the Labyrinth and Crevice. **Highlights:** An exciting and challenging scramble over rocks. Dramatic scenery of sheer cliffs and talus slopes and occasional open views facing south and east across the Wallkill Valley. **Downside:** The height, tough footing, and climbing make this route unappetizing to some. **Difficulties and hazards:** The scrambling can be challenging in spots. A lot of climbing on rocks. Footing is generally poor. You'll need to use your hands in places.

From the Birchen Trail (see above), the Staircliff Path continues west along the base of Sky Top cliff, passing a towering rock pinnacle on the right, separated from the main cliff. The route continues over rocks, passing another block disconnected from the main cliff. Cool air emanates from a hole underneath. The trail briefly climbs. Notice the overhangs above on the edge of the cliff. There are talus slopes below on the left. The route circumvents a large talus boulder then continues along the cliff base, passing beneath a slanting fallen boulder, briefly descending, and veers right to cross a rock field.

Climb boulders up to a "cave" covered by an enormous fallen rock slab, then descend into a "room" and up a wooden ladder. Continue following the base of the cliff, climbing talus boulders using your hands. The trail then bends away from the cliff and arrives at an intersection. A red-marked route on the left follows the talus slope down to the Spring Path (see above). The Staircliff Path continues along the base of the cliff. Again, you will probably need your hands to climb the steep rocks. Arrive at a flat, open slab with a fine east-facing view of the Wallkill Valley and Marlboro Hills. Just beyond is another intersection. The red-marked route on the left descends to the Spring Path. The other red-marked route is the Labyrinth Path (see above). The Crevice is above on the right.

Sunset Path

Length: 0.3 mile. **Markings:** Signs at both ends. **General description:** This trail starts from Pine Hill Drive just beyond the Fiddler's Green parking area and ends at Cope's Lookout Road by the basketball courts. **Highlights:** Close proximity to the Mountain House. A wonderful view from Sunset Rock and access to a number of other trails, useful for loop hikes. **Downside:** A little rough for some people. **Difficulties and hazards:** This trail is hard to follow in a few places.

From Pine Hill Drive (see above) just west of the Fiddler's Green parking area, turn left onto the trail (there's a sign). Follow it for a short distance. The red-marked Clove Path departs on the right (see above). Continue straight, crossing a tiny streamlet on rocks. The trail bends to the right and left, then passes Sunset Rock on the right with a gazebo. There's an excellent view from here looking north and west to Coxing Clove, the Rondout Valley, and the distant Catskills Range. Continue straight. Note the steep slope on the right as you pass through hemlocks and mountain laurel.

On the right is another branch of the trail, which descends a short distance to Laurel Ledge Road (see above). From the intersection, the Sunset Path veers to the left and climbs and bends more to the left. The trail finally comes into a clearing by the basketball courts. Just beyond, on the right, is Cope's Lookout Road (see above) and the end of the trail.

Tallman Path

Length: 0.2 mile. **Markings:** Signs at both ends. **General description:** This short but challenging trail starts from Huguenot Drive, crosses Garden Road, and later turns into the Whitney Path. **Highlights:** A challenging climb or descent with a good view from the top. **Downside:** This steep route is more difficult than what many people would prefer. **Difficulties and hazards:** The trail south of Garden Road is quite sheer, with precarious footing and dangerous cliffs. It is also not well defined. Use caution crossing Garden Road, an automobile route.

From Huguenot Drive (see above), the Tallman Path departs from the carriage road and heads north, passing a gazebo on the left perched on top of a rock with a fine west-facing view. Turn right and descend. The trail veers left. There is an open west-facing clifftop view to the Rondout Valley, with the Catskills Range in the distance. Garden Road is visible below. Cross a rock slab and bend to the right, following the edge of the cliff. Descend to the right of small cliffs and cross Garden Road. Watch out for traffic.

The trail resumes on the other side of Garden Road, descending through forest and soon arriving at an intersection. A trail on the left leads to a private residence. On the right is the Whitney Path (see above).

Undercliff Path

Length: 0.2 mile. **Markings:** Signs at intersections. **General description:** Not to be confused with Undercliff Road, which runs beneath the Trapps, this relatively easy and quite scenic walking trail built in 1874 follows the west shore of Mohonk Lake from the Mohonk Mountain House south and finally ending at the Lake Shore Path at the south end of the lake. Please note that the beginning of the trail, which traverses the hotel's bathing beach, is closed to all but hotel guests. Day visitors can circumvent the beach by taking Eagle Cliff Road to Lambdin's Path and descending the wooden staircase to the lakeshore, where it joins the Undercliff Path. **Highlights:** Easy to access from the Mountain House, this path is useful for walking trips around the lake and to other points of interest. There are many fine views of both the lake and Sky Top across the way. **Downside:** None. **Difficulties and hazards:** None.

Hotel guests wishing to access the trail may start from the Granary, a refreshment area reserved exclusively for guests. It is located south of the Mountain House off Eagle Cliff Road (see above). From the Granary, follow the trail down to the lake and the beach area. Cross the beach area and turn right and through the gate, entering the area that is also open to day visitors. The trail follows the shoreline of Mohonk Lake at the base of tall cliffs with overhangs. There's a short ascent through trees and mountain laurel, passing a gazebo on the left named Fort Washington with a westward view of the lake and Sky Top.

Reach Lambdin's Glen, a small trough in the cliff face. Lambdin's Path (see above) ascends a wooden staircase on the right. If you aren't a hotel guest, you may be accessing or departing the trail here, depending on what direction you're going. Continue south. The trail begins to descend. There are more superb views looking westward across the lake and north to the Mountain House. The trail reaches the lakeshore, passing a gazebo on the left. The Undercliff Path heads beneath a jumble of fallen blocks on the right and ends at the south end of the lake, intersecting the Lake Shore Path (see above).

Woodland Path

Length: 0.3 mile. **Markings:** Signs at intersections and at both ends. **General description:** A path through the forest starting from Lake Shore Drive and ending on Short Woodland Drive south of Mohonk Lake. **Highlights:** A pleasant jaunt in the woods, useful for a number of loop hikes. **Downside:** None. **Difficulties and hazards:** None.

From Lake Shore Drive (see above), the Woodland Path departs and continues between the road and the Lake Shore Path (see above), with Mohonk Lake below on the right. The Patridgeberry Trail (see above) crosses the trail. Continue straight. The Woodland Path veers to the left, with a small ascent. Again continue straight, climbing a slight, easy incline. Pass a ropes course on the left. It is strictly off-limits to everyone except those led by a trained instructor. The trail bends sharply to the left, continuing to climb steadily, then turns right and slowly descends. Pass more of the ropes course on the right. The trail ends at Short Woodland Drive (see above).

Zaidee's Path and Bower

Length: 0.4 mile. **Markings:** Signs, yellow blazes, and red arrows. **General description:** This trail starts from the Laurel Ledge Path, crosses Laurel Ledge Road and the Plateau Path, and turns into a loop that explores Zaidee's Bower—an area of rock outcroppings, small cliffs, and crevices. **Highlights:** Climb through a stunning and intriguing rock landscape separate from the other areas of cliffs and crevices. This route doesn't attract the crowds often seen in the Labyrinth, Rock Rift Crevices, or Giant's Workshop. **Downside:** More remote and more climbing than some people would prefer. **Difficulties and hazards:** Scrambling on rocks and through a tight squeeze are among the difficulties you will encounter. Use of hands is necessary in some spots. Obviously, this is more dangerous when icy or wet. Footing is poor. Should you be alone and injured, it may take a long time to be found and rescued.

From the blue-marked Laurel Ledge Path (see above), depart on the yellow-marked trail, which immediately crosses Laurel Ledge Road (see above). On the opposite side of the road, the trail descends, veering to the left and bending to the right. Cross the red-marked Plateau Path (see above) at an angle veering right. The trail continues to descend gradually, veering more to the right and then splitting as it enters Zaidee's Bower. Follow the right branch as it descends more steeply, soon entering an area of crevices and rocks, many covered with a bright emerald mantle of ferns.

Pass a narrow enclosed crevice on the left that spews cold air even in mid-summer. Descend between rocks and pass a second enclosed crevice on the left. Descend a rock "stairway" and turn left beneath a short cliff. The trail veers to the right, away from the cliff, through talus. Descend more steeply, meandering through jumbled boulders. The trail veers to the left then climbs up and into a cave "room." Follow the red arrows. Ascend a small wooden ladder and squeeze through a tight hole. You'll probably have to remove your backpack and go on a crash diet to get through this one. Follow the route between the cliff and boulders. Pass an overhanging ledge on the left and a miniature stone pinnacle. Cross a rock "bridge" and turn left. The trail circumvents a crevice, turns sharply to the left, and continues to ascend. There are steep slopes off to the left and a view looking north and west to the Hudson Valley, Rondout Valley, and Catskills Escarpment. The trail finally levels, veers to the right, and intersects the first branch of the trail. From here, follow the markers back to Laurel Ledge Road.

DUCK POND AREA

Located south of the Mohonk Lake and the Mountain House, the Duck Pond area is miles from any of the designated access points. Remoteness may be this area's primary downside, but it's also one of its greatest assets. The Duck Pond area doesn't attract the hordes you'll find around Sky Top and Mohonk Lake. Besides solitude, the area boasts a variety of scenery and experiences, from forests to open fields with satisfying vistas. The key feature and prime focal point for this area is, of course, Duck Pond (elevation 600 feet). In 1908, the Kleine Kill was dammed to create what was originally called Kleine Kill Pond, later renamed Duck Pond. Its chief purpose was aesthetic, though it was also used to raise brook trout. The rich soil around Duck Pond supports a variety of plant life. Cattails and purple loosestrife are aquatic plants found in the pond. Wildlife includes a variety of small fish, amphibians such as frogs and newts, gregarious snapping turtles, and numerous water snakes, all of which are easy to observe in the shallow waters along the edge of the pond.

When planning a trip here, keep in mind that it takes miles of travel just to get to this area from any of the designated access points. Allow yourself plenty of extra time. While there are no designated ski routes in the vicinity of Duck Pond, it sees a fair amount of use in winter by backcountry skiers. Duck Pond, Kleine Kill, and Glory Hill Roads are all designated bicycle routes.

Multiple-Use Roads and Trails

Glory Hill Trail

Length: 2.1 miles. **Markings:** Blue blazes and signs at intersections. **General description:** This trail ascends gradually from Pine Road to Old Stage Road, utilizing Glory Hill and Kleine Kill Farm Roads for part of its length. In other places, it is a woodland path. The Glory Hill Road segment and the section between Oakwood Drive and Old Stage Road are designated bike routes. The rest of the route is restricted to walkers only. This is not a designated ski trail, though skiers do sometimes use parts of it. Be forewarned that it's challenging and not groomed. **Highlights:** The chief highlight is the variety of scenery you'll pass along this trail, from forest to open fields with panoramic east-facing views of the Wallkill Valley. You'll also gain access to Duck Pond. Views from fields are best experienced when descending and are most exquisite at sunset, when the valley appears all lit up. **Downside:** The remoteness of this area may deter some. **Difficulties and hazards:** It's an uphill climb practically the whole way. Sun exposure and strong winds may be problems in the open fields.

From Lenape Lane (see above), proceed to the intersection with Pine Road, a short distance south of where the road intersects the Catskill Aqueduct. Turn right and follow unmarked Pine Road as it ascends, passing the ruins of an old aqueduct building on the left and soon crossing the Catskill Aqueduct at a diagonal. At this point, it becomes the marked trail. The trail continues to ascend to the right of the aqueduct. After a short distance, the trail levels and a blue-marked trail departs on the right. The road continues straight and descends, crossing a wooden bridge over the Kleine Kill and then intersecting the Historic Duck Pond Trail (see below). Follow the blue-marked trail as it climbs steeply and veers to the right, soon reaching Kleine Kill Farm Road. Go left on the road and immediately encounter a wire gate, easily bypassed to the left. Continue on the road. Bear right and pass an unmaintained field on the left, with the forest invading. An old driveway on the right leads to ruins of a former residence. The road descends, veers right, and crosses the Kleine Kill.

Intersect an old carriage road and turn right. Pass a stone bridge on the left. Just beyond, the dam for Duck Pond is on the left. The blue-marked trail then departs the road on the left, makes a brief ascent, and intersects Duck Pond Road, a designated bike route (see below). Just beyond on the right is an open view of Duck Pond, with a bench and other seating. The cliffs of Sky Top towering above create a sense of drama. Turn left onto Duck Pond Road and almost immediately intersect the Historic Duck Pond Trail (see below) on the left. From here, Glory Hill Road commences (see below).

A short distance farther, on the left, there is an outhouse; just beyond, on the right, lies a seating area. The road bends to the left and ascends through the woods. A green-marked nature trail that connects with the Duck Pond Trail departs on the right. The Glory Hill Trail continues to follow the carriage road, ascending and eventually crossing a small stone viaduct over a ravine. The road bends to the right and passes an open east-facing view on the left to the Wallkill Valley, with the Marlboro Hills on the horizon. The road continues to climb, following the edge of a field with the forest on the left. The road then turns right as a view across the field opens facing north and east.

The road climbs more steeply, spans a small concrete bridge, and bears right. The road continues to ascend, bending left and right. There are more views on the right, looking northeast. At this point, the blue-marked Glory Hill Trail departs from Glory Hill Road (for a description of the rest of Glory Hill Road, see below). For the next segment, the Glory Hill Trail is a woodland path suitable only for hiking; bicycles are not permitted. Follow this trail through the forest. Notice the plentiful white pine in the vicinity. Cross a seasonal stream. The trail ascends and then levels in an area of open oak forest. A old dirt road appears on the left. Veer right, joining the road and following it uphill. There are steep slopes on the left. Cross Oakwood Drive (see below). The trail becomes a bike route again as it continues to ascend gradually. You'll soon arrive at Old Stage Road (see below).

Glory Hill Road

Length: 1.1 miles. **Markings:** Signs at intersections. **General description:** This carriage road starts from the intersection of Duck Pond Road and the Historic Duck Pond Trail and ends at Old Stage Road. For most of its length, it is part of the Glory Hill Trail. The carriage road is a designated bike route except for the segment between Oakwood Drive and Old Stage Road. **Highlights:** Forest, fields, and panoramic vistas. **Downside:** The remoteness will deter some. **Difficulties and hazards:** It's uphill most of the way.

From the spot where the blue-marked Glory Hill Trail (see above) departs, the road bears right and crosses the field, with more expansive views behind you as you climb higher and higher. Cross a stone fence and continue across the field, reaching the intersection with Oakwood Drive (see below). The bike route turns either left or right onto Oakwood Drive. Hikers can continue on

Glory Hill Road by going straight. The trail ascends through a delightful open field, veering to the right. Turn about-face and observe stupendous views of the Hudson Valley, with the Wallkill Valley in the foreground and the Marlboro Hills in the distance. The village of New Paltz is plainly visible left of center. Just beyond, arrive at Old Stage Road (see below).

Home Farm Drive/Circle

Length: 0.5 mile. **Markings:** Signs at intersections. **General description:** This carriage road loops around fields and neighboring forest. Roads and trails connect it to Old Minnewaska Road, Forest Drive, and Old Stage Road. The road is a designated mountain bike route. It is also a designated cross-country ski route, rated more difficult. Home Farm used to be a horse pasture, and there were cultivated fields of corn and vegetables. Christmas trees were also raised here. **Highlights:** These are the closest fields to the Mountain House. The variety of flowering plants and wonderful east-facing views make this a worthwhile destination off the beaten track. **Downside:** Remoteness will deter some. **Difficulties and hazards:** None.

From Old Minnewaska Road (see above), Home Farm Drive departs and descends, passing a field on the left with a view of Sky Top and the Albert K. Smiley Memorial Tower. Fields soon flank both sides of the road. Arrive at a T-intersection. You can choose either direction. Going right, the road follows the boundary between field and forest; they're separated by a line of trees and barbed wire, with the forest on the left. The road bends to the left and crosses a field. Behold east-facing views of the Wallkill Valley with the Marlboro Hills, the Taconics, and the Hudson Highlands in the distance.

The road continues to bend to the left and reenters the forest. A trail on the right, the designated bike route, departs here and continues for a short distance to Old Stage Road (see below). Just beyond, arrive at another fork. A right turn leads to Forest Drive (see above). Turning left, a field appears on the right—the same field you observed on your way in. Just beyond, the road arrives at the intersection with the segment of road you started on. A right turn leads back to the beginning.

Oakwood Drive

Length: 3.3 miles. **Markings:** Signs at most intersections. **General description:** This long carriage road follows the east side of the ridge from Rhododendron Bridge to Lenape Lane. Though it crosses a field south of Duck Pond, it runs primarily through forest the whole way. The section from Rhododendron Bridge to Forest Drive is a designated bike and cross-country ski route. As a ski route, it is rated most difficult, though except for its length, I didn't find it overly taxing. **Highlights:** The primary attraction is access to remote areas on the east side of the Mohonk Preserve that see few visitors. It also serves as an important link between the northern and southern sections of the preserve and is therefore useful for extended trips. **Downside:** The remoteness of this carriage road will deter most visitors. **Difficulties and hazards:** Remoteness is the primary hazard. There are steep slopes off the side of the carriage road in some places. A few parts are strenuous.

From the east side of Rhododendron Bridge, Oakwood Drive goes right (south), soon bending to the left and then to the right again. There's a slope to the right of the carriage road. The road bends to the left again, staying fairly level, followed by a very gradual descent. The road loops around a ravine and bends to the right. There's a partial view on the right, looking south to the Trapps cliffs and Millbrook Mountain in the distance. The road loops around another small ravine, bends to the left and right, and starts a long, gradual descent. The road then bends right again and crosses a steep ravine with shale outcrops on the left. Veer left and continue your slow descent.

The road bends to the left and crosses a small stream, then bends to the right and left a number of times. It then stays level for a long stretch, eventually crossing the blue-marked Glory Hill Trail (see above). A right turn here leads to Duck Pond; a left goes to Old Stage Road. Just beyond, the carriage road turns right and a field appears on the left. The road bends to the left and arrives at an intersection with Glory Hill Road (see above). Again, turning right will bring you to Duck Pond. A left will take you up to Old Stage Road. Descend as you continue across the field. There's a row of trees to the left of the road.

Reenter the forest. There's a steep slope to the right of the road leading down to Duck Pond and the Kleine Kill. Old Stage Road (see below) appears on the left side of the road. There's a very long, gradual descent. The road eventually veers to the left, crosses a steep ravine, and turns right. The red-marked Duck Pond Trail (see below)—which on the right descends to Duck Pond, and on the left goes up to Forest Drive—crosses the road here. Continue to descend, eventually crossing a narrow V-shaped ravine containing a branch of the Kleine Kill. The road then bends sharply to the right and begins a steady ascent with a steep slope on the right. Climb a skinny section of road with a precipitous drop-off on the right. Just beyond, there's an open view of Sky Top and the Albert K. Smiley Memorial Tower. The road veers left and continues to ascend, with shale outcrops on the left. It then bends farther to the left, climbing more steeply. It intersects Duck Pond Road, which descends to Duck Pond (see below), and

Kleine Kill Road (see below), leading up to Rock Spring Bridge. Bicyclists have the option of following either of these routes.

Continue another 0.4 mile down to Lenape Lane. Approximately two-thirds of the way there, Forest Drive (see above) appears on the left. Oakwood Drive continues to descend, veering right and left. The road then bends sharply to the right, crosses an open gate, and joins Lenape Lane (see above). A left turn here leads to the Mohonk gatehouse; a right leads to Butterville Road.

Old Stage Road

Length: 0.8 mile. **Markings:** Signs at intersections. **General description:** This road, originally constructed in 1870 to provide guests more direct stage access to the (then new) Mohonk Mountain House, winds through forests and fields connecting Oakwood Drive and Forest Drive. Most of it is a designated bike route; the exception is the short section from Home Farm Circle to Forest Drive. **Highlights:** A fairly direct route from Duck Pond to the Mohonk Lake area, with a variety of scenery along the way. **Downside:** This road's remoteness may deter some. **Difficulties and hazards:** The route involves almost continuous climbing or a moderately steep descent, depending on which way you're going.

From the intersection with Oakwood Drive (see above), Old Stage Road ascends moderately through the forest. The road bears right, and a field soon appears on the left. The road follows the edge of the field, with lovely east-facing views of the Wallkill Valley in the foreground and the Marlboro Hills on the horizon. The road bends to the left and meets Glory Hill Road (see above), which descends left across the field. Just beyond, the blue-marked Glory Hill Trail (see above) also departs on the left. Old Stage Road bends to the right again and reenters the forest, continuing to climb a short distance to the crest of a hill. The road then descends briefly, bears right, and resumes climbing. The road eventually levels, bends to the right, and encounters on the left both a steep embankment and the beginning of a field (Home Farm). It then bears left and continues a slow ascent. In a short while, you'll arrive at the intersection with Home Farm Circle (see above). The bike route turns left here. Old Stage Road continues straight, soon reaching a T-intersection with Forest Drive (see above). A right turn leads to Rock Spring Bridge; a left goes to the Mohonk Lake area.

Duck Pond Road

Length: 0.9 mile. **Markings:** Signs at intersections. **General description:** The road (both a hiking trail and designated bike route) climbs from the Duck Pond dam up through forest and fields to the four-way intersection with Kleine Kill Road and Oakwood Drive. **Highlights:** Wondrous panoramic views of fields, with the Wallkill Valley in the distance as well as Sky Top. **Downside:** The remoteness will deter many. **Difficulties and hazards:** A long, grueling ascent and strong winds in the fields can make this climb an ordeal.

From the three-way intersection of Glory Hill Road (see above) and the Historic Duck Pond Trail (see below), go north along the top of the dam, enjoying fine views of the pond with Sky Top above in the distance. At the opposite end of the dam, the road intersects Kleine Kill Farm Road on the right. Follow the edge of the pond. Just beyond it, there's a wetland on the left. The road begins to ascend. The red-marked Duck Pond Trail departs on the left (see below).

The road then bends to the right and up a steep incline. Pass a shale outcrop on the left just before the road loops to the left. An open view appears on the right across a field, looking east to the Wallkill Valley with the village of New Paltz and the Marlboro Hills in the distance. The road continues to ascend, with fields on both sides of the lane and a narrow band of trees to the right of the roadway. A view of Sky Top appears on the left. There are continuous views on the right looking east. The road veers to the left, then bends sharply right. An unmarked branch of Kleine Kill Farm Road departs on the right for Lenape Lane. Continue uphill, veering right. The road then bends to the left; a more expansive view across the field opens up behind you, looking east and south with the Hudson Highlands in the far distance.

The road loops to the right and continues climbing steeply. Then it veers left and enters the woods. The road loops to the left and continues to climb a short distance before reaching a four-way intersection with Kleine Kill Road (see below) and Oakwood Drive (see above).

Kleine Kill Road

Length: 0.6 mile. **Markings:** Signs at both ends. **General description:** This carriage road climbs from the four-way intersection of Duck Pond Road and Oakwood Drive and ends at Rock Spring Bridge. It is a designated bike route and cross-country ski route, rated most difficult. **Highlights:** While useful for any number of circuit trips, it also has some fine west-facing views of Sky Top. **Downside:** None. **Difficulties and hazards:** Going uphill, it is a steep, taxing climb. For skiers going downhill, there are numerous curves, including one that may be difficult to negotiate.

From its intersection with Duck Pond Road and Oakwood Drive (see above), follow Kleine Kill Road uphill, veering right. The road levels, and the deep ravine of the Kleine Kill is on the left. The road continues veering to the right. Cross a small brook and bend to the left, ascending gradually. About a third of the way along, the road bends sharply to the right (skiers going downhill should note that this curve is very sharp and steeply banked). There's an open view of Sky Top standing prominently across the ravine. The road continues to ascend, gradually veering to the right. Pass a white pine "plantation" on the right. The road levels, bends to the left, climbs again, and veers to the right. Continue to ascend. The road curves a number of times and finally arrives at the four-way intersection at Rock Spring Bridge, where Forest Drive and Bridge Road (see above) meet.

Hiking Trails

Duck Pond Trail

Length: 0.9 mile. **Markings:** Red blazes; signs at intersections. **General description:** This hiking trail follows the narrow ravine of the Kleine Kill, connecting Duck Pond Road with Forest Drive. Enjoy beautiful forest scenery and rocky slopes along the upper reaches of the Kleine Kill, plus the most direct access from Duck Pond to the Mohonk Lake area. **Downside:** The long, rough ascent is more difficult than some people can handle. **Difficulties and hazards:** A nearly continuous ascent with few breaks, often on rocks with poor footing, and steep in places. However, no scrambling is required. Treacherous when wet or icy.

From Duck Pond Road (see above), just north of Duck Pond, the red-marked trail departs on the left down a short embankment, leveling then following a course parallel to the Kleine Kill. The green-marked nature trail appears on the left, crossing the stream on a wooden bridge and continuing to Glory Hill Road. The Duck Pond Trail veers to the right and begins to ascend, then levels. The trail departs from the stream. Then it bends farther to the right and climbs moderately. The red-marked trail bends to the left and down to the stream embankment. The trail then turns right, following the stream embankment on the left. It continues level through a hemlock stand. The trail turns right and ascends, then bears left and crosses the small stream on a wooden bridge. Two branches of the stream intersect just below the bridge.

The red-marked trail then veers to the right of the leftmost branch of the stream, crosses wooden boards, and begins climbing over rocks. The trail then bears left. There's a very steep slope to the left of the trail. The trail bends to the right and continues its moderate ascent over rocks. The Duck Pond Trail then crosses Oakwood Drive (see above). The trail continues uphill to the right of the stream, bearing left over rocks, then making an immediate sharp right. On the left is a steep, eroded shale embankment with hemlocks clinging precariously to it. The trail continues to meander upward through boulders. Some may be slippery with lichens and moss. Finally the end of the trail is reached at Forest Drive (see above). There's a gazebo to the right here, conveniently situated for those who need to stop and catch their breath. The red-marked Birchen Trail (see above) across the road continues to Sky Top.

Historic Duck Pond Trail

Length: 0.4 mile. **Markings:** A sign by Duck Pond; otherwise unmarked. **General description:** Part of the original stage route from the New Paltz train station to the Mountain House, this trail departs from Lenape Lane, crosses the Catskill Aqueduct, and ends at an intersection with Duck Pond Road and Glory Hill Road by Duck Pond. **Highlights:** A historic trail with lovely views of the Kleine Kill and Duck Pond itself. **Downside:** Remoteness and lack of markings may deter some. **Difficulties and hazards:** None.

Going south on Lenape Lane (see above), the Historic Duck Pond Trail departs on the right as Lenape Lane makes a hairpin left turn after crossing the Catskill Aqueduct. Follow the unmarked road as it slowly ascends. The aqueduct is on the right up the hill. Soon the road arrives at the aqueduct. Please note that while it may look inviting as a trail, no trespassing is allowed on the aqueduct. Do not linger on it. The trail briefly bears left on the aqueduct, then crosses the Kleine Kill. There are bridge ruins on the right. Just beyond, turn right on an unmarked but well-defined trail departing from the aqueduct. The old stage road soon departs on the left. Stay on the trail. The old stage road crosses a collapsed bridge missing its span—an interesting ruin if you want to check it out. A road appears on the right. It crosses the Kleine Kill above a former dam and continues for a short distance to the blue-marked Glory Hill Trail (see above).

Continuing on the Historic Duck Pond Trail, the old stage road rejoins on the left. Continue to ascend gradually, crisscrossing the stream four times. Another road on the right leads to the Glory Hill Trail. Bear left as a field appears on the left. You'll soon arrive at the T-intersection of Duck Pond Road and Glory Hill Road (see above). Duck Pond lies just beyond.

Woodside Trail

Length: 1.8 miles. **Markings:** Blue blazes and signs. **General description:** This moderately challenging path starts off Lenape Lane, where it crosses the Catskill Aqueduct and follows an undulating route across the gentle eastern flank of the Shawangunk Ridge, ending at Mountain Rest Road near the Mohonk Gatehouse. **Highlights:** While there are no views along this trail, it visits a variety of forest settings in some less visited parts of the Mohonk Preserve. Combined with Lenape Lane, it makes a good circuit hike; with the Northeast Trail (you'll have to spot vehicles), it makes a great long-distance one. **Downside:** The trail's isolation and lack of visitors may disturb some. **Difficulties and hazards:** Should you get hurt or lost, help may take a long time to find you.

To get there, follow Lenape Lane (see above) to where it crosses the Catskill Aqueduct. There's a description of the Catskill Aqueduct under Lenape Lane. (Please note that due to heightened security concerns in the wake of September 11, the entrance to the trail may be relocated. Turn left here and go around the gate. Follow the aqueduct east for about 0.3 mile. Go around another gate and cross a stream. As the aqueduct bends sharply to the right, turn left and follow the blue-marked trail into a hemlock grove. The trail continues level, parallel to the stream, climbs a short rise, bends to the right and left, descends, and crosses a small seasonal stream on rocks. The trail turns to the right, continues level, then climbs to the left away from the stream. An old dirt road is reached, and the trail turns right and follows it. Arrive at old stone bridge abutments on opposite sides of a small stream. Cross here with caution. Continue steadily uphill.

The trail levels and veers to the left and right of a deep ravine. The trail bends to the right and crosses a small drainage. Continue uphill for a short distance. The blue-marked trail departs from the road on the right and climbs a steep rise. At the top of the rise, bend to the left and continue fairly level for some distance through an area with abundant tall pitch pine and white pine. The trail then bends to the left and right and crosses a tiny drainage on logs. Cross another small stream and bend to the left. Pass a stone fence on the left and then cross it. Descend and ford a modest stream. Then ascend and veer left. Descend and cross another stream. Continue fairly level. The trail bends to the left and climbs, then veers to the right. Cross a wooden bridge over a very small drainage. Pass a foundation ruin on the left and, just beyond, arrive at Mountain Rest Road, across from the golf course. The blue-marked Northeast Trail (see below) continues across the road. A left on Mountain Rest Road will take you 0.2 mile to the Mohonk Gatehouse. To complete a circuit hike, return from the gatehouse via Lenape Lane (see above).

TRAPPS GATEWAY VISITORS CENTER

This parking area and access point features the Mohonk Preserve's Trapps Gateway Visitors Center, parking for 190 vehicles, and more than 2 miles of walking trails. The Gateway Center is definitely a must stop for all visitors to the ridge. Besides being the headquarters of the Mohonk Preserve, it also has educational, interpretive, and interactive exhibits, programs, and classrooms devoted to the history and ecology of the ridge, including a scale 52-square-foot topographic model of the preserve. Information, maps, and day passes are available. There are also rest rooms and a gift shop. Access to the visitors center and neighboring grounds is free. The area on which the Trapps Gateway Center is located was the result of a purchase and gift of the Beaverkill Land Conservancy, a branch of the Open Space Institute. The building, designed by Lee Skolnick, is heated through a environmentally friendly geothermal exchange system.

To get there from New Paltz, go west on Route 299 for 5.8 miles to the intersection with Route 44/55, then turn north on 44/55 and continue for another 0.6 mile. The visitors center is on the right.

Hiking Trails

Millstone Path

This very short trail leads from the parking lot up stone steps to the visitors center. The primary feature is a number of locally quarried millstones placed along the sides of the trail. A smoother alternate path is handicapped accessible.

Sensory Trail

Length: 0.2 mile. **Markings:** Signs. **General description:** This very short, smoothly paved loop through chestnut oak woodlands features interpretative signs with translations in Braille. It also provides access to the LaVerne Thompson Nature Trail (see below). It begins just outside the door at the bottom of the stairs to the lower level of the visitors center. Another feature of the trail is the Butterfly Garden, located adjacent to the center.

LaVerne Thompson Nature Trail

Length: 0.3 mile. **Markings:** Signs; green blazes. **General description:** This "rough" loop path was dedicated in memory of LaVerne Thompson, a member of the Mohonk Preserve's board of directors for 17 years until her death in 1989. For half its length, it coincides with the Foothills Trail, marked with yellow blazes. There are 16 labeled stops along the trail, described in an interpretive brochure available at the beginning of the trail and in the visitors center. **Highlights:** Learn about chestnut oak forests. See an old charcoal pit. **Downside:** None. **Difficulties and hazards:** None. This so-called rough path is really quite easy.

The trail starts from the Sensory Trail (see above), just southeast of the visitors center. Follow the mostly level trail through chestnut oak forest, with chestnut oak, red oak, black oak, hickory, and sugar maple trees and a few examples of American chestnut in the understory as well as wild grapes. Blueberries, huckleberries, and cushion moss are prevalent on the forest floor. There are also some fine examples of talus boulders and glacial erratics along the trail. At approximately the halfway point, the Foothills Trail turns off to the right (see below). There is a rustic wooden bench on the left. From here, the trail bends left and climbs briefly, passing an old charcoal pit on the right, dating back to the beginning of the 20th century. Burning wood to create charcoal was once a big industry in the Shawangunks. Just beyond, the East Trapps Connector Trail turns off to the right (see below). The trail passes another large talus boulder on the right with prominent fractures and then enters the lower parking lot. Proceed through the parking area with a view of the Trapps cliffs above. Bear left and then reenter the woods. Continue straight for a short distance, passing the visitors center on the right up the hill. You'll soon reach the intersection with the Sensory Trail and the beginning.

Foothills Trail

Length: 0.5 mile. **Markings:** Signs; yellow blazes. **General description:** This trail descends steeply from the area by the visitors center to a lowland area, passing through property managed by the New York State Department of Environmental

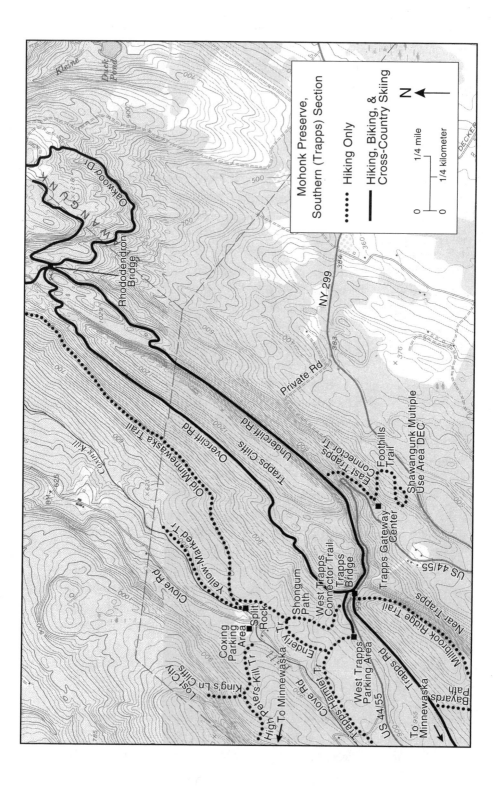

Mohonk Preserve,
Southern (Trapps) Section

········· Hiking Only

━━━━━ Hiking, Biking, &
Cross-Country Skiing

N

0   1/4 mile
0   1/4 kilometer

Kleine
Duck Pond

Oakwood Dr

S H A W A N G U N K

Rhododendron
Bridge

Old Minnewaska Trail

Coxing Kill

Overcliff Rd

Undercliff Rd

Trapps Cliffs

NY 299

Private Rd

East Trapps
Connector Trail

Foothills
Trail

Shawangunk Multiple
Use Area DEC

Trapps Gateway
Center

Clove Rd

Yellow-Marked Tr

Shongum
Path

West Trapps
Connector Trail

Trapps
Bridge

US 44/55

BM

Coxing
Parking
Area

Split
Rock

Enderly Tr

King's Ln

Lost City
Cliffs

High Peters Kill Tr

To Minnewaska

Clove Rd

Trapps Hamlet Tr

West Trapps
Parking Area

US 44/55

Trapps Rd

Millbrook Ridge Trail

Near Trapps

Bayards
Path

To
Minnewaska

DECKE

Conservation. **Highlights:** You get to see different forest habitats. **Downside:** For a short trail, it's fairly strenuous. **Difficulties and hazards:** To return, you must climb up a 200-foot slope. The footing may be challenging.

To get there, start from the north end of the parking lot north of the visitors center. The East Trapps Connector Trail (see below) turns left here, while the Foothills Trail, marked in yellow and green, turns right and proceeds downhill, passing the site of an old charcoal pit on the left and some glacial erratics. You'll soon reach another intersection, this one with the LaVerne Thompson Nature Trail (see above), which branches off to the right. The Foothills Trail, now marked with just yellow blazes, turns left, descends, and then levels. There's a steep slope to the right.

The trail then crosses into DEC property and begins another gradual descent on stone steps. It turns right and makes a very steep descent on stone steps to the right of a seasonal brook. The yellow-marked trail eventually levels, bends to the right, and crosses the small stream. It then passes a stone wall on the left and reaches an intersection with another trail. Take the right fork (marked) and continue, eventually arriving back on Mohonk Preserve land. Turn right and cross the stream again. The trail then bends to the left, loops around, and, after a short distance, rejoins the first branch. To return, you must climb back up the steep slope.

East Trapps Connector Trail

Length: 0.4 mile. **Markings:** Signs; yellow blazes. **General description:** This trail connects the Trapps Gateway Center to Undercliff Road. **Highlights:** Besides walking up the shoulder of Route 44/55, this trail provides the only access from the Trapps Gateway Center to the rest of the preserve's trails, especially the Trapps cliffs. **Downside:** A more challenging trail than you might expect. It's closed from December 15 to March 15. **Difficulties and hazards:** Steep and strenuous in places, mostly on stone steps. The last section traverses a talus slope, though when conditions are good, no scrambling is required.

The trail starts just to the north of the entrance to the visitors center. Follow the smooth gravel path to the left of the parking area. The trail then enters the parking area. Proceed up to its north end, where the East Trapps Connector Trail intersects the LaVerne Thompson Nature Trail (see above). There's a sign warning of the rough path ahead.

The trail veers to the left, climbing up stone steps and passing a huge boulder on the right. It enters a roadway and vehicle turnaround. Just before the boundary of private land, the trail climbs a wooden staircase on the left, then turns right and follows the base of a stone abutment with Route 44/55 above on the left. There's a private home below on the right. Cross a wooden bridge and climb stone steps. The trail veers to the left, climbing steep stone steps. Reach a tilted rock slab. The trail bends sharply to the left again, climbs more stone steps, then winds through large boulders, eventually reaching Undercliff Road (see below), with the Trapps cliffs towering above.

THE WEST TRAPPS PARKING AREA

This parking area takes the place of what once was primarily off-road parking along Route 44/55. It provides primary access to the area of the Trapps. The name *Trapps* comes from the Dutch *trapen,* which means "steps." The Trapps area was purchased by the Smileys in the 1880s and 1890s. The Trapps cliffs are the most popular rock climbing area in Mohonk and frequently crowded. For hikers, mountain bicyclists, and cross-country skiers, Overcliff and Undercliff Roads provide a fine multiple-use circuit route with access to the Trapps as well as other trails. There's also access to the beautiful Millbrook Ridge Trail and the historic Trapps Hamlet Path. Portable bathroom facilities are located just north of Trapps Bridge.

The West Trapps parking area and the neighboring Connector Trail represents a restoration of the old Wawarsing–New Paltz Turnpike, a former private toll road built in 1856 that crossed the mountains. The area of Trapps Bridge was once the site of a tollbooth. After a few years, the turnpike went bankrupt and became a public road. In 1929, it was realigned in its present form as Route 44/55. The parking area was constructed in 1993 with a special grant from the Access Fund, Inc. (Boulder, Colorado), for restoration of the Trapps area. There's a signboard with a map and educational exhibits.

To get there, follow Route 299 west of New Paltz to the intersection with Route 44/55. Follow 44/55 west for 0.9 mile up to the hairpin turn, then up another 0.5 mile and cross underneath the Trapps steel bridge. Continue 0.4 mile past the bridge; the West Trapps parking area appears on the right.

Multiple-Use Trails

Connector Trail

Length: 0.2 mile. **Markings:** None. **General description:** This very short uphill trail (less than a five-minute walk) connects the West Trapps parking area with the Shongum Path, providing access to Undercliff and Overcliff Carriage Roads and Trapps Road. Those with bikes or skis should note that there are steps at the end of the Shongum Path leading up to Trapps Bridge, though you can bypass these by turning right just before the steps and crossing Route 44/55; go under the bridge, turn right, and climb up to Trapps Road.

From the upper end of the parking area, follow the wide gravel path. After a short distance, the red-marked Shongum Path appears on the left. It goes down to the Coxing parking area (see below). You can follow the Shongum Path uphill the rest of the way to Trapps Bridge, approximately 200 feet.

Undercliff Road

Length: 2.4 miles. **Markings:** Signs at intersections. **General description:** This easy, primarily level carriage road follows the base of the Trapps cliffs from Trapps Bridge up to Rhododendron Bridge, where five carriage roads converge. It is suitable for walkers, bicyclists, and cross-country skiers and is perfect for beginners in all categories. Undercliff and Overcliff Roads were built in 1903, mostly by hand at a cost of $1 per foot, primarily so resort guests could enjoy the spectacular views of the cliffs and more distant sights. When Trapps Road was completed in 1907, Undercliff Carriage Road became part of the new main route between Mohonk and Minnewaska Lake. Undercliff Road was considered an engineering achievement when it was built—the only road in the Northeast to cross a talus slope. **Highlights:** The Trapps are the most accessible and popular cliff face in the Shawangunks for rock climbing; watching these acrobats cling to the sheer cliffs is one of the prime attractions of this carriage road. The magnificent cliffs themselves are best viewed in late fall, winter, or early spring when the leaves are down. Other attractions include the talus slopes at the base of the cliffs, as well as some fine open views looking east to the Wallkill Valley. **Downside:** The beginning section of the trail can be quite crowded on weekends in good weather. Those on bike should be especially courteous to those on foot. **Difficulties and hazards:** The traffic of many users can be a problem for both bicyclists and pedestrians. Cross-country skiers will have to tolerate numerous footprints in the tracks.

Undercliff Road begins at the intersection with Overcliff Road just north of Trapps Bridge and the end of the red-marked Shongum Path. Make a left at the top of the stone steps to the left of the bridge. Follow the carriage road, which immediately brings you to a huge boulder and an intersection of the two roadways. Go right on Undercliff Road, passing between a huge hunk of rock on the right and the main cliff on the left. Route 44/55 is below on the right, and a steady stream of traffic noise emanates from this busy highway. Slanting beds of conglomerate are on the left side of the road. There's a wire fence on the right, used primarily to prevent people from hiking up from the highway. Erosion caused by trampling has been very destructive to the steep slope, which now is being given a chance to recover. Notice shale outcrops on the left side of the road. There's an open view on the right side, looking south and east to the Near Trapps cliffs and Wallkill Valley, with the Hudson Highlands in the distance visible on clear days.

The road bends to the left and reaches the base of the Trapps cliffs, quite sheer in places, with overhangs that present exciting challenges for rock climbers. White marks on the rocks are chalk residue used by climbers to improve their handgrips on the rock. Often you can hear climbers shouting directions to one another: Safe climbing requires cooperation. This area along Undercliff Road beneath the climbing cliffs is popularly referred to as the Uberfall. A pipe spewing springwater appears on the right. A sign warns this water is untested, but many drink from it anyway. A bulletin board on the left has maps, information about climbing, and a message board that climbers use to communicate with one another. Rock climbers usually congregate here. There's a plaque dedicated in November 1991 to Hans Kraus and Fritz Wiessner, two rock climbers who pioneered many routes in the Gunks. You'll notice a number of access routes, many of them marked in yellow, on the left side of the road. These are used by climbers to reach the base of the cliffs. Following these routes cuts down on erosion and trampling in this sensitive environment. The road levels and crosses a talus field with enormous boulders on both sides of the road. A short distance beyond, the yellow-marked East Trapps Connector Trail appears on the right. It goes down to the Trapps Gateway Visitors Center (see above).

The road continues north across the talus slope. The crowds quickly thin as the road begins a slow, gradual descent. East-facing views eventually open up on the right; look for the Wallkill Valley below, with the village of New Paltz and the Marlboro Hills in the distance. Note the tall, stately white pine trees in the foreground. Cross another large talus slope. The road veers to the left of a deep ravine with a small stream. Having come approximately 1.8 miles so far, the road levels, makes an S-curve to cross the stream, and turns away from the cliffs, which disappear from view. Pass the Sleepy Hollow Trail on the left, closed for habitat restoration. Continue your slow descent. There's a view of the Smiley Memorial Tower on the right side of the road. Another ravine appears on the right, with a small stream.

Less than three-quarters of a mile from the last stream crossing, Undercliff

Road reaches Rhododendron Bridge (see above). Surprise, there isn't a rhododendron bush in sight. However, Rhododendron Swamp—which has numerous rhododendrons—is nearby, visible from Laurel Ledge Road. Overcliff Road is on the left. If you were to continue straight, you would stay on Laurel Ledge Road. Old Minnewaska Road and Oakwood Drive meet at the opposite end of the bridge. You can return to Trapps Bridge by taking Overcliff Carriage Road (see below). It is a total of 4.7 miles to complete the entire loop.

Overcliff Road

Length: 2.3 miles. **Markings:** Signs at both ends. **General description:** A relatively easy carriage road that connects Trapps Bridge with Rhododendron Bridge. Contrary to its name, it does not follow the top of the cliff. It is suitable for walkers, bicyclists, and cross-country skiers. **Highlights:** Almost the opposite experience from Undercliff Road—less crowded, with different kinds of scenery and excellent views looking north and west. It is often done as part of a loop with Undercliff Road. **Downside:** None. **Difficulties and hazards:** Winds can be quite strong.

From Trapps Bridge, go left on the carriage road at the intersection with Undercliff Road. Pass steep, slanting cliffs on the right as well as talus boulders on both sides of the road. The road bends right and continues north, ascending gradually. Pass a superb open view looking west to Coxing Clove, with Dickie Barrie and the Lost City cliffs on the left. The road loops to the right around a shallow trough and continues north, climbing steadily through deciduous forest. After 1.7 miles, the road begins a gradual descent, passing slanting rock slabs on the left rimmed with dwarf pitch pine, as well as more open views looking west and north to the Rondout Valley and distant Catskills Range. Below is Coxing Clove; opposite are Dickie Barrie and the Lost City cliffs.

Pass more slanting rock slabs and pitch pine on the right. An unmarked but well-trodden path on the left leads to one last open view of the mouth of Coxing Clove and the Catskills, with Ashokan High Point prominent in view. The road briefly levels and passes a small wetland to the right. After less than 2.25 miles, Overcliff Road bends to the right and crosses a small pass. It then begins to descend more steeply. The road loops to the right and passes cliffs with overhangs on the left; then it bends to the left and passes the Sleepy Hollow Trail on the right (closed in 1997 for habitat restoration). A unmarked road on the left provides a brief shortcut to Laurel Ledge Road below. Continue to descend, bending to the right and finally meeting Undercliff and Laurel Ledge Roads by the Rhododendron Bridge juncture. To return to Trapps Bridge via Undercliff Road, turn right here (see above).

Trapps Road

Length: 2.4 miles. **Markings:** Signs at both ends. **General description:** This carriage road starting from Trapps Bridge runs roughly parallel to Route 44/55, continuing to Lyons Road at the boundary of Minnewaska State Park Preserve. From there, it continues as the Awosting Falls Carriageway. It was built in 1907 to link Mohonk and Minnewaska and was originally called Minnewaska Drive. This route, which included Undercliff Road, became the primary link between the two resorts, replacing Old Minnewaska Road. The trail is open for cross-country skiing in winter, but is not groomed. **Highlights:** Pretty forest scenery and a useful connection between Mohonk and Minnewaska. It also provides access to hiking trails and may be useful for a number of loop hike possibilities. **Downside:** Traffic noise from nearby Route 44/55 disturbs the tranquility in places. **Difficulties and hazards:** None.

From Trapps Bridge, the carriage road bends right. An unmarked trail to the left leads to a camping area for rock climbers nicknamed Camp Slime due to the lack of sanitary facilities. After 100 yards, the blue-marked Millbrook Ridge Trail departs on the left (see below). Large tilted slabs of rock appear on the left with "islands" of pitch pine and other sparse vegetation. On the right, there's a steep slope down to Route 44/55 and a northwest-facing view of Dickie Barrie and the Lost City cliffs. After 0.25 mile, mixed deciduous forest of oak, pitch pine, maple, birch, striped maple, and mountain laurel appears on both sides of the road. After 0.5 mile, pass the red-marked Bayards Path (see below) on the left. It goes out to the Millbrook Ridge Trail, from which loop hikes are possible.

The road veers to the left. One mile from the beginning, the Coxing Trail, marked in light blue (see below), appears on the left. The road begins to descend, passing numerous hemlocks, and crosses the Coxing Kill on a wooden bridge. The road then veers right, crosses a small tributary stream, and bends to the left. Traffic noise from Route 44/55 can be heard. The road veers left and gradually ascends. The tributary stream is now on the left. Cross a small wooden bridge over it. The road bends to the right and crosses the stream again, then climbs out of the ravine and bends to the left. There are views below of the tributary stream and the branch of the road you just followed. Continue past an entrance sign for the Mohonk Preserve. There's a short, steep incline before reaching Lyons Road, which the carriage road crosses (be careful of occasional vehicular traffic); it continues on the other side into Minnewaska State Park Preserve (see the next chapter).

Hiking Trails

Millbrook Ridge Trail

Length: 3.6 miles. **Markings:** Signs; light blue blazes. **General description:** This trail begins at Trapps Road just south of the bridge and ends near the summit of Millbrook Mountain, following the top of cliffs for a good part of the way. **Highlights:** This is one of the longest and most spectacular trails in the Shawangunks. There are fine open views of the Wallkill Valley and points south and east. There are also a number of excellent long and short loop possibilities from the Millbrook Ridge Trail. The longest involves going all the way to Gertrude's Nose in Minnewaska State Park Preserve, approximately 10 miles. The shortest and easiest involves returning via the Bayards Path and Trapps Road, only 2.5 miles round trip. **Downside:** A rugged trail, longer and more challenging than many people would prefer, especially beginners. **Difficulties and hazards:** This trail involves a lot of steep walking on bare rock slabs. Be especially careful on the cliff edges, which feature sheer drops of up to 300 feet.

From Trapps Bridge, go south, crossing the bridge. The carriage road turns right. Follow it for 100 yards to where the trail, marked with light blue blazes, exits on the left on steep rock slabs with islands of pitch pine. Climb the smooth, rocky face with plentiful evidence of glaciation, including glacial scratches and polishing. Look behind you. There's a view west of the Lost City cliffs. The trail turns right and onto a huge, steeply angled rock slab with views looking north to Coxing Clove, Rondout Valley, and distant Catskills. Continue south across very smooth, steeply tilted rocks. The trail then veers left on a steeper pitch, climbing up the bare side of the incline, veering right, and then bending left to the crest of the ridge at Hawk's Watch. Here you'll find a dramatic view of the Trapps cliffs to the north; eastward to the Wallkill Valley, Marlboro Hills, and village of New Paltz; west to the cliffs of Lost City, valley of Coxing Clove, and Rondout Valley; and north to the distant Catskills. As you might guess, this is an excellent vantage for watching hawks and other raptors during their migration in late fall.

The trail turns right through mountain laurel and soon emerges near the top of the Near Trapps cliffs, with a view looking east to the Wallkill Valley. The trail temporarily leaves the rock and levels as it enters sparse woods of oak, pitch pine, and huckleberries. The trail climbs again on bare rock, with a north-facing view on the left that includes the Trapps cliffs. The trail levels again. An opening appears on the left with a very sharp drop (use caution). There's a view of the Near Trapps cliffs and the intersection of Routes 299 and 44/55 below, the Trapps cliffs to the north, and Sky Top and Eagle Cliff in the distance. Just beyond, a detour on the left leads to another precarious view.

Continue south through forest with mountain laurel and a thick undergrowth of huckleberries. There are partial views on the left through the trees, and some open ones looking south and east as far as the Hudson Highlands. After slightly more than 0.75 mile, the trail reaches a small saddle called Smedes Cove, which marks the boundary between the Near Trapps and the Bayards. The Bayards cliffs separate the Near Trapps from Millbrook Mountain; they were named for Mr. and Mrs. Bayards, who owned a tavern on Route 44/55 that climbers used to pass on their way to the cliffs. There's a partial view looking south to Millbrook Mountain, with its imposing precipice. You may need to use your hands to get over a small cliff face here. The red-marked Bayards Path (see below) joins on the right after a brief descent. It continues to Trapps Road, which you can follow for a short distance back to Trapps Bridge, making a short loop possible.

Follow the blue-marked trail as it bends to the left and climbs steeply angled rocks up to the crest of the ridge. Turn right and follow the crest, with partial eastward views on the left to the Hudson Valley. The trail continues to climb steadily through numerous pitch pines. Views open up on the left: the village of New Paltz, the Hudson Highlands in the south, and Heddens Lake below to the right. The tilted rocks are smooth and polished in places with glacial striations. The trail continues to follow the crest through deciduous forest of oak, maple, birch, tall pitch pine, and mountain laurel, with nearly constant partial views on the left through the trees. The trail dips briefly, and another open view appears on the left looking east and north: the village of New Paltz, the intersection of Routes 44/55 and 299, the wetlands of the Marakill, and the Taconic Range (in Connecticut and Massachusetts) in the distance. Continue south on the nearly level trail over bare rock slabs with frequent east-facing views. Pass a pair of cairns to the right of the trail. Thorny brambles appear to the left of the trail, with an open view looking eastward.

Enter a dense thicket of mountain laurel. Soon the trail opens up, with the dramatic profile of Millbrook Mountain's magnificent sheer cliff looming straight ahead. The trail turns right and away from the crest, descending gradually to the right of a shallow trough. A second red-blazed trail, the Millbrook Cross Trail (see below), appears on the right (cairn and sign). It exits to the Coxing Trail, which represents another loop possibility.

At this point, you've come slightly more than 1.75 miles. The Millbrook

Ridge Trail bends to the left, ascending rocks, regains the crest of the ridge then continuing south on open rock slabs, with numerous glacial erratics and sparse oak woods along the way. Enter another mountain laurel grove. The trail bends to the left and passes (on the right) a large rock with a tiny cave space underneath. The trail then skirts to the left of a dark hollow densely populated with hemlocks. A rocky cliff rises precipitously to the left; ascend on the right. The trail is very steep. Follow markers as the trail turns to the left. There's an open view looking east as the trail turns right just below the crest of the ridge. Continue to ascend more gradually. The trail finally reaches the crest of the ridge and continues its steep climb on smooth rock slabs. There's a good grip except when the rocks are wet or icy. Reach a high point on the crest and savor gorgeous panoramic views looking north to Sky Top, the Catskills, Dickie Barrie with the cliffs of Lost City, and Coxing Clove; east to the Hudson Valley; and south as far as the Hudson Highlands. However, this proves not to be the top.

The trail continues to climb the spine of the ridge with many open views on the left, finally reaching a second high point that also proves not to be the summit, but has fine views similar to those before. Descend on smooth rock slabs, which may be slippery. The trail continues to ascend. Nearly vertical rock slabs appear on the left, and there's a swampy basin of shrubs and pitch pine to the right. The trail begins to ascend again on rocks, soon reaching the crest; more open views here include the huge talus field that lies beneath Millbrook Mountain's dramatic cliff and, just beyond, a tilted rock ledge overhanging the sheer precipice. Beyond that is another thrilling view of the cliffs, with the boulder field straight below.

The trail turns right and continues level just below the crest, finally turning left and ascending what proves to be the actual "summit" of the mountain, a bit of a disappointment compared to everything you've seen thus far. The blue-blazed trail reaches its end, intersecting the red-blazed Millbrook Mountain Trail. This marks the boundary between the Mohonk Preserve and Minnewaska State Park Preserve. You can continue on from here for another 2 miles south to Gertrude's Nose, or return via the red-marked Millbrook Mountain Trail and the blue-marked Coxing Trail (see below), making a total loop of just over 6 miles.

Bayards Path

Length: 0.2 mile. **Markings:** Signs; red blazes. **General description:** This short trail connects the Millbrook Ridge Trail with Trapps Road. **Highlights:** This trail creates a possible loop from the West Trapps parking area using the Millbrook Ridge Trail and Trapps Road. **Downside:** None. **Difficulties and hazards:** A rocky path.

From a small valley called Smedes Cove, approximately 0.75 mile south of Trapps Bridge on the blue-marked Millbrook Ridge Trail (see above), make a right onto the red-marked Bayards Trail. The Bayards are a series of cliff faces located between the Near Trapps and Millbrook Mountain. The red-marked trail bends right and descends through a thick undergrowth of huckleberries. It then makes a sharp drop over a bare rock and continues to descend through mountain laurel, eventually coming out on Trapps Road (see above). A right here will return you to Trapps Bridge.

Millbrook Cross Trail

Length: 0.3 mile. **Markings:** Signs; red blazes. **General description:** This short, easy hiking trail crosses the Millbrook Ridge at a low point between the Bayards Trail and Millbrook Mountain, connecting the Millbrook Ridge Trail with the Coxing Trail. **Highlights:** Those wishing to hike the Millbrook Ridge while avoiding the most difficult part can use this bypass and still enjoy a great hike. **Downside:** None. **Difficulties and hazards:** None.

Where the blue-marked Millbrook Ridge Trail dips into a shallow trough between the Bayards and Millbrook Mountain, approximately 2 miles south of Trapps Bridge, the red-marked trail departs on the right and continues west, climbing gradually. The Millbrook Cross Trail veers right, eventually reaching a crest and making a gradual descent into more dense forest with plentiful hemlocks. Follow it for a brief while until you reach the blue-marked Coxing Trail (see below). Turning left here leads to Minnewaska State Park Preserve; a right will eventually take you to Trapps Road, which continues to Trapps Bridge.

Coxing Trail

Length: 1.7 miles. **Markings:** Signs; blue blazes. **General description:** This hiking trail connects Trapps Road with the Millbrook Mountain Path. It follows the upper valley of the Coxing Kill, much of its length via the old Van Leuven Road that once led to the James Van Leuven homestead. Though formerly cleared for timber and pastureland, today this area is primarily dense forest. The remains of stone walls that separated the fields are still very much in evidence. The upper portion of the trail is mostly on open ledges and exposed bedrock, with scattered pitch pine and mountain laurel. **Highlights:** Beautiful forest in the lower section, views in the upper section. It is especially useful as part of a 6-mile loop to Millbrook Mountain that also utilizes the Millbrook Ridge Trail. **Downside:** Some segments of trail in the lower section may be flooded at times. **Difficulties and hazards:** The upper section of the trail, which is mostly on exposed bedrock, is often obscure. Follow the markers carefully!

To get to the trailhead, follow Trapps Road (see above) south of Trapps Bridge for approximately 1 mile to the blue-marked Coxing Trail (there's a sign), which exits on the left. Follow the blue-marked trail through the forest. It's mostly a wide path that was once the old Van Leuven Road. After about 0.75 mile, the red-marked Millbrook Cross Trail branches off to the left. It continues over to the Millbrook Ridge Trail (see above) and can be used for possible loop hikes.

The trail passes through an area of hemlocks in varying stages of growth and then through an "enchanted" forest of tall deciduous trees with groundcover that's primarily clubmoss. A stone fence appears to the left of the trail. The nearby Coxing Kill can be heard tantalizingly close, but never seen. The trail narrows and bends sharply to the left through dense mountain laurel as it ascends gradually. The trail then turns right, and the forest eventually opens up to sparse oak, pitch pine, blueberries, and smooth, bare rock slabs. The trail continues to ascend to the right of a shallow ravine. Follow the markers carefully (easier to do when you're not taking notes like I was). At one point, you can turn around and observe a dramatic view of the upper reaches of Coxing Clove, with Sky Top in the distance. The trail continues its gradual ascent on bare rocks through a "garden" of pitch pine with cairns and glacial erratics on both sides of the trail, finally intersecting the red-marked Millbrook Mountain Trail (see next chapter). Here you can either go right for 1 mile to Minnewaska Lake, or left for less than 0.25 mile to the top of Millbrook Mountain. From there, you can return to Trapps Bridge via the Millbrook Ridge Trail (see above).

Trapps Hamlet Path

Length: 0.75 mile. **Markings:** Signs; light blue blazes. **General description:** A relatively easy hiking trail from the West Trapps parking area to Route 44/55, crossing Clove Road at roughly the midway point. **Highlights:** This quite scenic trail also features landmarks of historical interest, especially the Eli Van Leuven cabin, the only remaining residence of the Trapps Mountain Hamlet on Mohonk property. These landmarks tell the story of the former agricultural community, now abandoned, that once existed here. The area was probably first settled in the late 18th century. As the neighboring valleys were settled, families, many of them of Dutch descent, began moving farther up the ridge to the area of the Trapps Mountain Hamlet. The soil here was thin and not fertile, so farms had to struggle to survive. Families often supplemented their income by picking berries and nuts, harvesting maple syrup, lumbering, cutting and stripping hemlocks for tannin, cutting millstones, making barrel hoops and charcoal, laboring on local roads, and working at the nearby hotels. By the late 19th century, the hamlet featured a one-room schoolhouse, store/post office, chapel, inn/tavern, and sawmills. Unable to make a sufficient living, the farms were eventually sold. Much of the land was purchased by the Smileys and added to their resorts. A number of Trapps homesteads were demolished when Route 44/55 was built in 1929. In 1956, Irving Van Leuven, the last Trapps resident, died. Today, there are few remnants of the community left. Most of the land once cleared for timber and pasture has since returned to forest. A walking guide for the trail, titled "Trapps Mountain Hamlet," may be purchased at the Trapps Gateway Visitors Center. **Downside:** Traffic noise. **Difficulties and hazards:** Be careful of cars when crossing Clove Road.

From the north side of the West Trapps parking area, enter the forest opposite the gatehouse and descend gradually. The trail soon levels amid hemlocks, a shady area with no undergrowth whatsoever. It then veers to the left, passing a boulder pile. Farmers would remove these stones from their fields and either use them for making walls or leave them in a pile like this. Pass the yellow-marked Enderly's Path on the right; it leads to the Shongum Path (see below). Just beyond, cross a tiny seasonal stream on a small wooden plank. Past the stream, the trail veers left. Rock outcroppings appear on the right, as do some evidence of previous millstone cutting and a steep slope. Cross a second wooden bridge over a small stream. The trail then bends to the right and crosses a third bridge. This one was once part of a wagon road, and old stone bridge abutments are still present.

The trail veers left again and passes a stone wall on the right. You'll soon enter a more mixed forest of maples and birches as well as hemlocks. Another stone fence appears on the left. Cross a stone wall that once formed the boundary between two properties. Enter a more open forest that's mostly maples and soon arrive at Clove Road. This section was once part of the old Wawarsing–New Paltz Turnpike, built in 1856, which lasted until the newer Route 44/55 was built in 1929. Some parts of Route 44/55 follow the old turnpike. Be careful of car traffic when crossing.

The trail resumes on the opposite side of the road. It bends sharply to the left and enters the old unpaved Van Leuven Road. The road used to continue south approximately 1.5 miles to what was once the James Van Leuven homestead (see above). Unwilling to maintain this remote road, the town of Gardiner abandoned it in 1907. The Coxing Kill appears below on the right, gushing over rocks and through chutes. There is a steep slope between the trail and the stream. The trail begins a gradual ascent. On the left, about 100 yards up the hill, is an abandoned family burial ground. At least four headstones remain, but a number of other people, mostly children, were probably buried there. Stone fences also crisscross the area. The trail levels again and soon passes the Eli Van Leuven Cabin on the left. This simple two-story wooden cabin was built in 1889 or 1890. A porch in the rear features an interpretive sign and map of the community. Just beyond the cabin, on the right, is a short, steep trail leading to the spring that supplied the cabin's residents with water. There's a small parking area past the cabin, and from it a gravel road. Follow it. The road turns left and away from the old Van Leuven Road. You'll soon arrive at Route 44/55. On the right, just off the trail, lie the sunken basement and partial foundation of what was once the Coddington home, built in 1874. It is 0.4 mile back to the West Trapps parking area via the highway—but the safer and more scenic route is to simply return the way you came.

COXING PARKING AREA

The Coxing parking area is located on Clove Road, 1.1 miles north of its intersection with Route 44/55, 0.2 mile west of the West Trapps parking area. It is a trailhead for the High Peters Kill Trail, the Old Minnewaska Trail, and the Shongum Path, and it provides access to the Enderly Trail. The most prominent feature is Split Rock, where the Coxing Kill tumbles through a deep, narrow trough in the bedrock and empties into a pool perfect for wading. The Coxing Kill was originally named Coxen Kill for a local Dutchman. (*Kill* means "stream" in Dutch.) The rock slabs along the stream are ideal for sunbathing. There is no access to mountain bike or cross-country ski trails. This parking area can be utilized when the nearby West Trapps lot is full. Because of the swimming opportunities at Split Rock and other sites along the Coxing Kill, this area tends to be crowded on hot weekends in summer. There are portable bathroom facilities by the parking area.

The earliest evidence of European landownership in Coxing Clove (the name of the valley where the Coxing Kill is located) dates back to the early 18th century. Henry Harp was granted a 250-acre plot of land in the Clove in 1764. Much of Coxing Clove was part of the 1770 Nineteen Partners' Tract, which included 1,769 acres from the Trapps north to Sky Top and west to Dickie Barrie. In 1799, the Nineteen Partners' Tract was partitioned. In 1801, Johannis and Jacob Enderly purchased this site. By 1860, the Split Rock area was the site of a water-powered sawmill that produced boards and beams for local use. The blade from the sawmill is on display at the Trapps Gateway Visitors Center. This was also the site of the homestead of Hiram and Loretia Enderly. There was a sawmill, a blacksmith and barrel hoop-making shop, a springhouse, a large barn, additional residences, and a family burying ground. Foundation ruins of the Enderlys' barn and family residence can be seen along the trail between the parking area and Split Rock. In 1921, the land was purchased from the Enderly family by the Mohonk Mountain House.

Upper Coxing Clove was later settled in the 1930s by followers of Father Devine, a black religious cult leader. Devine's followers, who nationally numbered in the tens of thousands, believed Devine was God, had very strict morals, and practiced a communal lifestyle. Some of his followers established two resorts in the area: the Anderson Dude Ranch (which later became Smitty's Dude Ranch) and the Wickie Wackie Campground (named for a town in Jamaica). Both served a primarily black clientele. The Wickie Wackie Campground was a very genteel establishment that drew such notables as David Dinkens (the former mayor of New York City) and Duke Ellington. Upper Coxing Clove remained an exclusively black community into the 1960s.

Hiking Trails

Unnamed Trail

Length: 0.5 mile. **Markings:** Yellow blazes. **General description:** This hiking trail departs from the Old Minnewaska Trail just beyond the wooden bridge over the Coxing Kill and follows the stream northeast to the boundary of the Mohonk Preserve. **Highlights:** Wading and sunbathing at Split Rock and other smaller pools along the way. The clear stream lined with hemlocks and mountain laurel, flowing or tumbling over smooth bedrock, is enchanting. **Downside:** Boisterous or obnoxious individuals or groups sometimes spoil the atmosphere. **Difficulties and hazards:** Trampling plants and erosion pose threats to this fragile environment.

From the Old Minnewaska Trail, just beyond the bridge over the Coxing Kill, the yellow-marked trail departs on the left (north) side. It crosses a bare slab of conglomerate, skirting the Split Rock swimming area on the left. The trail descends from the rock slab into a hemlock grove to the right of the stream. The Coxing Kill splits here below the pool, reconnecting a short distance beyond. Cross wooden boards through a damp, fragile area. The trail continues north parallel to the stream. An old woods road enters on the right. The trail ends on an open area of streamside bedrock at the boundary of the Mohonk Preserve; beyond this is private land.

Old Minnewaska Trail

Length: 2.5 miles. **Markings:** Signs; occasional light blue blazes. **General description:** This trail, opposite the Coxing parking area, crosses the bridge over the Coxing Kill and climbs up to Laurel Ledge Road. It mostly follows an old carriage road (no bikes or skiing), built in 1879 to connect Mohonk with the (then new) resort at Minnewaska Lake. It was the first carriage road to connect the two resorts. Completion of Undercliff Carriage Road (1903) and Trapps Carriage Road (1907) created a new route between the two resorts, and Old Minnewaska Road faded in importance. **Highlights:** Among the trail's main attractions are fine west-facing views of Coxing Clove, Rondout Valley, and distant Catskills, as well as excellent blueberry picking along the way. It also provides access to the Shongum Path and the Undivided Lot Trail. **Downside:** None. **Difficulties and hazards:** Rougher than the other carriage roads. The ascent is long. Bears are known to frequent this area in mid- to late summer, grazing on blueberries.

From Clove Road opposite the parking area, the Old Minnewaska Trail passes foundation ruins of the Enderly barn on the right and a family residence on the left. It then crosses the Coxing Kill on a bridge. On the left is the Split Rock swimming area; just beyond the bridge is the unnamed yellow-marked trail described above. The trail climbs a very short steep incline before the red-marked Shongum Path (see below) appears on the right. The blue-marked carriage road soon levels and continues through an area of tall, thin deciduous trees and white pines. The road bends to the right, crosses two small streams, then bends to the left amid numerous hemlocks. It then begins a gradual ascent, veers to the right, and levels again. A larger stream appears on the left. The trail descends and crosses the stream on rocks. This was the site of a bridge, now removed, though stone abutments are still present. Climb a steep embankment and return to the carriage road.

The road continues fairly level, with a steep slope to the left. It then narrows and becomes a trail. At the same time, the forest opens up. There are mixed deciduous trees and mountain laurel, and scattered hemlocks and white pines. There are also numerous huckleberries and blueberries. Slanting rock slabs are seen to the right of the trail, which becomes rocky and begins a slow, steady ascent. Look for views through the trees on the left to Coxing Clove. Pitch pines begin to appear along the trail. There is a fine open view on the left of the lower section of Coxing Clove, the Rondout Valley, and the distant Catskills. The trail continues to climb steadily. Then it veers to the right with some brief ascents and descents, nothing steep. There is another superb view to the left of the trail looking north and west to the lower reaches of Coxing Clove, the Rondout Valley, and the Catskills, particularly the Devil's Path Range to the north.

The blue-marked Undivided Lot Trail (see below) appears on the left. The trail again starts to ascend, winding left then right amid slanting rock slabs with numerous pitch pines. As the trail loops to the right, a splendid north-facing view of the Rondout Valley and the Catskills appears on the left. The trail eventually levels, bends to the left—passing small wetlands on both sides, and then an area of hemlocks—and finally joins Laurel Ledge Road at the foot of a talus pile.

Shongum Path

Length: 0.6 mile. **Markings:** Signs; red blazes. **General description:** This trail connects the Old Minnewaska Trail with the Connector Trail, thus linking the Coxing and West Trapps parking areas. The Shongum Path follows an old Lenape Indian trail across the Shawangunks. It also marked the boundary between the 1730 Groote Transport Land Patent and the 1770 Nineteen Partners' Tract. From the Coxing parking area, it is uphill most of the way, though not steep. It is suitable for most beginning walkers. Estimated time is roughly 25 minutes if you're going uphill. **Highlights:** This trail provides access to the Trapps Hamlet Trail from the Coxing parking area. It is also useful for a number of loop hike possibilities. **Downside:** The steady uphill from the Coxing parking area may deter some. **Difficulties and hazards:** Slippery in some spots when wet.

From the intersection with the blue-marked Old Minnewaska Trail, just past the bridge over the Coxing Kill (see above), make a right onto the red-marked Shongum Path. There's a brief steep climb, and then the trail levels. A stone wall appears to the left of the trail, along with a stand of hardwoods with young white pine, striped maple, and hemlock; a steep slope down to the Coxing Kill lies to the right. The trail stays level, crossing a stone wall and then a seasonal brook on boards. It then turns left and enters a dense grove of hemlocks. The trail veers right, with large mature hemlocks on both sides of the path among many younger ones, then crosses a second seasonal brook on boards, larger than the first. There's a gradual ascent on boards veering to the left. Pass the beginning of the yellow-marked Enderly's Path (see below) on the right. It continues south to the Trapps Hamlet Trail.

Cross the same brook again on boards and continue your steady ascent, with the gurgling brook to the right of the trail. Turn right and cross the brook once more. The incline increases. The trail bends left and continues to ascend on open slabs of rock, with scrub oak and blueberries to the right of the trail. Mountain laurel appears on both sides.

The red-marked trail meets the Connector Trail between the West Trapps parking area and Trapps Bridge (see above). To go to the West Trapps parking area, turn right. To continue to Trapps Bridge, head left for 200 feet, soon reaching stone steps leading up to the bridge over Route 44/55 on the right. There are portable bathroom facilities to the left of the trail.

Enderly's Path

Length: 0.3 mile. **Markings:** Signs; yellow blazes. **General description:** This relatively easy, short hiking trail connects the Shongum Path with the Trapps Hamlet Trail. It was named for the Enderly family, who owned a farmstead with a sawmill located on the Coxing Kill by the Coxing parking area. **Highlights:** It can be used to get to the Trapps Hamlet Path from the Coxing parking area or to link the Coxing parking area with the West Trapps parking area. **Downside:** None. **Difficulties and hazards:** A short, steep ascent at the very beginning.

From the Shongum Path (see above), follow the yellow-marked trail, ascending a short incline on stones. Soon the ascent becomes more gradual and eventually levels off. Cross a tiny seasonal stream and continue level. There is a steep slope off to the right. After several minutes of nearly level hiking through hemlock stands, arrive at the blue-marked Trapps Hamlet Path. Turn right if you plan to follow the Trapps Hamlet Path; left if you're heading toward the West Trapps parking area.

High Peters Kill Trail

Length: 0.9 mile. **Markings:** Light blue blazes and signs. **General description:** This segment of the High Peters Kill Trail starts at the Coxing parking area and ends at the boundary with Minnewaska State Park Preserve. From there, it continues for another 2.1 miles to the Awosting parking area in Minnewaska Park. **Highlights:** The entire High Peters Kill Trail is one of the more wondrous and interesting hiking trails in the Shawangunks. The segment in the Mohonk Preserve offers a variety of forest scenery and evidence of prior agriculture usage. **Downside:** You will have to spot cars at both ends of this trail or take one of the long loops. **Difficulties and hazards:** While the segment in the Mohonk Preserve doesn't pose any special threats or chal-

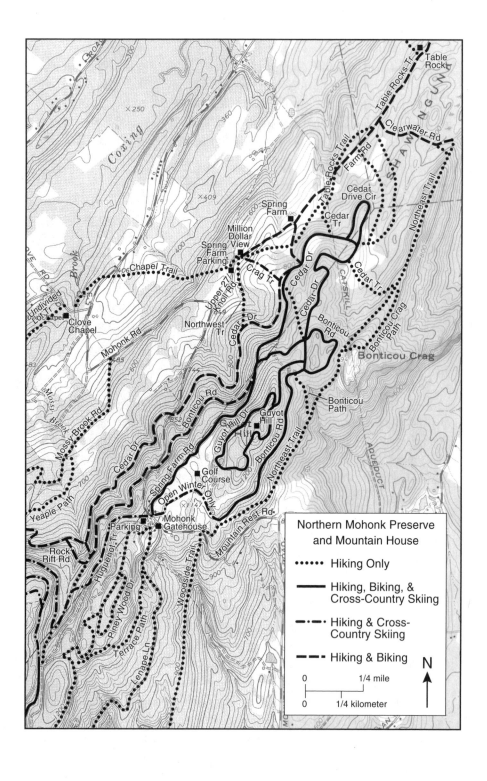

Northern Mohonk Preserve
and Mountain House

.... Hiking Only

———— Hiking, Biking, &
Cross-Country Skiing

—·—·— Hiking & Cross-
Country Skiing

– – – – Hiking & Biking

N

0   1/4 mile

0   1/4 kilometer

lenges, the rest of the trail in Minnewaska Park has steep ascents and descents, dangerous cliffs, and overall is fairly strenuous.

From the southwest corner of the Coxing parking area by the kiosk, the trail enters the forest as a wide, level path. It bends to the left and continues on wooden boards through a damp or wet area. Cross a tiny streamlet and then another, larger stream on a wooden board. The trail slowly ascends through a hemlock grove to the left of the stream. Pass a stone wall on the left. The trail bends to the right and crosses another small stream, then turns left, continues to climb to the right of the stream, and begins a steep ascent up a rocky path.

Cross a stone wall. The trail then splits. The 0.4-mile-long King's Lane (a climbing path marked with yellow blazes) departs on the right to the Lost City cliffs. Instead, take the left fork south between the stone wall on the left and the slope on the right. Cross a stone fence and proceed past an old field on the left. The trail then veers away from the stone wall. A spring is passed on the right. Cross another small stream. The trail bends to the right and begins a steep ascent to the left of the stream. Veer right and ford the stream. Veer left and right and climb more steeply. The trail enters Minnewaska State Park Preserve just before the rocky slope, where the blazes turn navy blue. For a description of the rest of the trail, see the next chapter.

SPRING FARM PARKING AREA

This parking area off Upper 27 Knolls Road (a branch of Mohonk Road)—1 mile downhill past the Mountain House Gatehouse and 5 miles from New Paltz—provides access to the trails and carriage roads of the northeast section of the Mohonk Preserve and Mountain House property. In the late 18th century, members of the Clearwater and Stokes families settled the area to farm. Albert Smiley bought the area around Bonticou Crag from Jesse Elting in 1881 and added it to the Mohonk resort. The trails and carriage roads of this section tend to see fewer visitors than other parts of the park. Don't let that deter you. (Some see it as a big advantage.) The area offers a rich variety of scenery, including forests and fields, expansive views, and excellent trails. Also, remnants of old farmsteads such as stone walls, abandoned fields, old roads, and foundation ruins are plentiful and obvious to even casual visitors. One of the primary destinations for hikers is Bonticou Crag (elevation 1,194 feet), whose rugged peak offers dramatic views. Another popular destination is Table Rocks, an area of sheer cliffs, deep crevices, and views. The nearly level carriage road loop that goes through the golf course and includes Spring Farm Road and Bonticou Road makes a superb cross-country skiing track, especially for beginners, while Cedar Drive and Guyot Hill Drive provide more challenging routes. There are portable bathroom facilities by this parking area.

Multiple-Use Trails

Spring Farm Road

Length: 2.1 miles. **Markings:** Signs at intersections. **General description:** This carriage road starts at the Spring Farm parking area and continues on to the Mohonk Gatehouse, where it intersects Bonticou Road. The entire road is open to hikers and mountain bicyclists; the 1.8-mile-long section from Cedar Drive to the gatehouse is also open for cross-country skiing. Skiers should note that Spring Farm Road can be accessed from the Spring Farm parking area via the red-marked Crag Trail. **Highlights:** A variety of scenery, from fields to forest, may be experienced on this road. There are broad panoramic views at the beginning of the roadway, a place aptly named the Million Dollar View. **Downside:** None. **Difficulties and hazards:** Some uphill climbing.

From the Spring Farm parking area, go through the gate and continue north on the unpaved roadway as it climbs a hill. The red-marked Crag Trail and blue-marked Table Rocks Trail (see below) depart on the right. From the crest of the hill, the "Million Dollar View" faces north and west overlooking the Rondout Valley and the entire Catskills Range.

The road descends briefly and forks. Continue straight. Pass a barn on the left. The road loops to the right. Farm Road, another designated bike route that continues out to Table Rocks (see below), departs on the left. Just beyond the intersection, there's a farmhouse on the left. This is Spring Farm (elevation 690 feet), which dates back to the 1850s or 1860s. In 1881, it was purchased by the Smileys and continued operating as a dairy farm until 1949. From 1949 to 1974, beef cattle were raised here. From 1974 to 1982, there was limited production of hay. Now it is part of the Mohonk Preserve. The fields are maintained by the preserve as a historical landscape. Just past the farmhouse is a garage; just past this, on the left, is the Slingerland Pavilion. Today, Spring Farm is used primarily for the preserve's educational programs.

Spring Farm Road bends sharply to the right and climbs. There's a field on the right. Cross the blue-marked Table Rocks Trail (see above). Continue straight, ascending. Cedars, maples, and shagbark hickory line the road. The road bends sharply to the left and, as it does, a magnificent view opens up from behind, across the field and north to the Rondout Valley and the Catskills Range. The road enters the forest and continues to climb. Turn right and after a short distance reach the intersection with Cedar Drive (see below), which approaches at a diagonal from the left, crosses, and continues to the right. Bear to the left and continue straight, ascending gradually. The red-marked Crag Trail (see below) crosses the road. The road bends to the left and then to the right, crossing the side of a steep slope. There are partial views through the trees. Pass small outcrops of shale on the left and continue through a hemlock grove.

The road continues to ascend. It crosses Bonticou Road (see below), which approaches from an angle on the left and continues off to the right. Continue straight, soon crossing the side of another steep slope with a partial view to the right through the trees. Spring Farm Road then bends to the left and levels. On the left is an unmarked intersection with Pine Water Reservoir Road, which leads up to Guyot Hill (see below). Continue straight. The Mohonk Golf Course appears on the left. The sound of traffic on Mohonk Road can now be heard emanating from the right. Garages appear on the right, with a view of the Catskills Range in the distance. Just beyond, pass cottages and other structures on the right. The road bends to the left and immediately arrives at the intersection with Bonticou Road and the wooden bridge over Mountain Rest/Mohonk Road. Just across the bridge, on the opposite side of Mountain Rest Road, is the gatehouse entrance to the Mountain House.

Cedar Drive

Length: 3.8 miles. **Markings:** Signs at intersections. **General description:** This unpaved carriage road actually starts from an intersection with Bonticou Road, then loops around, crosses Spring Farm Road and Mohonk Road, and finally ends at Mossy Brook Road. The entire road is open for hiking and mountain biking—but see "Difficulties," below. The section from Spring Farm Road to Bonticou Road is designated as a cross-country ski trail. Skiers should note that the section from Spring Farm Road to Mossy Brook is not groomed. **Highlights:** Access to some of the less visited areas in the northern part of the preserve. There's a fine view between Cedar Drive Circle and the intersection with Bonticou Road. **Downside:** Mohonk Road and Glenn Anna present a pair of interruptions (see "Difficulties"). **Difficulties and hazards:** The old bridge where Cedar Drive crosses Mohonk Road no longer exists, making this crossing (via steep, informal paths) very inconvenient, especially for skiers and bicyclists. Also, beware speeding traffic while crossing the roadway. Crossing Glenn Anna is a tough challenge, especially for bicyclists. The long uphill section from Cedar Drive Circle to Bonticou Road is considered fairly grueling for bicyclists and skiers.

Since this road is usually accessed from the Spring Farm parking area, I will begin its description from its intersection with Spring Farm Road. This section is open for hiking and mountain biking, and is a designated cross-country ski trail. Go left from this intersection, passing on the right the ruins of an 18th-century stone farmhouse once belonging to Louis Clearwater. The Clearwaters were farmers and millstone cutters; Clearwater Road was named for them. Cedar Drive continues level. There is a steep slope on the left with numerous young narrow-trunked hardwood trees. The roadway veers to the right. The red-marked Cedar Trail appears on the left (see below). The next section of Cedar Drive is also part of the Cedar Trail and is marked with red blazes. Cedar Drive turns right and intersects Cedar Drive Circle on the left (see below). Bicyclists must utilize Cedar Drive Circle to avoid the upcoming steep climb on Cedar Drive. As promised, Cedar Drive makes a rather steep, twisting climb. Cedar Drive Circle again appears on the left. Cedar Drive bends to the right and continues to ascend, though more gradually. The road bends more sharply to the right. There's a stone wall on the left. The red-marked Cedar Trail departs on the left.

The road continues its steep ascent, bending to the right. A stunning westward view opens up to the right of the carriage road, of the Rondout Valley and southern Catskills, framed by white pine and tall pitch pine trees. The road loops to the left, then bends to the right and continues to ascend. The road finally levels and bends left and right, then left again. There's another ascent, and then Cedar Drive bends to the right and reaches an intersection with the red-marked Crag Trail and Bonticou Road (see below). To shortcut to Bonticou Crag, go left. To continue on Cedar Drive, go straight, passing a wetland on the left filled with emerald vegetation in summer. The road bends to the left and climbs, then turns right and then left again. Guyot Hill Drive (see below) appears on the right. Just beyond is a second intersection with Bonticou Road and the end of Cedar Drive. A left turn here will take you to Bonticou Crag.

Spring Farm Road to Mossy Brook Road: This section is open for both hiking and mountain biking. It is not groomed for cross-country skiing, however, and presents obstacles and hazards that everyone should make note of. From the intersection, go right, soon crossing the red-marked Crag Trail (see below). Open views across old fields appear on the right. Soon a shale quarry is passed on the left; shortly after that, the red-marked Northwest Trail (see below) appears on the right and descends to the Spring Farm parking area. Continue fairly level, eventually reaching Mohonk Road. The carriage road used to cross the road here on a high wooden bridge, but it has been long since removed, though the buttresses remain. Descend to the right on a steep, rough path to the road.

Using caution, cross the road and turn left, following the road for a very short distance to where a trail marked by a sign ascends a small bluff on the right. At the top of the bluff, turn left. The carriage road continues as a fairly level path with a relatively steep slope off to the right. The road crosses two ravines, then turns right and reaches Glenn Anna, a stream that lies in a very steep ravine. A wooden bridge built in the 1930s once crossed the ravine. It collapsed in the 1960s and has been removed, though the stone buttresses remain. There are plans to replace it. It is a very steep and rough path down to the stream (bicyclists will have difficulty negotiating this). Cross the stream on rocks and ascend the equally steep, rough path on the other side. Finally reach the carriage road again, passing a large boulder in the middle of the path. Old Glenn Anna Road (see above) appears on the left. Pass through an area of talus boulders, with the most impressive slabs on the left. Just beyond, Rock Rift Road (see above) appears on the left. Continue for a short distance, noticing Mossy Brook Road (see below) below on the right. Cedar Drive soon intersects it and ends. The mountain bike route continues to the left.

Cedar Drive Circle

Length: 0.2 mile. **Markings:** Signs at both ends. **General description:** This short loop through the forest departs from and then rejoins Cedar Drive, thus circumventing a steep incline. The northernmost of any of the carriage roads, it is both a designated cross-country ski route and a mountain bike trail. **Highlights:** Views peering down steep slopes into the forest. **Downside:** None. **Difficulties and hazards:** None.

From Cedar Drive (see above), turn left onto this short loop road just before the incline. Continue fairly level, with a steep slope off to the left. The carriage road then begins to bend to the right. It loops around and continues in the opposite direction. Just before reaching Cedar Drive again, an unnamed yellow-marked trail appears on the left.

Unnamed Yellow-Marked Trail

Length: 0.5 mile. **Markings:** Yellow blazes. **General description:** This unnamed marked trail starts from Cedar Drive Circle and soon splits. One branch continues to Farm Road; the other ends at an unmarked road. This trail is ideal for backcountry skiing. **Highlights:** A chance to explore off the beaten track. There's plentiful evidence of prior agricultural use. **Downside:** This trail seems to begin nowhere and end nowhere. But those who view it that way are missing the point. **Difficulties and hazards:** None.

From Cedar Drive Circle, follow the yellow-marked trail for a short distance to where it splits. The left branch, which is far shorter, descends a slope, enters a field, and eventually joins Farm Road (see below). The right branch bends left, continuing through an old field grove of very young trees, then veering left and descending. A stone fence is passed on the right. The trail follows the fence, finally crossing it, and then crosses wooden boards over a wet area. Pass an alga-covered pond on the left.

The trail veers to the right, then descends again and crosses another stone wall. A seasonal stream appears on the right. The trail continues parallel to it for a short while, veering left. It then bends to the right and departs from the stream, climbs a small bluff, and bends to the left again. The trail then descends and meets an unmarked road. A left turn here leads to Farm Road; a right, to the Clearwater Road Trail (see below).

Bonticou Road

Length: 3.8 miles. **Markings:** Signs at intersections. **General description:** This carriage road begins at the intersection with Spring Farm Road by the wooden bridge over Mountain Rest Road. It continues through the Mountain Rest Golf Course and past Bonticou Crag, then loops back around, crossing Mohonk Road and continuing south and west to a three-way intersection with Rock Rift Road and North Lookout Road. The mostly level segment from the bridge, through the golf course, and on to the intersection with Spring Farm Road is part of a popular cross-country ski loop, rated easy. **Highlights:** A relatively easy route no matter how you're traveling. Some lovely forest is traversed. It may be used to access Bonticou Crag and the Rock Rift Crevices. In combination with other trails, it makes for some rewarding loop possibilities. **Downside:** The segment that goes through the golf course is closed from April to November. **Difficulties and hazards:** Use caution when crossing Mohonk Road due to speeding traffic.

From the wooden bridge over Mountain Rest Road, opposite the Mohonk Gatehouse, go east through the golf course. (Please note that this section of the road is closed from April to November, but makes an ideal cross-country ski route when snow conditions permit.) The road bends to the left past a steep hill used by hotel guests for toboggans and dishes when the snow conditions are right. It then bends to the right, passing a wooden shelter on the right. Just beyond, an unmarked road on the left departs for Guyot Hill. The road leaves the golf course and continues across the side of a steep slope. On the right is a ravine tempting those with downhill aspirations. Similarly, the hillside above on the left may be good for trying out your telemarking skills. The road continues and bends to the left with a field on the right, reaching an intersection with a road on the right that leads downhill to an intersection with the Northeast Trail (see below). From here, the carriage road is open for hikers and mountain bicyclists.

Bonticou Road bends to the left, crossing a pair of openings that were once downhill ski trails, part of the old Mohonk Ski Area, now closed. (The old ski trails are considerably overgrown.) There are views facing east to the Hudson Valley. Bonticou Road continues northeast. The road intersects Cedar Drive on the left (see above). The red-marked Bonticou Path appears on the right (see below). The road bends left and right, then continues to the left, passing an open view of Bonticou Crag's imposing white cliff on the right. Just beyond, the yellow-marked Bonticou Ascent Path departs on the right (see below). The road makes a sharp left past shale outcrops, also on the left. Bonticou Road then turns right and intersects Cedar Drive and the red-marked Crag Trail (see above).

To continue on Bonticou Road, go straight. The road bends to the right, passing shale outcrops on the left. Then it continues through a hemlock grove. The road makes a few turns and then crosses Spring Farm Road at a slant (see above). The ski trail ends here. Going left will bring you back to the Mountain House Gatehouse; going right, to the Spring Farm parking area. To stay on Bonticou Road, continue straight. There's a steep slope on the right with partial westward views through the trees. The road goes relatively straight and level for a while, then bends to the right, passing an old bridge abutment and Mohonk Road on the right. Continue straight. The road narrows and becomes an informal path just before it reaches Mohonk Road.

Cross the road to the left of the old bridge abutments. Watch out for speeding traffic! Pick up the road on the opposite side and continue level through the woods below the roadway on the left. There's a steep slope on the right. Following a slight ascent, the road bends sharply to the right, then veers to the left and then right again. Look for partial views through the trees on the right to the Rondout Valley, with the Catskills in the distance. There are shale outcrops on the left side of the road. The road continues level, then bends to the right and crosses a seasonal drainage through a steep-sided ravine. It continues through a hemlock grove. The road bends to the right and crosses Glenn Anna and, just beyond, Old Glenn Anna Road on the right, which descends steeply to Cedar Drive. Glenn Anna Ravine continues to the right of the carriage road. A short distance beyond, Bonticou Road ends at the intersection of North Lookout Road on the left and Rock Rift Road straight ahead (see above). The bike route continues on Rock Rift Road.

Farm Road

Length: 0.7 mile. **Markings:** Sign at intersections. **General description:** This unpaved road/trail, a designated bike route, links Spring Farm Road to the Table Rocks Trail and thus Table Rocks and the Clearwater Road Trail. **Highlights:** Varied scenery of fields and forest with many wildflowers. Direct access to Table Rocks. This trail is useful for any number of possible circular hikes. **Downside:** The fields can get a bit buggy. **Difficulties and hazards:** Bicyclists should note that this trail is not as well maintained or graded as the carriage roads. Use caution when riding to avoid spills.

To get there, follow Spring Farm Road up from the Spring Farm parking area. Just past the barn and farmhouse on the left and before the garage, Farm Road appears on the left. Turn left here. The Slingerland Pavilion will appear on the right. A trail branches off to the left across a field and continues to a woodland area, where a replica of a Native American longhouse, used for educational programs, is located. Make a left at the second trail, following it across the field.

Enter the woods and bear right, with stone fences lining both sides of the rough path. Enter a second field and cross. Reenter the woods. The road bends to the left, then bends to the right and climbs. The blue-marked Table Rocks Trail (see below) appears on the right. A right turn here will lead back to the Spring Farm parking area. For a short distance, Farm Road and the Table Rocks Trail are one and the same. Continue up the road to a second intersection at the beginning of another field. The Table Rocks Trail now departs to the left. The road veers to the right across the field. A yellow-marked trail enters diagonally from the right; you can follow this up to Cedar Drive Circle (see above). Veer left here and continue for a short distance along the edge of the field. A second trail, this one unmarked, departs on the right. Continue straight, eventually reentering the woods. The road winds through the woods for a short distance and reconnects with the blue-marked Table Rocks Trail on the left. Turning left, you can loop back to the Spring Farm parking area. Going right will take you to Clearwater Road, 0.1 mile, and Table Rocks, 0.75 mile.

Guyot Hill Drive/Pine Water Reservoir Road

Length: 2.7 miles. **Markings:** Signs at intersections. **General description:** Guyot Hill stands next to the Mohonk Golf Course and is part of the Mountain House property. With an elevation of 1,265 feet, it is the highest shale-based summit in the Shawangunks and the highest summit north of the gatehouse. Once it, too, was covered with conglomerate rock, but over millions of years the conglomerate eroded away, leaving the shale we see today. It was named for Arnold H. Guyot (1807–84), a professor of geology and geography at Princeton as well as a great lover of Mohonk and frequent guest of the Mountain House. The carriage road starts from Cedar Drive near its intersection with Bonticou Road. The road ascends and then loops around Guyot Hill. This is a designated bike route and ski trail. The ski trail is rated most difficult. **Highlights:** Guyot Hill used to be cleared and was a popular destination for its wonderful views. The forest has since grown back, and the views have mostly disappeared, although fine vistas down the steep wooded slopes into the forest and its canopy remain. Solitude is another feature. **Downside:** The remoteness of this road will deter most. Also, it may seem to meander aimlessly through the forest—though those who perceive it that way are missing the point. **Difficulties and hazards:** The long, steady climb to the top can be strenuous whether you are on foot, bike, or skis.

From Cedar Drive, Guyot Hill Drive climbs and veers left. The road then bends more to the left and continues to ascend. There's a steep slope off to the left. The road then veers to the right and left, and the incline steepens. The road slowly veers to the right again and continues to ascend slowly. It then bends more to the right, away from the slope, and arrives at a T-intersection with Pine Water Reservoir Road. From here on, the road makes a loop, so it doesn't matter which way you go. For our purposes, we will stay on Guyot Hill Drive and turn left.

The road continues to climb slowly. Another loop of the road appears below on the right. Guyot Hill Drive bends sharply to the left. A cairn (pile of stones) appears on the right; this is the summit. The road then bends sharply to the right. There may be east-facing views through the trees when the leaves are down. There are steep slopes on three sides of the summit. The road begins a slow descent, with a steep slope on the left. The road then veers to the right and left, bends sharply to the right, and loops around. Pass shale outcrops on the right side of the road. Another loop of the road appears below on the left.

The road makes a U-turn to the left and continues to descend slowly. There may be views on the right looking through the trees facing west. The road then bends to the left and right. It reaches a low point on the ridge, loops around, and begins to ascend. The road bends more sharply to the left, and then to the right, slowly climbing. There is a steep slope off to the left. Arrive at a small clearing. A short spur trail to the left leads up to a bench and a worthwhile and well-earned east-facing view of the Wallkill Valley, with the Marlboro Hills in the distance.

The road descends and loops to the right. Then it bends to the left and continues its descent. Notice a body of water below on the right: Pine Water Reservoir. The road loops sharply to the right and arrives at a T-intersection. The road on the left leads to the golf course and Bonticou Road. It is open only when the golf course is closed—from November to April—when it may be used as a skiing route. The bike route continues to the right, passing the reservoir on the right. Another road leading to the golf course enters on the left. Guyot Hill Drive continues to the right, circling the reservoir. Arrive at the intersection with Pine Water Reservoir Road. A left turn here leads to Spring Farm Road and the golf course. It, too, is closed except in winter. Turn right on Pine Water Reservoir Road, passing the shore of the reservoir on the right and the pumphouse.

Pine Water Reservoir Road then bends to the left and climbs away from the reservoir. It soon levels. There is a very steep slope on the left. The road continues mostly level for a while, then loops to the right and bends to the left. Then it bends to the right and left and finally arrives at the T-intersection where it joins the segment of Guyot Hill Drive that you already traveled on. A left turn here will return you to the beginning. Turn right if you wish to do the loop again.

Clearwater Road Trail

Length: 0.5 mile. **Markings:** Red. **General description:** This trail mostly follows Clearwater Road, crossing the ridge connecting the Table Rock Trail with the Northeast Trail. This is not a carriage road but an old public road that once crossed the northern section of the ridge from Mossy Brook Road to Springtown Road, named for a family of farmers and millstone cutters who lived along it. It is a designated bike route. **Highlights:** Ruins and other evidence of prior agricultural use. This trail provides a useful link with other trails in this section for some potentially rewarding loop hikes. **Downside:** Bicyclists will be tempted to continue on the unmarked, unmaintained portion. However, that section is very rough, often flooded, and crosses private land. **Difficulties and hazards:** Rougher and not as well maintained as the carriage roads. Bicyclists should use extra caution to avoid spills.

From the Table Rock Trail going north (see below), just beyond the gate that once formed the boundary of the Virginia Smiley Preserve, intersect the red-marked Clearwater Road Trail. Make a sharp right and follow this road uphill, soon reaching the crest of the ridge. Begin to descend. There's a stone wall to the right of the trail. An unmarked trail also appears on the right, which you can follow out to Cedar Drive Circle (see above). To the left of the trail are some rather enigmatic stone ruins and stone fences, remnants of a 19th-century Stokes family farmstead, one of three in the area. Continue downhill for a short way. The red-marked trail departs from the road, bending to the right and crossing a small stream on a wooden bridge. Then cross a wetland area on a wooden board and continue with the stream to the left of the trail and rocks on the right.

You'll soon intersect the blue-marked Northeast Trail (see below). Going right will take you south along the ridge, eventually to Bonticou Crag.

Hiking Trails

Chapel Trail

Length: 0.9 mile. **Markings:** Signs; blue blazes. **General description:** This trail starts at Upper 27 Knolls Road and ends at Clove Road by the Clove Chapel. It is mostly downhill following the described route, or mostly uphill if you're going in the opposite direction. **Highlights:** A mix of forests and fields as well as a lovely chapel and old family burial ground. It appears to see few visitors and thus is perfect for those seeking solitude. **Downside:** Traffic noise. **Difficulties and hazards:** There are some steep sections and a few muddy spots. Use caution when crossing Mohonk Road.

From Upper 27 Knolls Road, across from the entrance to the Spring Farm parking area, head east across the field and enter the woods to the left of two private residences. The trail bends to the left and enters a hemlock grove. Descend gradually and cross a stream. The trail continues to descend more steeply and crosses a second stream on a wooden bridge. There's a partial view on the right, looking west to the Catskills.

The trail continues to descend along the side of a steep north-facing slope, with Mohonk Road above on the left and traffic noise a constant reminder. The trail loops to the right, away from the road, and continues to descend. It then turns sharply to the left and descends more gradually. A stone wall appears to the left of the trail, which turns left and crosses the wall. Continue level for a short distance and then veer to the right. Descend gradually through an area of young trees with plentiful white pines.

The trail bends to the left and traverses a potentially muddy section. Another stone wall appears on the right. Turn right and cross the fence. A seasonal stream appears on the left, flowing past a stone fence. There's a lovely view of a farm through the trees on the left. Continue to descend gradually, parallel to the stream and fence (another potentially muddy area). Note the numerous cedars in the vicinity, a pioneer tree in old fields. Veer right and left, then cross the stream on wooden boards. There's another view of the farm on the left. Cross a stone fence and a second small stream. Turn left and right and begin a gradual ascent through a cedar grove. Turn left around the corner of the field. Look for barbed wire on the left. The trail veers right and continues uphill.

Arrive at an open field and cross it, following marked posts, with a view of the farm and the gentle side of the Shawangunk Ridge in the background. Reach Mohonk Road and cross diagonally. Use caution and look out for speeding traffic! The blue-marked trail resumes on the other side as a very wide path. Continue to descend gradually. An old Stokes family burial ground appears on the left (including John F. Stokes, the former owner of Mohonk Lake who sold it to the Smileys in 1869). On the right is a bluff with a view of cascades on Mossy Brook. Just beyond, the Chapel Trail ends at Clove Road. On the opposite side of the road on the right is picturesque Clove Chapel. It was built in 1876 by residents of Coxing Clove on property donated by Festus Stokes. The chapel was designed by James Freeland and features a Stick-style lych-gate above the entrance, tall pointed lancet windows, and board-and-batten siding. Today, the chapel stands partially hidden by trees, but when it was built it stood in the open, visible from afar. It was one of two chapels in the clove. The other, built in 1881 near present-day Route 44/55, burned down in the 1950s. The Clove Chapel was used for regular services by both Methodists and the Reformed Church until the early 1960s. It is owned by the Stokes family and used for occasional ceremonies. Just to the right of the chapel and across Mossy Brook is the trailhead for the blue-marked Undivided Lot Trail (see below).

Undivided Lot Trail

Length: 3 miles. **Markings:** Signs; blue blazes. **General description:** This is one of the longest hiking trail in the Mohonk Preserve. From its inauspicious beginning on Clove Road, it continues mostly through forest to its end on the Old Minnewaska Trail. The trail crosses land that local residents once considered too rugged to be used for agriculture, and so never divided into individual lots like the rest of the ridge. It remained open to local landowners for hunting and other purposes. George Washington was granted a share in the "common" to celebrate American independence. Because of the trail's length and isolation, you may need to spot cars at Spring Farm and Coxing Clove or West Trapps if you wish to hike the entire thing. **Highlights:** Superb views of Coxing Clove, the Rondout Valley, and the distant Catskills, especially in the last mile. **Downside:** The trail's isolation may be discomforting to some. **Difficulties and hazards:** The trail is moderately rough in a few places, though you shouldn't need to use your hands. The isolation may create dangerous situations should you get lost or injured. Getting help quickly may be impossible.

From the trailhead on Clove Road, enter the forest on boards through a sometimes wet area of very young forest, including birch and cedar. Begin a gradual incline. Hemlocks become more plentiful. The trail levels in a hemlock grove, then continues to ascend gradually. A short detour on the right will take you to an open vista on slanting slabs of conglomerate, looking west to the Rondout Valley and the distant Catskills Range with Ashokan High Point in the center of the view, a taste of what's yet to come.

The trail levels again. There's a stone wall to the left of the trail. Hemlocks and northern hardwoods are seen, eventually becoming almost exclusively hemlocks. The land slopes steeply to the right. The red-marked Stokes Trail branches off to the left (see below). The Undivided Lot Trail continues uphill through hemlocks and bears left. The blue-marked trail bends to the right and ascends a narrow ridge with steep slopes on both sides. It then levels again amid numerous blueberries and huckleberries. After a slight ascent, the trail bends to the left through thick mountain laurel and oak.

The trail crosses a tiny brooklet and climbs and bends to the right. It levels again amid low blueberry bushes, with rock outcrops on both sides. The trail then descends to the right, then the left, more steeply. The descent eases and finally levels. Cross another tiny stream on rocks. Just beyond is a gorgeous patch of ferns in an opening on the right. The trail continues level. Another stream appears on the right. The trail follows parallel to the stream, gradually rising. The red-marked Clove Trail appears on the left (see above).

A short distance beyond, the Undivided Lot Trail crosses the stream on rocks. It continues up the other side of the stream, and finally makes a sharp right turn away from the water. The trail bends to the left and then the right again with an open view on the right to the mouth of Coxing Clove. It begins a steady climb, passing another open view on the right, then makes a sharp left and ascends on rocks. The trail levels, with more open views on the right to Coxing Clove, Rondout Valley to the north, and the distant Catskills.

The trail climbs again, with a partial view on the right looking north. It continues to rise and then levels in an area of thick mountain laurel. The blue-marked trail climbs again on rocks amid pitch pine, white pine, and scrub oaks. There are partial views on the right of Coxing Clove below. The trail bends to the right, passing cliffs on the right. Approach a swampy area on the left and, just beyond, an old fireplace in fine condition. It's all that remains of the Straight Eight Cabin, once used by students of the Smiley Boys School at Mohonk. There are very steep cliffs off to the right. Continue level through hemlocks, crossing over the deep fissures in the rock with care.

The trail continues level through a hemlock grove and then a mountain laurel thicket. Make a right and descend steeply along the base of a cliff. At the bottom of the cliff, make a sharp left and continue to descend over rocks to a small, shallow stream. Cross the stream on rocks and climb up and out of the ravine. The trail bears left and out of the forest into an open area with steep slopes, bare rock slabs, scrub vegetation, and many views. The trail bears left again, then zigs and zags, bearing south. Blueberries, huckleberries, oak, pitch pine, white pine, and scrub oak are plentiful along this section of the trail. The trail ascends over some rock beds—known as the Outback Slabs—to an open view. Coxing Clove can be seen below, and the Coxing Kill can be heard roaring; in the distance lie the Rondout Valley and Catskills. A short distance beyond, the trail climbs and intersects the blue-marked Old Minnewaska Trail (see above). A right turn here leads down to the Coxing parking area. A left will take you up to Laurel Ledge Road.

Stokes Trail

Length: 1.2 miles. **Markings:** Signs; red blazes. **General description:** This trail begins on the Undivided Lot Trail, following an old road for much of the way to a power-line right-of-way. It continues from there as an unmarked trail to its junction with Mossy Brook Road. **Highlights:** A relatively quiet route to the Mountain House and other trails in the Mohonk Lake Area. Remnants of Yeaple Town, an abandoned community. **Downside:** This trail is more difficult than some would prefer. **Difficulties and hazards:** Be forewarned that the last 0.5 mile is somewhat strenuous and involves relatively steep elevation gain.

To get to the Stokes Trail, follow the blue-marked Undivided Lot Trail from Clove Road (see above). At its juncture with the Undivided Lot Trail, the red-marked Stokes Trails veers off to the left, descending right away into a dark hemlock grove. The trail levels and crosses a small stream, a tributary of Mossy Brook, on rocks. Just past the stream on the left and right are stone walls and foundation ruins—a few of the many remnants of Yeaple Town, an agricultural community made up of the Yeaple and Stokes families, who often intermarried. The community lasted from the late 18th century until the late 19th, when it was purchased by the Smileys and abandoned. The trail then begins to ascend. Pass through a deciduous forest, with stone walls to the left of the trail. The trail turns right, passing another foundation ruin on the right and becoming a very wide path with only a slight incline (an old road). There's a stream to the right. Continue through more hemlocks. The trail turns left (east) and narrows as it continues uphill through a rocky, more eroded section.

The red-marked trail widens again and passes on the left the remnants of a stone bridge where the old road departs from the trail and crosses a ravine. Here the Stokes Trail makes a sharp right turn and continues to climb. It then dips and bends to the left, through hardwoods. There's a small stream on the left.

The trail then makes a very sharp right turn. It continues uphill as an eroded, rock-strewn path. The trail then bends to the left, climbs a steeper pitch, and enters a patch of very young trees. It then steepens once more, meets a stone wall, and bends sharply to the right. It continues to climb steadily through forest, with oaks prominent. The red-marked trail bends to the left once more and ends at a power-line right-of-way, where it enters Mountain House property.

As an unmarked path, the Stokes Trail continues, crossing the right-of-way—a haven for the mountain laurel, which blooms spectacularly in June. The trail bends sharply to the right and continues to ascend to the left of the right-of-way. The trail levels and meets (on the left) the blue-marked Maple Path (see above), which continues for a short distance downhill to the Mossy Brook Road, part of a designated mountain bike route.

The unmarked Stokes Trail continues level a short distance. The blue-marked Maple Path veers off to the right. The unmarked path continues straight. Mossy Brook Road can be seen to the left and down the hill. The unmarked trail soon intersects a loop of the road. Just beyond the intersection, Mossy Brook Road becomes paved and continues into the heart of the Mohonk Lake area.

Mossy Brook Road (Lower Section)

Length: 1 mile. **Markings:** None. **General description:** A less used carriage road. The entrance is on Mohonk Road. The section described here continues up to its intersection with Cedar Drive. Bikes are not permitted on this portion of road. **Highlights:** The Yeaple Cabin; solitude. **Downside:** The sewage treatment plant. **Difficulties and hazards:** Some uphill climbing.

To get to Mossy Brook Road from the end of the Chapel Trail (see above), follow Mohonk Road for 0.3 mile south, then turn right onto an unmarked road. Follow this road, ascending gradually to the right of a field bordered by a barbed-wire fence. You'll soon pass an attractive private residence on the left (please do not disturb). Cross Mossy Brook. The road follows the stream on the left for a short distance, then crosses it again. About 0.5 mile from the entrance of the road, the rustic log Yeaple Cabin appears on the left. Despite the 1771 marking, the exact age of the cabin is unknown, though it was likely built in the 1770s. It is certainly by far the oldest structure on the Mohonk property. Log cabins like this one have come to symbolize American pioneer farming life and were prevalent in forested areas well into the 19th century. They of course used a lot of timber, still a plentiful resource in the Shawangunks into the 19th century. They were easy and quick to construct, requiring no nails, holes, or shaping, and with the help of a few neighbors could be built in less than three days. This was a typical one-room cabin with a fireplace and a loft for sleeping. Log construction for most represented a temporary solution to the habitat question, to be replaced later by more permanent dwellings. In this area they were fairly rare, because of the preference for stone and later clapboard homes. Several generations of the Yeaple family inhabited this one. The Yeaples were an old Dutch family who migrated into the area that came to be known as Yeaple Town; a number of Yeaple and Stokes family members resided here, often intermarrying. The community lasted until the late 19th century, when the Smileys purchased the property. The cabin itself was renovated in the 1940s; more recently, a new tar roof was added. Just beyond the cabin on the right is the entrance to the Yeaple Trail (see below). Those wishing to avoid the sewage treatment plant should take this shortcut.

The stream appears on the left. The road follows it for a short distance, then bends to the left. The sewage treatment plant with its accompanying stench is on the right. Just beyond, the road crosses the stream and bends left. Pass a private cottage on the right. The road bends left and then right. At the Birch Turn, the Yeaple Path reenters the road on the left. Mossy Brook Road continues uphill, with cliffs and talus slopes appearing above off to the left. Cedar Drive (see above) soon appears on the left. The upper section of Mossy Brook Road is described above.

Yeaple Path

Length: 0.4 mile. **Markings:** Signs at both ends. **General description:** This forest path departs from Mossy Brook Road next to the Yeaple Cabin and rejoins it at the Birch Turn. **Highlights:** A shortcut to the Yeaple Cabin. It also avoids walking by the sewage treatment plant. **Downside:** None. **Difficulties and hazards:** Some muddy spots and some uphill.

From Mossy Brook Road just beyond the Yeaple Cabin (see above), turn left and follow the path through a grove of tall white pine trees. Cross a small seasonal tributary stream, turn left, and climb. There's a stone wall on the right. The trail veers right and continues uphill. It then levels, crosses a stone wall, then briefly climbs again and crosses another stone wall. A short distance beyond, the Yeaple Path arrives at Mossy Brook Road at the Birch Turn. A left turn here continues to the Mountain House; a right leads to the sewage treatment plant.

Northwest Trail

Length: 0.6 mile. **Markings:** Signs; red blazes. **General description:** This short trail begins at the Spring Farm parking area and ends at Cedar Drive, passing fields and young forest. It tends to see few visitors. **Highlights:** Different field and forest habitats, solitude, and a useful shortcut to Cedar Drive. **Downside:** None. **Difficulties and hazards:** None.

From the west side of the Spring Farm parking area, cross Spring Farm Road and turn right on the red-marked path. The trail skirts an old field overlooking Upper 27 Knolls Road on the right, bordered by cedars and a barbed-wire fence. Cross a seasonal brook on wooden boards. The trail bends sharply to the left and climbs a slope through a young forest of skinny trees to the right of a stone wall. The trail bends right and continues to climb, turns left and crosses the stone wall, then bends to the right again and continues uphill. The red-marked trail veers to the left and passes through a hemlock grove. Climb stone steps up to Cedar Drive (see above).

Table Rocks Trail

Length: 1.9 miles. **Markings:** Signs; blue blazes. **General description:** This moderate trail through varied terrain of fields and forest begins from the Spring Farm parking area and ends at Table Rocks. Most of it is strictly a footpath, though the last 0.75 mile is also a designated bike route. **Highlights:** This is the most direct route from the Spring Farm parking area to Table Rocks—a stunning area of rock outcroppings with very deep crevices. Along the way, there are rewarding views and pleasant field and forest scenery, with many wildflowers. The Table Rocks Trail also provides access to a number of other trails in this northern section of the preserve, with possibilities for circular hikes. **Downside:** The fields can get buggy. **Difficulties and hazards:** The last section of the trail at Table Rocks involves some scrambling. The crevices are potentially dangerous. Stay on the marked path and don't get too close to the edge.

The Table Rocks Trail can be accessed from either end of the parking area, crossing Spring Farm Road and proceeding left, uphill, parallel to the road. There's an old field to the right of the trail; on the left lies the famed Million Dollar View to the Rondout Valley and distant Catskills Range. The red-marked Crag Trail (see below) departs on the right here.

Continue straight on the blue-marked trail, climbing uphill. The trail crosses an open field and bends to the left. Cross a wet area on a wooden board. Continue across the field to Spring Farm Road. You've now come about 0.5 mile. Cross the road and proceed into the woods. There's a field to the left. Pass the Slingerland Pavilion and other structures on the left, part of Spring Farm and used by the Mohonk Preserve for educational programs. The trail bends to the right and begins a slow ascent along the side of a steep slope. A third of a mile after crossing Spring Farm Road, the trail bends to the left and meets the red-marked Cedar Trail (see below), which departs on the right. You've now come about 0.75 mile from the parking area.

The blue-marked trail then begins a slow descent, crossing a number of water bars. The trail passes through dense woods, crosses a small stream on a wooden bridge, and continues downhill. Eventually it meets Farm Road, a designated bike route (see above), and makes a sharp right onto the road and into an open field. Follow the road for a short distance across the field. The blue-marked trail turns left and departs from the road, which veers to the right. Go straight along the left edge of the field next to a line of cedar trees. Cross a stone fence and continue straight into the woods. Farm Road reappears on the right side of the trail. The blue-marked trail goes straight, following this old dirt road through the woods and eventually reaching an open gate at the intersection of the red-marked Clearwater Road Trail (see below). You've now come 1.5 miles from the parking area. The 480-acre area to the north was once the Virginia Smiley Preserve, acquired by The Nature Conservancy in 1969 and managed by it until 1993; then ownership was transferred to the Mohonk Preserve.

This section of the trail at one time was part of Clearwater Road, a public road that crossed the ridge here. Continue on the road, marked in blue, as it turns left and descends. The road eventually levels, passing old stone walls on both sides. The unmarked remnant of Clearwater Road departs on the left onto private land. The Table Rock Trail continues on what was once a private woods road. Soon another woods road departs on the right. Cross a number of water bars. Pass a huge boulder on the left and descend. This and other large boulders in the area were deposited here by glaciers. The road then follows the narrow spine of the ridge, with a steep slope on the left. Descend again and enter a hemlock grove. The Table Rocks appear on the left. The road levels again, and the blue-marked trail turns left and departs. Bicyclists will have to dismount here in order to continue.

The Table Rocks are the product of a huge ancient rock slide. Following the retreat of the glaciers, this huge slab of conglomerate rock became unstable, broke into large blocks, and slid downhill. The slide was very gradual—a few inches per century. Descend, passing large rocks and crevices on the right. Pass a large rock slab on the left. Just beyond it, a second loop of the blue-marked trail departs on the left. Instead, turn right. Cool temperatures from ice in deep crevices may be noticeable; this ice lasts well into summer. The trail bends left and right, then turns left and climbs onto a huge tilted rock slab, cut by fissures—105 feet deep in places. Use caution here. There are fine open views looking west and north to the Rondout Valley and distant Catskills Range. A 55-foot-square block is separated from the others by a wide crevice 35 feet deep. There are numerous talus boulders around the main blocks. The trail bends left and descends from the rock slab through the woods. It then turns right and rejoins the other loop of the blue-marked trail.

Cedar Trail

Length: 1 mile. **Markings:** Signs; red blazes. **General description:** This forest trail starts from the Table Rocks Trail and ends at the Northeast Trail near its intersection with the Bonticou Ascent Path. Note that part of the trail follows Cedar Drive. **Highlights:** Generally quiet and not well traveled. The trail visits areas of very young forest (former pastureland) and sees other evidence of prior agricultural activity. Very useful for circuit hikes. **Downside:** None. **Difficulties and hazards:** None.

From the blue-marked Table Rocks Trail (see above), 0.9 mile from the Spring Farm parking area and 0.4 mile after crossing Spring Farm Road, the red-marked Cedar Trail appears on the right. Follow the red-marked trail 100 yards uphill to Cedar Drive (see above). Turn left onto the road. Cedar Drive Circle (see above) soon appears on the left. Cedar Drive starts to ascend gradually and meets a second loop of Cedar Drive Circle on the left. The road then bends to the right and continues to ascend. A stone fence appears on the left. A short distance beyond, the red-marked trail turns left and departs the road after following it for 0.3 mile. It immediately crosses the stone fence and enters an area of pioneer forest with numerous young trees and many cedars present.

The trail continues level. A stone fence appears on the right. The trail veers left and begins to descend gradually. The trail then bends to the right and left and crosses a small seasonal stream on rocks. Continue to descend and cross boards over a low, frequently wet area. Make a brief ascent. The trail bends to the right. Talus boulders and cliffs appear straight ahead. At 0.6 mile from Cedar Drive, the Cedar Trail intersects the blue-marked Northeast Trail (see below). A right turn here goes south toward Bonticou Crag; a left heads north to Clearwater Road.

Crag Trail

Length: 0.6 mile. **Markings:** Signs; red blazes. **General description:** This walking trail starts from the blue-marked Table Rocks Trail near the Spring Farm parking area; it continues to the intersection of Bonticou Road and Cedar Drive. **Highlights:** For hikers and skiers, it provides superb panoramic views from fields near the beginning of the trail, and also the most direct access to Bonticou Crag from the Spring Farm parking area. Cross-country skiers may use the beginning of this trail to access Spring Farm Road. **Downside:** None. **Difficulties and hazards:** Mostly uphill the whole way. Skiers using the beginning part should take note the grueling ascent or steep descent on the return.

From the blue-marked Table Rocks Trail (see above), make a right and proceed uphill. Look for a row of cedar trees to the left of the trail and a field on the right, with wonderful views looking west to the Rondout Valley and the entire Catskills Range.

The trail soon crosses a stone fence and bends sharply to the left; a view looks south across a field of the Shawangunk Ridge. The trail continues to climb, with a stone wall and a row of trees to the left. The trail briefly crosses the field and enters the forest, where it immediately crosses Cedar Drive (see above). Twenty-five yards beyond, the red-marked trail crosses Spring Farm Road (see above). You've now come about 0.5 mile. The trail continues uphill and along the side of a steep north-facing slope. It levels, bends to the right through hemlocks, and climbs again. It then bends to the left and meets Cedar Drive and Bonticou Road (see above). A left turn on Bonticou Road is the shortest way to Bonticou Crag.

Northeast Trail

Length: 2.2 miles. **Markings:** Signs; blue blazes. **General description:** This forest trail starts from Mountain Rest Road and continues all the way to Clearwater Road, following the eastern slope of the Shawangunk Ridge. **Highlights:** Impressive views from the base of Bonticou Crag and fine westward views from the Northeast Crags. There is access to the Bonticou Ascent Path, providing both easy and challenging routes to the top of this landmark. **Downside:** You'll have to spot cars in order to travel the entire trail. **Difficulties and hazards:** Footing is questionable in a few places.

From Mountain Rest Road across from the Woodside Trail (see above), climb the hill and pass the golf course on the left (no trespassing) as the trail bends to right. The blue-marked trail soon crosses an unmarked trail and enters a field. The trail descends, following the right perimeter of the field. A dirt road enters from the left. Follow this yellow- and blue-marked road (the Link). Continue to descend and reenter the woods. A short distance beyond, the blue-marked trail departs from the road and climbs a steep bluff on the left. The trail levels, then descends gradually. Mountain Rest Road, with abundant vehicular noise, is below on the right.

The trail levels, and veers to the left, away from the road, following the side of an east-facing slope. Cross an old overgrown ski slope now populated with young white pines, with a view looking east to the Wallkill Valley, the Marlboro Hills, and the Taconics in the distance. The trail ascends, turns right, and intersects an old woods road. Veer right, descend, and cross three "dry" ravines in succession. Enter an area with numerous white pines. Descend briefly and enter a hemlock grove. Descend a steep embankment and cross the red-marked Bonticou Path (see below). Continue your gradual descent and cross a small seasonal stream. The trail levels and crosses a second stream, then veers left. Ascend gradually, then more steeply, reaching the top of a rise with a partial view of Bonticou Crag straight ahead.

Descend to the base of the Crag with its large talus field of giant boulders. The trail turns left and veers right around the Crag's south face. Notice a prominent rock pinnacle separate from the cliff face. The trail ascends gradually, skirting the edge of the talus field, with wonderful views looking up at the cliffs. Cross the yellow-marked Bonticou Ascent Path (see below). The blue-marked trail continues to ascend briefly, then begins to descend, eventually leaving the talus field and views of the cliff. The trail veers to the right, then briefly levels and veers to the left. Descend briefly and veer right. Cross a small drainage. The trail veers to the left, stays level, and veers to the right. The red-marked Cedar Trail (see above) appears on the left. The blue-marked trail enters an area of talus boulders, turns left, arrives at the base of a small cliff, and climbs moderately, with tilted overhangs on the right. The trail makes a sharp left turn, then turns right and reaches the intersection with the yellow-marked Bonticou Ascent Path. The trail veers to the left, then turns north, following the spine of the ridge. There's a partial view on the right looking east to the Hudson Valley. Ascend briefly through white pine and mountain laurel. The trail bends to the left and right then crosses bare rocks, the Northeast Crags, with views looking west to the Rondout Valley and Catskills. The trail turns right and climbs to a higher vantage point with a superb open view. Follow the trail as it gradually descends, with continuous views looking west. It then enters a hemlock grove and descends more steeply. The red-marked Clearwater Road Trail (see below) appears on the left. The blue-marked Northeast Trail continues to descend for a short distance, crossing a small stream and ending at an intersection with the unmaintained Clearwater Road.

Bonticou Ascent Path

Length: 0.3 mile. **Markings:** Signs, yellow blazes. **General description:** This trail departs from Bonticou Road and ascends Bonticou Crag's gleaming white precipice. From the summit, it descends the narrow ridge through sparse vegetation, eventually intersecting the Northeast Trail. The name *Bonticou* comes from the Dutch *bonte koe,* which translates as "spotted cow." It was the name of a ship that brought Huguenot immigrants to America. The name originally referred to farms and fields along the Wallkill 4 miles north of New Paltz. That area later became a small hamlet. Since 1880, the name has been applied to the Crag. **Highlights:** A thrilling climb. Fantastic views from the top of one of the Shawangunks' must impressive landmarks. **Downside:** Certainly not for those who are squeamish about heights. **Difficulties and hazards:** A challenging scramble over a steep slope of giant boulders and then up the side of the cliff, less intimidating than it appears. Beware cliffs and overhangs with long drops.

The yellow-marked trail starts from Bonticou Road (see above), immediately descends, and crosses the blue-marked Northeast Trail (see above). It continues straight for a short distance to a large talus field at the base of the cliff, and then begins to ascend, bending to the left and scrambling over a pile of huge jumbled rocks. About a third of the way along, fine views are achieved, gradually improving as you ascend higher. Eventually you reach a ledge along the cliff with a superb open view. The trail turns to the right, then bends left again, and heads up to the left of a cleft in the rock you must squeeze through. The yellow-marked trail makes another sharp right and then bends to the left at the edge of the bare summit rocks. You can walk out to the end of this conglomerate peninsula with islands of bonsai-shaped pitch pines and expansive views of the Shawangunk Ridge to the south, the Rondout Valley to the west, the Catskills Range in the distance to the north, plus east to the Wallkill and Hudson Valleys, the Marlboro Hills, the Hudson Highlands far to the south, and Schunemunk Mountain. Be careful: Much of the ledge is overhanging and quite sheer.

The yellow-marked trail continues north along the mostly bare rock backbone of the ridge, gradually descending through thickets of scrub oak and mountain laurel. There's an open view on the right to the Wallkill Valley. The Bonticou Ascent Path continues to descend more steeply. The trail proceeds through dense mountain laurel to a partial east-facing view on the right to the Hudson Valley with the Taconic Range in the distance. The trail continues to descend, eventually reaching the intersection with the blue-marked Northeast Trail (see above).

Bonticou Path

Length: 0.3 mile. **Markings:** Signs; red blazes. **General description:** This easy forest trail connects Bonticou Road with the Northeast Trail. Please note that the lower section of the trail, which continues to the old Mohonk Preserve Headquarters, is closed. **Highlights:** This trail may be useful for circuit hikes in the vicinity of Bonticou Crag. It is generally quiet and not well traveled. **Downside:** None. **Difficulties and hazards:** Mostly uphill if you're going in the opposite direction from what's described below.

From Bonticou Road (see above), near its intersection with Cedar Drive, go east on the red-marked trail that descends and bends to the left. It then bends to the right and crosses a small seasonal drainage on rocks. The trail briefly levels then proceeds downhill. The trail veers to the left while descending. There's a partial seasonal view of Bonticou Crag on the left through the trees. The red-marked trail veers right and continues its gradual descent. It then crosses another seasonal stream on rocks and veers left, soon reaching the blue-marked Northeast Trail (see above). A left turn here will take you north to Bonticou Crag. A right goes south to Mountain Rest Road. The Bonticou Path is closed beyond this point.

MINNEWASKA STATE PARK PRESERVE

The 12,166-acre Minnewaska State Park Preserve is the largest single area of protected open space on the Shawangunk Ridge. It is also one of the most popular destinations for visitors. The park preserve serves the dual purpose of providing recreational opportunities as well as protecting significant habitats for plants and animals. The primary scenic features are Minnewaska and Awosting Lakes, both renowned for their lovely crystal-clear blue waters and stark white cliffs. Both feature swimming and other activities. There are gorgeous streams, waterfalls and cascades, and thousands of acres of forestland, pine barrens, and spectacular scenic vistas. Millbrook Mountain (which is partly shared with the Mohonk Preserve) has the highest cliff face in the Shawangunks. Other high points with open panoramic views include Gertrude's Nose, Hamilton Point, Cas-

Minnewaska Lake

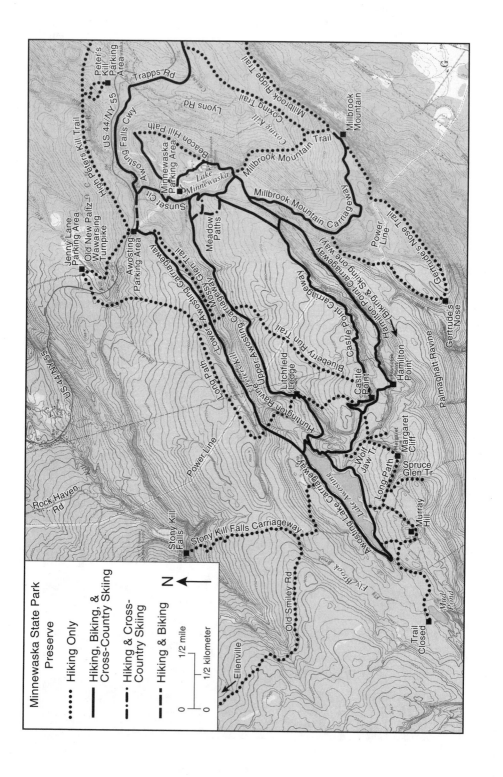

Minnewaska State Park Preserve

········· Hiking Only

━━━━━ Hiking, Biking, & Cross-Country Skiing

─ · ─ · ─ Hiking & Cross-Country Skiing

─ ─ ─ Hiking & Biking

N

1/2 mile

1/2 kilometer

0

0

Peter's Kill Parking Area

Trapps Rd

High Peters Kill Trail

US 44/NY 55

Lyons Rd

Coxing Trail

Millbrook Ridge Trail

Millbrook Mountain

Awosting Falls Cwy

Coxing Kill

Beacon Hill Path

Minnewaska Parking Area

Lake Minnewaska

Sunset Cir

Millbrook Mountain Trail

Millbrook Mountain Carriageway

Power Line

Gertrude's Nose Trail

Meadow Paths

Jenny Lane Parking Area

Old New Paltz Wawarsing Turnpike

Awosting Parking Area

Awosting Carriageway

Murray Glen Trail

Lower Awosting Carriageway

Upper Awosting Carriageway

Huntington Ravine

Blueberry Run Trail

Litchfield Ledge

Castle Point Carriageway

Hamilton Point Carriageway (Biking & Skiing one way)

Castle Point

Hamilton Point

Gertrude's Nose

Palmaghatt Ravine

Long Path

Power Line

Rock Haven Rd

US 44/NY 55

Stony Kill Falls

Stony Kill Falls Carriageway

Awosting Lake Carriageway

Wolf Jaw Tr

Long Path

Margaret Cliff

Spruce Glen Tr

Murray Hill

Old Smiley Rd

Fly Brook Rd

Fly Brook

Mud Pond

Trail Closed

Ellenville

tle Point, Margaret Cliff, Beacon Hill, and Murray Hill. Another major feature is the Palmaghatt Ravine, a cliff-lined gorge, the most dramatic in the Shawangunks. The park preserve is managed by the Palisades Interstate Park Commission (PIPC). The main entrance is located on Route 44/55, 4.6 miles west of the intersection with Route 299 and 10.4 miles west of the village of New Paltz.

HISTORY

The Minnewaska property was part of the "Groot Transport" Land Patent, a large land grant from the town of Rochester conveyed to one of its residents, Philip Dubois, in 1730. In 1785, the Groot Transport was partitioned and the Minnewaska land was divided among three landowners. Completion of the New Paltz–Wawarsing Turnpike in 1856 opened up this area, and George Davis, a resident of nearby Trapps Hamlet, operated a sawmill from the 1850s to the 1870s on the Peters Kill just north of present-day Route 44/55. In 1876, he led Alfred H. Smiley and his twin brother Albert, manager of the Mohonk Mountain House, with their families to a nearby lake on top of the mountain, then called Coxing Pond. They climbed up to the lake and beheld the magnificent view. Inspired by the scenery and wanting to create a resort similar to his brother's, Alfred expressed an interest in purchasing the land. Davis arranged for the property owners, including himself, to sell 2,200 acres to Smiley. Searching through old deeds in the city of Kingston, Alfred came across the Indian name *minnewaska*, meaning "frozen water." He renamed the lake. The Old Minnewaska Road was built in 1879 connecting the two resorts. That same year, Alfred opened the Lake Minnewaska Mountain House on the highest point overlooking the lake, approximately 1,800 feet above sea level, with a spectacular view of six states: New York, Pennsylvania, New Jersey, Connecticut, Massachusetts, and Vermont. The hotel eventually grew to accommodate 225 guests. Alfred and his family moved there, and he resigned his position as manager of the Mohonk Mountain House in order to operate his new resort on a full-time basis. Due to the popularity of the Lake Minnewaska Mountain House, a second hotel—the Wildmere—was erected on the north side of the lake eight years later. At this time, the Lake Minnewaska Mountain House was renamed the Cliff House; the two hotels were collectively known as the Lake Minnewaska Mountain Houses. The Wildmere grew to accommodate 350 guests.

Through additional purchases, the estate gradually expanded to its present size. Minnewaska's more rustic accommodations and wide expanse of untamed terrain offered guests a wilder experience than Mohonk, but many guests spent time at both resorts, traveling between the two and savoring the scenery. In 1907, completion of Undercliff Carriage Road and Trapps Road created a new primary route between Mohonk and the hotels at Minnewaska Lake, which took the place of Old Minnewaska Road. By 1926, recreational facilities included five tennis courts, four bathhouses, two long wharves with cushioned rowboats, a putting green, a baseball diamond, shuffleboard, quoit grounds, hundreds of summerhouses, and miles of carriage roads on which only horse-drawn vehicles were permitted. During this time, a number of blueberry pickers camped or illegally squatted on the property and harvested the wild berry crop, selling some to the resort.

The resort continued to operate under the management of Alfred Smiley's sons and later his grandson, Alfred Fletcher Smiley. By 1955, Alfred Fletcher was getting old and wished to retire. His daughters were not interested in taking on the huge task of running the resort, so he sold it to Mr. and Mrs. Kenneth Phillips. Phillips was an employee of the resort for 28 years, beginning as a chauffeur and later working his way up into management. In 1961, Phillips added a golf course, and in 1964 a downhill ski area, "Ski Minne," to widen the appeal of the resort. Both efforts failed to attract new guests. Given the high costs of maintaining the resort, Phillips found himself owing $1 million in back taxes and facing bankruptcy. In 1972, the Cliff House closed. Six years later, there was a huge fire likely caused by vandals. A heavy snowfall blocked the entrance road, preventing the arrival of fire-fighting equipment, and the entire hotel was destroyed. In 1979, the Wildmere also closed. Seven years later, it burned and had to be demolished.

In order to maintain the viability of the resort, in June 1970 Phillips sold 7,100 acres (including Awosting Lake) for $1.5 million to The Nature Conservancy, which then sold the plot to New York State; it became a state park under the management of the Palisades Interstate Park Commission. Though some users and residents of local communities demanded automobile, snowmobile, and ATV access as well as recreational facilities, the PIPC limited use of the new park to those activities that are primarily low impact. In 1975, an additional 1,570 acres, which included Ski Minne, were purchased by the state and added to the park. This was still not enough to stave off bankruptcy, however, and in 1977 Phillips sold another 1,300 acres of Minnewaska property to the state, with conservation easements on 239 acres of land around the lake preventing the use of powerboats and limiting future development. The $1.1 million price was funded half by the state and half by the federal government.

In 1979, the Marriott Corporation offered to purchase the remaining land and build a $31 million resort that would include a five-star, eight-story, 400-room hotel; a 500-unit condominium complex; and an 18-hole golf course, a disco, swimming pools, an ice skating rink, an indoor equestrian center, tennis and racquetball courts, and a brand-new ski center. The proposed project would have cleared 60 acres of forestland by Minnewaska Lake, including two stands of ancient pitch pines. According to one expert, it would also have consumed up to 80 percent of the lake's water in a decade, lowering the surface 23 feet. This plan was given general approval by the commissioner of the New York State Department of Environmental Conservation provided that Marriott could locate sufficient groundwater to supply the resort. Marriott also negotiated with the PIPC to amend the easement, allowing the expanded golf course but reducing the number of condominiums to 50.

Marriott's plan stirred up considerable political opposition, especially in the local community and among environmental groups such as the Friends of the Shawangunks. A private group, the Citizens to Save Minnewaska, was organized against the proposed development. These groups, along with the Appalachian Mountain Club, filed a lawsuit against the DEC. The Sierra Club and the AMC filed a second suit against the PIPC and funded a study of the northern Shawangunks by naturalist Erik Kiviat, which cited the ecological significance of the property. Meanwhile, projected costs for the new resort escalated to nearly $80 million. In 1983, the appellate division court struck down the decision of the DEC, stating that proof of sufficient water supply was required before the project could be approved. Marriott, which had already spent $1.5 million on legal fees and planning, was reluctant to spend additional money drilling wells. In 1985, the U.S. Circuit Court of Appeals stated that the amendment to the easement negotiated between Marriott and the PIPC required federal approval. Faced with the prospect of additional delays, court battles, and costs, the Marriott Corporation did the wise thing and withdrew its proposal.

Still facing bankruptcy and state-initiated eminent domain proceedings, Phillips was anxious to sell the remaining property. In 1987, 1,300 acres centered on Minnewaska Lake was purchased by The Nature Conservancy for $6.75 million and then sold to the state using bond-act funds. New properties were added later and the park, managed by the PIPC, grew to its present size. In 1993, the master plan for managing the new park called for the creation of a park preserve under Article 20 of the Parks and Recreation Law that would balance the needs for recreation with preservation of this unique landscape.

ACCESS, PERMITS, AND FEES

The primary access to the park is from Route 44/55. There is parking at Peters Kill, Minnewaska Lake, and Lower Awosting Parking Area. Those using these parking areas have to pay a per-car daily fee; you can also purchase an annual pass, also good for every state park in New York. Cross-country skiers in winter pay a per-person fee. The fees are higher on weekends. Rock climbers at Peters Kill also pay per person and require a special daily permit (for a small additional fee). Equestrians and scuba divers also require permits, but these are free. Kayak-

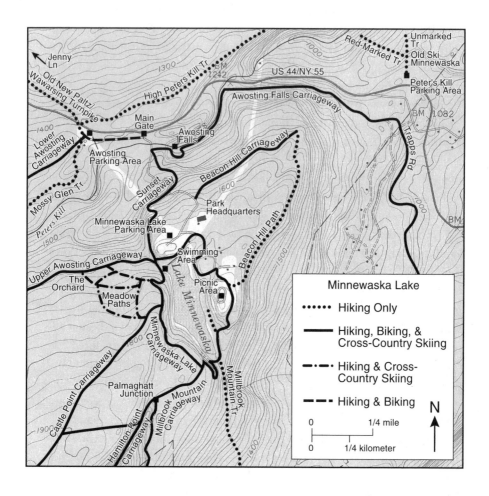

Legend on map:

Minnewaska Lake

•••••• Hiking Only

——— Hiking, Biking, & Cross-Country Skiing

—·—·— Hiking & Cross-Country Skiing

— — — Hiking & Biking

N

0   1/4 mile

0   1/4 kilometer

Labels on map: Jenny Ln, Old New Paltz/Wawarsing Turnpike, High Peters Kill Tr, BM 1242, US 44/NY 55, Red-Marked Tr, Unmarked Tr, Old Ski Minnewaska, Peter's Kill Parking Area, Awosting Falls Carriageway, BM 1082, Trapps Rd, Main Gate, Awosting Falls, Lower Awosting Carriageway, Awosting Parking Area, Beacon Hill Carriageway, Mossy Glen Tr, Sunset Carriageway, Peters Kill, Park Headquarters, Minnewaska Lake Parking Area, Swimming Area, Beacon Hill Path, BM, Upper Awosting Carriageway, The Orchard, Meadow Paths, Picnic Area, Lake Minnewaska, Minnewaska Lake Carriageway, Castle Point Carriageway, Palmaghatt Junction, Hamilton Point Carriageway, Millbrook Mountain Carriageway, Millbrook Mountain Tr, 1300, 1400, 1500, 1600, 1800, 1900, 1400, 1000, 1082

ing and canoeing permits are issued on a yearly basis. Jenny Lane features a small parking area for hikers accessing the Long Path. The park can also be accessed from Sam's Point Dwarf Pine Ridge Preserve; from the village of Ellenville via the Old Smiley Carriage Road; and from the Mohonk Preserve via Trapps Road, the Millbrook Ridge Trail, the Coxing Trail, and the High Peters Kill Trail. Note that access via any of these routes would involve miles of travel. The park opens daily at 9 AM. Closing times vary depending on the season and are posted at the entrance parking areas. Be forewarned that cars parked after closing time will be ticketed.

TRAILS AND FACILITIES

Minnewaska State Park Preserve boasts 27 miles of carriageways and more than 25 miles of hiking trails. The carriageways are the same as the carriage roads in Mohonk. They exclude motorized traffic (except for park vehicles), and most serve as multiple-use trails. They are, depending on the season, a primary destination for hikers, mountain bikers, horseback riders, and cross-country skiers. Most are marked with colored metal diamonds. There are also signs at most of the intersections. All carriageways are open for cross-country skiing. Most are groomed to make skiing easier, and are rated as easiest, more difficult, and most difficult. Call the park to get the most up-to-date ski trail conditions. Hiking trails are reserved specifically for hikers. These are maintained by volunteers from the New York–New Jersey Trail Conference and are marked with colored paint blazes and cairns. Many have signs at the trailheads. Please note that some routes in the backcountry are unmarked and unmaintained.

When hiking, cross-country skiing, or bicycling, please plan routes that take into consideration your ability and the amount of time available. Most of the trails and carriageways in the park involve miles of travel and may lead deep into the backcountry. If you're starting from the Minnewaska Lake parking area and interested in shorter routes, consider the Minnewaska Carriageway, the Beacon Hill Carriageway, and the Meadow Paths. Those starting from the Lower Awosting parking area and looking for short routes should try the Awosting Falls Carriageway or the Mossy Glen Trail. All accidents should be reported to park personnel.

Facilities are limited in this park preserve. Both lakes in the park have small swimming areas. There are rest rooms at the Peters Kill parking area and portable bathroom facilities at the other two parking areas, but none in the backcountry. Designated picnic areas are located around Minnewaska Lake. You'll also find a snack bar, a pay phone, an information center, and a nature center that serves in winter as a cross-country ski shop with equipment rentals, accessories for sale, and shoe storage (845-255-7059). Private ski lessons for small and large groups are available at 10 AM, noon, and 2 PM. You can call and reserve equipment and lessons in advance (845-564-5858). As of this writing, there are plans to build comfort stations at the Minnewaska Lake parking area. There is also a plan to construct a handicapped-accessible interpretive trail in that vicinity.

PROGRAMS AND ACTIVITIES

The park offers hikes, nature walks, and other hands-on educational programs led by the park interpreter and other staff to help foster understanding and appreciation of the region's history and ecology. These programs are for schools as well as the general public. The nature center is located in a small hut on the north side of Minnewaska Lake right by the parking area. It is staffed mostly by volunteers and features exhibits that would especially appeal to children and families. It is open on weekends from Memorial Day through Labor Day. There are also educational programs every Wednesday at 4 PM in summer, plus nature walks and hikes on weekends.

RULES AND REGULATIONS

1. Stay on established trails. No bushwhacking permitted.
2. Leave animals and plants alone.
3. All refuse must be carted out. Minnewaska has a "carry-it-in, carry-it-out" policy.
4. Glass containers are forbidden. No alcoholic beverages are permitted whatsoever.
5. At present there is no camping or overnight stays in the park.
6. Raised grills are permitted only in the designated picnic areas around Minnewaska Lake. You must bring your own. Otherwise, no fires of any kind are permitted in the rest of the park.
7. Bicyclists must travel on the carriageways only, never on the hiking trails. They must wear helmets and they must have signal bells to alert pedestrians. Bicyclists must always yield the right-of-way. The maximum speed is 15 miles per hour.
8. All pets must be leashed.
9. Only radios with earphones are permitted.
10. Parking is only permitted in designated areas. Most areas along Route 44/55 do not allow any parking.

In winter:
11. Sledding, tobogganing, hiking, bicycling, and pets are not permitted on trails groomed for skiers.
12. Skiing is permitted only on Minnewaska Lake (when conditions are suitable). Skiing is never allowed on Awosting Lake.
13. Avoid blocking ski trails. Allow faster skiers to pass. If someone is coming up faster from behind, step out the track and allow him or her to pass you.
14. Skate skiing is permitted on all trails open for skiing.

MINNEWASKA LAKE PARKING AREA

With space for 300 cars, the lot at Minnewaska Lake is the largest in the park. (Please note that there isn't enough space here for buses, which are *not* permitted.) The Minnewaska Lake parking area is reached by driving through the park preserve's main entrance and continuing up the winding, paved entrance road for approximately 0.8 mile to the parking area by Minnewaska Lake. The highlight and main attraction of this area is, of course, Minnewaska Lake (elevation 1,650 feet). Its exquisite emerald waters and spectacular views make it one of the scenic gems of the Shawangunk Ridge. It is the third largest of the sky lakes, covering approximately 34 acres. Its shoreline is just over a mile long. With a maximum depth of 78 feet, Minnewaska is the second deepest lake in the Shawangunks. Easy access also makes this one of the most popular destinations in the Gunks, and on busy weekends the parking lot can be full by as early as 10:30 AM. The Minnewaska Lake parking area also provides access to a number of trails. On the north shore of Minnewaska Lake is the sizable Cliffhouse cliff and talus slope. The private residence of former owners the Phillipses, built in 1987, overlooks the east side of the lake. The area of the parking lot was once the site of the Wildmere Hotel (see above). There is a nearby picnic area, portable toilet facilities, nature center (an outlet for cross-country ski rentals in winter), interpretive kiosk, snack bar, and main park office (information). As of this writing, comfort stations are planned for this area.

Multiple-Use Trails

Minnewaska Carriageway

Length: 2 miles. **Markings:** Red markers; signs. **General description:** Also referred to as Lake Shore Drive, this popular carriageway begins from the parking lot and circles Minnewaska Lake. It is suitable for walkers, mountain bicyclists, and equestrians, and in wintertime, when snow conditions are right, the road is groomed for cross-country skiing. **Highlights:** It is a mostly blissful jaunt with many excellent views of the lake, Cliffhouse cliffs and talus slope, as well as views looking east toward the Wallkill Valley. Short detours to the shoreline and swimming beach occur along this route, which also provides access to picnic areas and many of the park's trails. **Downside:** Not the place to go if beating the crowds is your goal. **Difficulties and hazards:** A generally easy trip—but be forewarned that for cross-country skiing, this is rated a most difficult trail. There are some short ascents and descents, and folks constricted by time or physical ability may find doing the entire road beyond their means. Also, the route around the east side of the lake is a bit confusing. Bicyclists and skiers, please note that there are a few tight curves. Beware the cliffs. In wintertime, skiers and walkers should be careful of the ice that tends to gather on the road at the south end of the lake.

From the west end of the parking lot, go left and descend a short distance on an unpaved roadway to an intersection with the red-marked carriage road.

You'll immediately encounter an expansive vista looking south to the lake, with the stately Cliffhouse cliffs off to the left rising up from the shore. To go clockwise around the lake, turn left and, after a short distance, bear right at the first intersection (there's a picnic area on the left here). Footpaths on the right descend on smooth stones down to the lakeshore or climb out to an open cliffside view of the lake. Pass on the right a small hut that serves as a nature center in summer (see above), and in winter as an outlet for cross-country ski rentals. Just beyond, you'll reach the intersection with a paved road. Portable bathroom facilities are on the left. A roadway on the right descends to the lakeshore at what's called Divers Cove and is used as a boat launch for canoeists and by scuba divers. (Both canoeing and scuba diving require a special permit.) Turn right. The red-marked carriage road veers right and away from the paved road, gradually ascending. Reach another intersection and go right. The road bends to the left, with a fine westward view of the lake from atop the Cliffhouse cliffs and a number of pitch pines in the vicinity.

Reach private property and bear left. Pass a park office on the right; it has a pay telephone. Bear right again. Reach a fork and bear left. (Pedestrians can go straight here: This trail takes you over a wooden bridge that arches across the roadway.) Enter the main road and turn right. The road bends to the right and descends underneath the picturesque wooden bridge. The road then bends to the left and climbs, passing a barn on the left, turning sharply right, and soon splitting. The left fork goes to a picnic area (located at the site of a former ball field), with a spectacular east-facing view of the northern ridge, including Sky Top and the Hudson Valley. This is also where you can start the Beacon Hill Path (see below).

If you go right at the intersection, the trail bears right and continues to ascend, then levels and bears left. On the right-hand side is a picturesque gazebo (here they're called summerhouses)—the only one left in Minnewaska State Park Preserve, though it's similar to the many in Mohonk. It is a perfect place to rest or snack, with a fine westward view of the lake. The road bears left and arrives at a big open grass field, the former site of the Cliffhouse Hotel, perched 130 feet above the lake. There's a picnic area straight ahead on the right side of the field, with fine views looking west and north to the lake and the distant Catskills. Bear left at the intersection and continue around the left side of the field. Behold the view looking east to the Hudson Valley and Sky Top in the distance to the north. The trail reaches another intersection with an unmarked road. Go left, into the woods. The road, which is fairly rough at this point, descends and then bends sharply to the left, intersecting another road. This one goes by the old ball field/picnic area mentioned above. Unless you want to loop back around, continue straight. The road bears left and descends. Pine Cliff—a historic trail on the left that is unmarked and unmaintained—leads to a cliffside view looking east to the Hudson Valley, with the Hudson Highlands in the distance to the south.

The road bends sharply to the right and continues to descend. Another informal path on the left leads to a cliffside, eastward view of the Hudson Valley that also includes the village of New Paltz and Sky Top to the north. The road bears left, and a view of the south side of the lake opens up on the right. The road levels. An unmarked road on the right runs along the lakeshore to an old docking area, with plentiful mountain laurel along the way.

The road bends to the right. Having come approximately 1 mile, you arrive at the south end of the lake. The road runs right along the lakeshore here, with a view of the entire lake looking north. There's a sign indicating the red-marked Millbrook Mountain Path (see below), which departs here on the left. Cross a drainage pipe. The road is just above the level of the lake, but this area tends to get rather wet; when it's cold, it's icy and can be treacherous for walkers or cross-country skiers. The road then climbs, bends sharply to left, and enters a hemlock grove. A vista opens on the left, looking east to the Hudson Valley. The road loops to the right and left and ascends. Then it turns right again. After going approximately 1.3 miles, the Millbrook Mountain Carriageway (see below), marked in yellow, appears on the left. Go right. The road levels, passing through thick mountain laurel and hemlock. The road begins a gradual ascent through beech, birch, maple, and oak trees. It then descends 0.4 mile from the last intersection, with the Castle Point Carriageway (see below), marked in blue, appearing on the left. Just beyond that intersection, the orange- and white-marked Meadow Path (see below) appears on the left.

Continue to descend. The road bends to the left and right, passes a rough shortcut route on the left, then loops to the left. The other end of the shortcut route then appears on the left. Just beyond, the Upper Awosting Carriageway (see below), marked in green, appears on the left. The beach area is on the right, as are a poor map of the park's carriageways and portable bathroom facilities. The road bears right and climbs (cross-country skiers will find this a thrilling or scary run when going down). On the left appears the orange-marked Scenic Sunset Carriageway (see below). Just beyond on the left is the parking lot where you started.

Beacon Hill Carriageway

Length: 0.6 mile, or 1.1 miles round trip. **Markings:** Orange markers; signs. **General description:** This carriage road starts from the entrance road, 0.1 mile from the Minnewaska parking area, and continues out to a viewpoint where it meets the yellow-marked Beacon Hill Path. In wintertime, when snow conditions are suitable, it is a groomed ski trail rated easiest. There are plans to develop this as a handicapped-accessible interpretive trail. **Highlights:** There's a magnificent panoramic viewpoint waiting at the end of the road, one of the easiest short trips visitors can take. Hikers using this carriageway, the Beacon Hill Path, and the Minnewaska Carriageway can complete a rewarding 2-mile-long circuit back to the parking area. **Downside:** In order to return, bicyclists and cross-country skiers will have to backtrack. **Difficulties and hazards:** None.

To get to the Beacon Hill Carriageway, follow the entrance road from the parking lot past the garage on the right. Just beyond, on the right, is the entrance to the orange-marked carriageway, clearly marked with a sign. Note that the 55-mile distance on the sign is clearly an error. The trail gently descends for more than 0.5 mile through the forest, finally terminating in a loop. There you encounter a spectacular 180-degree vista, one of the finest east-facing views in the Shawangunks. You can see the Catskills in the north, particularly Ashokan High Point, the Rondout Valley, the drainages of the Peters Kill and Coxing Kill, Dickie Barrie, Sky Top, the Millbrook Ridge, the Marlboro Hills in the distance, and the village of New Paltz, visible through a narrow notch. The Mohonk Mountain House is also visible. The name *Beacon Hill* comes from the Mountain House days when signal fires would be lit to send messages between the Minnewaska Mountain Houses and Mohonk. At the south end of the loop is the beginning of the yellow-marked Beacon Hill Path (see below).

Scenic Sunset Carriageway

Length: 0.8 mile, or 1.6 miles round trip. **Markings:** Orange markers; signs. **General description:** This carriage road used to be the main entrance road to the Minnewaska resort, later superseded by the paved entrance road. From the Minnewaska Lake parking area, it winds down to the main park entrance, where it connects with the Awosting Falls Carriage Road. In wintertime, when snow conditions are suitable, the Scenic Sunset Carriageway is groomed for skiing. As a ski trail, it is rated more difficult. Please note that pedestrians, skiers, and bicyclists restricted from using the paved entrance road must use this carriage road instead. **Highlights:** Nice west-facing views. This road provides the shortest connection between Minnewaska Lake and the Lower Awosting parking area, and also direct access to lovely Awosting Falls. **Difficulties and hazards:** Whatever comes down, must go up. It is a steep (for bikes), brake-burning descent or a grueling uphill climb—more than 270 feet—depending on which way you're going. Also, beware the many tight curves and traffic where the carriageway crosses the paved entrance road.

From the Minnewaska Lake parking area, go right on the red-marked Minnewaska Carriageway (see above). As the carriageway begins to descend toward the swimming area, the orange-marked Scenic Sunset Carriageway departs on the right. It briefly climbs, then turns right, passing two private structures on the right (no trespassing) as well as a fine open view on the left to the Rondout Valley and Catskills Mountains. Just beyond, the lower parking area appears on the right. The carriageway then turns left and begins to descend in earnest. The road bends to the right, passing another westward view of the Rondout Valley and Catskills.

The carriageway makes an S-curve, bends left, and crosses the paved entrance road. It continues to descend parallel to the road, bending right and left. You can hear the roar of Awosting Falls below. The road bends right and left again and finally ends at the entrance road, where it crosses the Peters Kill right by the main entrance. On the right is the red-marked Awosting Falls Carriageway, with Awosting Falls 0.2 mile away (see below). To get to the Lower Awosting parking area, make a right on the entrance road, then head left on the red-marked carriage road next to the entrance gatehouse. Follow this road a short distance to the Lower Awosting parking area.

Meadow Path

Length: Approximately 2 miles. **Markings:** Signs; orange- and white-marked posts. **General description:** Actually this isn't a single trail, but a small network of trails that explore the old golf course property between the Minnewaska and Castle Point Carriageways and the Upper Awosting Carriageway. The golf course is no longer maintained as such and is slowly returning to forest. Steeplebush (a purple native flower), pearly everlasting, sweet fern, blueberries, and grasses and sedges can be found in the fields. White birch and mountain laurel are common around the perimeter. Young pitch pines here are browsed by deer—the only place in the park deer are known to browse on this tree. Japanese barberry, a nonnative shrub, is invading the fields and is periodically removed by park staff. The trails are open for hiking and in wintertime are groomed for cross-country skiing. As ski trails, they are rated more difficult. Mountain biking is not permitted. **Highlights:** Easy to get to, easy to walk or ski, lovely fields, and fine views looking north and west are some of the attractions. There's not a lot of people traffic. This is a good place to observe early stages of forest succession. You can practice skiing using the telemarking technique. **Downside:** No map shows these trails very accurately. The open fields tend to be exposed to a lot of wind. Trails aren't always well marked. **Difficulties and hazards:** Skiers should beware a few steep sections and use caution.

From the Minnewaska Carriageway (see above), on the right (west) side of the lake less than 0.5 mile from the parking lot, the Meadow Path departs on the right just north of the turnoff for the Castle Point Carriageway. The trail immediately enters a clearing (the old golf course). Climb briefly. The trail seems to fork. Bear right and descend into the woods. Continue a short distance. Arrive at another clearing, bearing right and then left. Cross a small wooden bridge over a seasonal brook. Just beyond, the trail splits. The right fork descends, following the right perimeter of the field. At the bottom, it forks again. The right fork enters the woods, descends, turns right, and comes out on the Upper Awosting Carriageway (see below). The left fork continues up a steep hill and joins the left branch of the original trail. Here you can either go left and return to the beginning or go right and continue uphill into the woods, eventually coming to the end of a second big clearing. The latter trail is the one described below.

From the Castle Point Carriageway (see below), the orange- and white-marked trail departs on the right from a clearing (the old golf course) approximately 0.25 mile from the intersection with the Minnewaska Carriageway or 0.7 mile from the Minnewaska Lake parking area. Following the marked posts, the trail descends as it heads west with a pleasant view across the field to the Catskills in the distance. The trail approaches an ornamental pond, now largely overgrown; just before it, a segment of the trail turns to the right. Continue on a causeway across the pond and, on the other side, climb up to an intersection where the trail splits again. These last two intersections are the beginning and end of a trail loop described below.

If you go left, the trail passes another ornamental pond on the left. The trail briefly ascends and then levels. There's a large field on the left; to the right are woods with many white birch trees. The field begins to narrow, and the trail crosses to the left side. Just beyond, on the right, are wonderful views of the western Catskills in the distance. The trail then bends to the right and reaches the end of the field. Cross a short stretch of woods and enter a second field, once an old orchard, with a fine open view looking west; the Rondout Valley lies in the foreground, and the Catskills in the distance. The trail splits again. If you go straight, a short distance downhill you'll reach the green-marked Upper Awosting Carriageway (see below), in an area called the Orchard. A number of old varieties of apple trees grow wild here. A right turn will take you 0.7 mile back to the Minnewaska Carriageway.

If you go right where the trail splits, it bends to the right, enters the woods, and begins to climb, crossing a small seasonal stream—probably dry when you're there, but a regular torrent when I saw it with my daughter in December 2000. Continue uphill for a short distance, emerging at the end of another clearing. The trail encountered is part of the middle loop described below.

Regarding that trail loop I mentioned earlier: If you had gone straight after crossing the first pond (which way to start is arbitrary, of course), the trail continues to the left of a large field with woods on the right. There are views looking west across the field. Gradually the field narrows, and eventually the trail reaches its end. An unmarked trail departs on the left and descends toward the Upper Awosting Carriageway. The trail you're on makes a sharp U-turn and follows the markers uphill on the opposite side of the field. The trail bends to the left and levels, then turns left again into another open area and makes a gradual descent. This second field narrows, and the trail eventually reaches the corner, where it makes another sharp U-turn; another unmarked trail departs on the left, described above. You can go that way either to the Upper Awosting Carriageway or to the Minnewaska Carriageway. If you stay on the same path, it ascends along the left edge of the field. The field gradually widens again, and eventually the trail turns right, passes the first pond on the right, and reaches the first trail, where the loop ends.

Millbrook Mountain Carriageway

Length: 2.4 miles, or 6.3 miles round trip from the Minnewaska parking area. **Markings:** Signs; yellow markers. **General description:** This carriageway extends from the south side of Minnewaska Lake to Millbrook Mountain, mostly following the rim of the narrow ridge that separates Coxing Clove from Palmaghatt Ravine and then the ridge that separates Coxing Clove from the Hudson Valley to the east. It stays relatively level. In wintertime, it is groomed as a cross-country ski trail, rated easiest. **Highlights:** This is a fairly easy to moderate outing for walkers, bicyclists, and skiers. There are superb views from Millbrook Mountain and also of the Palmaghatt Ravine along the way, as well as access to the Gertrude's Nose Trail and Hamilton Point Carriageway. **Downside:** In order to return, bicyclists and skiers will have to backtrack. **Difficulties and hazards:** There are dangerous sheer cliffs at Patterson's Pellet and Millbrook Mountain.

From the right side of the Minnewaska Lake parking area, follow the red-marked Minnewaska Carriageway, which circles the lake (see above). Continue for just under 0.75 mile around the west side of the lake to where the yellow-marked Millbrook Mountain Carriageway branches off to the right. The roadway climbs steadily; 0.2 mile from the last intersection, it arrives at Palmaghatt Junction, where the carriageway to Hamilton Point and Castle Point forks off to the right (see below). The Millbrook Mountain Carriageway levels and continues left as the ridge between Coxing Clove and the Palmaghatt Ravine narrows. Less than 0.3 mile beyond, or 0.7 mile from the beginning of the carriageway, a large glacial erratic, Patterson's Pellet, appears on the right, perched on the edge of the cliff with a fine view of the upper section of the Palmaghatt Ravine, a cliff-lined gorge that widens and deepens to the southwest. The Palmaghatt Kill, a small perennial stream, descends through the gorge. No trails penetrate the ravine, and except for power lines that cross it, this is a largely pristine environment: On the opposite side of the ravine is Kempton Ledge.

Continue mostly level, passing more open views on the right. After another 0.4 mile, you'll pass the beginning of the red-marked Gertrude's Nose Trail on the right (see below). The carriage road makes a brief descent, bending right and then left. The road continues pretty level as the forest thins to scattered stands of pitch pine, oak, and birch. Eventually you'll arrive at the narrow ridge that separates Upper Coxing Clove from the Hudson Valley to the east. The red-marked Gertrude's Nose Trail runs closely parallel to the road here, and there are intermittent views looking east. The Millbrook Mountain Carriageway finally ends in a roundabout. The red-marked Gertrude's Nose Trail and the blue-marked Millbrook Ridge Trail (see the previous chapter) converge here, and the red-marked Millbrook Mountain Path (see below) begins nearby. The boundary of Minnewaska State Park Preserve and the Mohonk Preserve is also located in the vicinity.

Climb the stone steps to the right of the loop to the high point of the Millbrook Ridge (just over 1,600 feet in elevation) for an expansive, more-than-180-degree view looking north to the Catskills and Rondout Valley, the distant Taconic Range, the Shawangunk Ridge, Dickie Barrie, Sky Top, and the Near Trapps; east to the Wallkill Valley and village of New Paltz; and south toward the Hudson Highlands, Schunemunk, Sam's Point, and High Point, New Jersey. The cliff face is 0.75 mile long and more than 350 feet high, the tallest in the Gunks and one of the highest in the eastern United States. A huge talus field may be visible below. Turkey vultures are often seen launching themselves from ledges of the cliff. Be careful of the sheer drop!

Castle Point Carriageway

Length: 4.4 miles. **Markings:** Blue. **General description:** This very popular carriage road starts from the Minnewaska Carriageway on the west side of Minnewaska Lake and continues out to an intersection with the Awosting Lake Carriageway, passing Kempton Ledge, Castle Point, and Battlement Terrace. In wintertime, it is groomed for cross-country skiing and rated more difficult. **Highlights:** Spectacular views from Castle Point, Kempton Ledge, Battlement Terrace, and other points. This also makes for fine long loop trips, especially for cross-country skiers or mountain bicyclists, when combined with the Hamilton Point Carriageway or the Upper Awosting Carriageway. **Downside:** This is a long, moderately strenuous trip. **Difficulties and hazards:** Dangerous cliffs in a number of areas. Skiers and bicyclists should beware the many tight curves. Use caution.

To get there from the parking area, go right on the red-marked Minnewaska Carriageway, following it 0.4 mile around the west side of the lake to intersect the beginning of the Castle Point Carriageway on the right. The blue-marked road bends to the left and right and climbs a steep hill. The ascent gradually becomes more moderate. The carriage road soon crosses a grassy hilltop (the site of a former golf course), with views looking west to the Rondout Valley and Catskills Range. The orange- and white-marked Meadow Path (see above) departs on the right. The carriageway then enters a sparse woodland dominated by pitch pine and oak with an understory of mountain laurel, blueberries, and sheep laurel.

The road turns to the south. After 0.7 mile, it makes a brief descent, turns left, and reaches an intersection with a yellow-marked carriageway, which descends to the left and connects to the Hamilton Point Carriageway (see below). Continue south. Intermittent views open up on the left side of the road, looking down into the cliff-lined Palmaghatt Ravine. At 0.3 mile past the intersection, Kempton Ledge appears on the left, with a fine southeastward view of the Palmaghatt Ravine, Gertrude's Nose, and the Wallkill Valley beyond; the Hudson Highlands and Taconics lie in the far distance. The village of New Paltz is visible on the far left. The road runs close to the cliff on the left, so use extra caution.

The carriage road continues its gradual ascent in a westerly direction. At one point, the road bends sharply to the right and left. After traveling 0.8 mile past Kempton Ledge, pass underneath a Central Hudson power line built in the 1920s and 1930s. The road continues to climb, then turns sharply right. A fine open view on the left looks south and east, taking in the Palmaghatt Ravine, Gertrude's Nose, the Wallkill Valley, the Hudson Highlands, and the entire Shawangunk Ridge south, including Sam's Point and High Point, New Jersey. From here, expansive views continue as the road ascends, bending and twisting, with steep cliffs on both sides.

At 3.5 miles from the parking area, the trail finally reaches Castle Point (elevation 2,200 feet), the highest vantage point in the park, with a broad vista looking south and east toward the Wallkill Valley, with Sam's Point, the Hudson Highlands, Schunemunk Mountain, and High Point, New Jersey, in the distance; the Catskills and the Rondout Reservoir to the west; a dramatic view of Awosting Lake—Murray Hill and Margaret Cliff in the foreground—below; and Hamilton Point and Gertrude's Nose below on the left. This is arguably the single best view in the park, and is a popular spot for stopping. The turquoise-marked Long Path crosses the road here, making a short, steep descent from the side of the cliff down to the Hamilton Point Carriageway below (see below). Just beyond, on the right side of the road, the blue-marked Blueberry Run Trail ascends a small cliff (see below).

The Castle Point Carriageway continues west with more open cliffside views, gradually descending. A narrow cliff-lined ravine appears on the left, and the road descends in a tight hairpin curve. Just beyond, the Long Path departs to the right. Continue underneath the striking overhanging cliffs of Battlement Terrace on the left, often dripping a shower of water in spring, and sporting huge daggers of ice in winter. Approximately 0.7 mile from Castle Point, the carriage road intersects the yellow-marked Hamilton Point Carriageway (see below). Please note that bicyclists and skiers cannot turn left here onto Hamilton Point Carriage Road, which is one-way going in the opposite direction. Walkers can go left here to make a loop back to the Minnewaska Lake parking area, 8.3 miles total round trip. The turquoise-marked Long Path departs from the road here (see below).

The Castle Point Carriageway continues straight and descends. It then bends and twists, passing the unmarked Slate Bank Road (no bikes; see below), which departs on the left to Wolf Jaw. Half a mile from the intersection with the Hamilton Point Carriageway, the black-marked Awosting Lake Carriageway—which circles Awosting Lake (see below)—is reached. A left here will bring you 0.4 mile to the Awosting Lake beach. A right turn will take you to the Upper Awosting Carriageway (see above), a fine route for returning to Minnewaska Lake, 8.3 miles total round trip.

Upper Awosting Carriageway

Length: 3 miles. **Markings:** Green. **General description:** This carriage road connects the Minnewaska Carriageway with the Awosting Lake Carriageway. In wintertime, the road is groomed for cross-country skiing. As a ski trail, it is rated easiest. **Highlights:** This relatively easy, smooth, fairly level road provides the most direct route from the Minnewaska Lake parking area to Awosting Lake. Though views are infrequent, the forest—dominated by oaks, with fabulous stands of white birch and mountain laurel thickets—is quite breathtaking. Litchfield Ledge and the Overlook Cliffs are scenic landmarks. There are also fine detours possible to the Peters Kill and Rainbow Falls. **Downside:** None. **Difficulties and hazards:** Skiers should beware the ice that tends to gather underneath the Litchfield Ledge.

From the parking lot, go right on the red-marked Minnewaska Carriageway. Follow it downhill for a short distance to just opposite the lake's swimming area, where the green-marked Upper Awosting Carriageway branches off to the right. The carriage road turns right and then left, soon passing an open, north-facing view on the right to the Rondout Valley, with the Catskills in the distance. An unmarked road appears on the left, which connects with the Meadow Path (see above). The road bends to the left and, 0.8 mile from the beginning, crosses an open area that was once an old orchard. The Meadow Path (see above), marked in orange and white, appears on the left.

The road then reenters the woods. It crosses streams, bending to the right, left, and left again. The road then climbs, makes an S-curve, and bears left, crossing a stream flowing over large slabs of bare rock on the left. The road bends right and left and, 1.5 miles from the beginning, crosses the blue-marked Blueberry Run Trail (see below). A 0.25-mile detour here to the right will bring you to the lovely Peters Kill (see below).

Less than 0.5 mile farther, the Upper Awosting Carriageway crosses underneath a Central Hudson power line. The road bends right and left. The valley to the right begins to narrow, becoming Huntington Ravine. Cross a wooden bridge that traverses a picturesque stream cascading over moss-covered rock slabs. Note the rhododendron in the vicinity, as well as the tiny waterfall gushing on the right. Just beyond, there's a west-facing view on the right to Rainbow Falls plummeting from cliffs on the opposite side of the ravine, with the Catskills Mountains forming a distant skyline. Half a mile from the power line, the carriageway descends and crosses the Long Path, marked in turquoise (see below). A 0.2-mile detour on the right will bring you to the foot of Rainbow Falls. The steep, overhanging cliffs on the left are Litchfield Ledge. These may be dripping water in spring, or laced with icicles in winter. Because of the presence of ice on the road beneath the cliffs in winter, cross-country skiers or walkers should use extra caution here. Having reached the upper portion of Huntington Ravine, the Upper Awosting Carriageway loops to the right, crosses another stream, and climbs beneath the Overlook Cliffs on the left. The Upper Awosting Carriageway bears left and finally reaches the black-marked Awosting Lake Carriageway (see below), which circles Awosting Lake. From here, it is 0.4 mile to the Castle Point Carriageway and 0.8 mile to the beach. You can return to the Minnewaska Lake parking area by taking the Castle Point Carriageway (4.8 miles or 8.4 miles round trip) for a rewarding loop.

Hamilton Point Carriageway

Length: 2.8 miles. **Markings:** Signs, yellow markers with a black H. **General description:** This carriage road connects the Millbrook Mountain Carriageway with the Castle Point Carriageway. Starting in a narrow ravine densely populated with hemlocks, it follows the northern rim of the Palmaghatt Ravine most of the way. In wintertime, this trail is not groomed for skiing and is rated most difficult. **Highlights:** It offers a scenic experience distinct from the other carriageways: lush hemlock forest and dramatic cliffside views. **Difficulties and hazards:** This is the most challenging of the park's multiple-use trails. It is very rough and rocky and includes some steady inclines that most bicyclists and skiers will find grueling. Bicyclists and skiers, please note that to avoid some potentially dangerous downhill passages, the section from Echo Rock to the intersection with the Castle Point Carriageway is one-way, going south. Also note that following the entire carriage road from the nearest parking area (Minnewaska Lake) and back by any other route is at least 7.9 miles.

To get there from the Minnewaska Lake parking area, follow the red-marked Minnewaska Carriageway (see above) right for 0.7 mile to the south end of the lake, where the yellow-marked Millbrook Mountain Carriageway (see above) forks to the right and a sign points in the direction of Millbrook Mountain and Hamilton Point. Follow the yellow-marked carriage road as it climbs steadily for 0.2 mile to Palmaghatt Junction, where the carriageway to Hamilton Point forks to the right. Descend into the narrow cliff-lined Upper Palmaghatt Ravine. Almost immediately, there's another fork, this one not marked. The road on the right climbs steeply for a short distance to the Castle Point Carriageway (see above).

From the intersection, continue left on the yellow-marked carriageway as it descends through a picturesque dark stand of mature hemlocks. After 0.9 mile, the road begins to climb and passes Echo Rock on the left—an open rock slab with a dizzying sheer drop and a fine view across the cliff-lined Upper Palmaghatt Ravine. Patterson's Pellet, a large glacial erratic, can be seen perched on the rim of the opposite wall to the far left. For bicyclists and skiers, the Hamilton Point Carriageway is one-way-only from here. The yellow-marked carriage road continues to climb steadily, skirting the top of cliffs on the left with views of a hemlock forest in the ravine below. Be extra careful. This is an especially difficult and rocky section; if you're riding a bike, you may have to walk it in places.

About a mile from Echo Rock, the road passes underneath a Central Hudson power line. Gertrude's Nose is now visible on the left. The road finally levels amid sparser vegetation—pitch pine, birch, oak, scrub oak, mountain laurel, and berries. The road bends to the right, with an expansive view of the Lower Palmaghatt Ravine, Hudson Valley, and Hudson Highlands in the south, along

Hamilton Point from Castle Point

with the Taconics to the east. The road S-curves and briefly descends, then resumes climbing. Cliffs on the left have rock walls separated from the main cliff by wide fissures. There are expansive views of the Upper Palmaghatt Ravine with Gertrude's Nose across the way. The road winds up the rocky incline and eventually levels; leaving the cliffs, it continues through a pitch pine grove with trees averaging 8 to 12 feet tall. The road bends to the right and, 0.9 mile after crossing the power line, finally emerges at the top of Hamilton Point (elevation 2,020 feet). There is a panoramic view of Gertrude's Nose below, the Wallkill Valley beyond, and Margaret Cliff and Murray Hill to the west. Castle Point is visible above on the right. Sam's Point and High Point, New Jersey, can be seen in the distance. The rocks of Hamilton Point are cut by deep fissures, separating some sections from the main cliff.

The Hamilton Point Carriageway bends sharply to the right, and there's a brief winding descent. The road then bends to the left and climbs steadily again, then levels and bends to the right. The turquoise-marked Long Path appears on the right, just below the cliffs of Castle Point on the right. It joins the carriageway for approximately 600 feet to its juncture with the blue-marked Castle Point Carriageway, 0.3 mile from Hamilton Point (see above). You can go right here and return to the Minnewaska Lake parking area (4.3 miles, or 8 miles total round trip), or go straight and return via the Upper Awosting Carriageway (7.9 miles round trip).

Hiking Trails

Beacon Hill Path

Length: 0.8 mile. **Markings:** Signs; yellow blazes. **General description:** This hiking trail begins at the end of the Beacon Hill Carriageway and concludes at a picnic area by the Minnewaska Carriageway. **Highlights:** Hikers can use the Beacon Hill Path as part of a 2-mile-long loop from the Minnewaska Lake parking area that also utilizes the Beacon Hill and Minnewaska Carriageways. This trail has excellent views looking east and north. **Downside:** Beginners may find this route a bit challenging. **Difficulties and hazards:** The trail is moderately rugged in places, though no scrambling is required. Follow the markers carefully, since the route isn't always obvious.

From the Beacon Hill Carriageway (see above), the yellow-marked trail makes a short, steep descent on rocks, then bears right and climbs gradually. Bear left at a big rock. There's a partial view on the left looking east, with the village of New Paltz visible through a notch. Continue your ascent, bearing right through blueberries, sheep laurel, and pitch pine. Reach the crest and descend briefly. The trail ascends again, then more steeply on rocks. Look behind. There's a view of Dickie Barrie, with Coxing Clove and Sky Top in the distance. The trail levels. More views appear on the left, looking east to the Hudson Valley, Sky Top to the north, and the Hudson Highlands to the south. The trail continues as a cleared path on open bedrock. Glacial striations and polishing are quite noticeable in places, as are blueberries, scrub oak, and pitch pine. The trail remains fairly level for a stretch, then bends to the right and left and down a steep slope. After another bend to the right, the trail continues through a deciduous forest of birches, oaks, mountain laurel, scattered white pines, and hemlocks. There is a short, steep ascent. The trail bears left and then right again, levels, turns left, and finally turns right into the picnic area. The red-marked Minnewaska Carriageway (see above) is just beyond. Turning right on it will return you to the parking area in about 0.5 mile.

Gertrude's Nose Trail

Length: 3.4 miles. **Markings:** Signs; red blazes. **General description:** This remote trail begins on the Millbrook Mountain Carriageway, just over 2 miles from the Minnewaska Lake parking area, and later rejoins that same carriageway near the summit of Millbrook Mountain. **Highlights:** Numerous cliffside views, especially of the Palmaghatt Ravine. The nearly 1-mile-long section that closely follows the north rim of the Palmaghatt is one of the most spectacular sections of trail in the entire Gunks. Another prime feature is the trail's variety of vegetation, including pitch pine barrens, stunted forest, hemlock and white pine groves, numerous mountain laurel and blueberries, as well as certain rare species of plants. **Downside:** Only for the fit and determined, no matter which way you go. Despite the lack of serious elevation gains or losses and only a small amount of scrambling, this trail is rated as moderately difficult since getting there, hiking it, and returning will involve walking at least 7.7 miles and perhaps as much as 10, depending on the route chosen. **Difficulties and hazards:** Because of the nearby presence of steep and potentially dangerous cliffs, caution must be observed at all times. This is also a very remote part of the park; help may not be forthcoming should you get into trouble. Be sure to factor in the length of this hike along with other probable difficulties before coming.

The beginning of the trail is a cairn marked with red blazes on the right side of the Millbrook Mountain Carriageway (see above), 0.4 mile past Patterson's Pellet and 0.9 mile from the Minnewaska Carriageway (see above). Follow the red-marked trail through a stand of pitch pine to an opening on the right with an open view across the Upper Palmaghatt Ravine toward the opposite rim, where the Hamilton Point and Castle Point Carriageways are visible. The red-marked trail climbs to a high point, then descends a steep bluff with a south-facing view on the right; look for Sam's Point in the distance. The trail makes a sharp right into a beautiful hemlock grove at the base of the bluff, then zigzags through white pine, hemlock, birch, and pitch pine. After another brief descent, and 0.5 mile from the beginning, the trail crosses underneath a Central Hudson power line and continues across a small tributary of the Palmaghatt Kill. It climbs rock steps to the top of a bedrock slab. Follow markers as the trail traverses the edge of an upturned rock slab.

The trail climbs gradually on open ledges, some scraped incredibly smooth, that rim the Palmaghatt Ravine. On the right are steep, sheer cliffs, some with overhangs and views looking south of the Palmaghatt Ravine, which is lined with tall cliffs on both sides. Use caution, since these sheer drop-offs are potentially dangerous. To the left are groves of pitch pine and taller white pine, farther away from the cliffs. There are numerous deep fissures in the rock where sections have separated from the main cliff. Please stay on the marked path; areas just off the trail may be populated with rare plants that cannot tolerate trampling.

The red-marked trail winds from the cliff edge and in and out of pitch pine and hemlock groves, as well as thick stands of mountain laurel. There's a brief stretch that will require some rock scrambling. Continue out to Gertrude's Nose, 1.3 miles from the trail's beginning. Gertrude's Nose was possibly named for Gertrude Bruyn, a local resident. The Dutch word *noes* means "point" in English. From this V-shaped promontory that resembles a ship's bow, there are views across the lower section of the Palmaghatt Ravine to Hamilton Point and Castle Point, and south across the Wallkill Valley as far as the Hudson Highlands and Schunemunk Mountain, with High Point, New Jersey, visible in the far distance. Boulders left by the great ice sheet lay strewn across the smooth bedrock.

The trail makes a left (north) turn and continues close to the cliff edge; many open views look eastward to the Wallkill Valley, with the Marlboro Hills and Hudson Highlands in the distance to the south. The trail passes through some lovely hemlock and white pine groves as well as areas of stunted oak, maple, pitch pine, and mountain laurel. One mile beyond Gertrude's Nose, the trail makes a moderate descent into a shallow trough. Pass beneath another section of the Central Hudson power line, with an open view looking southeast. As the trail begins to ascend again, notice a deep cave off to the right of the trail exhaling chilled air in spring and summer. The trail then climbs a steep bluff to the southwest shoulder of Millbrook Mountain.

Turn sharply to the right, then the left, and climb on rocks. Arrive at an area of bare rock slabs with pitch pine and berries. Pass a number of cairns along the trail and continue through a stunted pitch pine forest. Enter another, larger area of bare rocks with "islands" of dwarf pitch pine. Cross a deep, narrow fissure in the rock. The trail bends to the left, passing another cairn on the right and eventually reaching the cliff edge, with views looking east to the Wallkill Valley, Marlboro Hills, and Hudson Highlands in the distance. There are also south-facing views of the ridge.

There's a brief, steep ascent on rocks. The yellow-marked Millbrook Mountain Carriageway appears again on the left and continues parallel to the Gertrude's Nose Trail. Continue north on smooth rock slabs with frequent open views. After a short distance, the summit of Millbrook Mountain—a slanted slab of rock to the right of the trail—is reached. There's a fine open view (described above under "Millbrook Mountain Carriageway"). The red-marked trail descends on rock steps down to the circle where the Millbrook Mountain Carriageway ends. To return to the Minnewaska Lake parking area this way would take 3.1 miles, or 8.5 miles total round trip. The red-marked Millbrook Mountain Path (see below) intersects nearby. It continues for less than 2.3 miles back to the Minnewaska Lake parking area (see above)—the shortest return route, but not necessarily faster than the Millbrook Mountain Carriageway, especially when it's wet and slippery.

Length: 1.25 miles. **Markings:** Signs; red blazes. **General description:** This trail of moderate difficulty begins at the south end of Minnewaska Lake and continues south to Millbrook Mountain, connecting the Minnewaska Carriageway to the Millbrook Ridge Trail. Access to the Gertrude's Nose Trail and the Millbrook Mountain Carriageway is near the end of the trail. The last section is on Mohonk Preserve land, though no permit is required to cross. **Highlights:** The shortest route from Minnewaska to Millbrook Mountain. There are views along the way looking north, east, and south. The trail crosses the Upper Coxing Kill. There's a variety of habitats. This trail is good for a number of possible loop adventures. **Downside:** Slow going. **Difficulties and hazards:** There's an approximately 300-foot descent and ascent. Certain sections of the trail on bare rock may be wet or icy, depending on conditions, and difficult to negotiate.

To get to the trailhead, follow the red-marked Minnewaska Carriageway (see above) around the right (west) or left (east) side of the lake, about 1 mile to a point on the south shore of the lake where there's a sign indicating the trailhead on the side of the carriageway right next to the pipe that drains the lake. The red-marked trail exits the carriageway and soon reaches the bank of the stream that drains the lake. Cross the stream on rocks, which may be slippery depending on conditions. The trail descends and veers to the right and away from the stream, which can be seen cascading over rocks. The path then levels amid hemlocks and enters a narrow ledge, running along a rock face covered with lichens, with steep cliffs above and below; beware slippery conditions and possible ice in spring or late fall.

The trail bends to the left of the ravine and continues to descend, then turns to the right in an area of dense hemlocks. An area of rock slabs and pitch pines is soon reached where you can see Dickie Barrie, Coxing Clove, and Sky Top to the north, and the village of New Paltz and the Taconic Range in the distance, looking northeast. The trail turns right again and crosses a second open area, with a view looking south and east to the Wallkill Valley, the Marlboro Hills, and the Hudson Highlands in the distance. The trail levels and winds through an area of mountain laurel. Millbrook Ridge appears straight ahead, visible through the trees.

The trail turns sharply to the left and descends gradually. The sound of the Coxing Kill can be heard. At 0.8 mile from the trailhead, the Coxing Kill appears to the left of the trail, which descends the steep embankment and crosses the stream on rocks. You've now entered the Mohonk Preserve. (No permit is required.) The trail loops around to the left, crossing a smaller tributary stream, then turns sharply right and up an embankment. The now rocky trail begins a gradual ascent through mountain laurel and hemlock, then turns to the right and continues to climb steadily on smooth, open rock slabs (slippery when wet). Enter an area of pitch pine, chestnut oak, and blueberries. Approximately halfway up the slope, the blue-marked Coxing Trail departs on the left (see the previous chapter), heading northeast toward the Trapps and other sites in the Mohonk Preserve.

Continue to ascend through pitch pine, chestnut oak, mountain laurel, birch, sheep laurel, and blueberries. Enter another area of slanting bedrock slabs with pitch pine and blueberries. Approximately 0.25 mile from the last intersection, reach the end of the trail as it intersects the blue-marked Millbrook Ridge Trail—which also heads northeast to the Trapps and other sites in the Mohonk Preserve (see the previous chapter). The blue-marked Millbrook Ridge Trail continues to the right 100 feet to a circle at the base of the summit rock and the beginning of the yellow-marked Millbrook Mountain Carriageway and red-marked Gertrude's Nose Trail (see above). The summit of Millbrook Mountain is nearby with its spectacular view (described under "Millbrook Mountain Carriageway").

To return to the Minnewaska Lake parking area, you can take the yellow-marked Millbrook Mountain Carriageway (3.1 miles, or 5.4 miles total round trip), or a combination of the Gertrude's Nose Trail and Millbrook Mountain Carriageway (5.1 miles, or 7.2 miles total round trip).

Slate Bank Road

Length: 0.5 mile. **Markings:** None. **General description:** This unmarked, unmaintained dirt road starts from the Castle Point Carriageway just south of Awosting Lake and ends at an abandoned shale pit. The Long Path crosses the trail near the end. Trail quality isn't as good as the marked carriageways, but it's better than most of the other hiking trails. Bicycling is not permitted, and the road is not groomed for skiing. **Highlights:** You'll encounter different rock formations—Silurian age Shawangunk conglomerate and Ordovician age Martinsburg shale—in close proximity to one another. Wolf Jaw is a dramatic rock outcropping along the road. Little used, the trail offers solitude and is good for some loop hike possibilities. **Downside:** The shale pit at the end is not an especially worthwhile destination. **Difficulties and hazards:** After heading downhill most of the way, you'll have a long uphill trek to return. Beware steep cliffs off the trail in the vicinity of Wolf Jaw.

Halfway between the Hamilton Point Carriageway and Awosting Lake Carriageway, Slate Bank Road departs from the blue-marked Castle Point Carriageway and heads south. Please note that there is no sign or marker at this intersection. The road descends and bends right and left a few times. Then it passes small cliffs on the left. Cross a seasonal brook. Wolf Jaw appears on the right—a magnificent cliff face with rock beds overhanging the road.

Continue to descend, passing a ravine on the left. There are large hemlocks in the vicinity. The road levels, and the turquoise-marked Long Path crosses the roadway (see below). A left turn here leads to Castle Point, a difficult scrambling route through a crevice and up a cliff. A right turn leads to Margaret Cliff, another challenging but rewarding route. Continue to descend a short distance to an abandoned shale pit on the right, where the road ends. Return the same way you came or use the Long Path for some loop possibilities.

LOWER AWOSTING PARKING AREA

This large unpaved parking area, with space for 240 cars, provides direct access to Awosting Lake via the Lower Awosting Carriageway (often referred to as the Peters Kill Carriageway), the High Peters Kill Trail, the Mossy Glen Path, and Awosting Falls. Practically all walks, ski trips, or bike rides from this parking area will have to cover some distance—not a bad option if you have the time, and the rewards are plentiful. This parking area is located 0.25 mile west of the park preserve's main entrance, on the left-hand side of the road. Due to the popularity of the Minnewaska Lake parking area, which often fills early on busy weekends, the Lower Awosting parking area frequently absorbs the overflow, but it's rarely filled to capacity. The Lower Awosting parking area was once the site of the Laurel Inn, a modest guest house built in the 1870s for those who could not afford the grander accommodations at Minnewaska Lake. It was demolished in the 1960s. Today, there is a signboard and portable bathroom facilities. A daily parking fee is charged. Often on weekdays and during winter, the entrance to this parking area is closed; you have to access it from the park preserve's main entrance, making a right and following the dirt road 0.25 mile to the parking area.

Multiple-Use Trails

Awosting Falls Carriageway

Length: 1.3 miles. **Markings:** Signs; red markers. **General description:** This carriage road begins at the Lower Awosting parking area and ends at the boundary of Minnewaska State Park Preserve in the vicinity of Lyons Road. From there, it continues as Trapps Road into the Mohonk Preserve and to the steel bridge in the Trapps area. It closely parallels Route 44/55 for much of the way. Also, for some of its length it follows the Peters Kill, an exceptionally lovely stream. In wintertime, it is an ungroomed cross-country ski trail rated more difficult. **Highlights:** The clear highlight is Awosting Falls, a picturesque gem and the most accessible waterfall in the Gunks. The carriageway also provides a potentially useful link to the Minnewaska Lake parking area via the Sunset Carriageway, and to Trapps Road linking Minnewaska and the Mohonk Preserve. **Downside:** There's plenty of traffic noise in certain parts. Swimming is not allowed in the tempting pool underneath the falls. **Difficulties and hazards:** The descent to the falls is relatively steep.

From the parking area, the red-marked carriageway departs on the left (east). It continues straight and level less than 0.25 mile to the park's paved entrance road. Go right here, soon cross the concrete bridge over the Peters Kill, and make a left on the carriageway immediately after the bridge. Note the orange-marked Sunset Carriageway to the right, which climbs up to the Minnewaska Lake parking area (see above). The red-marked carriage road follows the Peters Kill on the left for a short distance as the stream tumbles over rock slabs and winds its way through narrow chutes. From the top of the falls on the left, the road turns right (away from the stream) and begins a relatively steep descent, passing a rocky bluff on the right dripping water, with large icicles in winter. The road continues to descend, looping sharply to the left and then right, coming out by a large pool with the breathtaking 65-foot-high Awosting Falls towering above. The road continues to follow the Peters Kill, descending very gradually, then veers left and reaches a V- shaped fork in the road. The carriageway bends to the right. The other branch continues a very short distance out to Route 44/55. On the opposite side of 44/55 (beware speeding traffic) lie Sheldon Falls and the stone ruins of a power station built in 1922 to supply electricity for the hotels by Minnewaska Lake.

The Awosting Falls Carriageway bends right, staying very close to Route 44/55, then slowly begins to climb away from the noisy highway. The carriageway then crosses a talus-covered slope with cliffs above on the right and numerous hemlocks in the vicinity. Leave the slope and bend to the right, passing an area of exposed rock slabs on the right with pitch pine. The carriageway passes through a rock cut and descends briefly. The road continues to bear left and finally reaches the boundary of Minnewaska State Park Preserve. The road continues a short distance to Lyons Road, which it crosses, becoming Trapps Road as it enters the Mohonk Preserve (see last chapter).

Length: 3 miles. **Markings:** Signs; black markers. **General description:** This unpaved road was built in 1969 to provide automobiles with direct access to Awosting Lake, where a new beach and camping area were created. It follows a fairly straight route from the Lower Awosting parking area to the lake, where it intersects the Awosting Lake Carriageway. In wintertime, it is groomed for cross-country skiing and rated more difficult. **Highlights:** This is the primary gateway to Awosting Lake from the Lower Awosting parking area. In addition to Awosting Lake, it provides access to the Mossy Glen and Blueberry Run Trails and to the Long Path. Take your time and enjoy the mountain laurel and blueberries as well as the wildlife. **Downside:** As a road/trail, it's a less-than-stellar experience: Accompanied by a power line, it is wide with lots of sun exposure and relatively boring compared to the other carriageways. It also sees plenty of traffic from walkers, bicyclists, and equestrians. **Difficulties and hazards:** Cardiac Hill toward the end is a steep, rocky climb or a scary descent. Bicyclists are advised to walk this section.

The carriage road starts from the southwest end of the Lower Awosting parking area. Go through the gate just past the signboard and portable bathroom facility on the right. Just beyond, the yellow-marked Mossy Glen Trail (see below) departs on the left. The road veers to the right past tilted bare rock slabs, gradually ascending, then leveling. The Peters Kill appears downhill on the left, with numerous informal access routes on that side of the road. Cross a seasonal stream and begin a short, steep ascent. The road then veers to the right, levels again, and, about 1.5 miles from the beginning, crosses the blue-marked Blueberry Run Trail (see below). A short detour to the left—a steep descent—will bring you down to the Peters Kill, a perfect spot for wading on a hot day, or resting on the smooth flat rocks.

The road continues flat and uninterrupted for a while. Then it veers left and climbs another short rise with tilted rock slabs on the right. Just beyond, the road crosses underneath a Central Hudson power line. A short distance farther, the turquoise-marked Long Path (see below) enters from the right. The road then crosses Fly Brook on a causeway. Fly Brook, a tributary of the Peters Kill, drains Mud Pond (Lake Haseco). Just past the causeway, the Long Path departs on the left. The road then makes a long, steep ascent nicknamed Cardiac Hill. Tired, hot, out-of-shape walkers, and those carrying baby backpacks, may find this stretch a killer. Bicyclists should walk their bikes up it. As you near the top, a view from behind of the distant Catskills Mountains can be seen. Just beyond the top, about 0.5 mile from the causeway, the Lower Awosting Carriageway bends left and intersects the black-marked Awosting Lake Carriageway (see below), which encircles Awosting Lake. There is a rewarding view of the lake from here.

Awosting Lake Carriageway

Length: 3.5 miles. **Markings:** Signs; black markers. **General description:** Also known as the Awosting Lake Shore Road, this carriageway encircles Awosting Lake. At 93 acres, with a shoreline 2.7 miles long and a maximum depth of 91 feet, Awosting is by far the largest lake on the Shawangunk Ridge. It stands at an elevation of 1,867 feet. Albert Smiley offered to purchase what was originally called Long Pond from the owner, but the price was too high. In 1897, a fire broke out near the lake, and Albert organized a party of volunteers to fight the blaze. Following this, the owner, grateful for Albert's help, agreed to sell the lake and surrounding property to Albert for a lower price. Albert rechristened the lake after its original Indian name *Aawosting,* which means "flow waters." In 1967, it was home of the Mid-Atlantic Music Camp. In 1969, 5,000-acre Awosting Park was created by Minnewaska owner Ken Phillips, featuring camping and a new beach area. In 1971, Phillips sold it to The Nature Conservancy, which transferred ownership to the state as part of what later became Minnewaska State Park. In wintertime, only the section between the Lower Awosting Carriageway and Castle Point Carriageway is groomed for cross-country skiing. As a ski trail, it is rated most difficult. **Highlights:** For those willing to make the journey, there are many rewarding views of this impressive lake, especially from Overlook Hill, as well as numerous side trips to other interesting locales. In summer, the Awosting Lake "beach" is a popular destination. **Downside:** Swimming is allowed only at the beach area. Remote areas along the shore may appear very tempting for a dip, but you risk a severe penalty if you get caught by park personnel. Also, sections of roadway by the lake may be flooded in spring. **Difficulties and hazards:** This carriageway is nearly 3 miles from the nearest parking area. Therefore, traveling the entire carriage road around the lake involves at least a 9-mile trip. Those on bikes should beware a number of tight curves. There are dangerous cliffs in the vicinity of Overlook Hill and a few other spots.

Going clockwise around the lake: From the intersection with the black-marked Lower Awosting Carriageway (see above), the road bends left at the fork (the right heads counterclockwise around the lake). Immediately cross a causeway at the north end of the lake with a fine open view on the right of the lake looking south. The causeway crosses a tributary of the Peters Kill that drains from the lake. The road then ascends through a grove of hemlocks, bends to the right, and reaches a T-intersection with the green-marked Upper Awosting Carriageway (see above) on the left. Go right here and ascend Overlook Hill. There's a view of the lake on the right.

The road continues to ascend, zigzagging. A short detour on the right brings you to a fine panoramic clifftop view of almost the entire lake, with the Catskills off to the right and Sam's Point in the distance to the south. After more zigzagging, with more views, the road finally reaches the top of Overlook Hill and begins a short descent to a junction with the blue-marked Castle Point Carriageway (see above). Turn right and continue fairly level through an area populated almost exclusively by pitch pine. A short detour loop straight ahead leads to another clifftop view, this time looking down on the "beach" area.

The road turns sharply left then right and descends through a hemlock grove. Pass a tall cairn on the left. The road finally reaches the lakeshore and turns left, following the shore. Note that some sections of this road next to the lake may be flooded at times; also, swimming is strictly forbidden anywhere outside the designated swimming area. The road soon reaches the "beach" area—actually a slightly tilted slab of conglomerate dipping into the lake, perfect for wading. This swimming area was first opened in 1968. It is larger than any of the others in the Gunks, and many think it's the best. On a hot day after a long hike, it's certainly most welcome. There are portable bathroom facilities and a small changing hut. No pets are allowed in this area. Swimming is permitted only when a lifeguard is on duty.

The road continues along the lakeshore, then bends to the left. An unmarked road on the left leads to Spruce Glen (no bikes; see below). Pass a peninsula on the right with fine views of the north end of the lake and cliffs. The road then

Awosting Lake

departs from the shoreline and begins to climb. Note that this section is rough and rocky. From the top of the ascent, an unmarked road on the left (no bikes) departs for Murray Hill.

The road passes the south end of the lake on the right, then levels and continues to the left of a cliff-lined wetland. Notice the sharpened stumps of trees gnawed by beavers. The road soon loops to the right around the wetland and begins a steep and rocky climb. After a short distance, the road levels and bends to the left. There are some fine views here from the top of the bluff, looking northward to the lake with Castle Point in the distance. Continue fairly level for some ways, passing ruins of old Camp Awosting on the left. Established in 1899, it served as a camp for boys until 1947, when it went bankrupt. The road continues through numerous pitch pines, white pines, and birches, with intermittent views of the lake. Eventually you'll pass a cabin perched on a bluff on the left and, just beyond, a second cabin (both are closed); Old Smiley Carriage Road (see below) also lies on the left. It goes 7 miles to the village of Ellenville with interesting side trips to Stony Kill Falls, High Point, and Napanoch Point. This intersection is not marked. The cabin was at one time the infirmary for Camp Laurel, a boys' and girls' camp that succeeded Camp Awosting in 1950. There are ruins of this camp on the left just beyond the Old Smiley Road intersection. The road descends, passing detours on the right that lead down to the lakeshore. Soon the road comes to the end at the intersection with the black-marked Lower Awosting Carriageway (see above).

Hiking Trails

High Peters Kill Trail

Length: 2.1 miles, 3 miles including Mohonk Portion. **Markings:** Signs; blue blazes. **General description:** This trail begins on the north side of Route 44/55 opposite the Lower Awosting parking area. It climbs to the top of the Peters Kill cliffs and then descends and crosses the Peters Kill about halfway along. After climbing the ridge separating the Peters Kill from the Coxing Kill, it descends and ends at the Coxing parking area. *Important:* The last 0.9 mile of this trail is on Mohonk Preserve land and requires a day-use permit from the preserve. **Highlights:** There's a variety of scenery, from hemlock groves along the Peters Kill to open bare rock slabs with dwarf pitch pines. Enjoy fine views from the tops of cliffs. **Downside:** The trail can be quite an ordeal for new and inexperienced hikers. There's a disturbing amount of traffic noise along the beginning of the trail. This hike requires spotting cars at either end or a very long loop utilizing the Shongum Path and Trapps Road. **Difficulties and haz-**

ards: The length and amount of climbing make this a challenging experience. Beware dangerous cliffs in a number of spots, and use care crossing Route 44/55.

The trail starts next to the entrance gate. Follow the blue markers and soon cross Route 44/55. (Watch out for speeding traffic.) Bear right through deciduous forest dominated by oaks and maples, with a thick undergrowth of mountain laurel. The trail stays fairly parallel to the road, with the sound of speeding traffic frequently echoing through the woods. Ascend very gradually to the top of the High Peterskill Ridge. The trail bends to the left. There's a steep drop-off on the right. Pass through an open area of chest-high huckleberries. Sheep laurel is also present and in June bears clusters of tiny reddish-colored flowers.

Continue along open rock slabs bordering the edges of cliffs. Views begin to open up on the right to the Peters Kill Valley below, with Route 44/55, the Trapps, and Dickie Barrie off to the left. You can see the distant Marlboro Hills and Hudson Highlands standing beyond that ridge. Continue through sparse woods and open meadows of huckleberries and blueberries. There are steep cliffs on the right, and more views. The nearly bare slopes of what was once Ski Minne, a ski resort operated by the Phillipses as part of the Minnewaska resort, are prominent in these views. Pass a steep rock ravine on the right. The trail continues to bend left and briefly climbs. There's a very tall, sheer cliff on the right, with a tremendous panoramic view of the Peters Kill Valley below, Dickie Barrie, old Ski Minne, and the Trapps across the way.

Bend right, leave the meadows, and reenter the woods. Pass through a narrow rock cut. Descend from rock slabs and continue level along the cliff edge with more views. The trail becomes very rocky. Pass a slanted rock slab on the right with a splendid view of the valley of the Peters Kill below, old Ski Minne across the way, and the cliffs of Dickie Barrie beyond. There are more wonderful views looking south and east. The cliffs gradually give way to rocky slopes. The trail bends to the right and descends more steeply. At the base of the slope, the trail turns right and left and continues to descend gradually into forest dominated by hemlock and rhododendron. Turn right again and descend to the first of two wooden bridges over the Peters Kill. Cross the first bridge, turn left, and then turn right and cross the second wooden bridge. You've now come approximately 1.7 miles from the Lower Awosting parking area. The Peters Kill is a series of gorgeous cascades tumbling over smooth white bedrock.

After crossing the Peters Kill, the blue-marked trail intersects a unnamed red-marked trail (see below). From here, the High Peters Kill Trail begins a gradual ascent of the ridge that separates the valley of the Peters Kill from Coxing Clove. Departing the dense streamside forest, climb to a sparser one of oak and pitch pine with open rock faces. There are cliffs on the right facing south. Views open up, especially facing north and west, of the Rondout Valley and the distant Catskills. Pass through a gap between low cliffs at the top of the ridge. North of here, there once stood a wooden fire tower operated by the state from 1912 to 1923. After the Albert K. Smiley Memorial Tower on the summit of Sky Top was completed, it was used as a fire tower and the site on Dickie Barrie was abandoned. Continuing east, the trail arrives at a level area with a thick undergrowth of blueberries and huckleberries. As you reach the east-facing side of the ridge (elevation 1,270 feet), a small informal trail on the left leads to a fine view of Coxing Clove and the Trapps. The blue-marked trail then descends steeply, following part of a route used in the 1800s for transporting millstones quarried from the Lost City cliffs located just north of here, called Dug Way. The trail levels and enters Mohonk Preserve land. A day-use permit is necessary to continue. From here, it is less than a mile to the preserve's Coxing parking area.

Mossy Glen Trail

Length: 2 miles. **Markings:** Signs; yellow blazes. **General description:** This fairly new trail, completed in 1999, starts at the Lower Awosting parking area and ends at the Blueberry Run Trail. It follows the Peters Kill for much of its length. **Highlights:** Travel through a lovely shady forest populated with hemlock, white pine, rhododendron, and mountain laurel. The Peters Kill, which tumbles through rocks, shallow pools, and narrow chutes, is quite stunning, and there are plenty of opportunities along the way for wading in the stream and relaxing in the sun or shade on the smooth rocks. **Downside:** Beginners may find this trail a bit challenging in spots. **Difficulties and hazards:** Smooth bare rocks may be slippery in places, especially when damp. Markers may be hard to follow at times.

To get there, go to the end of the Lower Awosting parking area, past the signboard and the portable bathroom facilities and through the gate, and follow the Lower Awosting Carriageway. Just beyond the gate, the yellow-marked trail departs on the left from the carriage road, crosses a tiny meadow, and goes underneath a power line. The trail then enters the forest, gradually climbing and veering to the right. The path levels and bends to the right. An informal unmarked path departs on the left here and descends to the Peters Kill. The yellow-marked trail continues straight and level. At this point, the Lower Awosting Carriageway appears on the right, and the trail and road run roughly parallel for some distance.

Eventually the yellow-marked trail reaches a fork. An unmarked path goes right and soon joins the road. Turn left at this fork. The yellow-marked trail bends to the left and descends. Then it bends to the right and left and crosses the Peters

Kill on a wooden bridge erected by the New York–New Jersey Trail Conference. There is a lovely area of open rocks and a relatively deep pool located just downstream from here. After crossing the stream, the trail bends to the right and continues fairly parallel to it for the rest of the way. Please note that this section of trail, though well marked, isn't always obvious. It is also rougher and rockier, with exposed roots; some sections are muddy and slippery. About halfway along, the trail crosses an open rock slab that tilts into the neighboring stream. There are exceptionally nice opportunities for wading in the stream here as well as relaxing on the rocks. There is no trail at this point; you must follow the yellow blazes painted on trees. Eventually the trail veers to the left and departs from stream, climbing an incline and entering an area of relatively sparse vegetation dominated by pitch pine. Just beyond, the yellow-marked trail ends at the intersection with the blue-marked Blueberry Run Trail (see below). There is a stone cairn at this intersection. Turning left here provides a number of options, including hiking to Awosting or Minnewaska Lake, or out to Castle Point. A right turn will soon bring you to the Lower Awosting Carriageway and a 1.5-mile return to the Lower Awosting parking area, approximately 3.5 miles total round trip.

Spruce Glen Road

Length: 0.6 mile. **Markings:** None. **General description:** This unmarked, unmaintained dirt road goes south from the Awosting Lake Carriageway and ends at the park preserve boundary. The Long Path crosses the road and utilizes a small section of it. Overall trail quality is less than the marked maintained carriageways in the park, but better than most of the other hiking trails. Bicycles are not permitted, and the trail is not groomed for skiing. **Highlights:** Different vegetation habitats, including sparse pitch pine forest. Especially noteworthy is a damp lowland area that was once a small sky lake but is today populated with 60 species of plants, including 300-year-old red spruce trees, a remnant of postglacial boreal forests, and 400- to 500-year-old hemlocks. These trees are relatively diminutive in size. When combined with the Long Path, this trail offers some good loop hike possibilities. **Downside:** To return, you must backtrack. Also, you cannot continue beyond the park boundary. **Difficulties and hazards:** No signs or markers means that finding this road and staying on it may be difficult.

From the black-marked Awosting Lake Carriageway about 0.25 mile south of the beach area, Spruce Glen Road departs on the left. There are no signs at this intersection. Cross open bedrock slabs, climbing slowly. The road narrows. Some sections of roadway have eroded down to the bare rock. Huckleberries, pitch pine, birch, and chestnut oak are plentiful in the vicinity. The road veers left across bedrock. More dense forest appears on the right. The road bends to the right. The turquoise-marked Long Path appears on the right, heading south toward Murray Hill (see below). For the next brief stretch, the Long Path follows Spruce Glen Road.

The road veers left. There's a steep incline on the right side of the road. The Long Path soon departs on the left up a rocky slope; following it would eventually lead to Margaret Cliff. Continue straight on Spruce Glen Road. Small cliffs appear on the left. Damp moss and fern-covered lowlands appear on the right. Small trees in this area include ancient red spruce and hemlocks. Please do not leave the trail and trample sensitive vegetation.

Rocks partially block the roadway. The road continues as a causeway through the damp lowlands. The causeway crosses a small stream and then reaches a clearing on the right. The road narrows and becomes a trail, soon reaching private property and NO TRESPASSING signs. Return the same way you came.

Stony Kill Carriage Road to Stony Kill Falls

Length: 1.8 miles from the Awosting Lake Carriageway, 3.5 miles round trip, and nearly 10 miles (round trip) from the nearest parking area. **Markings:** None. **General description:** This unmarked, unmaintained carriage road route starts from the Awosting Lake Carriageway and uses a short section of Old Smiley Carriage Road. The road ends at the Stony Kill. Stony Kill Falls is located nearby. This route is not suitable for cross-country skiing, and mountain biking is strictly forbidden. **Highlights:** The 87-foot-high Stony Kill Falls is the second highest on the Shawangunk Ridge and the highest in Minnewaska State Park Preserve. There's also a deep pool perfect for taking a dip, scenic Fly Brook, a possible side trip to Napanoch Point and other sites, and a chance to see one of the more remote, less visited parts of Minnewaska Park. **Downside:** Only the very top of Stony Kill Falls is visible. **Difficulties and hazards:** Many will find the length of this trip a deterrent. The route is unmaintained, very rocky, and slippery in places. Downed trees and overgrown vegetation may be encountered. While hikers may find this route strenuous, they shouldn't have too much trouble. Bicyclists must park their bikes near the beginning of Old Smiley Road and walk the rest of the way. Because of the overall difficulties, hazards, and remoteness, I strongly recommend not doing this route alone.

From the Awosting Lake Carriageway, turn right on Old Smiley Carriage Road (see below) right after the wooden cabin on the right. Be forewarned that there's no sign at this intersection. Follow the carriage road as it briefly ascends.

The road turns left and briefly descends, then reaches a fork. Turn right and continue. You'll soon reach a second fork; this time, bear left. The road climbs a short distance to a crest. If you're riding a bike, I recommend parking it here, since the road is difficult from here on. The road then begins a rocky, sometimes slippery descent on rocks through an area of pine barrens. Less than a mile from Awosting Lake, the road reaches an area of bare rocks and Fly Brook. Cross the stream and arrive at an intersection. Old Smiley Road departs on the left for Napanoch Point, High Point, and the village of Ellenville (see below).

Continue straight. The road ascends gradually to the left of a steep ravine. Soon the road crests and starts to descend. The road bends to the left and levels, then veers left and continues its gradual descent. The road veers right, passing through an area of tall pitch pine, chestnut oak, birch, mountain laurel, huckleberries, and ferns. The road reaches a fork. Turn right and continue to descend. Cross a small seasonal brook. The road bends right and veers left, passing a cairn on the right and a discernible trail. (This is a very risky route to the bottom of the falls; I don't recommend taking it.)

The road continues to veer left, levels, and passes through a hemlock grove. Just beyond, it reaches the Stony Kill, a lovely stream with a deep pool lined with rocks and exotic-looking rhododendron. There are lovely small cascades nearby, but no falls. You're probably wondering where the falls are. To get there, backtrack up the road a very short distance to where a faintly visible informal path departs on the left. The path follows the stream down about 0.1 mile to a promontory. From the promontory, there's a lovely view behind you of a cascade; in front of you, Stony Kill Falls plunges through a narrow gap in the rock and into space. There's also a view of the southern Catskills only slightly marred by the presence of shale quarry in the foreground. Return the same way you came.

PETERS KILL PARKING AREA

This is the park's newest parking area (there's space for 80 cars) and developed access point. It is located 1.1 miles east of the park preserve's main entrance on the north side of Route 44/55, or 2.6 miles west of the hairpin turn. The Peters Kill parking area provides access to the part of the park preserve that lies north of Route 44/55. The neighboring Peters Kill cliffs provide the only rock climbing permitted in the park. The parking area overlies shale bedrock; the overlying conglomerate rock has long since eroded away. Nearby Ski Minne was Ken Phillips' ill-fated attempt to increase business for the Minnewaska resort. The ski slope opened in 1964 and closed in 1978; today, the mostly bare slope and old ski runs are slowly returning to forest. An old dirt road that leads from the parking area through a gap in the cliffs to the top of the old ski runs provides an excellent introduction to this area. There is a superb view from here of the valley of the Peters Kill, the Rondout Valley beyond, and the distant Catskills Range. The old ski slope is a good place to observe forest succession in process. The sun exposure and mostly shale base—which means the soil is less acidic—provide a favorable environment for new plants. Blueberries, the aromatic sweet fern, pitch pine, mountain laurel, and grasses are prevalent. Young white pines are quite abundant. Rare plants are also present, so be careful not to trample anything.

In addition to the ski slope, the red-marked trail provides a stunning experience walking along one of the most enchanting streams in the Gunks. Connecting with the High Peters Kill Trail, there are some wonderful loop possibilities. There are no opportunities for mountain biking or cross-country skiing from the Peters Kill parking area. There are rest rooms and a signboard. It is rarely crowded.

Hiking Trails

Unnamed Trail

Length: 1 mile. **Markings:** Red blazes. **General description:** The trail starts from the parking area and generally follows the Peters Kill down to the High Peters Kill Trail. **Highlights:** The Peters Kill is one of the loveliest streams in the Shawangunks. Numerous cascades, chutes, and rocks worn by stream action can be observed along the way. There are possible loop hikes with the High Peters Kill Trail in either direction. **Downside:** Beginners may find this trail a bit challenging. **Difficulties and hazards:** Some short, steep sections and bare rock that's potentially slippery, especially when damp.

The trail begins to the left (west side) of the parking area just beyond the gatehouse. Follow the carriage road past cliffs on the right and small wetlands populated with common reeds (phragmites). Continue to the end of the carriage road. The red-marked trail turns right and follows a small stream. The trail then turns left, crosses the stream, and climbs onto a huge tilted rock slab with islands of pitch pine and dwarf hemlocks. Follow the markers and descend on the left side of the open slab. Use caution as you approach the bottom, which often is wet and slippery. Turn right, then left, and make a steep descent to the Peters Kill. The red-marked trail follows the clear stream as it descends, cascading over slanting rocks slabs and boulders, bursting through narrow clefts in the rock, and swirling through pools. Hemlock, mountain laurel, and rhododendron are abundant along the stream. About halfway, an unmarked trail appears on the right. It climbs the old ski slope back to the parking area.

The red-marked trail briefly departs from the stream edge, traverses a small open area, and passes a second unmarked trail, which continues straight uphill. The red-marked trail turns left and descends to the stream edge again. A short while later, the trail bends to the right and crosses a small tributary stream on rocks. It then bends to the left and soon meets the blue-marked High Peters Kill Trail (see above). A left here leads to the Lower Awosting parking area. A right turn will take you to the Coxing parking area in the Mohonk Preserve.

JENNY LANE PARKING AREA

This small dirt parking area has room for several cars. Located off Route 44/55, 1.2 miles west of the Minnewaska State Park Preserve main entrance, it is at the end of short dirt and gravel drive that appears on the right without warning. It is sometimes closed in winter due to snow and ice, and at other times closed due to fire danger. The Jenny Lane parking area provides access to the Long Path, trails that connect to the Long Path, and the neighboring Sanders Kill and the old Wawarsing–New Paltz Turnpike.

Hiking Trails

Old New Paltz—Wawarsing Turnpike

Length: 0.8 mile. **Markings:** None. **General description:** This unmaintained section of the historic old road starts at the Jenny Lane parking area, crosses the Sanders Kill, and ends at the Lower Awosting parking area. It was a dirt-surfaced toll road originally built in 1856—the first official road to cross the Shawangunk Ridge in this area, though Native Americans and early settlers used a number of older, well-established trails. After just a few years of operation, the toll road went bankrupt and in 1861 became a public road. In 1929, the paved automobile highway Route 44/55, called the Minnewaska Trail, replaced the turnpike, though it used some of the same surface and closely paralleled the old route in most places. Bicycles are not permitted. **Highlights:** A pleasant stroll through some lovely mixed deciduous forest on a historic roadway. **Downside:** Nearby traffic noise for part of the way. **Difficulties and hazards:** Downed trees and overgrown vegetation will be encountered. Some parts are badly eroded and muddy.

The trail begins from the south side of the Jenny Lane parking area. It is a wide old roadway, easy to discern. Follow it to where the road once crossed the Sanders Kill. (The bridge is gone.) Turn right here and descend, crossing the Sanders Kill on rocks. Notice the old stone bridge abutments on the left along the stream. On the opposite side of the stream, rejoin the old road and turn right. Follow this wide path as it gradually ascends, soon turning left and continuing to slowly climb. Pass a small clearing and hemlock grove on the left. Gradually the sound of traffic can be heard as the trail approaches Route 44/55. The trail finally emerges from the woods on Route 44/55 opposite the Lower Awosting parking area.

Long Path

Please note that the small section of the Long Path beyond Mud Pond that crosses private land has been closed at the owner's discretion. That it may reopen at some point in the future is a remote possibility. Also, recent purchases of land in Witch's Hole and the Lundy Estate by the Open Space Institute will likely mean the future relocation of the Long Path to these properties, thus avoiding a significant amount of road walking that was necessary with the old route. Of course, the trail described below through Minnewaska State Park Preserve would continue to exist, but it could lose its designation as part of the Long Path.

Length: 9.2 miles. **Markings:** Signs; turquoise blazes. **General description:** Part of the 328-mile-long Long Path, the longest trail on the northern Shawangunk Ridge. The section through Minnewaska State Park Preserve starts from the Jenny Lane parking area and ends at Mud Pond. The section from the Jenny Lane parking area to the Lower Awosting Carriageway used to be called the Jenny Lane Trail. The rest used to be referred to as the Scenic Trail. **Highlights:** This adventurous trail traverses a variety of different terrains and habitats; visits some of the prime features of the park, such as Castle Point, Murray Hill, Rainbow Falls, and Margaret Cliff; and has many rewarding views. Many consider it one of the most spectacular sections of the entire Long Path. Some parts, especially south of Castle Point and Awosting Lake, are surprisingly tranquil. Parts of this segment may be combined with other trails to make some rewarding loop adventures. **Downside:** This long trail goes beyond some people's capabilities. **Difficulties and hazards:** The length of this trail makes doing the whole thing in one shot impractical for most people. Some sections of trail are quite rough and steep, and scrambling is sometimes required. The trail passes dangerous cliffs in a number of spots.

From the Jenny Lane parking area, the turquoise-marked trail proceeds southwest through tall pitch pine and crosses a stone wall, bends right and left, and meanders through chestnut oak woods and mountain laurel thickets. You'll soon cross Route 44/55, 0.2 mile from the beginning. (Be sure to watch out for speeding traffic on the roadway.) After crossing the highway, the trail continues through mountain laurel and sheep laurel and soon arrives at the Sanders Kill, which may be flood city or bone dry depending on the season. Turn right here, following the markers, and cross the stream on a log.

Pass a clearing with numerous young pitch pines on the right. The trail bends left and right a few times and begins to climb. It continues to make a gradual ascent through a hardwood forest with a dense undergrowth of mountain laurel. At 1.7 miles after crossing Route 44/55, the trail reaches the ridgeline, an open area of bare rock slabs and a cairn marker. Turn right and continue along the ridge, which is mostly level, to a second, larger opening. Notice that some bare rock slabs have been polished quite smooth by glaciation. Also notice the numerous dwarf pitch pines growing out of tiny soil patches in the rock. The undergrowth is largely blueberries and huckleberries. A short distance beyond, the trail makes a short descent to the intersection with the blue-marked Blueberry Run Trail (see below), 2.1 miles from the Jenny Lane parking area. A short detour left on the Blueberry Run Trail will bring you out to the Lower Awosting Carriageway and, just beyond that, the Peters Kill.

Continue on the turquoise-marked trail along the ridge. The trail gradually reenters more mixed forest, with white pine, white birch, red oak, maple, and mountain laurel. The trail bends to the left, makes a slight ascent to the spine of the ridge, and turns right. Soon there's a fine open view looking south and east toward Huntington Ravine, the Peters Kill, Litchfield Ledge, and the Lower Awosting Carriageway. At 2.8 miles from the trailhead, the trail reaches a clearing, with a Central Hudson power line towering above. The trail turns right and follows the power line for a short distance; then it makes a sharp left, reenters the woods, and becomes a wide path. Follow it through a pitch pine grove. The trail bends right and left a few times. Finally it descends and reaches a clearing. A well-trodden path on the right continues a short distance to a view overlooking Fly Brook. The Long Path turns left at the clearing and soon arrives at the Lower Awosting Carriageway (see above).

Make a right on the carriage road and cross a causeway over Fly Brook, a tributary of the Peters Kill. Immediately after crossing the causeway, the Long Path departs on the left from the road. Follow the turquoise-marked path as it bends to the left and passes Fly Brook on the left at the base of tilted slabs. The trail then veers right and away from the stream. Ascend bare rock populated with increasingly sparse vegetation: pockets of blueberries and dwarf pitch pine. There is plentiful evidence of glacial striations and polishing. Cairns and turquoise blazes painted directly on the rock mark the path in a number of places. The trail briefly levels, bends to the left and right, and crosses an outlet stream from Awosting Lake on rocks. Turn right and continue to ascend on open rock slabs.

Finally reach the top and savor an expansive north-facing view of the Catskills Range. There is a brief descent on rocks. You may have to use your hands here. The trail levels. Turn left and then veer right to the edge of a cliff, with open views looking east to Litchfield Ledge and Huntington Ravine. Veer left and follow the cliff edge, descending gradually on rock slabs. About 0.3 mile from the causeway, the trail turns right and descends more steeply. Then it turns right again and descends through a very steep cleft in the rock. Definitely use your hands here. Continue to descend to the base of the cliffs on the right, entering a hemlock grove. You are now in Huntington Ravine. The trail winds through the hemlocks, heading south, soon veering to the right and climbing past an enormous hemlock just before reaching the base of Rainbow Falls. Cliffs and overhanging rock ledges tower above, and plumes of water splash on the rocks below. Sparkling iridescent mists fill the air. Too bad you can't carry those cool mists with you on a hot day. From the base of the falls, the trail turns left and descends briefly, veers left again, and crosses a small drainage. Continue through the hemlock grove. The trail isn't always easy to follow here. Cross another small drainage and begin a gradual ascent, which becomes steeper just before reaching Upper Awosting Carriageway (see above).

The trail crosses the road, veers left, and continues climbing. The cliffs of Litchfield Ledge are to the right of the trail. Reaching the top, the trail turns right and becomes more level. Turn left and resume climbing. Then turn right and enter an area of bare rock slabs and sparse vegetation (dwarf pitch pine, blueberries, and huckleberries). There is a view looking north and west of the distant Catskills Range. Follow the markers to a superior cliffside view looking down into Huntington Ravine and a broad expansive view looking west and north of the Rondout Valley and the Catskills Range. Beware the sheer drop from the edge of the cliff.

The trail bends left and away from the cliff, reentering forest populated with hemlocks and mountain laurel. Bend to the right. There's a very steep slope on the right. Continue through forest, with hemlocks, maples, birches, and oaks prevalent. Finally bend left and climb onto a small open area. Follow cairns and then reenter the forest. Climb on rocks into a mountain laurel thicket, then head through a sparser area of open rock slabs. The trail levels and follows cairns into a pitch pine grove. Enter another opening and cross a smooth rock slab surrounded by dwarf pitch pine. The trail makes a right turn. Descend from the slab. Another rock outcropping appears ahead. The trail skirts to the left of it, then scales the side of the outcrop. You must use your hands. Continue along the top of the rock slab, then make a steep descent of the side. You won't need your hands here, just good balance. At this point, you've come approximately 5 miles from the Jenny Lane parking area.

Turn right and continue to descend. The trail bends right and left, then descends from a rock ledge. You may need your hands again. Arrive at the edge of Litchfield Ledge, with a panoramic view looking west and south; look for Awosting Lake in the distance and Sam's Point to the south. Be careful of long drops from the sheer cliff. There are overhanging cliffs on the right.

The trail bends left and away from the cliffs. Climb onto a slanting slab with a view on the right looking east to Castle Point in the distance, a future destination on this trail. The trail continues along the edge of the slab with better views of Castle Point above and on the right. The trail departs from the edge, turns left, and soon encounters another slab. Climb onto it, and using your hands again, follow the edge of this slab. There's a fine view looking across the way at the dramatic cliffs of Battlement Terrace, the ravine below, and the Castle Point Carriageway. The trail turns left. The trail turns right, descends, and joins the carriageway (see above).

The carriageway climbs, makes a U-turn, and continues to climb. There's an opening on the right with views looking west and south of the Catskills and Sam's Point. Beware the sheer cliffs. There are dramatic overhangs cut by narrow fissures, and a glimpse of Awosting Lake below. The view of the lake gradually broadens as you continue to ascend. The view now includes the Wallkill Valley on the left. The road bends to the left and right and continues to climb.

As the road bends to the left, the trail briefly departs from it on the right, then rejoins to enjoy another expansive south-facing view. The road bends left and right and briefly descends. Pass the blue-marked Blueberry Run Trail on the left (see below). Arrive at Castle Point, the highest viewpoint in Minnewaska State Park Preserve and arguably the best. You've come 0.5 mile from where the trail entered the Castle Point Carriageway.

The turquoise-marked path seems to abruptly terminate in thin air at the edge of the precipice. However, closer examination reveals that the route descends from here on steep ledges. (This is the most thrilling segment, and certainly not for the squeamish or those scared of heights. Actual exposure is negligible, however, and the route is far less dangerous than it appears. Use of hands is certainly required.) Turn left and follow a narrow ledge. Continue to descend, then turn right and begin a very steep descent on jumbled slabs, using your hands. The trail levels briefly, then descends another short distance and arrives at the yellow-marked Hamilton Point Carriageway (see above). A left turn here will take you to Hamilton Point. To continue on the Long Path, make a right and follow the carriage road for 600 feet. Arrive at an intersection with the blue-marked Castle Point Carriageway, which appears on the right. Continue straight on the Castle Point Carriageway. Just beyond, the turquoise-marked path departs from the carriageway and enters the forest on the left.

The next segment of the Long Path traverses an area that's considered very remote and sees few visitors. The trail continues to descend through huckleberries, scrub and chestnut oak, and pitch pine. The trail then levels and crosses a small area of open slabs with cairns as markers. It bends sharply to the right, with a view looking south across a ravine below to Margaret Cliff across the way, Sam's Point in the distance, and the Wallkill Valley on the left. Follow cairns along the edge of the rock slab. The trail turns left, descends, then squeezes down through a narrow cleft in the rock and continues level, skirting cliffs on the right. Pass beneath a huge overhanging ledge. Watch your head! Then turn right and continue through a narrow crevice. Turn left and descend through a short tunnel, too narrow for most backpacks. Emerge in an area of jumbled boulders.

The trail continues to descend, crossing a small brook and then Slate Bank Road (see above). A right turn here will take you to Wolf Jaw, a dramatic cliff face. The Long Path continues through an area of talus boulders at the base of Margaret Cliff. The trail turns right and climbs, then makes a sharp left turn at the foot of the cliff. It continues to climb steeply on fallen slabs, some of them loose. You'll need your hands for the final lift. Reaching the top, turn left. You're now more than 7 miles from the Jenny Lane parking area. The trail levels, with partial views looking east, then open views looking north to Castle Point and Hamilton Point, followed by fairly continuous views looking east and north.

Following cairns, continue through open bedrock, huckleberry fields, and then between cairn pillars. There's a view pointing south toward Sam's Point. The trail bends to the right and ascends to a flat area of exposed bedrock with a view looking north toward Castle Point. Follow cairns to a cliffside view overlooking Spruce Glen, with the distant Catskills Range off to the right. There's a deep crevice below on the left. The trail turns right and descends slowly, then left and continues its slow descent. Enter forest of mountain laurel, hemlock, oak, pitch pine, and birch.

The trail descends more steeply and arrives at Spruce Glen Road (see above). Spruce Glen, an intriguing detour, is off to the left. To continue on the Long Path, turn right instead, following the turquoise markers. There's a steep incline on the left. After a short distance, an abandoned carriageway, Murray Hill Drive, departs on the left. Follow this for a short distance to where the turquoise-marked path departs on the right and climbs onto open slabs. Continue to ascend slowly. Glacial striations are present on the smoothly polished rock. The trail bends to the right and slowly descends, then bends to the left. The trail climbs again to an area of diminutive plants: huckleberries, blueberries, mosses, lichens, and dwarf pitch pine. Behind you is a view looking north toward the Catskills Range. Arrive at Murray Hill Drive again and turn left. Soon you'll depart from the road, turn right, and climb to the top of the ridge and an open 360-degree view that includes Margaret Cliff and Awosting Lake in the foreground, Castle Point and the Catskills to the north and west, and Sam's Point, the Wallkill Valley, and Hudson Highlands to the south. The Long Path continues to ascend, bending to the left. Then it descends from open slabs, rather steeply. You must use your hands again. Reaching the old carriageway, turn left and continue for a short distance, descending. Following turquoise-colored blazes, depart from the roadway once more, climbing on rock slabs. Then return to the road, turn right, and arrive at the summit of the Murray Hill, with a remarkable view of the ridge and the Hudson Valley to the east. High Point, New Jersey, is visible on clear days. Murray Hill was named in 1900 for Francis Murray, a onetime owner of the land and a supervisor of the town of Shawangunk.

The carriageway descends gently, bending left and right and left. Arrive at a nice clifftop view looking south and at the ravine below. Sam's Point is observable in the distance. The road bends right and left. The turquoise-marked trail then departs from the roadway to the left. (Please note that this is a reroute. The Long Path used to continue from here down Murray Hill Drive to Awosting Lake Drive. This reroute is part of an effort to remove hiking trails such as the Long Path from the carriageways in the park preserve as part of the park's master plan.)

The new section of trail turns left, then right, and intersects the old section of trail. Turn left here and ascend slowly. The trail reaches a vantage point overlooking the ravine that lies beyond the southern end of Awosting Lake. The trail veers left here, continuing a gradual ascent on bare rock. There are views looking south of the "Antenna Farm" at Maratanza Lake. The trail briefly levels and then begins another slow ascent, veering left again.

Descend stone steps and veer right, then left. Make a steep descent. Follow cairns as you descend, more gently now on bare rocks. There's a precipice on the left. The trail veers right and descends slowly. Pass through a field of huckleberries, sheep laurel, small birch trees, and pitch pine.

Catch a glimpse of Mud Pond on the left. Mud Pond (elevation 1,845 feet) is also sometimes referred to as Lake Haseco (has echo). Covering 11 acres, with a shoreline 0.5 mile long, and a maximum depth of 4 to 5 feet, it is the smallest and most remote of the Shawangunk sky lakes. Continue through a small hemlock grove. The trail soon crosses an outlet of the pond on wooden boards with more glimpses of the pond on the left and wetlands on the right. Climb onto a rocky ridge with beds of conglomerate rock tilted nearly upright. There are some fine views of Mud Pond along this section of trail. The trail climbs to a high point with a view overlooking the south end of the pond. It then arrives at the boundary of the park preserve, beyond which is private land.

Blueberry Run Trail

Length: 2.3 miles. **Markings:** Signs; blue blazes. **General description:** This trail starts from the Long Path, 2.1 miles from the Jenny Lane parking area. It crosses the Lower Awosting Carriageway, the Peters Kill, the Upper Awosting Carriageway, and ends at Castle Point. **Highlights:** The Peters Kill is a perfect spot to relax and wade in the cool waters. There are numerous blueberries along this trail, as well as mountain laurel. Some sections with tiny islands of gnarled, stunted pitch pine on a sea of smooth white rock resemble Oriental gardens. There are many possible loop adventures when combined with other trails. **Downside:** None. **Difficulties and hazards:** Some short but steep ascents and descents. Some parts are fairly remote.

Starting from its junction with the Long Path, the Blueberry Run Trail turns left and soon descends a steep bluff. At the base of the slope, meander through a mountain laurel "jungle." Enter a shady hemlock grove and traverse a tiny stream on rocks in a muddy area. Turn left and right and cross the Lower Awosting Carriageway. Beware speeding bikes!

After crossing the road, the trail makes a short, steep descent to the lovely Peters Kill. A wooden bridge crosses the stream here; just beyond, the yellow-marked Mossy Glen Trail (see above) departs on the left. Continue up the slope of mostly bare rock with patches of pitch pine, following the blue blazes. The trail climbs some rock steps. The ascent becomes more moderate as it enters a sparse woodland of mountain laurel and oak. About 0.3 mile after crossing the Peters Kill, the Blueberry Run Trail reaches the green-marked Upper Awosting Carriageway (see above).

Cross the carriageway. The trail continues uphill and turns right (west) through a mountain laurel thicket, staying mostly level and parallel to the carriageway below. Less than 0.5 mile after crossing the Upper Awosting Carriageway, the Blueberry Run Trail goes underneath a Central Hudson power line. About 0.3 mile beyond, it enters a hemlock grove. The Blueberry Run Trail makes a sharp left here. Follow it uphill into an area of bare bedrock with patches of blueberries and stands of dwarf pitch pine resembling bonsai trees. There are views looking west to the distant Catskills Range.

The trail continues to make a gradual ascent, briefly dropping into another sheltered hemlock grove bordered by small cliffs. The trail eventually levels, crosses a rocky bluff, and, about a mile from the last intersection, makes a sharp descent to the Castle Point Carriageway across from Castle Point (see above).

Length: 7 miles. **Markings:** None. **General description:** This rugged, unmaintained carriage road climbing up from the village of Ellenville and ending at Awosting Lake was built in 1901 to bring guests arriving in Ellenville, via the railroad, up to the resort at Minnewaska. The road was later a main route for blueberry pickers, who built their seasonal "residences" in the vicinity between Mile Post 2 and Mile Post 5. Some remnants of these camps still remain. Unmaintained, the road became impassable by the late 1950s, which led to the closing of the blueberry pickers' camps. Today, Old Smiley Road crosses private land with a state-owned right-of-way. (Do not wander off the road onto private property!) Users may spot vehicles at the trailhead in Ellenville and at Sam's Point or at the Lower Awosting or Minnewaska Lake parking areas for rewarding all-day adventures. (Overall distances are more than 10 miles, depending on the route.) This road is not suitable for cross-country skiing, and mountain biking is strictly forbidden. **Highlights:** This trail provides back-door access to less traveled, more remote parts of Minnewaska State Park Preserve and Sam's Point Dwarf Pine Ridge Preserve. There are ruins of blueberry pickers' shacks, beautiful streams, and rewarding side trips to Napanoch Point or High Point (wonderful views), Stony Kill Falls, or the Shingle Gully Ice Caves (you must have a permit; see the next chapter). When the leaves are down, partial views looking west to the Rondout Valley and the Catskills may be savored along much of the route. This trail is great for solitude and, yes, there are still plenty of blueberries to pick. **Downside:** There are no short loop possibilities from this trail. You may need to spot cars and plan an entire day for this outing. **Difficulties and hazards:** The road climbs more than 1,600 feet, by far the longest ascent (or descent, depending on which way you're going) of any of the Shawangunk roads or trails. It is also steep and very rocky in places, and sections may be flooded. Stream crossings are unbridged. Downed trees and overgrown vegetation are also certainties on this unmaintained trail. The absence of signs and markings makes getting lost a real possibility, and the absence of other humans means that finding help may be difficult. I strongly recommend not traveling this carriage road alone.

From the intersection of Routes 299 and 52 in Ellenville, go south on Route 52 through the heart of the village. Just past some old warehouses and before the road makes a sharp right-hand turn and begins to climb, you'll see Berme Road on the left. Make a left here and go a short distance. On the right, just before the firehouse, is Berme Road Park, which has parking and picnic tables. Behind the picnic area, the Old Smiley Road begins rather inauspiciously. Follow it for a very short distance as it climbs. The carriage road enters the woods and reaches a T-intersection. Go left. The road immediately becomes steep and rocky, then loops to the right and intersects a woods road on the left. Just beyond, it intersects another woods road on the right. Go left and continue uphill at a steady grade, passing numerous mountain laurel.

After several minutes of straight uphill walking, the road turns sharply to the right and then left. It continues for several more minutes then switchbacks left, and then right again. Notice the pitch pine in the area. A beautiful steep ravine named Shingle Gully appears to the left of the road, with water cascading over rocks and small ledges. The road bends to the left and, amid abundant rhododendron, crosses a small tributary of the stream on an old wooden bridge (in very poor shape, but the only remaining bridge on this road). Just beyond, it crosses the main stream on rocks. Continue straight, passing large pitch pine on either side of the road. There's a partial view of the airport off to the left. The roadway here is very rocky and in places has eroded down to bedrock. Pitch pines appear in increasing numbers. A short distance past the stream, on the left side of the road, was the Two Mile berry pickers' camp, the first of these camps along Old Smiley Road. Pickers moved on to the higher camps as the berries ripened at the higher elevations.

At approximately 1,300 feet of elevation, the road enters a section that is part of the Catskill Forest Preserve. The road veers right, with Louis Ravine, also called Witch's Hole, on the left. Pass a lovely hemlock glade on the left, with a gurgling stream that empties into the ravine. The road makes a sharp left and crosses a tributary stream on rocks in an area populated by hemlocks. At 2.5 miles from the beginning, a pipe gushing springwater—reputed to be safe to drink—appears on the right. It was referred to as Rickety Spring and supplied water for the blueberry pickers' camps. Cross Beaver Creek, which drains Louis Ravine, on rocks and enter property that has been purchased by the Open Space Institute and may eventually be added to Minnewaska State Park Preserve. Be sure to stay on the roadway. Hemlock, rhododendron, and mountain laurel are abundant in the area. At 3.1 miles from the beginning, the unmarked High Point Carriageway appears on the right. It continues for 1 mile over to High Point and the Sam's Point Dwarf Pine Ridge Preserve (see the next chapter).

Just beyond this juncture on the right was the former site of a store, and the largest of the blueberry pickers' camps, Mile Post 3, abandoned in 1931. Pass a large rock on the left. The road bends sharply to the right and then left with a slight ascent. A discernible, but unmarked, path on the left departs toward Napanoch Point. Be forewarned that this path is unmarked, unmaintained, probably overgrown, and difficult to follow. It meanders through the forest and over bare rock ledges for about 0.1 mile out to an open clifftop (elevation approximately 1,885 feet), with a fine view looking south into Louis Ravine and westward to the Rondout Valley and Catskills Mountains.

From the turnoff to Napanoch Point, Old Smiley Road enters Minnewaska State Park Preserve and continues fairly level. A dirt road departs on the left onto private land. Enter an area of pitch pine barrens followed by more diverse forest. Pass the ruins of a blueberry picker's shack on the right with a rusty old stove still standing upright. The road continues mostly level. Some sections here may be flooded. Cross a small brook and reach a fork in the road. Bear right. There's a slight ascent to 1,925 feet, the highest elevation along Old Smiley Road. The road then levels again and passes through more pitch pine barrens with scrub oak and plentiful berries. Some parts of the road here may be flooded.

The road briefly descends and reenters more mixed forest, passing a conglomerate cliff on the right with a black bear, marked 1957, painted by Meinard Broghammer, a berry picker. Continue to descend, finally reaching the Stony Kill with open rock ledges and small cascades. Cross the stream and pass a dirt road that enters on the right. Just beyond, on the left, was the last camping area for blueberry pickers on the road, abandoned in 1951. From here, the road stays pretty level, but is rocky and may be flooded. Cross four tiny seasonal streams.

Less than a mile after crossing the Stony Kill, you will hear a stream on the right. The trail bears left, descends, and finally reaches the intersection with the Stony Kill Carriageway (see above). Turn right here. (A left turn leads to Stony Kill Falls.) Wade across the stream, named Fly Brook. A bridge used to span the stream here, but was removed by the Smileys to prevent poaching of timber and hoop saplings on their land. Ascend the smooth, bare rock on the opposite shore, eventually locating the road again. Continue uphill through more pitch pines. The road briefly levels, then proceeds at a steeper pitch. It's very rocky in places; some of the rocks may be slippery when wet. The road finally attains the crest, then begins to descend soon reaching a T-intersection with an unmarked dirt road. Go right and continue your descent, soon reaching a second intersection. Turn left. The road continues to descend, bends to the right and left, and arrives at the intersection with the Awosting Lake Carriageway (see above) a little over 0.5 mile after crossing Fly Brook.

Author's Note

In January 2001, the Open Space Institute—with financial help from the New York–New Jersey Trail Conference—purchased a 90-acre parcel of land adjacent to Minnewaska State Park Preserve. The parcel, located at the end of Shaft Road, northwest of the park preserve, will provide access to the base of Stony Kill Falls. A parking area off the road and a foot trail to the falls are in the works. It is also planned that this parcel will eventually be transferred to the Palisades Interstate Park Commission, which manages Minnewaska State Park Preserve, thus becoming a new part of the park preserve.

CRAGSMOOR AND SAM'S POINT DWARF PINE RIDGE PRESERVE

6

For many, the Shawangunks stop at Mohonk and Minnewaska. Lying just to the south, however, the area that includes the community of Cragsmoor and Sam's Point Dwarf Pine Ridge Preserve has scenery and attractions that certainly rival those other places. This area, often referred to as Ice Caves Mountain, is the highest part of the Shawangunk Ridge. And for those seeking a quieter experience, it doesn't attract the crowds you often find at Mohonk and Minnewaska.

CRAGSMOOR

Cragsmoor is the only surviving mountaintop community on the Shawangunk Ridge. It was primarily an agricultural community, later becoming one of the first documented arts colonies in the United States. Today, it is a quiet neighborhood of attractive residences of performing artists and others who appreciate natural beauty. Highlights include the Sam's Point Dwarf Pine Ridge Preserve, the Old Stone Church, Cragsmoor Free Library, and the Bear Hill Preserve. Cragsmoor is located 5 miles south of Ellenville off Route 52.

History

Cragsmoor was first settled in the 18th century by hunters and trappers. By 1770, much of the land in the neighboring valleys had already been cleared for farming and for timber. New settlers arrived in the area to harvest the uncut forests of chestnut, oak, and maple that still populated the ridge. Fresh-cut timber was transported down to lumber mills and tanneries in neighboring valleys. As the population in these valleys grew, the demand for timber also rose. This was especially true after the completion of the D&H Canal. By 1820, John Manse had built a sawmill on the South Gully stream. A small community of settlers there was called the Manse Settlement, because members of the Manse family made up a huge portion of the population.

As the forest was removed and timber became scarcer, families began raising crops on the cleared land and grazing sheep and cattle. Others manufactured hats, linens, carpets, wagons, sleighs, and coffins. By 1852, a wooden plank toll road was built linking Newburgh and Ellenville, roughly following the same route as present-day Route 52. This improved access to the community and made it easier for local residents to market their goods to the neighboring valleys.

Due to the thin soil, short growing season, and competition from other places, farming activity was insufficient to support the local population. To supplement their income, some farm families began taking in summer boarders. Residents of New York City and other large population centers often left the crowded, unhealthy city to visit the countryside, where the air and food were still fresh and the scenery unblighted. Completion of the O&W rail line to Ellenville in 1871 improved access for visitors to the Cragsmoor area.

In the 19th century, romantic depictions of American landscapes were very popular. These included works by artists of the Hudson River School, who used landscapes from the Hudson Valley and neighboring mountains as subjects. When some of these painters traveled to the Shawangunks in search of new scenery, they found the community of Cragsmoor—with its proximity to New York, splendid views, and rural open space—an attractive place to visit and stay. Many started as summer boarders, eventually building their own summer homes. A prime mover in the development of Cragsmoor as an arts colony was Mrs. Eliza Hartshorn, who was friends with a number of artists. She purchased land in the community and either sold it or gave it to her friends. One of those friends, and one of the first to settle in Cragsmoor, was Edward Henry (1841–1919), a popular genre painter, who built his Victorian summer residence here in 1884 and used it until his death. Through his encouragement, his friend Frederick Dellenbaugh (1853–1935), the noted artist, writer, and explorer who traveled with William Powell on his famed expedition through the Grand Canyon and helped found the Explorers' Club, built a summer residence here in 1882. In 1892, Dellenbaugh gave the community the romantic name of Cragsmoor. He also designed the Stone Church and summer homes of a number of other artists who settled in the area. Most of the summer residences were built with native stone masonry, frame construction, and cedar shingles, often in the Queen Anne and Colonial Revival styles. In addition, a number of older farmhouses and other buildings were enlarged and converted into summer residences. Many of the summer residences of the artists had quaint names like the Barnacle, Peanut Shell, and Rest-A-While. Because of the long, harsh winters, these homes were used only six months of the year. Their owners would spend the winters in the city or in warmer climates.

Dellenbaugh designed a summer home for his friend Charles Curran (1861–1942), who used Cragsmoor's clifftop landscapes as backgrounds for his idealized paintings of young women. George Inness Jr. (1854–1926), son of the famed landscape artist, was an excellent painter in his own right. In 1900, he purchased the Chetolah estate, expanded it to 350 acres, and built an elaborate 42-room mansion, the most opulent Cragsmoor residence. Other residents of the Cragsmoor arts colony included Helen M. Turner (1858–1958), an impressionist, and Eliza Pratt Greatorex (1820–97), one of the earliest female members of the National Academy of Design. Artist residents of Cragsmoor formed a close-knit community. Many of the original local residents who predated the arts colony found employment constructing, remodeling, repairing, cleaning, and maintaining the homes of the artists.

Not all of the artists who visited or stayed in Cragmoor had summer residences. Many stayed in the boarding homes and hotels that were very much a part of this community. The largest and most famous of these was the Cragsmoor Inn. Previously a farmhouse and boarding home, the inn opened in 1904 with more than 100 guest rooms. It offered fresh food from its own garden, fresh milk from its own herd of cows, and fresh water from nearby springs. There were parties, concerts, and theater. It was a center of social activity for local residents as well as guests. Unfortunately, business declined during the Depression, and by 1958 the facility had become a boarding school for boys (the school moved to Wallkill in 1963). The inn burned down in 1964.

As the original artist residents passed on, Cragsmoor lost its identity as an arts colony. By the 1950s, use of the snowplow had opened up Cragsmoor as a year-round community. Many of the summer residences were winterized and became primary residences. In 1996, the Cragsmoor Historical Society formed and Cragsmoor was accepted on the National Register of Historical Places.

Historical Sites

The Cragsmoor Federated Church is located on Cragsmoor Road 1.4 miles east of Route 52 and just east of the intersection of Dellenbaugh Road and Henry Road by the Cragsmoor post office. It dates back to 1880 as a Methodist church. In 1906, it became a federated church to serve the various religious affiliations in the community. Today, it is a playhouse and headquarters and meeting place of the Cragsmoor Historical Society.

Next to it, the Cragsmoor Free Library was first formed in 1914 and chartered in 1915. The small building was designed by Frederick Dellenbaugh and completed in 1925. It houses an excellent collection of books and documents related to local history and displays works by local artists including E. L. Henry, Dellenbaugh, Curran, George Inness Jr., and others. A dozen round columns of native American chestnut (mature chestnut trees have been extirpated from the Shawangunks) supporting the interior balcony is one of the highlights of this structure. There is a cathedral ceiling and a one-and-a-half-story rubble stone fireplace. In summer, it is open Tuesday through Saturday.

The Gothic Revival Stone Church, also known as the Chapel of the Holy Name, is located on Henry Road, 0.8 mile north of the intersection of Henry, Dellenbaugh, and Cragsmoor Roads where the post office is located. Be sure to follow the signs! It is certainly one of the loveliest churches in the region. Designed by Dellenbaugh, its construction was supervised by local resident John Keir. It was built of locally quarried stone by Italian stonemasons and completed in 1897. The chapel has a high vaulted ceiling and two-story bell tower. There are stained-glass windows, including one designed by Tiffany. Eliza Hartshorn, a summer resident of Cragsmoor, had the chapel built as a memorial to her late husband. In 1922, ownership was transferred to the Episcopal Church. There are currently Sunday services in summer; the church is also used for weddings, concerts, and other special events. Behind the church is a fine view of South Gully, with Sam's Point Dwarf Pine Ridge Preserve in the background and the village of Ellenville and the Catskills Range in the distance.

Bear Hill Preserve

The 50-acre Bear Hill Preserve (elevation 1,950 feet) is owned by the Cragsmoor Historical Society and managed by the Cragsmoor Free Library. Bear Hill was a popular recreation site for residents of this community for many years. The threat of losing access to this property due to planned development in 1978 galvanized the Cragsmoor Association to purchase the land. In 1983, the association donated it to the library, which opened it as a nature preserve. It features two unnamed trails totaling approximately 0.8 mile, as well as a section of the turquoise-marked Long Path. There are areas of chestnut oak forest as well as stunted forest of scrub oak, birch, pitch pine, and mountain laurel. The preserve's highlight is the sheer white cliffs, the southernmost tall cliffs in the Shawangunks. From these cliffs, expansive views face south and west. There are also a pair of crevices called Devil's Kitchen and the Lemon Squeeze. Those planning to explore the crevices should be forewarned that the routes are not marked and rock scrambling will be necessary—more difficult when the rocks are icy or wet. The preserve opens daily 30 minutes before sunrise and closes 30 minutes after sunset. There is no admission fee.

To get to the Bear Hill Preserve, follow Dellenbaugh Road north for 0.4 mile from the intersection with Henry Road and Cragsmoor Road by the Cragsmoor post office. There is a parking lot on the left-hand side of the road.

Hiking Trails

From the parking area, enter a dirt roadway blocked to vehicular traffic. This roadway is also part of the Long Path. The turquoise-marked Long Path soon departs on the right, descending 0.5 mile to Route 52 and continuing south along the ridge. Continue straight on the dirt roadway, which stays fairly level. Pass an informal trail on the left that used to go to the Cragsmoor Inn. The surrounding forest is populated with red oak, chestnut oak, white pine, maple, mountain laurel, and wild azalea. Another trail appears on the right. Turn right here and leave the roadway.

The trail bends sharply to the right and climbs, then loops to the left and soon levels. Vegetation rapidly thins to scrub oak, mountain laurel, birch, pitch pine, and blueberries and huckleberries. Pass an area of bare open rock with pitch pine on the left. You're tracing the edge of a plateau with a steep slope on the right, mostly obscured by vegetation. Follow this relatively straight, level trail to an intersection with another trail on the left. This is the trail you'll probably return on.

From the intersection, the trail veers right and briefly descends. An unmarked trail appears on the left. The trail then veers left and climbs onto bare bedrock with an open view looking south. Notice the rock pillar below on the right called Pulpit Rock, a well-known landmark often appearing in photographs and paintings. Once a glacial erratic was balanced on its top; unfortunately, vandals removed it. From open rock ledges, there are views of the ridge looking south, including High Point, New Jersey, on clear days, the old Roosa Gap fire tower, and the valleys on either side of the ridge.

A trail on the left descends through the narrow crevice known as Devil's Kitchen; overhanging ledges feature boulders wedged between them, suspended over you precariously. There's also an angled crevice on the right, the Lemon Squeeze. Near the base, a small cave emits chilling air. There's a view from the base of the cliffs of crevices towering above, Devil's Kitchen on the right and the Lemon Squeeze on the left. The distant traffic of Route 52 can be heard below.

To return, backtrack to the trail intersection and go right. The trail climbs briefly, veers left, and descends. Pass a woods road on the right that leads to private property. Soon arrive at the intersection with the trail on the left you used previously. Continue straight for less than 0.5 mile to the entrance.

SAM'S POINT DWARF PINE RIDGE PRESERVE

Sam's Point Dwarf Pine Ridge Preserve is a large 4,600-acre, 8-square-mile tract located south of the village of Ellenville and roughly west of Minnewaska State Park Preserve. The highest elevation points on the Shawangunk Ridge are located here, as well as some of its rarest and most notable features. These include the so-called ice caves, plus spectacular views from Indian Rock, High Point, Sam's

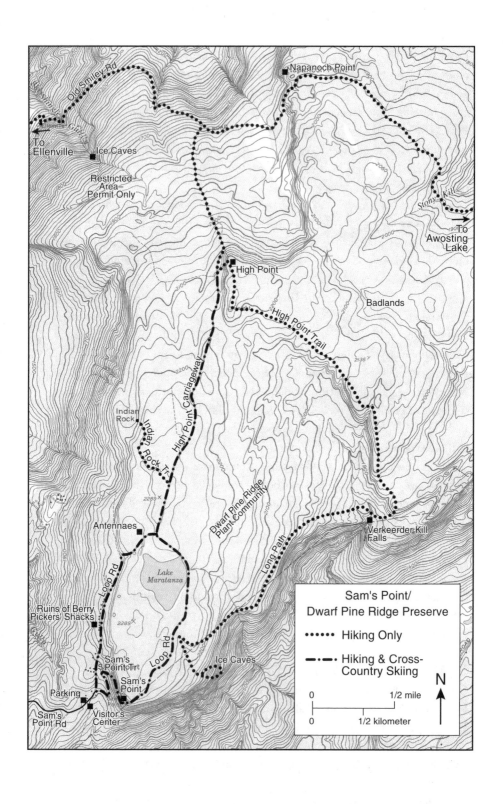

To Ellenville
Old Smiley Rd
Napanoch Point
Sunset Grill
Ice Caves
To Awosting Lake
Stony Kill
Restricted Area– Permit Only
High Point
Badlands
High Point Trail
High Point Carriageway
Indian Rock
Indian Rock Tr.
Dwarf Pine Ridge Plant Community
Antennaes
Long Path
Verkeerder Kill Falls
Lake Maratanza
Loop Rd
Ruins of Berry Pickers' Shacks
Loop Rd
Ice Caves
Sam's Point Trt
Parking
Sam's Point
Visitor's Center
Sam's Point Rd

Sam's Point/ Dwarf Pine Ridge Preserve

••••• Hiking Only

—·—·— Hiking & Cross-Country Skiing

N

0   1/2 mile
0   1/2 kilometer

Point, Verkeerderkill Falls (the highest waterfall in the Shawangunks), Maratanza Lake (a glacially carved sky lake), and the world's largest area of dwarf ridgetop pitch pine barrens. It is owned by the Open Space Institute and managed by The Nature Conservancy. Sam's Point Dwarf Pine Ridge Preserve is more remote and less developed than Mohonk or Minnewaska, and tends to get fewer visitors, but in terms of spectacular scenery and views it clearly rivals those other places, especially in midsummer when berry bushes in the pine barrens produce their delicious crop, and in fall when they form brilliant carpets of vermilion color.

The ice caves of Sam's Point Dwarf Pine Ridge Preserve are a federally designated National Natural Landmark. They are deep fissures in the conglomerate bedrock that contain ice more or less all year long. These "caves" are caused by masses of rock sliding down the slope and breaking. The Shawangunk conglomerate overlies softer, older shale. When the shale erodes, it creates unstable conditions; thus slides like this can occur. The ice caves are in fissures between rock masses, but not all fissures of this type on the ridge contain ice. The National Landmark ice caves are on the southeastern side of Ice Caves Mountain. The Devils Den Ice Caves are on the southwest end, and the Shingle Gully Ice Caves are on the north side of the preserve.

Another unique but historically underappreciated feature of this Nature Conservancy preserve are the dwarf pine ridge barrens, a sparse habitat dominated by stunted pitch pine trees, 6 feet or less in height, some very ancient— more than 300 years old. This type of ridgetop pine barrens is extremely rare. By far the largest such area of ridgetop pine barrens is located here, covering much of the upland plateau east of Sam's Point and Maratanza Lake. A particularly remote, wild, trailless area of dwarf pine ridge barrens is the Badlands, located southeast of High Point and northeast of Verkeerderkill Falls. Dwarf pine ridge barrens are a strange, alien type of environment. The absence of landmarks and relative sameness of this primarily horizontal landscape can liberate you from any sense of familiar place. One of the plants that populates this area is rhodora (*Rhododendron canadense*), a flowering shrub, a member of the heath family, and a cousin of the more plentiful mountain laurel. Rhodora is considered rare in New York State, but a number of fine examples may be seen around Maratanza Lake. Its beautiful dusty purple blossoms on the ends of leafless stems appear in May.

Sam's Point itself is the highest-elevation viewpoint on the Shawangunk Ridge (2,255 feet). The imposing white cliff is visible from the entrance. This clifftop vista on clear days offers superior views of the southern Shawangunk Ridge all the way to the tower at High Point, New Jersey, as well as fine views of the neighboring Wallkill and Rondout Valleys and southwestern Catskills.

Dwarf pitch pine barrens at Sam's Point Dwarf Pine Ridge Preserve

Sam's Point is named for Samuel Gonzalus (1733–1803), a famous hunter, scout, and Indian fighter. The Gonzalus family—of Spanish descent—were the first European settlers in what's now Sullivan County. Samuel Gonzalus was the first person of European descent to be born in Sullivan County. According to legend, in 1758 during the French and Indian Wars, Sam, in order to escape from a Lenape war party, leaped 40 feet from the precipice to the safety of hemlocks below, which broke his fall. He survived with only bruises. The Natives, who themselves were being hotly pursued by militia, mistakenly gave Sam up for dead. A diorama depicting this famous leap is on display at the Ellenville Museum. In 1910, Blanche Desmore Curtis published a popular epic poem about Sam's leap that was illustrated by local Cragsmoor artist Charles Curran.

Another prime feature of the preserve is Maratanza Lake, the highest sky lake in the Shawangunks (elevation 2,242 feet) as well as the second largest. It is 46 acres in size, 17 feet deep, with a shoreline length of approximately 1 mile. A natural lake situated in a glacially gouged depression, it was artificially enlarged in the 1920s. Cranberry bogs inhabited by carnivorous sundew plants can be found along the shoreline. Today, it serves as a reservoir for the village of Ellenville; swimming is not permitted.

Still more features of the preserve are the ruins of shingle-sided shanties built and used by blueberry pickers during the late 19th and early 20th centuries. Most have collapsed into heaps but a few are still standing, rare remnants of this once prolific activity.

Sam's Point Dwarf Pine Ridge Preserve is primarily reached via its main entrance at the end of Sam's Point Road. From the village of Ellenville, go south on Route 52 for 5 miles, then turn left on Cragsmoor Road. Follow this for 1.4 miles to its intersection with Dellenbaugh Road. Follow this for 0.1 mile, make a right on Sam's Point Road, and continue for 1.3 miles to the entrance of the preserve. The preserve is also accessible from Old Smiley Road, which starts in the village of Ellenville and can also be reached from Awosting Lake. These routes are described in chapter 5, "Minnewaska State Park Preserve." There's an interpretative center at the entrance to Sam's Point Dwarf Pine Ridge Preserve. Information, maps, books, souvenirs, and snacks are available here. A new interpretive center is planned for 2004. Portable bathroom facilities are available by the parking area. The preserve has 10.3 miles of hiking trails, including 3.2 miles of the Long Path. The trails are maintained by the New York–New Jersey Trail Conference and the Adirondack Mountain Club. Because of the ecological sensitivity of the area, no bicycling or rock climbing is permitted. There is a program of staff- and volunteer-led outings on weekends. The preserve is open dawn to dusk. There's a small parking fee.

History

Artifacts found next to Maratanza Lake, including a spearpoint dating back to the Archaic period (3,000 to 3,300 years ago), show that the area in what's now Sam's Point Dwarf Pine Ridge Preserve was used by Native Americans for hunting and gathering. By the 18th century, Europeans began visiting the area, also for hunting, trapping, and gathering of berries and other edibles. John Saeger built a shanty by Verkeerderkill Falls; by the 1830s, a road called Saeger's Road went from the entrance out to Saeger's shanty. Numerous hemlock trees along Saeger's Road were cut and their bark stripped to supply tannin for the tanning industry. The bark was also used by shingle weavers. A number of cabins were built along the road to house these workers.

In 1858, Thomas Botsford purchased 300 to 500 acres in the Sam's Point area. That same year, he built the first wagon road to Sam's Point, opening the area as a tourist attraction. In 1860–61, Botsford built a stairway from the end of the road to the top of Sam's Point, which became a popular destination for sight-seeing and picnicking. Up to 50 horses a day would bring visitors on horseback or carriage up to the base of Sam's Point. In 1871, Botsford built an observatory on top of Sam's Point; he also constructed a unique hotel into the side of the cliff, which burned a year later. Commercial berry picking started in the area in the 1850s, and by the 1870s pickers had begun establishing seasonal camps along Saeger Road. In 1902, LeGrand Botsford—Thomas's son—constructed a road up to Maratanza Lake and built a hotel there. The lake featured rental boats and swimming and sand imported from the New Jersey shore. The hotel lasted only two years before it, too, burned to the ground. Around this same time, the gatehouse was constructed, the oldest surviving structure at Sam's Point. It is to the left of the entrance gate.

LeGrand sold the land to John Stedner. He and his family lived in the gatehouse. They maintained the road up to the fire tower at High Point and operated a small store by the gate that supplied the needs of berry pickers. In 1922, the village of Ellenville purchased the area as part of its watershed. From that point on, the area was known as the Ellenville Watershed or simply the Ellenville Tract. Between 1923 and 1925, Maratanza Lake was dredged and enlarged. Other alterations were made to drain the lake into Gully Brook, and Maratanza became a backup reservoir for the village. Besides the lake, much of the land was considered worthless, though the village tried to make money off it by leasing it to various private enterprises. An oil company explored the area for natural gas, erecting a 131-foot-high oil drilling rig. An underground gas storage facility was proposed but never built. A glider port was constructed but never used. These schemes left lasting scars on the landscape.

In 1947, the last devastating fire swept the ridge, burning 7,405 acres between Maratanza and Awosting Lakes. In the mid-1960s, AT&T built the first tower at Maratanza Lake. Other towers soon followed, including ones built by the DEC and the New York State Troopers. In 1967, Frederick Grau, a local resident, purchased a 25-year lease from the village to open Ice Caves Mountain as a rather flamboyant commercial tourist attraction. A mountaintop drive was built to the ice caves, and a number of natural features there were given ludicrous names like Cupid's Rock, Rivers of Mystery, and Wall Street Canyon. Visitors were not permitted to leave their cars except at certain designated attractions. Thus much of the property was off-limits to the public.

In 1972, the ice caves became a federally designated National Landmark. In 1983, energy company FloWind East proposed the construction of a 1,200-acre wind energy farm north of Sam's Point. This proposal was supported by Grau. The Friends of the Shawangunks and other groups strongly opposed this plan, which fortunately—due to decreasing oil prices—failed to win the necessary financial support and died. In 1992, the Cragsmoor Association (led by its president, Paula Medley) and a coalition of other environmental groups successfully prevented Cellular One from building a tower in the vicinity of the Shingle Gully Ice Caves. As early as 1970, the state expressed interest in purchasing the Ellenville Tract. In 1991, the Open Space Institute (OSI) began negotiating with the village of Ellenville. In 1997, OSI acquired the 4,600-acre property and all of the stock of the Ice Caves Mountain Inc. (The commercial concession ceased operating in 1996.) It is currently managed by The Nature Conservancy as a day-use preserve.

Hiking Trails

Sam's Point Trail

Length: o.6 mile. **Markings:** Turquoise blazes; signs. **General description:** This short, easy hike from the entrance follows a rough paved roadway up to Sam's Point, where it meets the Loop Road. The Sam's Point Trail is a designated part of the Long Path. Though ungroomed, it may be used for cross-country skiing or snowshoeing in winter. **Highlights:** At 2,255 feet, this is the highest viewpoint in the Shawangunks and has spectacular south-facing views, especially from the top of the cliff. There's a dramatic change in plant communities, from oak-dominated forest below to dwarf pitch pine on the top. **Downside:** None. **Difficulties and hazards:** An uphill ascent the whole way.

From the entrance, the road immediately forks. Left is Loop Road, which circles Maratanza Lake. Continue straight. As the road ascends, it zigzags through deciduous forest of oak, maple, tulip tree, birch, mountain laurel, striped maple, and ferns. Eventually the cliffs reappear to the left of the road, which follows their base. (Note that no climbing is permitted.) There are deep fissures in the rock and overhanging cliffs. Unfortunately, there is also graffiti damage. In 1860, Thomas Botsford build a 75-step stone stairway up through the cliff to the top. Today, this stairway has greatly deteriorated and is overgrown. In 1871, he built a hotel 92 feet long and 25 feet wide that was fastened directly to the cliff. A couple of the original anchors are still present in the rock. Natural elements were a part of the hotel's unique design. The cliff actually served as its back wall. A spring ran through the main room. Fissures in the rock were used as chimney flumes, and there were ferns growing on the walls. The hotel was open in summer only. It was destroyed by fire after only one season.

Eventually, unobstructed views to the right appear from atop bedrock slabs. You can see south and east, down along the spine of the Shawangunk Ridge and as far as High Point, New Jersey, if it is clear enough. The vegetation changes to pitch pine, mountain laurel, scrub oak, berries, and birch. The roadway continues to climb and bends to the left. To the left, from atop the cliffs, are fine views looking west, south, and east. A large glacial boulder on the top was in 1871 enclosed by a 20-foot-square, 30-foot-high wooden observatory with a railing around the outside. Meals were served on the top. It was reported that the observatory could be seen from as far away as Cold Spring and Newburgh. Exposed to strong winds, the observatory didn't last through the winter. The stone walls that are still present date back to the 1960s, when the ice caves were a commercial attraction.

The area to the north of Sam's Point is a dwarf pitch pine barren. From here, the roadway becomes Loop Road.

Loop Road

Length: 2.3 miles. **Markings:** Signs at intersections. Turquoise blazes along the short segment that is part of the Long Path. **General description:** This roadway starts at the entrance gate, climbs through forest past extensive remains of old berry pickers' camps, then continues past an area of antenna towers and circles Maratanza Lake. It intersects the Long Path and finally arrives at Sam's Point, where it meets the Sam's Point Trail. Loop Road may be used for snowshoeing or cross-country skiing in winter. **Highlights:** This relatively easy walk acquaints visitors with some of the prime features of the preserve: the blueberry pickers' camps, the dwarf pine ridge habitat, Maratanza Lake, the ice caves, and Sam's Point. This roadway also provides access to the Long Path and High Point Carriageway, making longer excursions possible. **Downside:** The antenna towers, most would agree, are an unsightly feature, as are the dredge spoils on the east side of Maratanza Lake. **Difficulties and hazards:** The length of this loop may deter some. Relentless sun and strong winds are often experienced in the unsheltered horizontal landscape of the dwarf pine ridge area.

From the entrance, the road forks. Go left and follow the road as it slowly climbs through forest dominated by oak trees. After 0.5 mile of walking, remnants of blueberry pickers' shacks are encountered to the left of the roadway. Blueberry pickers started building their seasonal camps here in the 1870s; they were used until the 1970s, when the last resident died. A number of simple shanties were built. Some were mere shelters, while others were like tiny homes and boasted gas stoves, iceboxes, and other amenities. Their construction was generally flimsy, and they weren't intended to last long. Most have collapsed into piles, though a few are still standing. Forest has grown up around these areas that were previously cleared.

Pass a shale quarry on the right. The shale, which underlies the Shawangunk conglomerate, was used to pave the roads here. In 1902, this section of what was called Saeger's Road was improved to provide access to a new hotel at Maratanza Lake. In the 1930s, the Civilian Conservation Corps (CCC) enlarged and improved it to provide better access to High Point, where a fire tower was located.

Continue up the road, passing more ruined shacks on the left and small cliffs on the right. The road continues to climb, bending to the right and finally reaching the plateau. By now you've departed from the forest and arrived in the area of dwarf pitch pine barrens. Pitch pines are the dominant trees, and few are taller than 10 or 12 feet. Pass a number of antenna towers on the left. A trail on the right provides access to the shore of Maratanza Lake. There's also a glimpse of the lake from the road. Maratanza doesn't have the prominent cliffs of the other sky lakes, and dredge spoils and the antenna towers somewhat mar the views, depending on which way you're looking. Dragonflies use the lake for mating, and ducks can often be seen there. Alpine sandwort, triffid rush, and rhodora are among the rare plants found in the vicinity. The lake was a tourist attraction around the turn of the 20th century; for a brief time, there was a hotel here, along with swimming and other recreational activities. Points north and south of the lake are the highest on the Shawangunk Ridge (elevation 2,289 feet).

The road reaches an intersection with the High Point Carriageway (see below). Turn right here and continue around the lake. Pass an area of dredge spoils on the right—the result of the enlargement that took place when the village of Ellenville developed the lake as a backup reservoir. Twenty-foot-high snowdrifts are often seen in the vicinity in wintertime. Pass another access trail to the lakeshore on the right. This leads to an area of cranberry bogs. The sundew, a type of carnivorous plant, can be found in these bogs.

Continue a short distance to another fork in the road, 0.8 mile from the last intersection with the High Point Carriageway. A left turn here leads to the ice caves and to Verkeerderkill Falls via the Long Path (see below). A right turn continues 0.4 mile to Sam's Point. This last section of Loop Road is designated part of the Long Path and is marked with turquoise blazes. It passes through dwarf pitch pine barrens. Blueberry, huckleberry, and sheep laurel comprise much of the ground cover. Just before arriving at Sam's Point, you'll find some open fields of huckleberries and blueberries, along with "islands" of pitch pine and fine views of the Wallkill Valley and points east. From Sam's Point, you can follow the Sam's Point Trail (see above) back to the entrance.

The Ice Caves

Length: 0.6 mile. Markings: Signs. General description: This unique area of cliffs, crevices, and talus boulders was opened to the public in 1967 as a commercial attraction. It closed in 1996 and then reopened in 2002 by The Nature Conservancy as part of the Sam's Point Dwarf Pine Ridge Preserve. The new version is more low key than the old commercial attraction. It can be reached via a spur from Loop Road, the former automobile road that connects it to the entrance. It is 1.3 miles from the entrance to the caves. **Highlights:** One of the most impressive rock formations in the Shawangunks, it features cliffs, talus boulders, and deep fissures that contain ice throughout the summer. Unlike the Labyrinth and other rock scrambles at Mohonk, this one is user friendly. There are steps, boardwalks, guardrails, and motion-sensitive solar-powered lamps. You don't have to be especially skillful or fearless to make it through. **Downside:** Ice may not be present in especially warm or dry years. **Difficulties and hazards:** Short ladders and possible slick footing in a few places. Please stay on the trail.

Inside National Landmark Ice Caves

From Loop Road (see above), 1 mile from the entrance, the Ice Caves Trail departs on the right (east). Just beyond the intersection, the turquoise-marked Long Path (see below) departs on the left for Verkeerderkill Falls. Follow the road as it descends slowly through dwarf pitch pine barrens, bending to the left. Panoramic views open up north to Castle Point and Gertrude's Nose in Minnewaska State Park Preserve, and to the Wallkill Valley in the east. The road ends after 0.3 mile in an old parking lot. There is an information kiosk by the entrance to the ice cave trail.

The trail descends and bends to the left and right. Descend stone steps into a wide crevice. There are wooden guardrails. Pass a narrow side crevice on the left and descend underneath a rock wedged overhead. Pass another large crevice on the right, perfect for exploration with a flashlight. The route turns left and continues to descend. You'll soon arrive at an opening amid talus boulders. You're shocked by the sudden lush presence of an oak forest that offers a dramatic contrast to the dwarf pitch pine barrens at the entrance to this trail.

The trail bends to the left, skirting overhanging ledges. Climb onto wooden bridges over talus. The trail winds through talus beneath the cliff. Cross a tiny stream on wooden boards. The trail veers left and enters a cave "room" illuminated with motion-sensitive lighting. Turn right and descend through a narrow crevice. Arrive at another opening and turn left, following the base of the cliff. Descend wooden steps, which turn into stone steps, and continue beneath overhanging rock ledges. Climb a wooden ladder and follow a boardwalk through a wet area. Pass beneath a rock ledge with a dripping pool on the left and then continue underneath a second rock overhang. Veer left and climb stone steps through talus boulders. Arrive at a doorway. Once you're through, be sure to close the door to prevent the escape of cold air. Turn right and follow a boardwalk through a crevice where ice is usually clinging to the sides. Be prepared for chilling temperatures. Turn sharply left and follow the boardwalk into a second ice-laden room. Ascend stone steps, followed by a wooden ladder. Veer left and cross a wooden bridge. Arrive on top of open rock ledges, perfect for relaxing and savoring a view facing north and east. The trail turns right and ascends, eventually arriving at the kiosk from which the other branch of the trail departed.

High Point Carriageway

Length: 1.7 miles. **Markings:** Signs at both ends. **General description:** This roadway connects Loop Road by Maratanza Lake with the High Point Trail just below High Point. It was constructed in the 1930s by the Civilian Conservation Corps (CCC) as part of the route from Sam's Point to High Point, improving access to the fire tower there. It is wide and generally level and thus easy to walk. Cross-country skiing and snowshoeing are also possible in wintertime. The area it crosses is primarily dwarf pitch pine barrens, though a variety of vegetation may be encountered. **Highlights:** Access to the Indian Rock Trail, High Point, and Shingle Gully Ice Caves, as well as back-door access to Minnewaska State Park Preserve and Napanoch Point. This trail is used by hikers as part of an 8.2-mile-long loop that traverses a good portion of Sam's Point Dwarf Pine Ridge Preserve. **Downside:** The relative straightness, absence of landmarks, and unrelenting sameness of the terrain can be wearisome or liberating depending on your perspective, but many find it dull. There are no good views along this road except of antenna towers, although some fine views located nearby are noted below. **Difficulties and hazards:** Hiking back and forth to High Point is almost 6 miles. The last 0.1 mile up to High Point, following the High Point Trail, is steep and rocky.

From Loop Road by the east side of Maratanza Lake (see above), just over a mile from the entrance, the High Point Carriageway turns left, crosses under power lines, and passes antenna towers on the left. Continue straight through dwarf pitch pine barrens with numerous sweet ferns, sheep laurel, and birch trees along the side of the road. After 0.4 mile, the Indian Rock Trail appears on the left (see below).

The road continues fairly level, veering to the right with occasional views of the Catskills Range. Pass a clearing on the right, once a natural gas drilling site. There's a view of Castle Point in Minnewaska State Park Preserve in the distance. At 1.3 miles past the intersection for the Indian Rock Trail, the High Point Carriageway widens. Access to the Shingle Gully Ice Caves is on the left (see below). Please note that this is a restricted area open only to those with special permits. Just beyond, on the right, is the High Point Trail, marked with red blazes (see below). There's a sign. If you follow this trail for 0.1 mile up a steep rocky incline, you'll arrive at High Point, which has excellent views. If you continue straight, the High Point Carriageway continues 1 mile out to Old Smiley Road (see below).

Indian Rock Trail

Length: 0.5 mile. **Markings:** Yellow blazes and cairns. **General description:** This short trail starts from the High Point Carriageway 0.4 mile north of Maratanza Lake and ends at Indian Rock, a large glacial erratic. **Highlights:** Indian Rock is clearly the highlight, but there are also some wonderful views from neighboring cliffs. This trail is a very worthwhile detour. **Downside:** None. **Difficulties and hazards:** The trail is a little tough to follow in places. There is also some rock scrambling; Indian Rock itself is an especially challenging scramble.

From the High Point Carriageway (see above), 0.4 mile north of Loop Road by Maratanza Lake and about 1.5 miles from the entrance, the Indian Rock Trail departs on the left. Wooden boards cross a bog area, a project of the Mid-Hudson Adirondack Mountain Club. Continue through pitch pine barrens. There's a south-facing view on the left. Bear right. The trail zigzags, passing more views. Turn right again. Cross bare roots and come out on open ledge. Follow cairns. Indian Rock is prominent on the left. The trail descends to the left. It is steep enough here that you must use your hands. Arrive in an area of scrub oak and birch.

Indian Rock is perched over a substantial crevice. There is a fine south-facing view of the Rondout Valley and southern Shawangunk Ridge. Those contemplating climbing the rock should be warned that it's no piece of cake.

Long Path from Loop Road to the High Point Trail

Length: 2.2 miles. **Markings:** Turquoise blazes, cairns, and signs. **General description:** This section of rocky trail begins at Loop Road near Maratanza Lake and the ice caves, continues out to Verkeerderkill Falls, and ends at the intersection with the High Point Trail. It is well marked and easy to follow. **Highlights:** This gem of the Shawangunk trails is the most scenic hike in the Sam's Point Dwarf Pine Ridge Preserve and one of the most spectacular sections of the entire Long Path. It features dwarf ridgetop pitch pine barrens, magnificent Verkeerderkill Falls, and amazing views. It can be done as part of an 8.2-mile loop that also includes High Point and takes you around much of the preserve. **Downside:** If you aren't traveling the long loop, you must backtrack. Also, the length (6.4 miles round trip) and roughness of this trail will deter some. **Difficulties and hazards:** This trail takes you into some pretty remote places; don't travel alone. Also, beware dangerous cliffs in the area near the falls.

From Loop Road, 0.4 mile from Sam's Point and 1 mile from the entrance, where the road turns left for the High Point Carriageway, instead go right toward the ice caves. A short distance from the intersection, the turquoise-marked Long Path departs from the road on the left.

Berry fields immediately appear to the right of the trail, along with "islands" of pitch pine that in fall appear to be floating in a vermilion sea. Descend into the dwarf pitch pine. Views to the east and north include the Hudson Valley and Shawangunk Ridge, with Awosting Lake, Castle Point, Hamilton Point, and Gertrude's Nose most prominent. On a clear day, the Berkshires and Taconics may be visible. The trail veers left, crossing the slope. Enter an area of taller, 8- to 12-foot-high trees forming a canopy. Sweet fern may be observed or scented among the other ground cover. Ford a small brook that drains Maratanza Lake and enter a grove of normal-sized oak and birch with fields of ferns and otherwise sparse undergrowth. After a short distance, reenter the pitch pine forest with fine open views north and east. The trail bends to the left and arrives at a T-intersection with an old trail. Make a sharp right here and descend as you enter another area of taller pitch pines with scrub oak, witch hazel, and mountain laurel. The numbers of oaks and maples increase; eventually you enter a grove dominated by thin white birch trees.

Descend more steeply into a forest of normal-sized trees, including white pine and hemlock, oak and maple, along with striped maple, sassafras, mountain laurel, and huckleberries. The sound of rushing water can be heard. Finally you reach the Verkeerderkill, a braided stream among islands of trees and rock. Notice the many rhododendron bushes. The stream is shallow and not difficult to cross. On the other side, you can go right, off the trail, to some ledges with fine views of Verkeerderkill Falls—at 180 feet the highest waterfall in the Shawangunks. Be especially careful of the sheer drops. The remote, steep ravine through which the Verkeerderkill flows is a rich mosaic of colors in fall.

The trail turns left and climbs through mixed forest of birch, oak, pitch pine, hemlock, striped maple, mountain laurel, berries, and sheep laurel. Climb a steep incline and arrive at an area of open rocks with a view behind you facing south. The trail turns left, with a fine view looking southeast to High Point, New Jersey, in the distance and Veerkederkill Falls Ravine in the foreground. The trail follows the edge of the ravine with constant views on the left, then veers right and climbs again; there are great views from the top of rocks off the trail on the left. The trail levels in an area of pitch pine barrens. The red-marked High Point Trail (see below) appears on the left as three red blazes marked on a rock. From here, the Long Path used to continue into Minnewaska State Park Preserve, but the section that crosses private land has now been closed. There are plans to reroute the Long Path using the High Point Trail; see chapter 5 for more information.

High Point Trail

Length: 2.6 miles. **Markings:** Red blazes and a sign at the north end. **General description:** This trail connects the Long Path near Verkeerderkill Falls with the High Point Carriageway near High Point. **Highlights:** Besides providing wonderful panoramic views, especially at High Point, the trail crosses an expansive stretch of dwarf pine barrens. It also provides a useful link for circular hikes using the High Point Carriageway and Long Path. From the main entrance, this would total 8.2 miles, a good daylong hike. **Downside:** Remoteness and rough hiking make this trail unpalatable for some. Lack of shade on sunny days and no water are other considerations. **Difficulties and hazards:** This trail's scarcity of people and remoteness make it especially dangerous if hiked alone. Beware sheer cliffs. Also, the trail is rocky, and a little bit of scrambling is necessary.

From the intersection with the Long Path (see above), 0.4 mile east of Veerkeederkill Falls, the High Point Trail travels north, turns left, and continues along the edge of the rock slab. Then veer right, following cairns that mark the path along the edge of a slab. Climb a short cliff (no hands necessary). Enter a birch grove. Climb tilted rocks (these may be slippery if wet). The trail bends left and right.

Continue through taller 10- to 15-foot pitch pine trees. There's a view on the left looking south and east. Continue your gradual ascent. There are more open views on the left from bare rock slabs. A number of cairns and glacial erratics (sandstone from the Catskills, distinguished by their orange color) appear by the side of the trail. Antennae are visible on the left. The ravine that contains the Verkeerderkill is also visible on the left in the foreground. Follow the edge of the escarpment that borders the ravine. There's a pitch pine forest on the right. The cliffs on the left grow taller as you proceed.

Climb a rock ledge with a view from the top. Continue north along the edge of the escarpment. There are tall cliffs on the left with overhanging ledges. Climb rock steps up to a ledge. On top are diminutive plants: mosses and lichens, dwarf pitch pine, and huckleberries. The trail continues along the top of the ledges with continuous views on the left and straight ahead. Climb another rock ledge; you will need your hands here. Depart from the escarpment. Climb yet another rock ledge, easier than the last. Enter a mixed forest of stunted trees: birch, oak, and pitch pine. The trail bends left, with views looking southeast. Turn left and descend from the ledge. The trail bends to the right, with views of the Wallkill Valley and the Hudson Highlands in the distance. The antennae are visible on the right. The Verkeerderkill watershed is below in the foreground. There are more views on the left from atop ledges.

To the west, there's a partial view of the Catskill peaks over the tops of dwarf pitch pine trees. The trail veers left and descends into a mixed forest of pitch pine, birch, white pine, and oak. The trail climbs into another area of dwarf pitch pine. There are constant view on the left, including the towers behind you and cliffs you've already climbed. Ascend gradually through dwarf pitch pine, 6 to 8 feet high, following the edge of a rock ledge. Oak trees are on the left, dwarf pitch pine to the right. Enter another area of dwarf pitch pines, many only as high as your chest or waist. Behind you lies a panoramic view of Castle Point, the Hudson Highlands, the Wallkill Valley, and areas you've already traversed. The antenna towers stand on the horizon to the left.

Cross the ridgeline. Views looking west of the Catskills open up, especially to the right. The trail bends right and climbs. There's an excellent north and west view of the Rondout Reservoir and Catskills. Climb to the top of the rocks, the highest point on the trail (elevation 2,246 feet), surrounded by dwarf pitch pine barrens, and enjoy a 360-degree view of the eastern Catskills and northern Shawangunks, including Sky Top, the Berkshires, the Taconics, and the Hudson Highlands. Follow rock slabs marked with red blazes. The trail reenters the pine barrens and veers left, remaining level. Emerge on a rock with west-facing views. Notice the sandstone erratics.

The trail bends to the left. Soon you'll climb over rocks to the top, where the High Point fire tower once stood. The first tower was constructed here of trees in 1912. This was in response to a number of forest fires in the vicinity, including one in 1908 that destroyed 2,000 to 3,000 acres near the Ellenville zinc mines. In 1919, the state built a new 47-foot steel tower. This tower closed in 1971 and was disassembled in 1988, though some foundation remnants still exist. There is a fine, more-than-180-degree, panoramic view looking north and west that includes the entire range of the highest Catskills peaks, from the east-facing escarpment to the western Catskills. The Rondout Valley and Rondout Reservoir can also be seen below to the north and west; to the south lies the broad, uninterrupted sweep of pitch pine forest. You may feel you're on top of the world. Actually, some of the Catskill peaks to the north are nearly twice as high.

Follow the trail straight, then veer left and join a rough road that descends steeply over rocks. The road finally levels and crosses an often flooded area on wooden boards to a clearing where the High Point Carriageway (see above) and High Point Trail intersect.

High Point Carriageway from Old Smiley Road to High Point

Length: 1 mile. **Markings:** None. **General description:** This unmaintained route from High Point provides access to Old Smiley Road, Napanoch Point, and the eventually the village of Ellenville. The road was built in 1912 by the state to provide access to the High Point fire tower. Because it crosses private land, staying on the roadway (or as close as possible) is a necessity. **Highlights:** This road creates some possibilities for loop hikes or continuous long-distance hikes, including access to the Shingle Gully Ice Caves (you must have a permit; see below) and Napanoch Point. **Downside:** Only for the hardy. **Difficulties and hazards:** This unmaintained roadway passes beaver-created wetlands that necessitate a number of detours.

From the High Point Carriageway (see above), descend and veer left. The roadway steepens. There's a view over your shoulder of High Point in the background. The road departs from Sam's Point Dwarf Pine Ridge Preserve and enters what is currently private land. Please stay on the road. Continue to descend. A detour appears on the right around a flooded portion of roadway. Wind through a hemlock grove and cross a stream on rocks. On the left appears a patch of wetland with bleached-white skeleton tree trunks, diminutive pitch pine, and other shrubs.

Rejoin the roadway and continue your descent, departing from the pitch pine area and entering an impressive forest dominated by hemlock and birch with sphagnum moss on the ground. Again, you'll likely encounter sections of roadway underwater and will have to detour to the right over a log bridge. Rejoin the road, passing a stream on the left. Climb a short incline and veer left to arrive at Old Smiley Road (see the previous chapter). You can turn left here and follow it for 3.5 miles to Berme Road Park in the village of Ellenville, or turn right and continue to Awosting Lake in Minnewaska Park Preserve.

The Shingle Gully Ice Caves: This restricted area in the north part of Sam's Point Dwarf Pine Ridge Preserve is accessible only to those with permits. The primary attraction is the ice caves, though the area is laced with crevices—the deepest and most spectacular in the Shawangunk Ridge. The Shingle Gully caves are associated with a large slide block sometimes referred to as the Ellenville Landslide. This is the largest block landslide in the East, and possibly the whole United States. The course of a small stream was altered 200 degrees by this slide, perhaps the only example of such a stream alteration east of the San Andreas Fault. The caves themselves are marred with graffiti but nonetheless quite stunning, in some places more than 100 feet deep. At least three rare plant species are associated with the Shingle Gully Ice Caves, as well as some rare species of mammals.

To get there, follow an unmarked rough path that begins near the juncture of the High Point Carriageway and the High Point Trail, approximately 0.1 mile west of High Point (see above). You can obtain directions (as well as the necessary permits) from the Sam's Point Interpretive Center. The trailhead is marked with rocks and a red arrow painted on the rock. Follow the rocky trail (vegetation may intrude upon the path in places) as it winds through a forest of medium-height pitch pines, with undergrowth of berries, sheep laurel, and sweet fern. Some brief sections of the trail may be flooded, necessitating short detours. The trail gradually descends for more than 1.25 miles.

Eventually some west-facing views of the Rondout Valley, Rondout Reservoir, and Catskills Range open up. Just beyond is the area of crevices and caves. There's a maze of informal paths leading to the crevice rims. Use caution: The area is laced with numerous precipices, sometimes hidden, and accidents have occurred. Be sure to see the "Sunken Forest" of hemlocks, which lies at the base of the largest crevice—more than 100 feet deep and 100 feet wide. The ice cave itself is the most impressive. Over 100 feet deep, it's just a few feet wide in places, with overhanging shelves and ledges and hemlocks growing from the walls. The bottom rarely sees light and thus is devoid of plants except for some moss. Unfortunately, it is also defaced with graffiti. It can be entered by climbing down on rocks. Flashlights and possibly a rope are necessary for going all the way into this cave, which contains ice until late summer. On hot summer days, the damp cold at the entrance of the cave can be unbearable. Other, smaller crevices in the area may also be worth exploring.

THE SOUTHERN RIDGE

7

South of Sam's Point Dwarf Pine Ridge Preserve, the Shawangunk Ridge does-n't stop. It narrows to roughly 1 mile in width and continues southward for 30 miles to the New Jersey border. This part of the ridge passes through three dif-ferent New York counties: Ulster, Sullivan, and Orange. The southern Shawan-gunk Ridge is not as well known or studied as the northern. More of it is developed, too, especially the eastern side of the ridge. Two major highways—Route 17 and Interstate 84—cross the southern ridge, as do a number of other important roads. The fact that much of the southern ridge is privately owned, the absence of certain key features like sky lakes and towering cliffs, and (until recently) the lack of a trail network have discouraged recreational use in this section. However, the southern ridge has many of the same features as the north-ern ridge in terms of exposed bedrock, rare vegetation communities, historical sites, and spectacular views. It also joins the northern ridge to the 245-mile-long ridge that starts in Pennsylvania and ends in Rosendale. In fact, this is what connects it to the Appalachian Range. Without this connection, the northern Shawangunk Ridge would be an isolated bump on the map. Some visionaries see the entire ridge that the Shawangunks are part of as a kind of greenway—an archipelago of protected lands and parks connected by a trail corridor.

Thanks to recent efforts by the Open Space Institute and New York–New Jersey Trail Conference, some important tracts of land on the southern Shawan-gunk Ridge have been protected and are now open for public use. The Trail Conference has also constructed the Shawangunk Ridge Trail and Long Path, creating 37.6 miles of continuous hiking from High Point State Park in New Jersey to the entrance of Sam's Point Dwarf Pine Ridge Preserve. These offer the rewards of long-distance hiking, varied scenery that's both similar to and different from areas to the north, and incredible views. All of this makes the southern Shawangunk Ridge well worth exploring.

Geologically, the southern ridge is in some ways similar to the northern part. The Shawangunk conglomerate that dominates northern sections is present here, too, but the area it underlies is smaller and narrower—generally less than a mile wide—and the rock beds are thinner and not as well exposed. Here much of the Shawangunk conglomerate has, over millions of years, eroded away. What's left is the top of an anticline: a very narrow, sharply crested ridge of steeply tilting conglomerate, which, as we've seen before, is hard and highly resistant to erosion. Smaller ridges of mostly Helderberg (Lower Devonian) limestone exist parallel to the main ridge west of Otisville and east of Port Jervis.

The Shawangunk Ridge Trail follows the southern Shawangunk Ridge from its intersection with the Appalachian Trail in New Jersey's High Point State Park, north to its intersection with the Long Path, 2 miles northeast of the village of Wurstboro, a total distance of 28.6 miles. The Long Path continues from there for another 11.9 miles to the entrance to Sam's Point Dwarf Pine Ridge Preserve. Both trails generally follow the western side of the ridge, just below the ridgeline. The SRT sometimes follows roadways and old railroad right-of-ways. Both trails cross private land and sometimes newly acquired state land. Originally conceived as a new route for the Long Path, the SRT is now considered an alternate route and part of the Long Path system.

Trails

High Point Monument to Greenville Turnpike

Length: 4.3 miles. **Markings:** Red and green discs, turquoise blazes, and occasional signs. **General description:** This segment of the Shawangunk Ridge Trail starts from the High Point Monument in New Jersey's High Point State Park. Some may quibble that this ventures outside the purported scope of this book—High Point State Park is located on the Kittatinny Ridge, which technically is not part of the Shawangunks. The trail does eventually cross into New York State, however, where the ridge becomes the Shawangunks. It passes through the property of a private sporting club and ends at Greenville Turnpike. **Highlights:** Wonderful views from High Point and a host of other locations. The trail passes through a unique white cedar swamp in the Dryden Kuser Natural Area. You'll observe many of the characteristic plant communities—chestnut oak forest, scrub oak thickets, and pitch pine groves—that are prominent farther north, as well as areas of exposed bedrock similar to their more extensive northern counterparts. There are opportunities for loop hikes in High Point State Park. **Downside:** You will have to spot cars or backtrack to hike this entire segment. **Difficulties and hazards:** The trail is rough and rocky in places, with unsteady footing. The risk factor increases because of the remoteness of this trail.

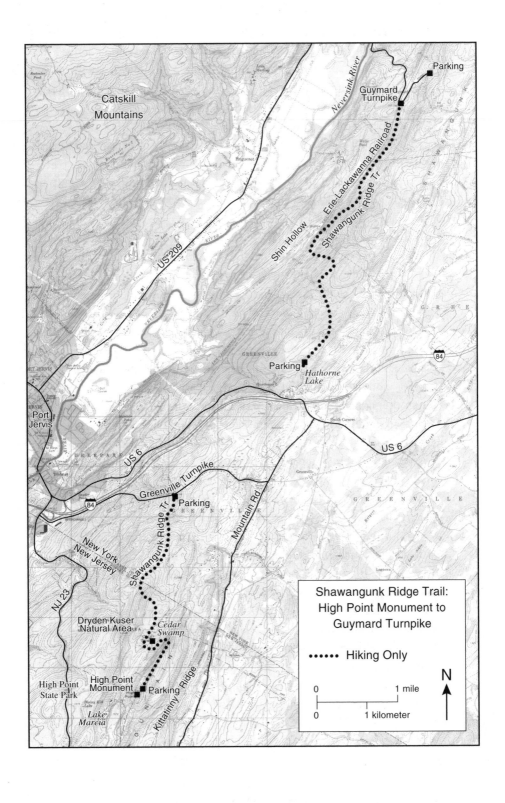

Catskill
Mountains

Neversink River

Parking

Guymard
Turnpike

Erie-Lackawanna Railroad

Shawangunk Ridge Tr

Shin Hollow

US 209

GREENVILLE

84

Parking

Hathorne
Lake

Port
Jervis

Smith Corners

DEERPARK

US 6

US 6

84

Greenville

GREENVILLE

Greenville Turnpike

Parking

GREENVILLE

Shawangunk Ridge Tr

Mountain Rd

New York
New Jersey

NJ 23

Dryden Kuser
Natural Area

Cedar
Swamp

High Point
State Park

High Point
Monument

Parking

Kittatinny Ridge

Lake
Marcia

Shawangunk Ridge Trail:
High Point Monument to
Guymard Turnpike

•••••• Hiking Only

0   1 mile

0   1 kilometer

N

To get to the trail, you must start in High Point State Park in New Jersey. To reach this state park, located in the extreme northwestern corner of the state, you can take Interstate 80 west and exit on Route 23 in Wayne. Follow Route 23 west to High Point State Park. Or follow Interstate 84 to exit 1 in Port Jervis. Go south for 4.3 miles on Route 23 to the park's main entrance.

High Point State Park is situated on the crest of the Kittatinny Range, New Jersey's counterpart to New York's Shawangunks. It covers 14,213 acres. The park is rather intensely developed for recreation: You'll find a campground, picnic facilities, paved roads, rest rooms, playgrounds, a large interpretive center, swimming beach, and 50 miles of hiking trails, including 18 miles of the Appalachian Trail, as well as 24 miles of groomed cross-country ski trails (half are covered with manufactured snow) in winter. There is also a ski lodge and ski rentals. For information about the ski center, call 973-702-1222. The park was created when Colonel Anthony R. and Susie Dryden Kuser donated the land, which was dedicated in 1923. The landscape design was by the Olmsted Brothers firm, sons of the famed landscape architect who created Central Park in New York City. A large portion of the park remains in its natural state, particularly the 800-acre Dryden Kuser Natural Area, which includes a unique white cedar swamp. Dryden Kuser was Colonel Anthony's son as well as a New Jersey state senator and conservationist. For more information about the park, call 973-875-4800.

Enter the park and follow signs past 20-acre spring-fed Marcia Lake. Follow the road uphill to the end, where the High Point Monument is located. A large parking area features rest rooms with a water fountain, a concession stand with picnic tables, and—towering above it all—the 220-foot High Point Monument, which resembles the Washington Monument. It was completed in 1930 and stands at 1,803 feet above sea level, the highest elevation in New Jersey. It is dedicated to New Jersey's war veterans. If it is open, you can climb the huge tower. Even from the base, there's an amazing view in all directions. What you see is labeled in four signs around the stone perimeter. You can gaze northward along the spine of the ridge at least as far as Mohonk. To the south, you can easily see the Delaware Water Gap and beyond, far into Pennsylvania. Nowhere else can you see as much of the ridgeline as here. The Appalachian Trail is located 0.25 mile south of the monument, where it intersects the Monument Trail, the official beginning of the Shawangunk Ridge Trail.

From the north end of the parking area, bypass a barricade and enter the woods next to a sign indicating the beginning of the Monument Trail, marked with red and green discs. This is also part of the Shawangunk Ridge Trail, marked here with occasional turquoise discs. Continue north, following the trail along the ridge, sometimes to the right of it, more often to the left of it, and sometimes along the spine itself. Pass a sole mountain laurel bush on the right. Mountain laurel is very common in the northern Shawangunks, but practically absent here. The forest here is largely stunted, with chestnut oak, scrub oak, and pitch pine the most common trees and shrubs. There are numerous small outcrops of conglomerate rock tilted at steep angles. After 0.5 mile, a side trail on the left leads to a view looking west to Port Jervis and the Delaware River. Just beyond, a couple of side trails on the right lead to panoramic east-facing views.

One mile from the parking area, the trail descends more steeply into denser forest with a greater variety of trees, shrubs such as striped maple, and seedlings sprouting from the moss-covered ground. Arrive at a four-way intersection. The Monument Trail goes straight here. The Shawangunk Ridge Trail, marked with turquoise blazes, turns left and follows an old road that skirts the edge of the Cedar Swamp, which lies in a valley between two parallel ridges.

The Cedar Swamp, part of the 800-acre Dryden Kuser Natural Area, appears lush and tropical, densely packed with rhododendron, large hemlocks, black spruce, and Atlantic white cedar. The damp floor of the swamp is thickly covered with moss and ferns. White cedar is normally a coastal plain tree, and its occurrence here at a high elevation is reputed to be unique in the world. Thus the swamp contains an interesting mix of both highland and lowland species. Arrive at a T-intersection with a road and turn right. This old road crosses the swamp on a wooden boardwalk, part of a nature trail that loops around the swamp. There is a self-guiding booklet available that explains the numbered markers you'll encounter.

The road continues with the swamp on the left and more typical chestnut oak forest on the right. Then it departs from the swamp altogether, soon arriving at another intersection with a bench. Turn right and leave the road, shortly reaching an intersection with the red- and green-marked Monument Trail again. At this juncture, turn left onto the Monument Trail and follow it as it ascends the ridge to an open patch with skeleton trees and grass. The SRT turns left and descends. The trail then bends to the left and continues its descent. Pass a New York–New Jersey Trail Conference register on the left. Proceed for some distance across a fairly level area to the left of the ridgeline.

The trail bends to the left and descends, soon bending to the right and continuing its gradual descent. Arrive at a level spot in lush forest. Cross a small stream (possibly dry in mid- to late summer and fall). The trail ascends gradually, veering left, then right, and then left. Cross into New York State, passing a stone border monument on the right. You're now officially on the Shawangunk Ridge. You've also entered the property of a private sporting club. Departing from the marked trail is strictly forbidden in this area, and especially risky during hunting season: mid-November to mid-December. The trail winds through a thick scrub oak thicket, climbing to the top of the ridgeline.

Turn right and continue north along the ridge through more scrub oak, pitch pine, and chestnut oak, as well as bare, upturned rock beds. There are partial west-facing views here. The trail then bends to the right and crosses a small col. Cross another trail and veer left. Turn right and ascend rock slabs, then veer left again at the top. Pass the best west-facing view of Port Jervis and the Delaware River on the left. The trail bends to the left and descends, then bends to the right and levels for a long stretch. Descend again and cross a rocky slope. Beware poor footing, especially in wet or damp conditions. Cross another rocky slope, and arrive at an unpaved road and turn right. Soon you'll cross the road at a diagonal and descend a slope on the opposite side. Cross a small brook lined with ferns. Continue through the forest, descending very gradually. Finally arrive at Greenville Turnpike. To continue on the Shawangunk Ridge Trail, turn right and follow it for 0.7 mile. Then turn left onto Old Mountain Road and continue for 0.9 mile to Route 6. Turn left here, head underneath Interstate 84, and, just beyond, arrive at Hathorn Road. (See below for further directions.)

Lake Hathorn to Guymard Turnpike

Length: 4.6 miles. **Markings:** Turquoise blazes. **General description:** From the end of Lake Hathorn Road, the Shawangunk Ridge Trail follows the ridge to Conrail tracks. It then follows Shin Hollow Road and returns to the forest, continuing parallel to the tracks and ending this section at the Guymard Turnpike, where the next segment of trail picks up. **Highlights:** A diversity of experiences and forest habitats, including some chestnut oak and slab rock environments that are more characteristic of areas farther north. Berry picking in midsummer is another plus. **Downside:** A boring stretch alongside a railbed. Litter, traffic noise, and gunshots may mar the experience in a few places. **Difficulties and hazards:** The trail may be overgrown with prickly vegetation in some spots. Make sure you wear long pants for protection. Also, watch your footing: The trail is rocky and/or steep in several places, and there are a few stream crossings.

To get to this section of trailhead, follow Route 6 east as it climbs 3.5 miles from its intersection with Route 84 in Port Jervis to Lake Hathorn Road on the left. Or get off Route 84 at exit 2, Mountain Road. Turn left on Mountain Road and follow it for a short distance south to Route 6. Turn right on Route 6 and continue west for a short distance to Lake Hathorn Road on the right. Follow Lake Hathorn Road for 0.4 mile to a cul-de-sac at its end, where there's plenty of parking available.

From the parking area, the turquoise-marked trail follows an old woods road briefly, then turns left and leaves the road. A new home is passed on the right with a multitude of parked trailers. The trail skirts the property and crosses a collapsed stone wall, then climbs a hillside, levels, and crosses another stone wall. Evidence of prior agricultural use in the form of stone walls and old roads is plentiful in this area. Descend into a small valley with a lovely open meadow on the left. Cross another stone wall. There is an old road on the floor of the valley. The trail intercepts the road and continues straight. Pass an aspen grove on the left, then depart from the road and cross another stone wall.

The trail turns left and descends, crossing wooden planks over a wet area populated with skunk cabbage. It then turns right and faces a familiar outcrop of slanting slabs of Shawangunk conglomerate. The trail climbs to the top of this small face, turns right on a dirt road, and heads north through a dry, level plateau. You'll immediately encounter a different forest community—the chestnut-oak-dominated forest typically seen farther north. The undergrowth is thick with huckleberries. Pass another private residence off to the right.

The trail crosses another old road and bends to the left, slowly descending. Cross the bottom of a small valley through dense fern foliage. Notice gypsy moth damage to oak trees left of the trail. Continue to descend through a field of ferns. The trail bends to the right and levels. Cross another old road and then a stone field. There is a rise on the left. The trail suddenly veers left and climbs the rise. Encounter more tilted rock beds on the left, then veer left and follow the ridgeline for a short distance. Descend steeply on a rocky path. There is a seasonal stream to the left of the trail, which veers right on an old road. Descend, passing mountain laurel on the right growing on a rocky slope. The trail veers to the right again, with partial views on the left through the trees. Traffic noise from Shin Hollow below can be heard.

The trail crosses another rocky slope. Suddenly, there is an opening with slanting slabs of conglomerate, dwarf pitch clinging to tiny soil-filled cracks in the bare rock, and views looking down into Shin Hollow and across the way to a parallel ridge composed of younger bedrock, with Port Jervis and the Poconos in the distance to the left. This is the trademark Shawangunk Ridge landscape, a perfect place to stop and savor the view. Continue north through dense blueberries.

Descend and veer left, then right, following an old road. The road departs on the left. Continue straight, descending . A rail line appears below on the left. The trail turns left, descends, and then climbs up to the rail line. Follow the service road next to the tracks, heading north. Metro-North passenger trains running from Hoboken to Port Jervis use these tracks. Continue for 0.7 mile; a variety of colorful flowers along the tracks may help relieve the monotony.

A bridge crosses the tracks. At this point, the trail turns right and departs from the tracks, climbing the steep embankment underneath the bridge through some especially nasty, prickly vegetation onto Shin Hollow Road, which is a dirt four-wheel-drive track here. Follow the road as it ascends, passing a cottage with an outhouse on the right. All this property is privately owned, so please stay on the road. After 0.5 mile, just as the road levels, the turquoise-marked trail turns left and departs from the road. There is a rock cairn at this point. The trail soon arrives at a dirt road, turns left, and follows it downhill. The trail then veers right and continues its descent.

The trail levels. There's a steep slope on the left, and partial views looking west through the trees. Cross a road. There's a view of the tracks below on the left. Cross a small seasonal stream, followed by a hemlock grove along the side of a steep slope. Continue level along the side of the slope, with the railroad tracks visible below on the left. Cross another road, and then another picturesque seasonal stream tumbling over large rocks. The trail gradually descends, staying in close proximity to the railroad tracks but remaining in the woods. Pass an open area on the right and then a seasonal pool on the left with frogs. Continue parallel to the tracks, finally arriving at Guymard Turnpike.

Guymard Turnpike to Route 211

Length: 5.3 miles. **Markings:** Turquoise blazes. **General description:** This segment of the Shawangunk Ridge Trail follows the abandoned Erie Railroad Port Jervis line for 1.25 miles, then leaves the old railroad right-of-way and climbs the ridge, which it follows for the next 2.7 miles. Then it rejoins and follows the railroad right-of-way again for the last 1.4 miles to Route 211. Mountain bicyclists have the option of bicycling the entire way on the abandoned rail line. This segment of the Erie Railroad closed when a tunnel through the Otisville Notch was completed. The new line runs slightly west and a little below the old line. **Highlights:** Varied forest habitats and scenery and a few west-facing views. Blueberries in summer. Walking the rail line is easy. **Downside:** Power lines, ATVs, traffic noise, and illegal dumps. **Difficulties and hazards:** Some strenuous hiking. Also, this section of trail doesn't appear well trodden and may be overgrown in places. Keep your eyes on the blazes and stay off the tracks of the newer rail line.

To get to Guymard Turnpike, go south from Wurtsboro on Route 209 for 11.8 miles. Turn left and follow Guymard Turnpike east for 2.2 miles, crossing the Neversink River and passing Guymard Lake on the right. The road crosses a bridge over the railroad tracks; just beyond, the Shawangunk Ridge Trail crosses the road. There is limited off-road parking on the left about 0.1 mile past the bridge. From Guymard Turnpike, the turquoise-marked trail descends an embankment, crosses a small wooden bridge over a drainage ditch, and climbs

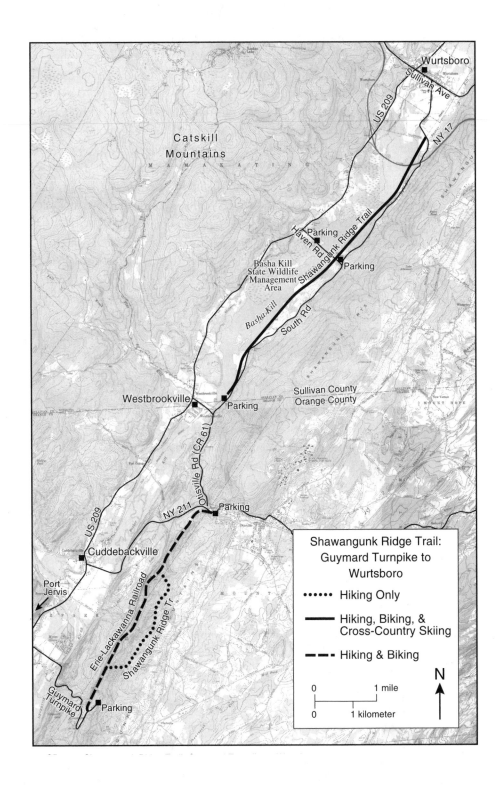

Wurtsboro

Sullivan Ave

US 209

NY 17

Catskill
Mountains

M A M A K A T I N G

Parking

Haven Rd

Shawangunk Ridge Trail

Parking

Basha Kill
State Wildlife
Management
Area

Basha Kill

South Rd

SHAWANGUNK MTS

Westbrookville

Parking

Sullivan County
Orange County

MOUNT HOPE

Olisville Rd (CR 61)

NY 211

Parking

US 209

Cuddebackville

Erie-Lackawanna Railroad

Shawangunk Ridge Tr

Port
Jervis

Guymard
Turnpike

Parking

Shawangunk Ridge Trail:
Guymard Turnpike to
Wurtsboro

•••••• Hiking Only

——— Hiking, Biking, &
Cross-Country Skiing

– – – Hiking & Biking

N

0   1 mile

0   1 kilometer

the embankment on the other side up to the abandoned rail line, which here runs right next to the new line on the left. Turn right here and follow the old rail line north. This old rail line is suitable for mountain bikes, which can follow it north all the way to Route 211. The rail line is also used by ATVs. The old rail line soon departs from the new one and enters the woods, continuing slightly above and east of the new line. Unfortunately, illegally dumped refuse may be visible in a number of spots along the next mile of trail. Pass a short gravel road on the right and, just beyond it, a private residence.

The railroad right-of-way crosses a small gurgling stream. Pass outcrops of slanting rock beds on the right reminiscent of those on the northern Shawangunk Ridge. At 1.25 miles north of the intersection with the Guymard Turnpike, the turquoise-marked trail turns right, departs from the old rail line, and enters the forest. The trail climbs uphill gradually, veering first to the right and then the left, then more steeply across a hemlock-covered slope. Past the hemlock grove, you'll enter an open oak forest. Continue up a more gentle slope. The trail is easier to follow here.

The trail bends left and right. The angle of the slope increases. Finally, about 0.25 mile after departing from the abandoned rail line, the trail bends left just below the ridgeline and soon begins to level out. Pass through an area with a lush undergrowth of ferns. Just beyond is a partial view looking west. Cross an old road, then a second one. Both lead to heaps of stones from an abandoned lead mine. Cross a field populated with stunted chestnut oak, scrub oak, and huckleberries. Reenter the woods and begin a gradual descent. Pass occasional mountain laurel. Cross another old road. The trail climbs briefly to the top of a small bluff and continues level for a short distance. There are partial views on the left of the western Catskills and Neversink Valley.

The trail turns sharply right, veers left and continues north, then bends left and down a rocky slope. Cross another old road and pass through an area of conglomerate slabs, followed by a small hemlock grove. The trail veers left. Cross a tiny seasonal stream, probably dry in midsummer and fall. Climb another small bluff, veering left and then right. Chestnut oak, scrub oak, and huckleberries are abundant here. There are partial views of the western Catskills above the trees. Notice small blueberry bushes along the trail. Power lines appear ahead. Cross an old road and, just beyond it, an open corridor beneath the power lines. Follow the turquoise blazes through this area, which is populated with a wide variety of native and nonnative vegetation.

Reenter the forest and descend. Turn right and continue descending. The trail bends left, crosses a small stream, and continues through a muddy section. Pass a hemlock grove on the left and cross a pair of shallow, rocky ravines. The trail continues through an area of open forest and gentle slopes. Traffic noise may be heard in the distance. The trail descends gradually and veers right. It then bends to the right and levels, following an old road for a short distance before departing left. You'll soon turn left and descend steeply onto the old railroad right-of-way—the same one you left 2.7 miles ago.

Turn right and quickly reach power lines towering overhead. The trail follows these for 0.6 mile. Finally the power lines turn left and continue west across the Neversink Valley. Follow the old rail line north for another 0.75 mile, veering to the right and around a metal gate. Route 211 is just beyond. There's a parking area here, with enough room to accommodate several cars.

To pick up the next section of the Shawangunk Ridge Trail, go left on Route 211 for a short distance to the intersection with Otisville Road (County Road 61) on the right. Follow Otisville Road north for 1.6 miles to South Road. Make a right here and continue for a short distance to the Basha Kill Wildlife Management Area, where the next segment of the Shawangunk Ridge Trail begins (see below).

Basha Kill Wildlife Management Area to Wurtsboro

Length: 6.7 miles. **Markings:** Turquoise blazes. Blue discs in the Basha Kill Wildlife Management Area (state-owned land). Markings are often infrequent, but the trail is fairly obvious in most places. **General description:** This section of the Shawangunk Ridge Trail mostly utilizes the old abandoned Ontario & Western railbed as it traverses this large protected area of forests and wetlands. The railroad opened in 1871 and operated until 1957. Bicycling and cross-country skiing are permitted along this section of trail, and a number of parking areas along South Road provide access. South Road is accessible from Haven Road and from County Road 61. Please note that Haven Road, a causeway, may be closed at times of high water, usually in spring. **Highlights:** Many opportunities for observing this spectacular wetland area, rich in aquatic plant life and wildlife. It is especially renowned for bird-watching. The trail crosses a number of habitats, including red maple swamp forest. There is more information about the Basha Kill and its wildlife in the next chapter. **Downside:** Some may find the miles of level hiking monotonous. **Difficulties and hazards:** Though hikers will find this section relatively easy, those on bicycles will find it a bit of a challenge. The trail is rough, with protruding roots and wooden rail ties in a number of places, and deeply eroded in others. Downed trees and overgrown vegetation may also be encountered. Only experienced bicyclists with durable bikes should attempt this. Those who do may find the challenge more satisfying than the easy carriage roads at Mohonk and Minnewaska. Skiers should note that this trail is not groomed. Also, be forewarned that hunters are often the primary users of this area. Be aware of scheduled hunting seasons and avoid if necessary.

To get to the beginning of this segment, follow Route 209 south for 6.5 miles from Wurtsboro to Westbrookville. Turn left on Otisville Road (County Road 61) and continue for 0.5 mile to South Road. Turn left on South Road and follow for a short distance. A parking area for the Basha Kill Wildlife Management Area appears on the left, with a view of the south end of the wetland, relatively narrow here. There's access for canoes and kayaks and wooden observation platform. From the parking area, continue north along South Road for a short distance, following the turquoise-colored blazes. The trail soon turns left, departs from the road, and enters the forest. Blue DEC discs mark the trail up to Route 17. Follow this trail for a short distance until it arrives at an abandoned railbed, part of the old New York, Ontario & Western rail line. This is the Basha Kill Rail Trail. You will be following this most of the rest of the way.

Turn right on the rail-trail and continue north. Pass a second parking area on the right (direct access to the trail for bikes). There's an open view of the now broad wetland on the left, with the Mongaup Hills (western Catskills) just beyond. Pass a smaller wetland on the right. The trail continues north, following the old railbed for another 0.5 mile. A wooden bridge then appears on the right, leading to another parking area. On the left is a nature trail that follows the edge of the marsh. Continue straight through the forest. This is the roughest section of the trail, overgrown with vegetation and poorly defined in places with numerous downed trees, a nightmare for bicyclists. Pass a private residence on the right. The nature trail appears again on the left.

The rail-trail improves somewhat and arrives at the shore of the wetland with fine west-facing views. Pass another parking area with a boat launch on the left. There is another open area with wonderful views. Note the many small wooden bridges over tributaries—these present no problem for the hiker but are major obstacles for the bicyclist. Reenter the forest. Another open area with west-facing views of the wetland appears on the left, but it's tough for bicycles on account of exposed ties and tree roots. Reenter the woods once more.

Cross another wooden bridge and follow the now rocky railbed just before arriving at Haven Road, a causeway across the Basha Kill. There are excellent views of the marsh and neighboring mountains from the causeway, which is also a popular fishing spot. The trail crosses Haven Road and follows a gravel road north for 0.25 mile to another parking area on the right. Pass through the parking area and continue straight, bypassing a gate. There are intermittent views of the wetland on the left and a partial view of the Shawangunk Ridge on the right. A short nature loop trail appears on the left. There are no signs or markers. The nature trail passes labeled trees and eventually leads to an elevated platform that provides a view of several bird-feeding stations. Just beyond, a concrete ruin appears on the right. A short distance later, the rail-trail passes

The Basha Kill wetland

the north end of the nature trail on the left. You'll also find canoe or kayak access to the wetland on the left and a fine open view of the marsh with the Mongaup Hills beyond.

Continue north, entering the forest and passing floodplain forest on the left. This is an area of forest with mature trees that may be inundated by water at certain times of the year, but are dry the rest of the time. Pass multiunit housing up the hill on the right. This section of trail is more eroded and rough. Bikes may again have a tough time of it here. A smaller wetland area appears on the right, with abundant fish and amphibians. Cross a pair of wooden bridges. There's swamp forest on the left. These mature trees, primarily red maple, are at least partially inundated by water most of the time. Swamp forest habitats are normally very difficult to access because of mud and dense vegetation, so hikers and bicyclists rarely get to experience them. Cross a third wooden bridge over a small stream, then another pair of bridges over streams.

Five miles north of the first parking area, the rail-trail crosses underneath Route 17 through a noisy tunnel. The trail continues north, passing a wetland area on the right and floodplain forest on the left. Cross another wooden bridge over a small stream. There are partial views of the Mongaup Hills on the left beyond wetlands. Bypass a gate and arrive at Walker Lane, 0.6 mile north of Route 17. The rail-trail ends here.

Turn left on the road, following turquoise markers. Pass more wetland areas on the left and right. The road then bends to the right. There's a view of the Shawangunk Ridge on the right and behind you. Pass a pond on your right on private land (no trespassing). There are more views of the Shawangunk Ridge on the right. Then pass a large open field on the left with fine views of the Mongaup Hills. A field appears on the right with more views of the Shawangunk Ridge. Pass an elementary school on the left and cross the old channel of the D&H Canal. There's a marker and old stone snubbing post on the left here. Enter the village of Wurtsboro. You'll soon arrive at the corner of Pennsylvania and Sullivan Avenue, the main street in Wurtsboro; a left turn here will bring you to the heart of town, which offers numerous shops and places to eat, as well as the Catskill Hiking Shack. There's ample parking along Sullivan Avenue.

Wurtsboro to Summitville—Roosa Gap Road

Length: 4.1 miles. **Markings:** Blue discs. Turquoise blazes at the very end. **General description:** This section of the Shawangunk Ridge Trail begins at an old O&W rail station, now a VFW post located approximately 1 mile east of Wurtsboro off old Route 17. It ends at the Summitville–Roosa Gap Road. Parking is available at both ends. The first 0.9 mile is part of the Shawangunk Ridge Trail, while the rest is part of the Long Path. Practically the entire section is located on the Wurtsboro Ridge, a 2,300-acre property acquired in 1985 by the Open Space Institute. Ownership transferred to the state in 1989. It is managed by the New York State Department of Environmental Conservation. There was once lead-mining activity in this part of the Shawangunks; some of the old lead mines are purported to date back more than 300 years. **Highlights:** Excellent views from the ridgetop looking west and south as well as north toward the Catskills. Also, there are a number of diverse habitats, including northern hardwoods, chestnut oak forests, and open areas featuring rocky-summit communities of pitch pine, oak, and heath along the ridgetop. Views of planes and gliders from the nearby Wurtsboro Airport are another highlight. **Downside:** Noise from planes often disturbs the tranquility. **Difficulties and hazards:** A number of inclines and descents make this a rather strenuous outing. Not for everyone. The footing can be a little challenging in a few steep sections.

From Sullivan Avenue (Old Route 17) in the village of Wurtsboro, head east, passing the old railroad station on the right and continuing out of town. Follow Old Route 17 as it climbs and bends to the left. Just before old rail abutments, there's a gravel road on the left. The abutments are part of the old O&W; a bridge once carried the rail line over the road here. This portion was known as

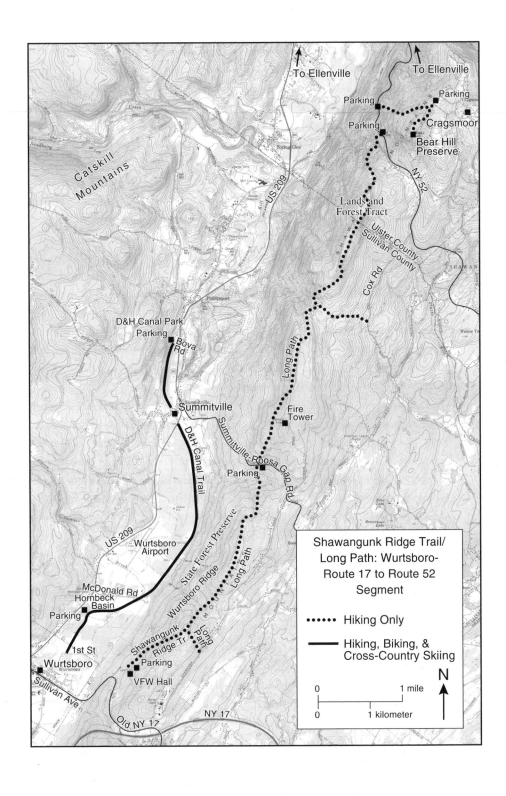

**Shawangunk Ridge Trail/
Long Path: Wurtsboro-
Route 17 to Route 52
Segment**

••••• Hiking Only

—— Hiking, Biking, &
Cross-Country Skiing

N

| 0 | 1 mile |
| 0 | 1 kilometer |

the High Line because of the tunnel that was blasted through the Shawangunks. A short distance east of the old bridge abutments are the remains of the 3,750-foot Highview Tunnel Portal, which opened in 1872. The O&W rail line ran from the West Shore Railroad in Cornwall through the western Catskills to Lake Ontario. It closed in 1957.

Turn left on the gravel road and follow it for a short distance to a parking area at the end, an old rail station that's now a VFW post. There is ample parking. ATV users also use this parking area. Follow the old railroad right-of-way just beyond the old station. A trail marked with white blazes and blue discs departs on the right into the forest. Follow it. It ascends gradually for 0.1 mile to an intersection with the Shawangunk Ridge Trail. There's a green L/P sign at the intersection. If you go straight, it will take you 0.2 mile back to old Route 17. Instead, go left.

Continue to ascend gradually as the trail crosses the side of the ridge. Cross a small ravine with a seasonal stream. The trail then bends sharply to the right and continues to climb. The forest gradually thins to chestnut oak and other oaks. There are partial views of the Mongaup Hills to the west, part of the western Catskills. The trail bends left and enters open fields of scrub oak, pitch pine, and berries. The top of the ridge is on the right. The trail bends right again, climbing more steeply. There's an open view on the left, looking north to the Catskills Range. Continue through scrub oak and pitch pine. Another panoramic view opens on the left looking both north and south, including the valley below and the Catskills to the north. The Basha Kill is visible to the south, as well as the village of Wurtsboro and a partial view of the Wurtsboro Airport to the west. Planes with gliders in tow may be observed. The Wurtsboro Airport is the oldest gliding center in the United States, established in 1927. The narrow valley with steep ridges on both sides creates updrafts and favorable conditions for gliding. It is reported that this vantage is also excellent for viewing migratory raptors in fall.

The trail continues to climb for a short distance through scrub oak and pitch pine to the top of the ridge, much of it on tilted slabs of conglomerate. An old gravel road appears on the right. It was once part of a planned residential development, which prompted its purchase by the Open Space Institute in 1985 to ensure protection. Just beyond, the turquoise-marked Long Path enters from the right. The Shawangunk Ridge Trail ends here, approximately 0.8 mile from the last intersection or 0.9 mile from the VFW post.

Continue north, now following the Long Path. The blue disc markers remain the same. Note that this area was recently hit by forest fire in 1997. The trail veers to the left, enters chestnut oak forest, and descends gradually. The trail veers to the left again and makes a steeper descent. It then bends to the right; the descent continues. The forest becomes taller and thicker. Gray birch and red oak are present in this more varied forest. The trail bends left, then right, and crosses a woods road. At the bottom of the col, cross a seasonal stream. The forest floor is covered with ferns in some places. Trees such as white oak, gray birch, maple, and hemlock, and shrubs like striped maple are present.

Begin a gradual ascent again. Cross an old logging road. The trail bends right and left and climbs more steeply. As it does so, the forest begins to thin once more, chestnut oak becoming the predominant tree; you'll also see red oak and scrub oak. Gradually it thins to mostly scrub oak. Views open up on the left, looking west to the valley below and the Mongaup Hills (western Catskills) on the opposite side of the valley. Continue through fields of scrub oak with berries and scattered pitch pines. The trail ascends and veers to the right. Just under 2 miles from the VFW post, the trail crosses another wide path. Continue to climb and veer right through fields of scrub oak and berries. There are more open views on the left looking west and north. The Catskills Range is visible in the distance to the north. There's a great view of the Wurtsboro Airport with planes often flying below you. Cross tilted beds of conglomerate rock with more fine views. The trail enters more chestnut oak forest, with pitch pine and scrub oak also present. There's another view looking north and west. This one includes the ridge north. The Roosa Gap fire tower is visible in the distance, as are the Catskills and Rondout Valley. The remains of the old abandoned Delaware & Hudson Canal lie below on the left.

The trail veers left and descends. After a large glacial erratic on the left. the trail bends to the right, then veers to the left and continues to descend. Pass a ravine on the right with a seasonal stream. Maple, birch, and mountain laurel become prevalent. The trail crosses two branches of the seasonal stream. Bright emerald ferns are especially abundant in the area. Cross another woods road and begin to ascend. The trail leaves state land and enters private land. From here on, markers are turquoise blazes. Climb moderately. Veer left and then bend to the right. The trail bends left again and makes a short, steep climb up to the dirt-and-gravel Summitville–Roosa Gap Road. There is parking available for a number of cars here. Summitville–Roosa Gap Road descends west for approximately 1.25 miles to Route 209. Note that if you're going in the opposite direction, this trail crossing is not marked; the only sign is a warning not to litter. Highly motivated individuals in great shape may want to continue through the next section (see next page).

Long Path from Summitville—
Roosa Gap Road to Route 52

Length: 5.5 miles. **Markings:** Mostly turquoise blazes. Blue discs when crossing the DEC parcel. **General description:** The Long Path continues north from the previous section, mostly following the ridge, to end at Route 52 south of Ellenville. It crosses private land, a 160-acre parcel managed by the DEC, and the 1,300-acre Lands and Forests Tract purchased in 2000 by the Open Space Institute with help from the New York–New Jersey Trail Conference and the Trust for Public Land. Ownership of this property has recently been transferred to the DEC. Eight natural communities have been identified on this property, with 27 rare species of plants and seven rare species of animals. **Highlights:** Arguably the most spectacular section in this chapter of the book. Marvelous views in all directions; varied scenery; rocky-summit communities of pitch pine, oak, and heath; chestnut oak forest; cliffs; and crevices are just some of the things that make this a very rewarding hike. It also sees few visitors, so solitude and viewing wildlife may be other benefits. **Downside:** Have to spot cars at both ends in order to hike the whole thing. Also, this strenuous hike is not everyone's cup of tea. **Difficulties and hazards:** Rough trail on rocks, with steep inclines in places. Beware dangerous cliffs and crevices in certain spots. The trail's isolation means that discovery and rescue may be prolonged should you be alone and get into trouble.

To get to the beginning from Summitville, go east on Summitville–Roosa Gap Road as it climbs 1.3 miles up the ridge. The road starts out paved but is dirt and gravel for much of the way. It is also quite steep. Most cars, however, should have no problem. The Long Path crosses the road 0.7 mile before the top. This crossing is poorly marked; finding it is one of the bigger challenges of the hike. Just before the crossing, there's parking along both sides of the road, with room enough for several cars.

After crossing the road, the turquoise-marked trail veers right and climbs steeply through the forest on rocks. Chestnut oaks and red oaks predominate in this forest. You'll soon arrive at an opening with a view southwest of the Wurtsboro Ridge, the valley of the Neversink, the Basha Kill wetland, and the Wurtsboro Airport. Just beyond, a second opening provides a rare southeast-facing view through the Roosa Gap, with the mostly flat profile of Schunemunk Mountain in the distance. Half a mile after crossing the road, the trail arrives in an open area dominated by scrub oak with pitch pine, blueberries, and huckleberries. The north and south views are magnificent. In the distance, the monument at High Point State Park in New Jersey can be seen on clear days. The Catskills are visible to the north. From here, the trail levels and runs parallel to the ridgeline, about 100 feet below the top of the ridge with intermittent openings through the taller shrubs with views looking west. The 47-foot-high Roosa Gap Fire Tower appears on the top of the ridge to the right, mostly obscured. It began operating in 1948, providing an excellent view of the ridge south of the High Point Tower. In 1971, the DEC closed the tower. Today, it is leased by the Sullivan County Department of Public Works, which uses it as a base for radio antennae facilitating emergency and police communication.

A mile from Roosa Gap Road, the trail bends to the right and climbs on top of the ridge. It then turns left and continues north. Pass a memorial to John Hennessey (1931–96), a volunteer builder and maintainer of the Shawangunk Ridge Trail. Continue over slanting slabs of conglomerate. Enter a woodland of stunted oak trees. Arrive at a dirt road and veer left. The marked trail soon departs from the road on the right, following the top of the ridge through a grove of pitch pine trees. Slowly ascend for a brief while, then begin a short, gradual descent, crossing open bedrock marked with a cairn. The trail remains fairly level, continuing through fields of scrub oak, pitch pine, chestnut oak, and huckleberries. There are partial views on the left of the southern and western parts of the Catskills Range.

After another brief ascent into pitch pine barrens, the trail bends to the right. From the top, the trail bends left and right. Enter a woodland of chestnut oaks and gray birch. The trail turns left and soon departs from the woodland. Then it veers right. There's a cairn on top of a glacial erratic and a view looking west and north of the Catskills. Continue through more stunted woodlands—trees generally less than 30 feet high. Depart the woodlands and enter scrub oak thickets once again. There are more views on the left. Ascend briefly, veering to the right. There are fine open views among fields of shrubs no more than waist high. Sam's Point becomes visible ahead, and you attain a sense of northward progress. Continue to a Y-intersection and veer left. There's another, better view looking north toward Sam's Point that also takes in the towers by Maratanza Lake and Gertrude's Nose. The Catskills are visible to the north and west, including Slide Mountain and many others.

Continue through waist- or knee-high shrubs, with nearly uninterrupted glorious views in front of you. The trail veers left, and soon you arrive at another area of open beds of slanting conglomerate rock with views looking west, north, and south. The trail veers to the right and ascends briefly. There are west- and north-facing views of the Catskills and the Rondout Valley below. Pass a large erratic by the side of trail with a cairn on top. Excitement builds as you reach another excellent vista looking north to Sam's Point, the Maratanza towers, Gertrude's Nose, the Wallkill Valley, and the Catskill high peaks. Cross a shallow, forested ravine and then return to scrub oak thickets. The trail veers left and then right, with nearly uninterrupted north-facing views. The trail meanders then veers left and slowly descends, passing a view on the left of the Rondout Valley below. Descend once more into woodlands, dominated by chestnut oaks, red oaks, and mountain laurel. The trail bends right and left, continuing to descend, then turns right and briefly levels as it enters state land managed by the DEC. The turquoise blazes change to blue discs.

The trail descends through a steep notch in rock and enters a shallow forest ravine. Turn right. There are small cliffs on the right, some with overhangs. Cross a stone fence with a cairn and continue through a talus field at the base of the cliffs. The trail ascends to the base of the cliffs, turns left, and gently descends a forested slope to the bottom of the ravine. It then climbs the opposite slope to the right of a stone wall. The trail levels amid a mixed forest of beech, maple, oak, birch, pitch pine, and hickory. Striped maple is the predominant shrub. Stone walls crisscross the area. The trail crosses an old dirt road. A right turn here leads 0.6 mile to a point on Cox Road 1.2 miles south of Route 52, another possible entry point. The trail then makes a gradual ascent, crossing a stone wall along the way, then veers right and continues level to the right of the ridgeline, finally leaving the older DEC property. Turquoise blazes replace the blue discs. You've now entered the Lands and Forests Tract, which has recently been transferred to the DEC, though at this point the markers remain turquoise blazes.

Pass a mountain laurel thicket on the left. The trail begins climbing again to the top of the ridge. It passes through an open area of scrub oak, chestnut oak, pitch pine, sheep laurel, and berries, with a partial view looking west. The trail continues through sparse oak forest to the right of the ridgeline. There are steep east-facing cliffs on the right. Veer left again to the top of the ridge through an open area with wondrous views facing west, silhouetted by tall pitch pine trees. The trail veers right and follows the top of an east-facing cliff, then veers left and climbs back to the top of the ridge. Cross areas of bare bedrock with fine west- and north-facing views. Pass a number of glacial erratics along the trail. Bend left and descend. Turn right and continue level through scrub oak, pitch pine, and berries. Pass forest on the right and a small narrow crevice. Ascend gradually to the top of the ridge once more.

Pass cliffs on the right with rock walls separated from the main cliff by wide crevices. There's a view into a slanting crevice on the right. Encounter a superb east-facing view looking out upon the Wallkill Valley. The distant cluster of large buildings is Watchtower Farm, a headquarters of the Jehovah's Witnesses. Two immense rock pinnacles are encountered on the right, both separated from the main cliff with a fine east-facing view behind them. When late-day light shines on these pale rocks, it's definitely a camera moment; or just take your time and savor this delightful vista.

More cliffs and talus are encountered on the right. The Long Path veers left back to the top of the ridge, with partial views looking west and north. From the top of a rock, you'll encounter an open view of sparkling white cliffs in the Bear Hill Preserve (see the previous chapter), as well as private residences in the community of Cragsmoor. The trail veers left and descends, entering an area of steeply slanted slabs of conglomerate and sparse vegetation dominated by pitch pine, blueberries, and huckleberries, very reminiscent of ridgetop areas in the northern Shawangunks. There are fine open views looking north and west to the Catskills Range and Rondout Valley. Descend some distance on one large, tilted slab. The trail veers right (north) again. The cliffs of the Bear Hill Preserve appear straight ahead.

Descend and enter the forest once again. There's a brief opening with a view looking north toward the Catskills Range. The trail continues to descend, gradually at first, then more steeply. Continue the long, steady descent. There's an open view on the left of the Rondout Valley and Catskills Range silhouetted by tall pitch pines. Cross more steeply slanted slabs of conglomerate and then enter a more mixed forest of oaks. Cross a gravel road. The trail continues mostly level through a partially open area of grasses and young, thin-trunked trees. The trail crosses another small spine of ridge, with west-facing views and numerous pitch pines and berries. Then it veers left and descends once more.

Cross a rocky stream in a deep ravine shaded by hemlocks. Climb a steep old road and then cross the gravel road once again. Continue straight up a rocky slope. Veer left and cross a small seasonal stream. Ascend another small ridge with sparse forest, a thick shrub layer of berries, and partial views facing west. Bend right and cross more slanting slabs of conglomerate. Pass a register box on the left and descend a short distance to Route 52. A left turn here leads to a vista and parking area in less than 0.1 mile.

To continue on the Long Path, follow Route 52 north for 0.5 mile. The Long Path then leaves the highway and reenters the forest. A steep 0.5-mile climb leads to the Bear Hill Preserve, covered in the last chapter.

THE NEIGHBORING
VALLEYS

8

While the Shawangunk Ridge has much to entice, focusing solely on it leaves out an important part of the experience. The valley of the Wallkill located east of the ridge, and the valleys of the Rondout and Neversink to its west, provide a lot in terms of experience and places. Your perspective of the ridge will be incomplete unless you view it from below or from some distance away. Also, to better understand and appreciate the Shawangunk Ridge, it is necessary to study its relationship with and connection to the surrounding lowlands. Besides wonderful scenery and rich habitats, the neighboring valleys abound in historical sites, and local communities offer shopping, dining, accommodations, entertainment, special events, and other attractions. For hikers, mountain bicyclists, and cross-country skiers, a number of trails provide excellent opportunities to experience the valleys' charms.

Geologically and physically, the valleys that flank the Shawangunk Ridge are distinctly different. The Rondout and Neversink Valleys form the 50-mile long valley west and north of the ridge from Stone Ridge to Port Jervis. Shales and sandstones from the Middle Devonian Hamilton Group underlie the floor of the valley from Ellenville south. North of Ellenville, Lower and Middle Devonian limestones of the Helderberg and Onondaga Groups form the base of the valley. These rocks of the valley are softer and more erodible than the hard Shawangunk conglomerate that forms the top of the ridge. The floor of the valley is filled with glacial outwash and relatively flat, especially from Ellenville south. East of Ellenville, the Shawangunk Ridge rises 1,800 feet from the valley floor to its highest point.

Between Wurtsboro and Ellenville, there is a high point where the valley constricts. North of this point, water flows into streams that in turn drain into 66-mile-long Rondout Creek, whose point of origin is high in the Catskills near Peekamoose Mountain. Rondout Creek flows north and east, eventually draining into the Hudson River at Kingston. South of the divide, water flows into streams that drain into the 69-mile-long Neversink River. The Neversink, whose

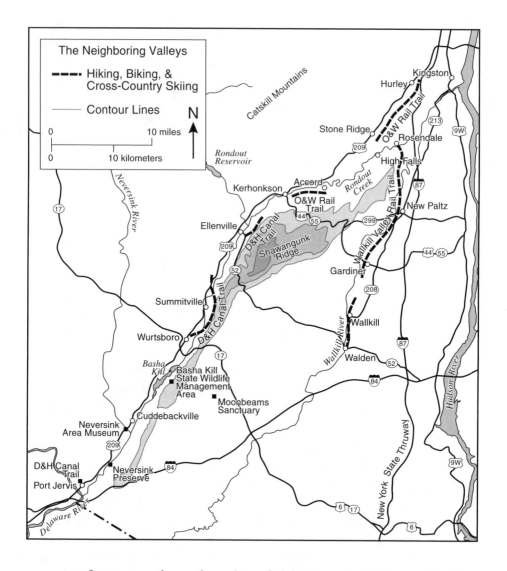

point of origin is on the southern slope of Slide Mountain (highest peak in the Catskills), continues southwest, emptying into the Delaware River at Port Jervis. Important communities in this valley include Rosendale, High Falls, Stone Ridge, Kerhonkson, Ellenville, Wurtsboro, and Port Jervis.

According to some historical accounts, the valleys west of the Shawangunks were crossed by a road built by the Dutch as early as the mid–17th century. Called Old Mine Road, it was used to transport copper ore from a mine in New Jersey north to Kingston. It is reputed to have been the first 100-mile-long road in America. The road was soon abandoned; not a trace remains. In 1828, the D&H Canal following the valley north of Port Jervis was completed. The canal brought commerce and industry to the valleys, and communities along it experienced large increases in population and commercial activity. The canal was unable to compete with the railroads, however, and it eventually closed in 1898. Today, 35 miles of the historical canal route in Ulster County between Kingston and Ellenville have been designated the D&H Canal Heritage Corridor. Remnants of the D&H Canal were designated a National Historic Landmark by the National Park Service in 1968. The corridor also includes the abandoned rail line of the New York, Ontario & Western Railroad and scenic Rondout Creek. It offers a number of hiking, biking, and cross-country-skiing opportunities on old canal towpaths and abandoned railbeds as well as scenery, wild habitats, and historical landmarks.

The Wallkill Valley lies east and south of the ridge. It is approximately 65 miles long and 20 miles wide, much broader than the valleys west of the ridge. It is bordered on the south by the New Jersey Highlands and on the east by the Marlboro Hills. Relatively soft and easily erodable Ordovician age shales from the Martinsburg and the older Austin Glen Formations underlie this large lowland area. These rocks are even more ancient than Shawangunk conglomerate or those of the valleys west of the ridge. What we see today is largely the result of ice age glaciers that gouged and depressed the land, leaving behind a thick layer of sediment. It is drained primarily by the 88-mile-long Wallkill River and its many tributaries. The Wallkill originates in the Highlands of New Jersey and flows north and east—one of the few rivers in the eastern United States to flow northward. It eventually joins the Rondout just a few miles west of the Hudson near Kingston. Its many tributaries include a number of streams that flow east from the Shawangunk Ridge and into the Wallkill. Communities in the Wallkill Valley include New Paltz, Gardiner, and Wallkill. The 15-mile-long Wallkill Valley Rail Trail offers hiking, biking, and cross-country skiing as well as scenic vistas, varied habitats, and historical landmarks. Two nonprofit organizations, the Wallkill Valley Land Trust and the Orange County Land Trust, protect the valley's unique habitats, viewsheds, and agricultural land from sprawl development.

ROSENDALE AND HIGH FALLS

These two small communities located on Rondout Creek north and west of the Shawangunk Ridge are both largely the product of the D&H Canal and the natural cement industry. Rosendale is located along Route 213 west of Route 32, 6 miles north of the village of New Paltz. High Falls is 2 miles west of Rosendale on Route 213.

Rosendale

The village of Rosendale was an important shipping center on the D&H Canal and the headquarters of the once thriving natural cement industry. The town's

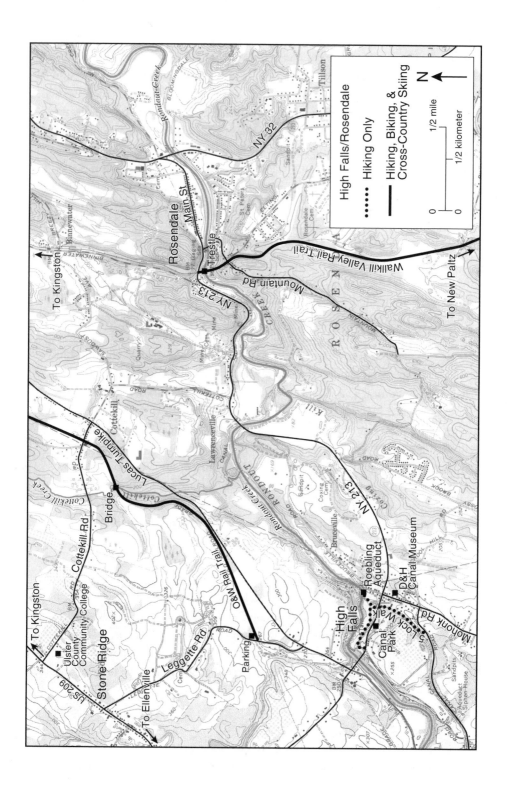

High Falls/Rosendale

······· Hiking Only

——— Hiking, Biking, &
Cross-Country Skiing

N

1/2 mile

1/2 kilometer

0

0

main street has a wonderful assortment of homes and buildings that date back to this period. Remnants of the D&H Canal, plus ruins of old cement kilns and abandoned cement mines, are found in this area. The Wallkill Valley Railroad Viaduct towers over the village, an impressive monument to the railroad age. Rosendale offers shopping for antiques and crafts, cafés, nighttime musical entertainment, and one of the last remaining family-owned small discount movie theaters in the Hudson Valley. North of town is Williams Lake, an old resort active since 1925 which offers 600 acres of woodlands, a 42-acre lake, and easy hiking, biking, and cross-country skiing trails. Call 1-800-382-3818 or visit www.willy-lake.com. Table Rock Tours at 292 Main Street is a bicycle shop and hiking, biking, and climbing guide service for the Shawangunk Ridge. The 15-mile-long Wallkill Valley Rail Trail (see below) can be accessed from Mountain Road.

The Rosendale area was first settled by Jacob Rutsen (1650–1730). He was born in Albany and moved in 1677 to Kingston, where he became a successful merchant. Later he served in the militia and was promoted to a colonel. In 1680, he purchased 960 acres along the Rondout between the Coxing Kill and Lefevre Falls. He leased this property to Direk Keyer in return for the construction of a stone house and barn. In 1685, Rutsen expanded his purchase, and in 1700 he moved to his new property, later increasing the size of the home.

The area remained thinly settled and primarily agricultural until the D&H Canal was completed in 1828. Prior to this, there were only two residences in the town. With the advent of the canal, things changed rapidly. In addition to the new transport route, the discovery of natural cement in the area was a primary impetus for the town to grow and prosper. In 1825, during the construction of the canal, blasting on the property of Jacob Snyder uncovered rock that was first thought to be limestone. The workers took their find to a local blacksmith in High Falls. After the rock was crushed and burned and water poured over it, it was found to harden. The workers had discovered the single largest natural cement deposit in the United States—32 square miles of it between High Falls and Kingston that included Rosendale and a number of other small communities. This cement was used in the building of locks and other structures for the canal. The village and town were formally incorporated in 1844, the result of lands ceded by the state from neighboring towns so the booming cement industry would be under the authority of a single municipality.

At first the cement was quarried, but eventually deep mines were dug. Kerosene lamps provided light, and stone pillars held up the vast ceilings. A number of local gristmills were converted to use by the cement industry, and millstones that formerly ground grain into flour were used to grind the cement. At its peak, during the second half of the 19th century, the cement business involved the operation of at least 19 large companies and several smaller ventures, employing 4,000 to 5,000 workers. Four million barrels of cement were produced and shipped yearly, most of it via the D&H Canal. This represented nearly 50 percent of the total production of natural cement in the United States. Rosendale natural cement was used in the construction of the Brooklyn Bridge, the pedestal for the Statue of Liberty, the Washington Monument, wings of the U.S. Capitol, the Croton Aqueduct, Grand Central Terminal, and many other projects. By 1872, Rosendale had a population of 550, three churches, two hotels, and a number of specialty shops.

In 1875, Portland cement was first developed, and by 1895 a million barrels a year were being produced. Portland cement takes only seven days to reach 65 to 75 percent of its full strength. Natural cement takes far longer, reaching only one-eighth of its full strength in the same amount of time. Thus Portland cement gradually replaced natural cement. The production of natural cement declined from 8.5 million barrels in 1900 to only 1 million by 1910. Many of the Rosendale area's mines and plants closed; by 1920, only the Andrew J. Snyder plant remained open. Some mines have seen further use for mushroom farming, as bomb shelters, and for storing records and other goods. The closing of the canal in 1910 and the demise of the natural cement industry led to the economic collapse of the town. The population dropped from 6,278 in 1900 to 1,959 in 1920. Some local families supported themselves taking in boarders as much of the area struggled to survive by turning to tourism. A devastating fire in 1895 destroyed many of the buildings on the north side of Main Street.

The recent prosperity of the region has benefitted Rosendale, which has seen its Main Street become gentrified while also maintaining some of its low-key 19th-century charm.

High Falls

This tiny, compact community features the most extensive and best-preserved remnants of the D&H Canal as well as many restored homes and buildings from the canal period and prior. The center of town is a designated Historic District listed on the National Register of Historic Places. Today, High Falls boasts a fine assortment of antiques and upscale crafts shops, restaurants, and cafés. There are bed & breakfast and other accommodations in the local area. Highlights of this town include the D&H Canal Museum, Roebling Aqueduct, Five Locks Walk, and Rondout Creek, which has noteworthy scenery as well as sites of geologic and historical interest. The O&W Rail Trail, which offers hiking, mountain biking, and cross-country skiing, is located just north of the town (see below).

High Falls was called Great Falls by the early European settlers. In 1679, Frederick Hussey purchased 50 acres of land in the vicinity. In 1776, Jacob Hasbrouk settled in the area. In 1783 he built a gristmill to harness the water-

The ruins of Canal Lock #16 on the Delaware & Hudson Canal at High Falls

power generated by the falls. By 1796, two more mills flanked the lower falls. These powered machines for washing and felting wool as well as for grinding grain. High Falls remained a tiny, primarily agricultural community until 1827, when the construction and opening of the D&H Canal caused the town to sprout up almost overnight. In addition to the canal, the discovery of natural cement nearby also became a basis for the local economy, and many earlier gristmills were converted to use as cement plants. Besides cement, coopers (barrel makers), dye works, and leather tanneries all used the power of Rondout Creek falls. Raw materials often came from the neighboring Shawangunk Ridge. The canal was used to ship cement, locally quarried bluestone and millstones, timber, manufactured goods, and farm products.

John Burroughs, the famed poet-naturalist, resided here in 1857 and served as schoolmaster. It was during his brief stay that he married his wife, Ursula, who lived in Olivebridge. By 1872, High Falls had a population of 400, two churches, two hotels, two meat markets, a gristmill, and a number of cement plants. The town was very dependent on the canal; when it closed in 1899, the town lost approximately half its population over the next 30 years. The growing popularity of the Shawangunk Ridge since the 1970s has led to a return of population and considerable gentrification in the area. The community now very much caters to tourists and upper-class local residents.

Historical Sites and Walking Trails

The D&H Canal Museum

This Gothic-style building was once the chapel of St. John's Episcopal Church. It was completed in 1885 on property owned by the D&H Canal Company, which quarried limestone there. Today, the museum is owned and operated by the D&H Canal Historical Society, a nonprofit organization. A registered Ulster County landmark (1969), it received congressional recognition in 1977, two years after the D&H Canal Historical Society purchased the building for its museum. The museum features artifacts, maps, historical photographs, and other memorabilia telling the fascinating story of the history of the D&H Canal. Some of the noteworthy exhibits include a working model of Lock #16, scale models of the Roebling Aqueduct Bridge in High Falls, canal barges, and the gravity railroad that brought anthracite coal to the canal. There is also a diorama of a typical canal boat cabin (rustic furnishings include bunk beds and a tin bathtub) and a replica of a telegraph office featuring the original desk. A beautiful watercolor by William Ricarby Miller shows High Falls during the height of the canal period; there's also a full-sized oil painting of New York governor De Witt Clinton holding the D&H Canal Company charter. The museum is located on Mohonk Road, one block south of the village center. It is open 11 AM–5 PM, Thursday through Monday (on Sunday it opens at 1 PM), May 30 through Labor Day. In September and October, it is open weekends only (Saturday 11–5, Sunday 1–5). There is a small admission fee.

Five Locks Walk

Length: 0.2 mile. **Markings:** A sign at one end. **General description:** Owned and maintained by the D&H Canal Historical Society, this short trail follows a section of the D&H Canal towpath through High Falls from Route 213 to Depuy Road. The five canal locks that can be viewed from this trail are a designated National Historic Landmark. Brochure guides with maps are available from the D&H Canal Museum. **Highlights:** A very pleasant, easy-to-walk, simple-to-follow trail. Ruins of canal locks and other historical landmarks are the primary draw. These include the best-preserved locks along the D&H Canal. **Downside:** There's so much to see, you wish it went on longer. **Difficulties and hazards:** There are no guardrails along the tops of the locks, so use caution and don't get too close to the edge. There are plans to improve the trail to make it more accessible to seniors as well as remove debris from the locks and channel.

Due to the popularity of the D&H Canal and the resulting congestion, between 1847 and 1852, the canal was enlarged to accommodate new 140-ton barges. The section of the canal through High Falls was rerouted through town to provide a more direct route, with fewer of the turns that the new bigger boats would have difficulty negotiating. The new section included five locks, one right after another, which collectively raised or lowered barges a total of 73 feet. Construction was accomplished with great difficulty due to a riot by Irish laborers and wetter-than-average weather that turned the soil into quicksand. The improvements ended up costing almost twice as much as expected. Once the new section of canal was operating, the old section was abandoned, though ruins of it are still visible (see below).

The trail starts to the left of the Depuy Canal House off Route 213. The Canal House was built in 1797 as a tavern. With the construction and completion of the D&H Canal in 1827, it was expanded to serve workers and travelers on the canal. Indentations made by ropes used to tow the canal barges can still be seen on the cornerstone of the building. Today, the Depuy Canal House is an upscale restaurant.

Canal Lock #16 is located to the left of the beginning of the trail. It is the finest preserved of all of the D&H Canal locks and is made of locally quarried, precision-cut Shawangunk conglomerate. The blocks fit so tightly together that no mortar was required in the construction. There's a working replica of this lock on display in the D&H Canal Museum (see above). The trail climbs steps to the right of the lock. Notice the indented section of wall on both sides of the lock that the doors would have folded into. Larger canal boats fit rather snugly into these locks—often with only inches to spare—requiring great skill on the part of locktenders who walked boats through the locks. Also notice the stone snubbing posts used for tying mules, and the metalwork embedded in the caprock that lines the top of the lock walls.

Just past Lock #16 are the remains of a loading slip used to load cement and locally quarried bluestone onto barges. The trail skirts this section, though there are plans to build a bridge over the entrance to the slip, which would allow the trail to follow the towpath more directly. Just beyond the loading slip and to the left of the trail lies a waste weir, a ditch partially covered with bluestone slabs. It was used to drain excess water from the lock. As you continue, notice the rough-hewn stone on the left lining the canal's retaining wall. Lock #17, on the left, is in the poorest condition of the five locks. Tree roots and erosion have damaged the lock walls. Plans are to maintain this lock in a dilapidated state to contrast it with the locks that have been restored.

At Lock #18, you can compare the rough-hewn stones that line the channel with the precision-cut stones lining the lock. All four snubbing posts are still present at this lock. The metalwork embedded in the capstone is also preserved. Lock #19 features a wooden bridge built by a local Boy Scout troop. It is located where the lock's gear house would have been. The gear house is where the machines that operated the doors to the lock were situated. From the bridge, there's a fine view looking down into the lock as well as of the whole section of the canal above and below the lock. From the opposite side of the bridge, a trail continues uphill for a short distance to Canal Road, where a small parking area is planned.

From the end of Lock #19, you can observe an underground waste weir. South of Lock #19, the canal cuts through solid bedrock. Holes drilled in the bedrock, still visible, were used to insert explosives that blasted out the channel. Planting and lighting these explosives was a dangerous job; a number of workers were injured or killed. Just below Lock #20 on the left are stones quarried from the channel. To save time, effort, and money, canal builders would often leave stones like these instead of carting them away. Above the canal on the left is a white residence built in 1848 to house the locktender. Locktenders walked boats through the locks, operated the machinery, and maintained the locks. During the shipping season, they were on call 24/7. Naturally, they had to live close by, so their homes were supplied by the canal company on company-owned land. Just below the house are the foundation ruins of a general store; to the right of the trail are the foundation ruins of the store's warehouse. Enterprising locktenders could make extra money operating businesses like this that served workers and travelers on the canal.

Just past Lock #20, the trail bends to the left and crosses another waste weir. Just beyond are stone abutments of a former bridge where the towpath crossed the canal. If you continue straight for a short distance, you'll reach Depuy Road. You can return the same way you came or turn left here and continue to the D&H Canal Museum.

Though they're not officially part of the Five Locks Walk, the canal ruins north of Route 213 are well worth visiting. These include remains of the old 1826 canal and the stone abutments of the Roebling suspension aqueduct that carried the canal over Rondout Creek. On the north side of Route 213, opposite the Depuy Canal House, next to the old canal channel filled with water, the remains of Lock #15 can be observed from a wooden platform on the side of the road. To the left of the pool is a locktender's cottage built in 1865. Affiliated with the Depuy Canal House (see above), it now serves as a bed & breakfast.

From the parking lot of the B&B, a trail follows the original old canal channel constructed in 1826 and abandoned in 1847 when the new section of the canal was completed. On the right, the rough-hewn stones that lined the retaining wall are in remarkably good condition. Above on the right was the new canal's towpath; on the top of the rise is the old telegraph office, currently in a dilapidated state. This is the same one that is replicated in the D&H Canal Museum.

Just beyond on the right is where the old and the new channel merged. A stone pillar on the right was the abutment from a bridge that once crossed the canal here. A trail on the right climbs up to the stone abutment for the Roebling Aqueduct—a timber trough used to carry the canal over Rondout Creek. The trough was supported by a revolutionary system of steel-wire suspension cables. The iron anchors for the cables are still visible. Three other similar suspension aqueducts were used on the D&H Canal, including one that spanned the Neversink, described below. The aqueduct designer, John Roebling, later went on to use a version of the suspension cable design in the construction of the Brooklyn Bridge, perhaps the finest engineering feat of the 19th century. From the abutment, there's a dramatic view of Rondout Creek below as well as the abutment on the opposite shore. The aqueduct itself, unfortunately, was destroyed by fire in 1917. Below and to the left of the aqueduct is the abutment for an earlier stone arch aqueduct designed by John B. Jervis that the new suspension aqueduct replaced. Ironically, the stone aqueduct—though never used once the newer aqueduct was complete—actually lasted much longer than its partner. It was finally demolished in 1956 by Central Hudson as an eyesore. The area below the abutments is a popular, though very dangerous and illegal swimming area where a number of drowning deaths have occurred. Unfortunately, there often is a lot of refuse present.

High Falls Hydroelectric Facility and Historic Site

Length: 0.3 mile. **Markings:** Signs. **General description:** This park and trail along Rondout Creek provide access to views of the creek, two waterfalls, as well as historical sites and areas of geologic interest. The trail starts 0.2 mile west of the Depuy Canal House off Route 213, follows Rondout Creek, and ends on Route 213 opposite the Canal House. The pathway is relatively easy, and there are benches and interpretive signs. It connects with the Five Locks Walk; it's well worth doing the two walks together. The facility is owned and maintained by the High Falls Civic Association and the Central Hudson Gas and Electrical Company. It is open from dawn to dusk. **Highlights:** The waterfalls and cement industry ruins. **Downside:** The hydroelectric plant. **Difficulties and hazards:** Swimming in the creek is illegal and dangerous. There have been drowning deaths.

From the parking area off Route 213, there are benches, views of the upper falls on the left, and an interpretive sign explaining local history. You'll also find a boat ramp and canoe portage to get around the falls. A passage through a chain-link fence provides access to the trail. The trail turns right and downhill past an outcrop of Upper Silurian age Binnewater sandstone on the right. A fairly continuous sequence of Middle to Upper Silurian rock formations are exposed along this section of Rondout Creek. The rock underlying the falls is dolostone of the Rondout Formation—the area's primary source of natural cement. On the left are ruins of the F. O. Norton Cement Mill, one of the largest of the area's cement companies. Just beyond the ruins on the left, you'll find a bench, a millstone, and an informal path that leads to an open view of the upper falls. Waterpower from the falls fueled a number of local industries, including cement plants, and is still used today to generate electricity.

The road levels. On the left is the Central Hudson generating plant; just beyond it on the left are the lower falls, which are not as tall as the upper ones. A view looking downstream takes in the stone abutments that once supported aqueducts carrying the D&H Canal over the Rondout.

The trail passes through another chain-link fence. You'll pass underneath some power lines; just beyond them, a trail on the left leads up to the top of the old stone abutments as well as other remnants of the D&H Canal. These are described above. The trail bends to the right and continues uphill, eventually reaching the parking lot for the Locktender's Cottage, a bed & breakfast. You are now facing Route 213 opposite the Depuy Canal House. Return the way you came or continue across the road on the Five Locks Walk (see above).

Other Historical Sites in High Falls

In addition to those already mentioned, a number of other sites dating back to the canal period and before are worth checking out. Canal Park, located between Route 213 and Old Route 213, just west of the Depuy Canal House, has the remains of Locks #17 and #18, which were part of the original 1826 canal that was abandoned in 1847. Both are in a rather dilapidated condition. Viewing them may help you appreciate how much smaller the older canal was before it was enlarged.

The Towpath House, located on the west side of block-long Firehouse Road, was originally a farmhouse built in 1787. During the period of the canal, the bottom level was used to stable mules that pulled the canal barges. Canal workers often stayed in rooms upstairs. Today, it's a gift shop. Across the street is the Hasbrouk Store, originally built in 1850 by the D&H Canal Company as a feed and grain store. Now the shop sells antiques. On the south side of Route 213, just east of town, is the Elmendorf House, an impressive example of Greek Revival architecture built in 1849. With its tall white columns, it looks like a southern plantation home. It is a private residence.

O&W RAIL TRAIL

There are currently three segments of rail-trail here: a 2.1-mile segment from Kingston to Hurley, a 4.1-mile section from Hurley to Marbletown, and a 3.5-mile segment from Accord to Kerhonkson. The rail-trail segments follow the old bed of the Ontario & Western Railroad, which operated from 1902 to 1957. They're part of the D&H Canal Heritage Corridor. The old railbeds are open for public use and are suitable for hiking, mountain biking, and cross-country skiing.

The O&W began as the New York & Oswego Midland Railroad, the vision of New York politician Dewitt C. Littlejohn. It was planned as a direct route across New York State, serving areas that didn't have rail service. In 1868, construction on the "Midland," as it was popularly called, began. By 1871, a branch to Ellenville was completed; later that same year, the 3,857-foot Highview Tunnel through the Shawangunk Ridge opened, providing a more direct east–west route. Construction costs on this railroad proved to be higher than expected, and within a month of completion the Midland went bankrupt. It was reorganized in 1880 as the New York, Ontario & Western Railroad. Hauling coal and perishable farm goods, especially dairy products, was the prime focus of this railroad. Carrying tourists to the resort areas of the Catskills and Shawangunks was also a major part. To increase ridership, the railroad was heavily involved in promoting these areas as tourist destinations.

By 1898, the D&H Canal was closing and a new branch of the O&W from Ellenville to Kingston was proposed to take the place of the canal for hauling Pennsylvania coal. In 1901, the O&W purchased the Cornell Steam Company and a 25-mile segment of the D&H Canal between Ellenville and Algierville. On June 28, 1901, the construction contract was awarded to the J. M. Jackson Company, employing 45 workers. The new rail line was completed on October 24, 1902. Much of it ran closely parallel to or literally on top of the old canal. Economic decline in the region served by the railroad, competition from automobiles, and a decrease in coal traffic hurt the O&W's business. Eventually it came to be called the "Old and Weary." In February 1937, the O&W Railroad defaulted on its financial obligations and entered a period of voluntary bankruptcy from which it would never emerge. It finally ceased operating in 1957.

O&W Rail Trail—Kingston to Hurley

Length: 2.1 miles. **Markings:** A sign at the beginning. **General description:** This section of the rail-trail starts from the parking lot of the Super 8 Motel off Washington Avenue in Kingston, just east of the traffic circle. It ends on Route 209 just north of the village of Hurley. **Highlights:** Old fields and wetlands with colorful flowers such as purple loosestrife, goldenrod, and Queen Anne's lace. The historic 17th- and 18th-century village of Hurley is a worthwhile detour. **Downside:** Power lines and an electrical generating plant mar the view. **Difficulties and hazards:** This section of trail, especially the first 0.7-mile segment, is very much a work in progress; parts may be fairly rough and overgrown. If you're biking, it may be necessary to walk your bike at times.

Start from the back of the parking lot of the Super 8 Motel. There's a sign-board next to the trailhead. Follow the trail to the right of power lines as it passes a pair of artificial ponds on the left, populated with common reeds (phragmites) and loosestrife. Cross a bump and pass through a concrete tunnel underneath the New York State Thruway. Then cross a makeshift bridge and reach an unnamed road. Cross this road and follow the left side of a grass field to the corner of the field. The trail bends sharply to the left and right, becomes wider, and continues to the right of the power lines.

Cross a wooden bridge and pass an 18th-century stone farmhouse on the left. Cross a second wooden bridge and then pass underneath power lines and a power station on the left. The trail continues underneath power lines. There's a floodplain forest on the right next to Esopus Creek. Pass a house on the left and cross a dirt road. Continue to the right of the power lines. Pass fields of loosestrife on the left and a tunnel on the right underneath Route 209. The trail bends left and right and continues to the left of the power lines, passing another huge loosestrife field on the left. The trail finally bends to the right and comes out on Route 209 right across from a cornfield. Follow Route 209 for 1.7 miles to the next section of trail. On the way, pass through the historic village of Hurley. It's hoped that eventually a paved walkway will follow this section of the rail-trail that runs parallel to Route 209.

Hurley was founded in 1662 by Dutch settlers and Huguenots as Nieuw Dorp, a fortified satellite of their main settlement, Wiltwyck (later renamed Kingston). It was attacked and burned by Esopus Natives in 1663. In 1669, it was rebuilt and renamed Hurley. In 1777, during the Revolutionary War, Hurley briefly served as the capital of New York State after Kingston was burned by the British.

Stone architecture was very popular among the Dutch and Huguenot settlers, and all of the older residences in the village are of stone. In fact, Hurley contains the largest concentration of original 17th- and 18th-century stone residences in America. Most are privately owned. The Hurley Heritage Society Museum is located in the Elmendorf House on Main Street. It has historical exhibits and free brochures for walking tours of the town. It is open on Saturday 10 AM–4 PM and Sunday 1–4 PM from May through October. For information, call 845-338-1661. There is an annual Hurley Stone House day on the second Saturday in July when a number of the stone houses are open to the public. There are tours, demonstrations, period costumes, refreshments, and crafts sales. For information, call 845-331-4121.

O&W Rail Trail—Hurley to Marbleton

Length: 4.1 miles. **Markings:** Signs at both ends and at some intersections; mileage markers. **General description:** This section of the rail-trail starts off Route 209, 1.4 miles south of the village of Hurley. It ends at Leggett Road about 1 mile north of the village of High Falls and 1.2 miles from Stone Ridge. There is also access from Marcott Road off Route 209. This segment of rail-trail was built and funded by the 1986 Environmental Bond Act. It is in excellent shape for hiking, biking, horseback riding, and cross-country skiing and appears to be well maintained. **Highlights:** Forest, fields, and wetlands. Numerous cardinal flowers are a late-summer delight. The village of Stone Ridge is a worthwhile detour. **Downside:** Plenty of mosquitoes in summer. **Difficulties and hazards:** A steep descent before crossing the Cottekill and a steep climb after.

Turn off Route 209 onto the dirt entrance road, passing through the parking area, past a signboard on the left, and through the open gate. Pass a swamp on the left and enter the forest. By now you've noticed how easy and wonderfully well maintained this segment is compared to the last. Cross two wooden bridges through a forested wetland area, pass a 0.25-mile marker on the left, and then pass a house on the right. A 0.5-mile marker appears on the left. There's a steep slope on the right with many hemlocks.

The 1-mile marker is reached. Pass limestone cuts on the left side of the trail. There's a partial view on the right through the trees facing west of fields and the Catskill peaks in the distance. Pass the 1.5-mile marker on the right, then a wetland area—also on the right—featuring the upright trunks of dead trees, common reeds, and purple loosestrife. Pass the 2-mile marker on the right. There's a hitching post and wooden bench on the left, perfect for resting. Continue past the 2.5-mile marker on the right. Just beyond, also on the right, is a drainage ditch with brilliant red cardinal flowers in bloom from mid- to late summer. Pass through a dark hemlock tunnel and soon reach a small parking area, crossing paved Marcott Road. A right turn here will lead a short distance to Route 209.

Continue straight and soon cross another wooden bridge over a tiny stream. Pass houses on the left. The trail reaches a paved driveway and the back side of the Cottekill Volunteer Fire Station. Follow the driveway, passing the old train station on the right, now restored as a quaint private residence. You'll soon reach Cottekill Road. A right turn here on Cottekill Road will bring you 1.5 miles to the outskirts of the lovely historic hamlet of Stone Ridge, where a number of 18th-century stone residences line the main street. A left turn will bring you a short 0.1 mile to an intersection with Lucas Avenue, where there's a deli on the corner. To stay on the trail, turn right and make an immediate left onto the next section of trail. There's a sign.

Pass another loosestrife field on the right. An old stone abutment appears straight ahead. The trail makes a sharp right at the abutment and descends steeply to a new wooden bridge over the Cottekill; when it was completed in 1998, it opened up this whole section of trail for use. For safety, please walk your bike down this part. After crossing the bridge, the trail ascends to a second stone abutment on the left. It then levels and passes limestone cuts on both sides, some covered with emerald moss. A steep slope appears on the left and then Lucas Avenue below, gradually drawing closer to the trail. Pass a farmhouse and field on the right. Then cross a private driveway and another wooden bridge. A small parking area is soon reached; just beyond is Leggett Road, where this section of trail ends. A right turn on Leggett leads 1.2 miles to Stone Ridge; a left will bring you 0.4 mile to Lucas Avenue. A right turn on Lucas will take you 0.3 mile to the outskirts of High Falls. Please note that there are plans to extend the trail to Route 213 on the outskirts of High Falls.

O&W Rail Trail—Accord to Kerhonkson

Length: 3.5 miles. **Markings:** Signs at both ends. **General description:** This segment of the O&W Rail Trail follows the former rail line from the Town of Rochester Park in Accord to the hamlet of Kerhonkson. Kerhonkson is located right off Route 209, just north of its intersection with Route 44/55. This section also closely parallels the old route of the D&H Canal. In fact, the railbed covers the old canal channel and towpath in a number of places. It also closely parallels Rondout Creek for much of its length. Besides the access from either end, there is additional access from Berme Road at roughly the midway point. The trail, which is generally wide, flat, and smooth, is very suitable for hiking, mountain biking, equestrians, and cross-country skiing. You'll find basic facilities for picnicking, and access to Rondout Creek for fishing and nonmotorized boating. Motorized vehicles are not permitted. **Highlights:** There are beautiful views of the Rondout, field and forest scenery, and historical landmarks relating to the history of the canal and railroad. Great for solitude. **Downside:** Buggy in summer. You will have to backtrack or spot cars at either end. **Difficulties and hazards:** None. This is a very easy trail.

To get there, turn left (if you're going south; right if you're going north) onto Main Street in Accord. Accord is 6 miles south of the intersection of Routes 213 and 209, or 6.8 miles south of the hamlet of Stone Ridge. It has some crafts shops and at least one restaurant. There is also a bike shop—the Accord Bicycle Service—located on Route 209 (845-626-7214). Follow Main Street, which immediately crosses Rondout Creek. Right after the bridge, turn right on Scenic Road. If you continue straight, the Accord train station is on the left. During the canal period, Accord was known as Port Jackson and was the site of two rather extensive basins used for loading and unloading goods to and from boats on the canal. Follow Scenic Road for a short distance, turn right at the next intersection, and continue briefly to the Town of Rochester Park, where you'll find a playground, a small parking area, and a sign for the rail-trail to the left of the Highway Department. There's also an interpretative sign with a map and historical data about the railroad and canal.

Starting on the trail, you immediately enter the forest and pass through a section cut in limestone rock. This part of the old railbed was blasted to provide a more direct route for the rail line and avoid a sharp turn in the old canal channel called Fiddler's Elbow. The trail soon leaves the forest, passing fields on the right and left. The old D&H Canal and towpath soon appear on the right and join the old railbed. The rail-trail closely parallels the old canal channel for the rest of the way. After the canal closed, the railroad company purchased the section from Ellenville to Algierville and used parts of it as the bed for the new line. This segment of the D&H Canal was fairly level and had no locks. The rail-trail passes another field on the right; beyond is Rondout Creek, just out of view. A trail appears on the right. It detours to a picnic bench and a view overlooking the creek.

The rail-trail crosses Spring Brook, a tributary stream. There's a slope on the left, with the creek below on the right. There are continuous views of the creek for some distance, as well as access to the stream for fishing and boating on the right. Soon a second, smaller trail appears on the right running parallel to the rail-trail between it and the creek. After a short distance, it rejoins the rail-trail. Canoe access to Rondout Creek appears on the right. Just beyond lies another picnic bench, also on the right. A gravel road appears on the left with a small parking area. It leads to Berme Road, another access point.

The trail crosses a wooden bridge over Mountain Brook. On the left are old stone abutments for a small aqueduct where the canal once crossed the stream. Pass another field on the left. There are more views of Rondout Creek below on the right. Cross a second wooden bridge. There's a stone abutment on the right in a collapsed, very eroded condition. You'll soon pass a cornfield on the right and an alga-covered pond on the left, once part of the old canal channel, with its retaining wall of rough-cut stone. There are some old railroad ties in the trail here. Pass a private residence on the right and a small D&H Canal sign on the left. Enter a paved roadway. Pass a red barn on the right, then a fire station. There's plentiful parking here. This was also the site of former Lock #24, which then became the site for the railroad station. The hamlet of Kerhonkson was known as Middleport during the canal period. Today, the center of town offers little, but along Route 209 there's a grocery store, a pair of convenience stores, and a few restaurants. The Hudson Valley Resort, formerly the Granite Hotel, is located nearby.

ELLENVILLE

Situated in the narrow valley between the Catskills and the Shawangunk Ridge's highest elevations, the village of Ellenville enjoys a splendid setting. Historically it has been an important transportation, industrial, and tourist center. Today, the town boasts accommodations, dining, and shopping; access to the Shawangunk Ridge via nearby Sam's Point Dwarf Pine Ridge Preserve; and back-door access to Minnewaska State Park Preserve via Old Smiley Road. There's also a section of the old O&W Railroad/D&H Canal that's open for hiking, biking, and cross-country skiing, as well as other historical sites related to the town's colorful past. For more information, contact the Ellenville Chamber of Commerce (see "Resources" at the back of this book). Interested in hang gliding in the Shawangunks? Ellenville is the center. Check out the Mountain Wings Inc. & Eastcoast Paragliding Center located on 150 Canal Street; contact 845-647-3377 or www.flightschool.net.

The Warwarsinck (the name means "where the streams wind") tribe of Esopus Native Americans populated this area when the first Europeans arrived. Following the Second Esopus War, the Natives vacated, and the Europeans gradually settled it. In 1684, William Beek purchased land in the town of Wawarsing; it was inherited by his daughter and became the Anna Beek Patent in 1685. By 1754, there was a gristmill in neighboring Napanoch. By the time of the American Revolution, the area that's now Ellenville was still unsettled frontier. Nearby Napanoch, however, was a thriving settlement, and there was a small satellite community located on the neighboring Fantine Kill. On May 4, 1779, a party of Native Americans allied with the British with Tory help surprise-attacked that community, killing 11 settlers and destroying four homes—the worst such massacre in the region.

American victory in that war removed the threat of raids by Native Americans, thus opening the area for settlement. In the 18th century, the Dewitt family owned land in the Ellenville area. By 1798, John Dewitt, a blacksmith, sold his Ellenville property to Alpheus Fairchild. Ellenville was called Fairchild City, or "The City" for short. In 1806, the town of Wawarsing (which includes Ellenville) was created from part of the town of Rochester.

In 1817, Fairchild sold his land to Nathan Hoornbeek and Jacob Bogardus. Hoornbeek's tavern became a meeting place for the community. By 1823, The City was a small community with one general store. Applying for a post office, community leaders settled on the name *Ellenville*, for Ellen Snyder, Hoornbeek's sister-in-law.

In 1828, the D&H Canal was completed and Ellenville became the busiest port on the canal between Port Jervis and Rondout (Kingston). Lock #31 was located near the center of town. In the adjacent area was a busy dry dock and slips, factories, stores, and warehouses. Almost overnight, the community grew to the second largest in Ulster County. By 1852, a plank turnpike crossed the Shawangunk Ridge east of Ellenville, thus improving the community's links with areas east of the ridge. In 1856, the village was incorporated, with a population of 1,500. By 1870, the population had reached 3,000 and stores occupied both sides of Canal Street, the town's main thoroughfare. Timber and lead-mining activity on the neighboring Shawangunk Ridge, along with the canal, supported the growth of local industries. Ellenville became the world's leading producer of barrel hoops. The Ellenville Glass Company (1836–96) depended on the canal for transport and timber harvested from the ridge for fuel to produce flasks and bottles. The Ellenville Pottery Company produced stoneware crocks, jars, jugs, and pots. There was also a cutlery.

By 1871, Ellenville was connected to the Ontario & Western Railroad; service was extended to Kingston in 1902. Now within a day's journey of New York City, the village at the foot of the Shawangunks became an important tourist center. Hotels and boardinghouses sprang up throughout the area. In 1891, 40 boarding homes were advertised in the vicinity; by 1900 there were 60. Smiley Road was built to create access from the west side of the ridge to the hotels at Minnewaska Lake. The Terwilliger House was the town's flagship hotel. It burned in 1904 and was replaced by the Wayside Inn in 1908. Outside of town were large resorts—Mount Meenahga, built in 1881; the Cragsmoor Inn, built in 1901; the 1885 Lackawack; and the Nevele, which opened in 1901 and later became part of the famed Borscht Belt. It's the only one that's still standing.

At the turn of the 20th century, the Eastern State Correctional Facility at Napanoch was completed. It, along with the Schrade Company, a tool and cutlery manufacturer, are presently the town's largest employers.

Historical Sites and Multiple-Use Trails

The Terwilliger House Museum

Located in a late-19th-century Queen Anne Victorian home, the museum features a collection of glassware from the Ellenville Glassworks, stoneware from the Ellenville Pottery, historical lithographs, and other items related to the history of the community as well as temporary art exhibits and period furnishings. There is also a fine collection of historical materials and books in the museum's research library. Located at 40 Center Street, the museum is connected to the Ellenville Library. It is open noon–3 PM on Wednesday, Friday, and Saturday, April through November. Contact 845-647-5530.

D&H Canal Trail

Length: 1.5 miles. **Markings:** None. **General description:** A section of the old O&W Railroad and D&H Canal that starts at the end of Edward's Place and concludes at Bennet Lane off Berme Road. This segment of trail follows the rail line. The O&W Rail Company bought this section of the canal after it closed as a route for the proposed rail line. Some of the rail line runs directly over the old canal. In other parts, it lies in close proximity. The trail is open for low-impact recreational use including hiking, mountain biking, and cross-country skiing. The trail opened in 1998 and is maintained by volunteers. **Highlights:** Varied scenery, tributaries of Rondout Creek, wildlife, wildflowers (trillium and jack-in-the-pulpit), and historical sites related to the railroad and canal. The birding is excellent due to the variety of habitats. **Downside:** The stench of the sewage treatment plant is an unfortunate way to begin. Also, refuse and ATV damage mar the scenery in some spots. Mosquitoes are annoying in summer. **Difficulties and hazards:** One short rough area and a small stream crossing may challenge some. Those on bikes will have to walk a brief section.

To get there from Route 209, follow Canal Street (Route 52) east for 0.4 mile and turn left on Edwards Place. Continue 0.4 mile to the end, passing ball fields on the right. At the end of the road is a sewage treatment plant. You may park off the road here. A small wooden sign marks the beginning of the trail to the right of the sewage treatment plant. Things unfortunately get off to a rather foul start as you inhale the stench from the treatment plant and observe refuse scattered about. Just past the treatment plant, there is a short detour on the left to a small bluff overlooking the Beer Kill—a large tributary of Rondout Creek and an excellent spot for bird-watching if you can stand the fetid odor. Mallards, sandpipers, red-winged blackbirds, orioles, mourning doves, Carolina wrens, and yellow warblers are among the birds you might see.

The trail and old rail line veers to the right and enters the forest. The stench decreases and soon can no longer be detected. Pass on the right an old exit weir (stream) from what was once the Terwilliger Feeder, which supplied water for the canal. A short distance beyond, pass an open field on the left with west-facing views. On the opposite side of the trail are partial views of the Shawangunk Ridge through the trees. Pass a long wooden fence on the right. Just after the fence, the embankment of the old D&H Canal appears on the right. This part, unfortunately, was used as a dump, and is decorated with old tires and various appliances. Cross another small tributary stream. The canal channel approaches the trail, crosses it at an angle, and continues to the left. Pass another exit weir on the left. Cross an ATV trail. Then cross a wooden bridge over a flood channel. The trail then departs from the old rail line, which was washed away by flooding, and follows the canal towpath (more like a hiking trail). Those on bikes will probably have to walk them through this brief section.

Cross a small tributary stream on old railroad ties and climb an embankment back up to the railroad grade. Remnants of Canal Lock #28 appear on both sides of the trail, mostly buried by the rail line that crosses it. The canal channel continues to the right of the trail, much of it flooded as a stagnant pool. The stone retaining wall is largely intact. A branch of Rondout Creek appears on the left. On the right, there's a steep embankment over the canal channel, with Berme Road above it. Pass a bench on the left overlooking the creek. The canal channel crosses the trail again and continues on the left. Arrive at a gate. Here you'll find a wooden bridge built by Eagle scouts over a drainage ditch and Bennet Road, just off Berme Road, where this section of trail ends. Return the same way you came.

D&H CANAL LINEAR PARK (SULLIVAN COUNTY)

There are two segments of trail, located north and south of the hamlet of Summitville. These follow the old towpath of the D&H Canal. They are located about 7.5 miles south of Ellenville, off Route 209. The two access points are from Bova Road and a parking area off Route 209. The trails and linear park they're located in is owned and managed by the Sullivan County Department of Public Works—Parks and Recreation. The trails are wide and flat and suitable for walking, mountain biking, cross-country skiing, and snowshoeing. For more information about the park, contact the Sullivan County Parks and Recreation Department (see "Resources" at the back of this book).

Length: 0.9 mile. **Markings:** Signs. **General description:** This segment of trail north of the hamlet of Summitville follows the towpath of the old D&H Canal. Equestrian use is not permitted, nor are motorized vehicles. **Highlights:** An easy, pleasant walk or bike ride. Ruins of a canal lock and other landmarks are the primary features. **Downside:** Traffic noise from Route 209 often spoils the otherwise quiet atmosphere. Many will find the trail too short—a situation you can remedy by walking 0.3 mile to the next segment, described below. However, you will have to spot cars or backtrack. **Difficulties and hazards:** The trail, which is unpaved, is a little rough for bikes. Beware tree roots in a few places.

From Route 209, turn right (left if you're going north) onto Bova Road. You'll soon cross a bridge over the former canal channel and enter the park. The road bends to the right and into the parking area. There are picnic facilities on the left. A gravel trail leads directly from the parking area for a short distance to the stone ruins of an old dry dock where canal boats were repaired. Return to the parking area. Across the bridge is the old towpath and trail. If you go left and follow the towpath trail for a short distance on the left, you'll soon encounter the ruins of Lock #50. This lock would raise or lower boats 12 feet. The 17-mile stretch of canal between this lock and next one south is by far the longest lock-free section of the D&H. It is also the highest elevation of the canal between the Hudson and Delaware Rivers and was referred to as the Summit Level.

The trail continues for a short distance out to Route 209, where it ends. Backtrack to the bridge and continue in the other direction, going south. This section of towpath trail goes 0.8 mile. On the right is the old canal channel. Remnants of the retaining wall built of rough-cut stone are visible. On the left is a wetland with purple loosestrife. Traffic noise from nearby Route 209 unfortunately mars the tranquility of this otherwise idyllic scene. Follow the trail to old Route 209 in Summitville, where it ends. You can backtrack to the parking lot. Those wishing to continue can turn left here and follow the road to Route 209, then turn right and continue a short distance—about 0.3 mile total—to where the towpath trail picks up again on the left side of Route 209 (see below).

Length: 3.6 miles. **Markings:** A few signs. **General description:** This parking area accesses a segment of the D&H Canal Linear Park that runs both north and south from here. This multiuse trail follows the old towpath of the D&H Canal. It is suitable for hiking, mountain biking, and cross-country skiing. Equestrian use is not permitted, and there are no motorized vehicles. **Highlights:** This is by far the longest segment of restored towpath along the D&H Canal. It is quite scenic and features forests, fields, and wetlands, numerous animals and diverse plant life, views of the Shawangunk Ridge and southern Catskills, and historical landmarks relating to the history of the old canal. **Downside:** Buggy in summer. You will need to spot cars or backtrack. **Difficulties and hazards:** Bicyclists may find it a bit rough in a few spots.

The Hornbeck's Access parking area is located on the east side of Route 209, just over 11 miles south of Ellenville and 0.9 mile north of Wurtsboro. The parking area itself is located on a site that was once a boat basin along the canal. Today, it is a nice shady forested area with picnic and portable bathroom facilities.

From the parking area, a trail enters the woods and continues a short distance to a bridge over the old canal channel. On the opposite side of the bridge is a trail that follows the canal's former towpath. This old section of the canal and towpath is part of a 17-mile-long section between Locks #50 and #51, called the Summit Level. The Summit Level was by far the longest lock-free section of the canal. It was also the section with the highest elevation between the Delaware and Hudson Rivers. Turning left at the intersection, follow the trail south, passing remnants of the old retaining wall on the left built of rough-cut stone. The canal channel is flooded and remains so the rest of the way. Ironically, this section of the canal had few reservoirs and feeder streams and therefore was more subject to drought than other segments. As a result, there were a number of times when the water level was too low for boats to navigate; this section had to be closed.

Pass a wetland on the left, then a field on the right with a view of the Shawangunk Ridge in the background. Just beyond, pass a private residence on the right; please do not disturb. The trail then departs briefly from the towpath, bends to the right, crosses a small wooden bridge over Gumaer's Brook (a tributary stream), and then bends left and rejoins the towpath. The trail continues straight for another 0.25 mile to a gate at McDonald Road, passing another nice view of the Shawangunk Ridge on the right. Go through the gate and cross McDonald Road. By now you've traveled approximately 0.7 mile. Continue straight on a paved road for a short distance, passing private residences on the right. Soon the road passes through a gate and becomes an unpaved trail again.

The canal channel is flooded with stagnant water and thus supports a variety of aquatic plants such as water lilies and the brilliant cardinal flower as well as wildlife like fish, amphibians, turtles, and snakes, which are numerous in the warmer months. From here, the canal curves into the Mile Straight, the longest straight section of the canal. This is also where it crosses the divide between the drainage of the Delaware River to the south and the Hudson River to the north. Pass through an area of intermittent forests and wetlands on both sides of the channel. A couple of trails on the right lead to the old O&W railbed, now abandoned, which runs parallel to the D&H Canal through this section. Cross a number of small wooden bridges over ditches and tributary streams. Pass a large stone abutment on the left that was once part of the Swamp Bridge. Continue passing through forests and wetlands, and eventually encounter an open view on the right to the Shawangunk Ridge. Just beyond on the right is a portable bathroom and picnic table; beyond that lie a gate and Route 209. You can continue on from here to the other D&H Canal Linear Park segment (see above) by turning right on Route 209, following it for 0.2 mile, and then turning left onto old Route 209 in the hamlet of Summitville. From there, you can pick up the next section of the towpath trail.

If, instead, you backtrack back to the intersection near the beginning and continue south on the towpath trail, the trail continues another 0.5 mile through forest, passing a lovely view on the left to the Shawangunk Ridge; in the foreground lies a partially submerged forest with skeleton tree trunks. The trail ends at a gate at 1st Street in a residential subdivision on the outskirts of Wurtsboro. You can turn right and left and proceed into the village of Wurtsboro.

THE NEVERSINK VALLEY

The areas described below are all part of the Neversink watershed, which has been designated one of the world's "Last Great Places" by The Nature Conservancy. Besides offering scenic beauty, views of the Shawangunk Ridge, and historical landmarks including ruins of the old D&H Canal, its habitats support rare and endangered species.

Wurtsboro

This small, attractive village located at the intersection of Routes 209 and 17 is an important crossroads. In the early 18th century, it was very much a frontier area. The Gonzalus family, of Spanish descent, settled nearby. They were primarily fur traders with the local Native Americans. Eventually a small community called Rome was established. In 1801, the Newburgh–Cochecton Turnpike was chartered, which crossed the Shawangunk Ridge east of town. The turnpike became an important east–west route of commerce, and the community became an important crossroads and shipping center for the tanning industry in Sullivan County. In 1828, it became a port on the newly completed D&H Canal and was renamed for Maurice Wurts, one of the founders of the canal. By 1871, the O&W Railroad built a line from Port Jervis to Ellenville that ran through the town; the following year, the Highview Tunnel created a significant east–west rail route that passed nearby. Though not a tourist town, tourists on their way to the resorts in the Catskills and Shawangunks often passed through Wurtsboro, and many stayed at a number of boardinghouses and hotels located in the town and surrounding area. By 1872, Wurtsboro contained three churches, a district school, eight stores, a tannery, a gristmill, two wagon shops, three blacksmiths, and 650 inhabitants.

Wurtsboro has a number of nearby hiking, biking, and cross-country skiing possibilities: The Basha Kill is located just south of town, and to the north and east lies the 2,300-acre Wurtsboro Ridge, a DEC tract. Just north of town are two segments of the D&H Canal Linear Park. The Shawangunk Ridge Trail even passes right through town. Wurtsboro makes for a pleasant destination or stopover. There are a few restaurants and crafts and antiques shops along Sullivan Street, the primary commercial artery. The Catskill Hiking Shack at 259 Sullivan Street has equipment, clothes, and maps for the hiker as well as information about local hiking destinations from its friendly and knowledgeable staff. Call 845-888-HIKE or visit www.catskillhikers.com. The Wurtsboro Airport, located 2 miles north of town along Route 209, is a renowned center for gliding. It was established in 1927 and is the oldest gliding center in the United States. The amazing spectacle of motorless gliders silently circling above the town is a frequent treat for visitors. Short trips and instruction are available. It is open daily, weather permitting. For more information, call 845-888-2791.

Basha Kill Wildlife Management Area

Lying at an elevation of approximately 500 feet, between the Shawangunk Ridge to the east and the Mongaup Hills to the west, is the 2,179-acre Basha Kill Wildlife Management Area. It includes 1,333 acres of wetlands—the largest freshwater wetland area in southeastern New York State. These wetlands include marshes, swamps, and swamp forest. There are also 842 acres of uplands including forests, old fields, and former orchards. The area of wetlands is approximately 5 miles long and 0.75 mile wide at its widest point. In early spring and sometimes in late fall, the Basha Kill resembles a shallow lake, but in summer the entire marsh, except for major channels, becomes crowded with 19 species of soft-stemmed aquatic shallow-water emergent plants—primarily purple loosestrife, arrow arum, pickerelweed, sedge, water lilies, smartweed, cattails, common reeds, and the radiant cardinal flower. There are also five species of submerged aquatic plants, including pondweed, coonstail, and bladderwort. Neighboring woodlands include 42 species of trees: red maple, swamp hardwoods, yellow birch, elms, white pine, and a number of oak species. There are 21 species of shrubs, including buttonbush, alder, sumac, spicebush, and witch hazel.

Wildlife is plentiful. Thirty-three species of fish have been reported, including largemouth bass, pickerel, and bowfin. The iron-colored shiner is found here, the northernmost locality for this fish and the only known site in New York State. There are 31 species of reptiles and amphibians reported, including 6 species of turtles, 11 species of snakes, and 7 species of salamanders. When it comes to birds, 140 species have been reported, though one source claims 220. It is reputed to be the finest bird-watching spot in the vicinity of the Shawangunks, if not one of the finest spots in all of New York State. Aquatic birds include pied-billed grebes, great blue and green herons, and least and American bitterns. Virginia rails and common gallinules are among the birds that nest in the marsh. Northern harriers and other hawk species are often seen. Other species to watch for, depending on the time of year, include killdeers, plovers, woodcocks, snipe, yellowlegs, cuckoos, hummingbirds, belted kingfishers, flycatchers, vireos, warblers, wrens, shrikes, grosbeaks, goldfinches, and sparrows. Ospreys and bald eagles use the Basha Kill to feed and rest. There are 39 species of mammals, including muskrats, otters, raccoons, deer, gray foxes, cottontail rabbits, and beavers. The Indiana bat, a federally listed Endangered Species, has been reported roosting in limestone caves in this area.

The name *Basha Kill* is from *bahsaba,* which is an Eastern Algonquian term for "ruling sachem" or "chief of a nation." In other words, *Basha's land* refers to a particular chief's land. The Basha Kill is owned by the state and managed by the Department of Environmental Conservation. The land was acquired by the state between 1974 and 1981 with funds from the 1972 Environmental Bond Act. The wildlife management area is open for a number of activities, including hunting, fishing, trapping, hiking, mountain biking, cross-country skiing, snowshoeing, canoeing and kayaking, wildlife observation, nature photography, and research. Probably the best way to experience the Basha Kill is to explore the many channels and open areas by canoe or kayak. However, there are also 15 miles of multiuse trails, suitable for hiking, where mountain biking and cross-country skiing may also be practiced. Bicyclists should note that these trails are very rough; only experienced bicyclists with very sturdy bikes should attempt them. The primary trail on the east side of the management area is the O&W Rail Trail. It is also part of the Shawangunk Ridge Trail and described in the previous chapter. In addition, there are some trails on the west side of the wetlands. These may be accessed from a parking area on the north side of Haven Road, 0.3 mile from Route 209. The trails utilize some old roads and forest paths. They provide access to the wetlands and some upland forest areas. They are only occasionally marked with rust-colored DEC discs. While some brochures and maps show a more extensive trail system, it appears that at least some of it is no longer used and has become overgrown. The rules of the management area include:

- Park only in designated parking areas.
- No gas-powered boats.
- No launching of boats except from designated launch sites.
- No motorized vehicles on the trails.
- No swimming or bathing.
- No camping.
- No overnight mooring or storage of boats.
- Do not damage vegetation or harm or frighten wildlife.

The 200-member Basha Kill Area Association (BKAA), founded in 1972, is committed to protecting the wetlands and promoting environmental education. Primary access to the east side of the Basha Kill, where the O&W Rail Trail is located, is from Haven Road, 3.3 miles south of Wurtsboro from Route 209 and from South Road, which features a number of parking areas and access points. South Road can be reached from Haven Road and from Otisville Road (County Road 61), 0.5 mile east of Route 209 in Westbrookville about 6.5 miles south of Wurtsboro.

Neversink Valley Area Museum and D&H Canal Park

The museum and 300-acre park is owned and maintained by the Orange County Department of Parks, Recreation, and Conservation. It is located in Cuddebackville, about 10.7 miles south of Wurtsboro off Route 209. Going south, turn right off Route 209 just after a school on the right and just before a big bridge crossing the Neversink River. The small road goes a short distance parallel to the river to the park and museum on the right.

A prime attraction of this site is the mile-long section of the old D&H Canal towpath that is relatively well preserved and open for walking, biking, or skiing. There's even a facsimile of an old canal barge, the *Neversink Kate,* which still plies this section of the canal carrying guests. Other prime features are the dramatic stone bridge abutments of what was once an aqueduct that spanned the Neversink River here. The aqueduct was completed in 1852 as part of an overall plan to enlarge the canal. Three other aqueducts were also built as part of this plan. One was located in High Falls (see above). All four aqueducts used a revolutionary design of steel-wire suspension cables like modern suspension bridges. They were designed by the famed engineer John A. Roebling, who later designed the Brooklyn Bridge. Photographs of the aqueduct are on display in the museum.

The museum actually consists of a number of buildings that date back to the time of the canal. The Carpenter's House by the first parking lot was built around 1840 in the Greek Revival style. A carpenter who probably made his living building and repairing canal boats is believed to have resided here; today, it's a museum of D&H canal history as well as hosting changing exhibits. There are many fascinating historical photos of the canal in operation. There is also a small gift shop/bookstore. Next door is a blacksmith's shed still used to demonstrate the blacksmith's craft. Beyond lies the Blacksmith's House, originally built in 1799 as a one-room structure, with other rooms added later. A blacksmith resided here. Blacksmiths shoed the horses and mules that pulled the canal boats as well as repairing tools and implements used in the operation of the canal and on local farms. Across the road from the Blacksmith's House, a small trail leads down to the river and views of the aqueduct mentioned above. The aqueduct is gone, but the stone abutments can be seen towering over the Neversink.

Follow the road uphill. Ruins of the canal can be seen on the left. The road climbs up to where it meets the canal. Here was Lock #51, which was buried in the 1920s and is no longer visible. This is the beginning of the southern end of the Summit Level, a 17-mile-long section of the canal that was level and had no locks. The next lock, #50, is described above under "D&H Canal Linear Park." The white house to the right of the road was built by the canal company for the locktender, who had to be available at all times to operate the lock. The garage next door was a grocery store built in the 1830s to serve canal boat operators. In the 1860s, the store was run by two women who sold legendary baked goods—made in a backyard beehive oven—to those waiting to use the lock. Lock #51 became known as the Pie Lock.

Just beyond, the trail departs from the road and follows the towpath next to a water-filled channel that used to be the canal. You'll soon pass the dock with the replica of the canal barge on the left. On the right is a pavilion for those waiting to ride the barge. Continue along the towpath. Notice the stone retaining wall on the opposite side of the channel. Stones helped keep the soil in place and prevented erosion of the embankment, which would have also caused the canal to fill with sediment. The channel widens to a pond with an island in it. This was a holding basin called Island Basin where canal barges waiting to use Lock #51 would sit. The towpath trail bends to the right. The channel narrows again to its normal width. There's a steep embankment to the right of the trail.

The trail slowly bends to the left. There's a cemetery on top of the opposite bank. The sound of traffic can be heard, growing louder as the trail approaches Route 209, below on the right. Finally you arrive at a gate, the end of the trail. On the right is an outhouse and a private residence that was once a canal store. Just beyond is Oakland Valley Road. Beyond the road was the Cuddeback Freight Basin, where bluestone was loaded on barges for shipping. To return to the museum and parking, follow the same trail back in the opposite direction.

Neversink Preserve

This 370-acre preserve is owned and managed by The Nature Conservancy, whose Neversink River Program is dedicated to protecting the river's 435-square-mile watershed and habitat, designated as one of the world's "Last Great Places." The watershed, which includes part of the Shawangunk Ridge, is home to 40 species of fish and 30 rare species of plants and animals such as the endangered dwarf wedge mussel. The Neversink is also a world-class trout stream where the sport of fly-fishing was perfected in the 1800s.

The Neversink Preserve is a lush, diverse lowland environment consisting of old fields, young successional forest, older mature forest, and wetlands. Wildlife, especially birds, and a wide variety of plant life that includes dozens of wildflower species, can be seen here. Human beings, however, are scarce. The Neversink Preserve is a wonderful opportunity to observe lowland habitats and compare and contrast them with ones encountered on the Shawangunk Ridge.

Until recently, the preserve was farmland. In 1871, the Port Jervis–Monticello Rail Line crossed the property (it followed the roadbed you drove in on). Later it became part of the O&W Railroad. The Ogden Fields family donated the initial 35 acres of land to The Nature Conservancy in 1990. In 1994, the Conservancy purchased an additional 170 acres that had been a hunting camp. Finally in 1997, 131 acres of land along the opposite side of the river that had been slated to become a sand-and-gravel quarry was purchased and added to the preserve.

To reach the preserve, go south on Route 209 for 11.8 miles from Wurtsboro. Make a left onto Guymard Turnpike about 1 mile south of where 209 crosses the Neversink. Travel 0.2 mile, turn right on a gravel drive (a sign here features the pleasing Nature Conservancy logo), and follow this all the way to the parking area, where there is a kiosk with maps and brochures.

There are approximately 2.5 miles of trails in the preserve. No pets or horses are allowed; bicycling, camping, hunting, trapping, and fires are also prohibited. Fishing is by permission only. Motorized vehicles are not allowed. Please stay on the trails and do not disturb plants or wildlife. Trails are mostly color-coded and marked with colored blazes and arrows. They may be somewhat overgrown in places, partly due to infrequent use. A brochure available at the kiosk has a map and guide to local wildflowers.

The route described here circles the preserve and is approximately 1.5 miles in length. From the kiosk, follow the road for a short distance. A field appears on the left. There is a blue arrow on the left; the blue-marked trail starts here. The trail immediately splits. The right branch goes through the center of the field and rejoins the main branch in the corner of the field. Follow the main branch north. There is a view looking east to the Shawangunk Ridge in the distance. When you arrive at the northwest corner of the field, the other branch of the blue trail rejoins the main branch.

Cross a line of trees and enter a second field. The trail crosses the center of the field diagonally. There is an east-facing view of the Shawangunk Ridge in the distance. On the right is a large shed. An unmarked trail enters from the right. It follows the east edge of the field out to the road. The blue-marked trail then crosses an embankment and enters the forest. Birch and white pine are plentiful. The ground is dense with ferns in many places. Notice the large nests in the tall dead trees on the left. The trail bends to the right; there's no sign. You'll soon cross Spring Brook on a wooden bridge with a bench for sitting. There's a wetland on the left. The water appears shallow and stagnant.

The blue-marked trail veers to the right and left, then crosses another, smaller wooden bridge over a tributary stream. Continue on wooden planks for a short distance. The blue-marked trail makes a sharp left. The white-marked trail departs on the right. It goes through the forest and ends at the red-marked trail. Continue through forest, with gentle topography. The trail bends to the left and then to the right of a small rise. There are some very tall white pine trees in the vicinity. When this area was a hunting camp, the forest was allowed to replenish itself. Thus we have relatively mature growth—perhaps 80 or more years old. The blue-marked trail bends to the right and ends at its juncture with the yellow-marked trail. The Neversink River is just beyond.

Follow the yellow-marked trail as it bends left toward the river; it then turns right and follows the river south. Maple, beech, hemlock, white pine, and birch are among the many mature trees found along the river's edge. Across the river rises a ridge that runs parallel to and lower than the Shawangunk Ridge. It is composed of bedrock slightly younger (by tens of millions of years) than the Shawangunks. Once these rock beds covered the entire ridge, but as the Shawangunk rocks were folded and uplifted, these younger, softer rocks, over a period of hundreds of millions of years, eroded away, exposing the older, harder underlying rock—though in some places leaving these parallel ridges as remnants. In other places, these rocks have eroded away entirely, leaving a relatively flat valley floor that's filled with glacial outwash.

About halfway along, the yellow-marked trail turns inland briefly and intersects the red-marked trail. The red-marked trail goes through dense forest with lush undergrowth, crosses Spring Brook below a pond with a beaver dam, and ends in a field where it intersects the orange-marked trail and the road you came in on. Continuing on the yellow-marked trail, follow it along the river for another 0.2 mile until it ends at the intersection of the orange-marked trail, which turns right and away from the river. The orange-marked trail goes a short distance and meets a white-marked trail, which goes north through the forest and ends at the red-marked trail.

The orange-marked trail continues west through dense forest with a wide variety of trees, including red maple, oak, hickory, white pine, beech, basswood, sycamore, and ash. Shrubs include spicebush, winterberry, and alder, while among the dense undergrowth you'll find a variety of ferns, herbs, mosses, and grasses. The trail turns right, then bends sharply to the left and crosses a shallow trough. There is a view of agricultural fields on the left through the trees. The trail then veers to the right and left and crosses a small tributary stream on a wooden bridge; following another turn to the right, it crosses the Olivia P. Millard Bridge—a long, elegant wooden structure over Spring Brook with a bench for resting and viewing the idyllic stream. Beyond the bridge, the trail veers again to the right, then turns right along the edge of an old field bordered by tall shrubs and pioneer trees. The trail veers left and cuts diagonally across the field, arriving at a four-way intersection. You can veer right here to pick up the red-marked trail that leads back to the Neversink, or veer left and continue out to the road. Or you can make a sharp left and follow the orange-marked trail—which strangely is unmarked the rest of the way—as it veers to the left into a dense young forest of skinny trunks that includes birch, maple, oak, and black cherry. The trail veers to the right, bends more to the right, and passes a small overgrown field on the right. The trail ends as you go through a gate. The kiosk and parking area are on the left.

PORT JERVIS

Situated where the Neversink empties into the Delaware, where three states meet, Port Jervis is a natural crossroads and transportation hub. It is the only incorporated city in the region. The Shawangunk Ridge towers over the community; Port Jervis refers to itself as the Queen of the Shawangunks but seems to identify more with the Delaware River, which flows past the town. It also calls itself the River City. The Delaware Water Gap National Recreation Area begins 8 miles south of the city, and the Upper Delaware Scenic and Recreational River begins 6 miles to the north. These areas provide wonderful opportunities for canoeing, kayaking, and rafting. The best nearby hiking opportunities are on the Kittatinny Ridge in New Jersey's High Point State Park. You'll find 50 miles of trails there, including the famed Appalachian Trail. The Shawangunk Ridge Trail is also located there, described in the previous chapter. The park is approximately 5 miles south of Port Jervis off Route 23. The city's commercial heart is centered near the railway station. Passenger trains stop here several times a day. The city's heart has seen some efforts to gentrify in recent years. On weekends, traffic through the town can be onerous: urbanites and sububanites headed for nearby weekend retreats, or canoeists, rafters, and kayakers pursuing water adventures. The city offers accommodations, dining, and shopping. For more information, call or write the Tri-State Chamber of Commerce (see "Resources" at the back of this book), open weekdays only, or visit the city's official web site.

As a crossroads, Port Jervis has a long and colorful history. It was a frontier settlement, a scene of Indian raids, a prosperous port on the D&H Canal, and later a significant railroad hub. Remnants of its proud past are scattered about the town, but for a city with as much history as Port Jervis, there are few real historical attractions. The 5-mile-long Delaware River Heritage Trail begins and ends at Fort Decker, passing some of the more noteworthy historical sites in the town. It is marked with orange blazes and described on the city's official web page. For more historical information, check out the web site of the Minisink Valley Historical Society (see "Resources").

In 1690, a 1,200-acre patent named Pecnpack was granted to seven settlers. It was located northeast of Port Jervis, north of Huguenot and south of Cuddebackville. Most of the settlers were Dutch or Huguenots. Around that same time, William Titsoort, a blacksmith refuge from the Schenectady Massacre, arrived in the area. The local Natives voluntarily granted him some land 1 mile north of the present city, which he formally purchased in 1698. In 1713, he sold his land to Jan Decker and moved away. Twenty years after the first settlers, Dutch from Ulster County settled land on both sides of the Neversink River between the city and the neighboring hamlet of Huguenot.

In 1755 the colony of New Jersey built Cole's Fort in what was then called Minisink, for protection during the French and Indian Wars. New Jersey claimed the area, and the border dispute with New York wasn't resolved until 1769. By the time of the Revolutionary War, there were an estimated 18 families living in the area. On July 20, 1779, Joseph Brant, a Mohawk chief, led a party of Indians and Tories that raided the community. Houses, barns, a church, a sawmill, and crops were destroyed. There were perhaps two or three fatalities among the settlers. The Decker House, which was used as a fortress, was pulled down by the victorious Indians and set ablaze.

The Deckers were a Dutch family who owned much of the property where the present city lies. By the early 1800s, they sold it and moved away. Completion of the D&H Canal in 1828 was the catalyst for the town's long rise to prominence. In 1826, it was renamed for John B. Jervis, the chief engineer of the canal. The canal company laid out the original plan for the city. Port Jervis became a major stop. For nearly 40 years, the canal dominated the area's economy. In 1851, rail service via the Erie Railroad arrived in the town. In 1868, the Port Jervis Monticello Railroad transported farm goods and tourists from Port Jervis to the heart of Sullivan County. Railroad service expanded and eventually eclipsed the canal's role as a vital transportation artery. By 1922, there were 20 passenger trains passing through Port Jervis every day; an estimated 2,500 workers employed by the railroads resided here.

The city became an industrial center with glassmaking, silk manufacture, bottling, baking, cigar making, stove manufacture, a tannery, a brewery, and clothing and shoe factories among it's diverse industries. In 1907, there were 82 industrial establishments. Port Jervis had the oldest continually operating savings and loan association, formed in 1869. There were numerous hotels and retail establishments in the downtown area.

In 1853, Port Jervis was incorporated as a village with a population of 2,585. By 1870, the population had grown to 6,377; in 1880, it had had risen to 8,678, and to 9,000 by 1890. In 1907, Port Jervis was chartered as a city. It was also a cultural center with a library, music conservatory, opera house, moving-picture house, and vaudeville theater. Taking advantage of easy rail access from New York City and the spectacular scenery and wonderful recreation opportunities nearby—including swimming, canoeing, hunting, fishing, hiking, and golf— Port Jervis promoted itself in the late 19th century as the Scenic Queen of the Shawangunks. Many boarding homes located in the vicinity catered to tourists seeking scenery, outdoor recreation, and a healthy environment.

The city's fortunes declined along with those of the railroads. In the 1960s and 1970s, many of the city's finest historical buildings were demolished as a part of urban renewal schemes. Still, the city's location on the fringe of the New York metropolitan area; its importance as a transport hub, with access by rail and interstate; and the wonderful scenery and recreation opportunities in the vicinity hold some promise for Port Jervis's future.

Historical Sites

Fort Decker

This stone house, located at 127 West Main Street, northwest of the downtown area, is the city's oldest structure. The original stone house was built in 1760 by Frederick Haynes. It was used as trading post and military outpost during the French and Indian Wars. During the Revolutionary War, a log palisade was built around the house. On July 20, 1793, a party of Native American warriors and Tories, commanded by Joseph Brant, captured the fort, pulled down the outer walls, and set it ablaze. In 1763, it was rebuilt by Martinus Decker (1734–1802). Between 1826 and 1828, it was a hotel and tavern used by the traveling public and laborers on the D&H Canal; it also served as a headquarters for engineers supervising canal construction. John B. Jervis, chief engineer on the canal, for whom the town is named, stayed here while this segment of the canal was being built. It was referred to then as the St. John Canal Hotel. It was later used as a residence until 1965. It was purchased by the Minisink Historical Society in 1970.

Today, you'll find historical exhibits here, including a replica of the hotel sign that was used when it was a tavern and residence of engineers overseeing the construction of the D&H Canal. There are also old lithographs and 19th-century maps. The basement was excavated from 1982 to 1999, uncovering a number of artifacts from the late 19th and early 20th centuries. The house is open on Saturday 1–4 PM. There is a small admission fee. For more information, call the Minisink Valley Historical Society.

The D&H Canal and Gravity Railroad Trail

Two and a half miles of the former canal channel and towpath lie within the city. Most, about 1.5 miles, now lies buried beneath city streets, but the route is marked by 4-inch-square metal signs with the D&H logo embossed on a white background, should you choose to follow it. Sites related to canal history have the familiar blue and yellow signs. A 1-mile section of the canal route in the northwest corner was acquired by Port Jervis in 1999 and opened in 2000 as a linear park. The trailhead and parking area are located off West Main Street just before it crosses the railroad tracks and just uphill from the Fort Decker Historic site (see above).

The trail follows 1 mile of the former towpath. It is a pleasant and easy walk, bike ride, or cross-country ski outing. The path is wide with a firm gravel bed, and almost perfectly level. No pets are allowed, and currently there are no facilities. A kiosk by the entrance is bare. The trail's highlight is a chance to walk the towpath and observe the abandoned canal channel. Other perks include solitude and lovely forest scenery. Sometimes you can imagine you're deep in a forest somewhere. The downside is that this is a dead-end trail that concludes at the city boundary with no place to go except to backtrack. You'll also have to endure some traffic noise and litter. There are no difficulties or hazards except those which are human created.

From this trail, located some distance above the valley with the Delaware River and railroad tracks far below, you can more fully appreciate the magnificent effort involved in constructing the canal. The former channel has been reclaimed in a number of places by vegetation that has obscured it from view. In other spots, the growth has been cleared, exposing stone retaining walls that protected the embankments from erosion—which would have also filled the channel. Where the canal cuts through a hillside, about two-thirds of the way along the trail, unusually intricate and well-preserved stonework may be seen.

Mahackamack Churchyard

The neighboring church, named for a local Indian tribe, was destroyed in an Indian raid in 1779 during the Revolutionary War. The graveyard, located on

East Main Street at the corner of Jersey Avenue, is one of the oldest in Orange County, with burials dating from the 1740s until the mid–19th century. A number of Revolutionary War veterans are buried here, including Martinus Decker, who built Fort Decker. Unfortunately, the near proximity of a busy roadway mars the atmosphere. It is owned by the Deerpark Reformed Church.

Laurel Grove Cemetery

Believe it or not, one of the most worthwhile places to visit in Port Jervis is the cemetery. It is located off East Main Street in one of the more stunning spots in the city, where the Neversink River empties into the Delaware. It was built in 1856 and designed by New York architect Howard Daniels. It is a fine example of the type of beautifully landscaped cemeteries that became popular then and were the predecessors of large public parks like Central Park in New York City. From points overlooking the Delaware, you can watch the flotilla of canoes drifting past. The 35-acre cemetery is landscaped with hemlocks, pines, and laurel. Carpenter's Point is located in the cemetery where the Neversink empties into the Delaware and where New York, Pennsylvania, and New Jersey all meet. The Tri-State Monument built in 1882 marks this location. Route 84 towers above, and the constant loud drone of traffic overhead destroys any atmosphere. There is a fine view looking south along the Delaware with the Kittatinny Ridge in the distance.

Orange Square

Orange Square, the city's most impressive park, located at the corner of Broome and Pike Streets, was donated by the D&H Canal Company in what was then the center of the village. There is a fountain; at the center of the park is a 45-foot-high monument, built in 1886 and dedicated to veterans of the Civil War.

Elks-Brox Park

The city's largest park is located on Point Peter and Mount William overlooking the city. It can be accessed by 2.5-mile-long Skyline Drive. The city's Elks Club purchased the land for a park in 1914. In 1934, it was donated to the city. It features lovely forest scenery, picnicking, and wonderful views from the top looking down on the city with the Delaware River flowing past and the Shawangunk Ridge and Kittatinnies in the background, topped by the High Point Monument.

Stephen Crane Home

Stephen Crane (1871–1900), author of *The Red Badge of Courage* and other works, often visited and stayed with his youngest brother, William H. Crane, who lived at 19 East Main Street. Crane spent more time here than anywhere else and considered Port Jervis home. It was here on the porch that Crane wrote some of his most famous works, including *Red Badge*. Crane based his book on accounts he read and on conversations he had with Civil War vets he met at the foot of Soldier's Monument in Orange Square.

Port Jervis Free Library

The Port Jervis city library is located on Pike Street near Orange Square. It was built with funds donated by Andrew Carnegie and completed in 1903. The library was designed by the architectural firm of Ackerman and Ross, who designed a number of other Carnegie libraries as well. Of the 1,679 Carnegie libraries, less than a third are still standing and functioning as libraries. This one houses the archives of the Minisink Valley Historical Society as well as a collection of works by Stephen Crane.

Erie Depot

Located at 15 Jersey Avenue on the edge of the city's restored downtown area, the Port Jervis Erie Depot was the town's third railway station. The first was a wooden frame structure at the base of Pike Street. The second, a brick-and-stone structure, opened in 1889 but burned a year later. This one, a two-story brick station, opened in 1892. It is a mix of a number of architectural styles that were popular at the time. By the 1970s, after the closing of the Erie Lackawanna, there was talk of demolishing it, but thanks to efforts of the Minisink Valley Historical Society, the Depot Preservation Society, and the Port Jervis Development Corporation, the depot has reopened as shops and offices.

NEW PALTZ

Located right off the New York State Thruway, this bustling town perched on bluffs east of the Wallkill River's broad alluvial plain wears a number of different hats: university town, tourist town, cosmopolitan counterculture outpost, New Age center, commuter suburb. Separately or collectively, none does it justice. The village has many fine views of the Shawangunk Ridge, the most prominent being the familiar profile of Sky Top, which towers above the valley. New Paltz may be rightfully called the Gateway to the Gunks: Route 299 passes right through town, channeling a steady stream of visitors on their way to Mohonk and Minnewaska, which are located just a few miles west. For visitors on the way to the Gunks, it's a good place to stop for coffee and a bagel or after the outing for dinner, shopping, and evening entertainment. There are plenty of accommodation options in the area. Please note that on fine weekend days, the traffic can be horrendous. To find out more about the community, check out the New Paltz Chamber of Commerce (see "Resources" at the back of this book).

The town offers a wide assortment of crafts shops, antiques shops, and art

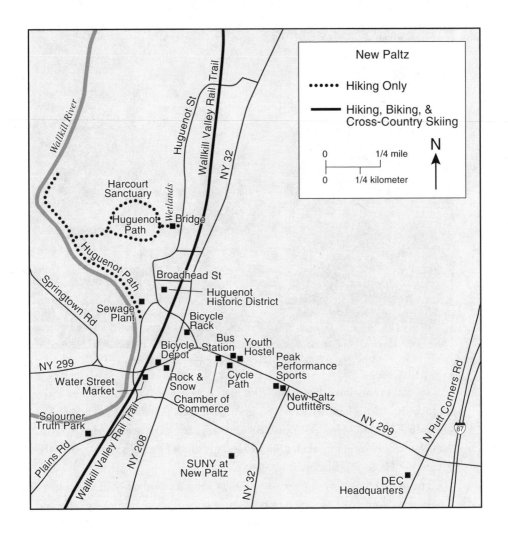

galleries, mostly along Main and North Front Streets and in the Water Street Market. There's also a vast array of restaurants and cafés. South and west of town are orchards, farm markets, and wineries. Check out the Shawangunk Wine Trail; 845-255-2494 or www.shawangunkwinetrail.com.

The town also has a number of taverns and clubs, some offering live entertainment and dancing. These, plus the university and activities in the nearby Gunks such as rock climbing and mountain bicycling, make New Paltz a magnet for throngs of young people. Main Street—especially on weekend evenings—is a crowded, lively scene. Finding parking can be a challenge. If you're looking for accommodations, there are a number of motels on Route 299 in the vicinity of the Thruway. You'll also find bed & breakfast establishments in town and nearby, as well as the area's only youth hostel.

Historic homes along Huguenot Street in New Paltz

Special events are a big part of the life of the town. The most noteworthy include the Ulster County Fair held in August, the New Paltz/Woodstock Arts & Crafts Fair held Memorial Day weekend and Labor Day weekend, A Taste of New Paltz held in September, and a Colonial Street Festival sponsored by the Huguenot Historical Society in August.

The State University of New York at New Paltz, located off South Manheim Boulevard (Route 32), is very much a centerpiece of the community's life and culture. The town's earliest school was in the community's church in 1689. In 1812, the first school building was built on North Front Street. It still stands. In 1828, the New Paltz Classical School was established to meet a growing need for secondary education. Classes were held on the second floor of the school building. In 1833, a separate new building was built overlooking the Wallkill, which became the New Paltz Academy. It was expanded in 1840, but in 1884 the school was demolished by fire. Suffering declining enrollment and financial difficulties, the school applied to become a state-funded teacher training program. In 1885, it was named the first such program, called a Normal School, in southeastern New York State. The school grew and by 1907 moved to its new and present location. In 1942, it became a four-year teachers' college; in 1948, it joined the new New York State University, along with 47 other teachers' colleges. In 1959, the name was changed to the State University College of Education at New Paltz.

Today, approximately 8,000 students attend the 216-acre campus. There are 150 fields of study. Theater productions, concerts, sports, and some lectures are open to the public. The hilltop location has many fine views of the Shawangunk Ridge and surrounding area. While you're there, be sure to visit the Samuel Dorsky Museum of Art. This new museum—established in 2001—features year-round exhibitions and programs from the museum's permanent collection as well as works by contemporary and local artists in 9,000 square feet of modern gallery space.

Bike Shops
- Bicycle Depot, 15 Main Street, 845-255-3859, www.bicycledepot.com. Sales, service, and rentals.
- Cycle Path, 138 Main Street, 845-255-8723, www.cyclepathny.com. Sales, service, and rentals.
- The Bicycle Rack, 13 North Front Street, 845-255-1770. Sales and service.

Other Outdoors Shops
- Rock & Snow, 44 Main Street, 845-255-1311, www.rocksnow.com. Outdoor wear, equipment, cross-country ski rentals.
- Peak Performance Sports, Inc., 184 Main Street, 845-255-8200. Outdoor wear, equipment, cross-country ski rentals.
- New Paltz Outfitters Inc., 188 Main Street, 845-255-2829.

History
Archaeological evidence shows that prehistoric Native Americans used the bluffs overlooking the Wallkill for thousands of years for hunting and gathering, while the river was used for fishing, washing, and transport. The Esopus Natives populated the area and cultivated fields along the Wallkill. On June 7, 1663, during the Second Esopus War between the Dutch and the Esopus Native Americans, there was a surprise attack on the Dutch settlements of Wiltwyck (Kingston) and its satellite, Nieuw Dorp (Hurley); a number of women and children were taken hostage by the Esopus. Louis Dubois, whose wife was one of the hostages, was part of the expedition that pursued the hostages and their captors through the valley of the Wallkill to the mouth of the Shawangunk Kill, eventually gaining their release after a bloody struggle.

Impressed by the rich alluvial plain in the New Paltz area, Dubois and his associates purchased a large tract of approximately 39,683 acres of land (the Paltz Patent) from the Esopus Native Americans in 1677 for an assortment of goods, including kettles, clothing, blankets, tools, horses, tobacco, flintlocks, wine, and the like. From our modern-day perspective, the price seems ridiculously cheap. For the Native Americans, however, it was generous deal. The Huguenots were especially anxious to please them, since good relations were highly valued. The purchased land included all of the property between Mohonk and the Hudson River. Shortly thereafter, in the spring of 1678, Dubois, a French Huguenot, and his Huguenot associates (called patentees)—12 families in all—moved from Nieuw Dorp and Wiltwyck and settled in the New Paltz area. In establishing their own community separate from the Dutch, the Huguenots hoped to preserve their religion, language, and culture.

The Huguenots were French Protestants who were members of the Reformed Church established by John Calvin in the 16th century. They faced extreme persecution in their home country, which was largely Catholic; there had been massacres in which thousands of Huguenots were slaughtered. The New Paltz Huguenots resided in the Walloon region, an area of northern France that borders the Netherlands and was under the control of the Spanish Hapsburgs, who were Catholic. Spain brutally suppressed Calvinism in the area under its control. In 1609, following a long and bitter struggle, the Netherlands won its independence from Spain, although the southern provinces that bordered France remained under Spanish control. From 1620 to the 1630s, there were numerous border conflicts between France and Spain; the Walloon region frequently changed hands. Many Huguenots fled to neighboring Protestant countries, including Die Pfalz, the German Palatinate (also referred to as the Rhineland), which had been devastated by the Thirty Years' War; French Protestants with skills as merchants and artisans were invited to the Palatinate with promises of tax breaks and exemptions from military service.

Perhaps fearful that Louis the XIV, the Catholic French king, would eventually conquer the Palatinate, and under the threat of reprisals against Protestants, especially former French citizens, the Huguenots began emigrating to colonial America. The first group that would eventually occupy New Paltz arrived in New Amsterdam in 1660 aboard a ship named the *Gilded Otter*. A few months later, they settled in Wiltwyck, then moved to neighboring Nieuw Dorp (new village), and finally to New Paltz.

The New Paltz Huguenots were farmers and merchants who mostly dealt in land. They lived in a cluster of dwellings and cultivated fields in the neighboring floodplain. Living in a small cluster provided security from raids by Native Americans as well as more social opportunities and a sense of community. Wheat and flax were the primary crops. Their first dwellings were likely earthen dugouts—square pits in the ground with walls and floors lined with timbers and a wainscot ceiling. Simple wooden structures were eventually built on top of these. Before long, the community they established became quite prosperous; by 1692, the first permanent stone dwellings, in the style of local Dutch residences, were erected over the original dugouts. These were initially one-room structures: The cellar area was the kitchen and eating area, and the room above became a family bedroom. Attics were used for storing grain. Other rooms would eventually be added on as families grew and the community became more prosperous.

Worship services began in 1683, and by 1717 a permanent stone chapel was erected. Early services were conducted in French. Despite efforts to maintain their language and culture, by the late 1720s Dutch had replaced French in services, and by the 1750s the congregation had become part of the Dutch Reformed Church. In 1799, English finally replaced Dutch.

Originally the nearby fields were held and worked in common, but due to the expanding population, in 1703 the land was divided among the 12 patentee families. As the population continued to grow and the original patentees died, disputes over wills and landownership increased. In 1728, the New Paltz townsmen elected a council of 12 men called the Duzine that was responsible for surveying and subdividing the land and defending the boundaries of the patent against "encroachments" by neighboring landowners. This governing body functioned until 1824.

The New Paltz Huguenots were slave owners. The 1790 census showed that of a population of 1,253, there were 179 slaves—13.1 percent of the population. Slaves obviously performed a huge share of the agricultural work as well as the more odious domestic duties. Providing this necessary labor obviously helped make this a viable community. Slaves usually resided in the basements beneath the stone houses, or in the attics.

In 1807, a turnpike was built from New Paltz to Paltz Landing, located on the Hudson opposite Poughkeepsie (today the village of Highland). In 1856, the turnpike extended across the Shawangunk Ridge between New Paltz and the Rondout Valley west of the ridge. Called the Wawarsing–New Paltz Turnpike, it was a toll road. Where it crossed the Wallkill River west of town, there was a covered bridge and a tollbooth. The stone bridge abutments and tollbooth can still be seen today. By 1861, the turnpike had gone bankrupt and become a public road. Prior to the turnpike, Huguenot Street was the town's primary thoroughfare. Now business activity shifted to Main Street. In 1870, the Wallkill Valley Railroad arrived in the town. One of its primary functions was bringing guests to the Mohonk Mountain House and hotels at Minnewaska Lake. Tourism wasn't the only industry, however: The village also had a creamery and a fruit processing plant.

As noted above, the New Paltz Normal School—later part of the New York State University system—and its contribution to the local economy helped offset the decline seen in most Wallkill Valley communities through the 20th century.

The Stone Houses of Huguenot Street

The chief historical attraction in New Paltz is the Huguenot Historic District, which includes eight structures along Huguenot Street (a National Historic District) dating from the late 17th to the late 18th centuries, including six of the original residences plus a reconstruction of a 1717 church. The Stone Houses continued to be inhabited by descendants of the original Huguenot settlers into the 20th century. Collectively, the homes tell the fascinating story of the first European settlement of the area. The Stone Houses are owned and maintained by the Huguenot Historical Society. All eight are open to the public as part of guided tours led by volunteers. Tours run from 45 minutes to two hours, depending on the number of structures you wish to visit, and vary accordingly in price. They originate from the Dubois Fort Visitors Center on Huguenot Street (see below). A booklet with a map, drawings, and information about the individual homes is on sale here for a small fee. Don't expect to see the insides of all the homes in one visit. There is parking on the south side of Broadhead Street two blocks north of the village center. Guided tours are available from late May to September, Tuesday through Sunday 9 AM–4 PM. The rest of the year, the homes are only open on weekends. The Huguenot Historical Society sponsors a street festival in August with food, exhibits, and entertainment, at which all of the homes are open. There is also an evening candlelight tour that is especially worthwhile. Huguenot Street itself provides very pleasant walking and biking, especially in combination with the Wallkill Rail Trail or the Huguenot Path (see below). For more information, contact the Huguenot Historical Society (see "Resources" at the back of this book).

The Deyo House

The foundation of this residence was built in 1692, making this the oldest structure on Huguenot Street. In 1894, Abraham Deyo Brodhead, a wealthy descendant who later served as mayor of New Paltz, had the original dwelling gutted and restored as a fashionable Victorian showplace in the Queen Anne style with all the "modern" conveniences of the time. Legend has it that Gertrude M. Deyo, Abraham's first wife, who died of consumption, still haunts the house. Her gloomy portrait hangs on the second floor. The expensive refurbishment, which took years, bankrupted Abraham, who was forced to sell the house in 1915. The home has a wonderful display of original Deyo family furnishings, reflecting the culture and social morality of the late-19th- and early-20th-century Victorian and Edwardian periods.

The Jean Hasbrouck House

This square structure with a steeply pitched roof was built in stages between 1694 and 1712. It originally consisted of four sizable rooms and a wide hallway and is much larger than it appears from outside. One room served as a tavern and general store. There is also a fine kitchen with the huge jambless fireplace that was typical of the time. A copy of the original 1677 Paltz Patent signed by the Huguenot settlers and the Esopus Native Americans hangs in the hall. Upstairs was a crude sleeping quarters for male travelers, as well as a huge storage area. There's a display of antique spinning wheels and a 200-year-old hand loom. Most impressive is the brick chimney, supposedly the largest of its type in North America. The bricks were made locally. Furnishings range from the 17th to the 19th centuries. All are from the original Huguenot settlers and their descendants. This was the first structure acquired by the Huguenot Historical Society and was opened to the public as a museum in 1899.

Bevier-Elting House

This home was built in 1698 by Louis Bevier, who became the wealthiest of the 12 original settlers. In 1760, Louis's son Samuel sold the house to Roelif Elting; it remained in the Elting family until 1963, when it was donated to the Huguenot Historical Society. Originally a one-room house, it features a second room added between 1715 and 1720, and a third in 1735. The home displays its tiny original windows as well as furnishings dating back to the period of 1735. Most unusual is a wooden cradle used for rocking sick or invalid adults. There's a side porch that provided the women covered access to the kitchen area and a sheltered place to do spinning and other domestic chores.

Dubois Fort

Dubois Fort was built in 1705 by Daniel Dubois, son of one of the original patentees, on orders from the English governor to construct a fortress for the protection of the community from feared attacks by Native Americans. Gunports can still be seen today on either side of the original two ground-floor windows facing Huguenot Street. Fortunately, relations with the local Native Americans were good, and the fort never saw military action. While it served as a fortress, it was primarily a residence for the Dubois family. The building was greatly expanded during the 19th century, including the two-story porch. Today, the building serves as a quaint gift shop, gallery, and site where guided tours originate.

Lefevre House

This Federal-style home was built in 1799 with brick on the outside in the front and on one side of the house. Brick was more expensive and a status symbol of the time. In this case, it was used only in the facade of those parts of the house that were visible from the ferry, which crossed the Wallkill nearby. Emphasis in Federal-style architecture was on symmetry. The large rooms, high ceilings, and long, wide hallway reflect the growing affluence of the community by this time. Ezekial Elting, the original owner, was a merchant and mill owner; he owned slaves as well. The house was both a residence and a store. The dining room features a plate warmer and original dinnerware. There's a bedcover from an 1823 community wedding. In 1968, the Lefevre family purchased the home and donated it to the Huguenot Historical Society.

The French Church

This replica of the original stone church built in 1717–18 was constructed in 1972. It's a square structure with a triangular, raised roof. There was practically no adornment. A stairway leads to the top, where a member would call the congregation to worship by blowing a tin horn. It could accommodate 55 to 60 people. The large windows flood the chapel with light. This contrasts with the private residences, whose small windows provide at best only dim lighting. Church was a very important element in the life of the early settlement. Besides being a social gathering place, the church reminded residents that they were a part of a community. The small scale of the structure, its simple design, and the use of native stone in its construction reflect the close relationship and dependence of the community on the land. As the community grew, this church became too small and was replaced by a larger church built nearby in 1772. The original church was eventually dismantled and the stones used to build the community's first school (1812–74), which still stands on North Front Street. Today, the church is used for special nondenominational services, weddings, and other special events. Next to the church is an old burial ground with original headstones, some dating back to the 1700s.

Beyond the Stone Houses

While New Paltz's Stone Houses are truly noteworthy, there are a number of other historical residences and buildings worth checking out if you have the time and inclination. On Huguenot Street near the corner of Broadhead Avenue and Huguenot, the Huguenot Historical Society maintains a small library with 6,000 volumes of early and local history specifically related to the Huguenot settlers and their descendants. It is open by appointment only. The main office of the Huguenot Historical Society is located next door at 18 Broadhead Avenue. The Reformed Church across from the Abraham Hasbrouck House was built in 1839 in the Greek Revival style. It replaced an earlier stone church that was built next door in 1772. On Huguenot Street 0.5 mile north of the Stone Houses is the site of an African American burial ground used until after the Civil War. A number of slaves owned by the community's white residents are presumed to be buried there. Today, there is a commemorative plaque. At 0.6 mile north of the Stone

Houses is the Jacob Hasbrouck home, built in 1788. Hasbrouck served in the militia during the Revolutionary War. The home was also the birthplace of Jacob M. Hasbrouck, who served as New Paltz's first mayor in 1887. Along the west side of Huguenot Street are fine views of the Shawangunk Ridge across fields.

Beyond Huguenot Street, The Bakery at 13A North Front Street has a brochure guide focusing on noteworthy sites in the downtown area. Most of the buildings on Main Street date back to the late 19th or early 20th century, though some are older. Many residences in the heart of town have been converted to apartments and rooms for young people, primarily college students. Outside town, you may want to visit Locust Lawn, an impressive neoclassical Federal-style home built in 1814 for Josiah Hasbrouck (1755–1821), who served as a congressman. It contains a fine collection of period furnishings. It is owned by the Huguenot Historical Society, which also owns the Terwilliger House located nearby on the same property—a stone house built in 1738. Terwilliger was a farmer of Dutch descent; his wife was the granddaughter of Hugo Freer, one of the original Huguenot patentees. Eighteenth- and early-19th-century furnishings are displayed in the home. The property includes a wildlife sanctuary and family burial ground that includes slaves. Locust Lawn and the Terwilliger House are found 3 miles south of New Paltz on Route 32. If you want to visit, contact the Huguenot Historical Society.

Also outside of town is the Testimonial Gateway, a medieval-looking stone tower and arch, built in 1908 to commemorate the 50th wedding anniversary of Albert and Eliza Smiley. It spans the stage road that once was the primary route to the Mohonk Mountain House. The gateway is not open to the public, but it can be viewed from neighboring Gatehouse Road. Fine vistas of the Shawangunk Ridge with Sky Top may be observed nearby. To get there from the village, go west for 1.3 miles on Route 299 to the corner of Gatehouse Road. Follow Gatehouse Road for views of the gateway.

Hiking Trails

You don't have to travel to the Gunks to hike or mountain bike; New Paltz features a number of pleasant walks or bike rides on quiet residential streets. The 15-mile-long Wallkill Valley Rail Trail passes right through the heart of town. Also, the Harcort Sanctuary and Huguenot Path offer peaceful hiking and a variety of habitats and views.

Huguenot Path

Length: 1 mile. **Markings:** Signposts. **General description:** A pleasant, easy hiking trail through the Harcourt Sanctuary that begins and ends on Huguenot Street. The

Harcourt Sanctuary includes 50 acres of former agricultural land: old fields, flood-plain forest, wetlands, and the Wallkill River. It was acquired by the Huguenot Historical Society in 1976 from Hastings Harcourt to provide a protective buffer against expansion of the waste treatment plant. In 1977, it was established as a wildlife sanctuary, and in 1991 the Huguenot Path was opened to the public. It is maintained by the Huguenot Historical Society, the New Paltz Environmental Commission, and other volunteer groups. **Highlights:** A variety of habitats, with diverse plant and animal life. Surprisingly tranquil for being so close to town. There are fine views of the Wallkill River and the Shawangunk Ridge in the distance, and ice skating in the wetlands area during the winter. The trail is best combined with a stroll on Huguenot Street past the Stone Houses, or on the Wallkill Rail Trail. **Downside:** None. **Difficulties and hazards:** Sections of this trail may be flooded in spring and at other times of the year. Mud is certainly a factor anytime after it rains or the snow melts; beware poison ivy. It's also hot and buggy in summertime, especially in the old fields bordering the wetlands.

The trail begins on the west side of Huguenot Street, 0.2 mile north of Main Street, just before the turnoff for the village waste treatment plant. It ends on Huguenot Street 0.2 mile north of the Stone Houses (see above). There is parking at the waste treatment plant and in a small lot on the left side of Huguenot Street just north. The trail parallels the entrance road to the waste treatment plant, following the Wallkill River on the left. Pass the waste treatment plant on the right. There's a view of the Wallkill River on the left, with cultivated fields on the opposite bank and the Shawangunk Ridge to the right. Enter the parking lot for the Gardens for Nutrition. Parking is restricted to those who maintain plots here. Pass the gardens on the right. Continue into an area of floodplain forest, soon arriving at a wooden bridge. There's access to the river below on the left. If you cross the bridge, the trail continues for another 0.25 mile following the river on the left, with open fields on the right. There are views of the river, with the Shawangunk Ridge in the background. Eventually the trail peters out on the edge of a large field.

To follow the main branch of the trail, turn right just before the bridge and continue on the broad path as it bends to left and intersects another road on the right. There's an old dam site on the left, supposedly once used for trapping fish from the river so they could be harvested easily. The trail veers to the left and enters an old field populated with many flowers in summer. Another intersection is soon reached. A left turn here takes you across the field and into a lush floodplain forest populated with red maple, locust, cherry, and ash. The trail winds through the forest and then follows the edge of the field to where it intersects with the original trail. There are fine views toward the end looking west across the field, with the Shawangunk Ridge in the background.

If you stay on the main path at the last intersection, the trail slowly veers to the left with fine views over your shoulder of the Shawangunk Ridge, Sky Top dominant in the center. Pass a small, narrow pond and wetland area on the right. It is all that's left of a loop that was once part of the Wallkill River; it was separated from the main channel by sediment and now stands isolated. If it were larger, it would be called an oxbow lake. By midsummer, the pond is covered with duckweed. Purple loosestrife, an exotic aquatic plant, is plentiful along the shore. The trail bends more to the left. A wooden bridge appears on the right. Just beyond it, the trail meets the forest loop described above. You can return by crossing the bridge over the pond and wetland—which makes a perfect natural ice skating rink in winter. On the opposite side of the bridge, the trail ascends a hill and soon arrives at Huguenot Street. Turn right there and walk 0.5 mile, passing the Stone Houses, to get to where the Huguenot Path begins.

Wallkill Valley Rail Trail

Gardiner to Rosendale

Length: 15 miles. **Markings:** Signs at every intersection except in the town of Rosendale. **General description:** This popular multiple-use trail follows the old bed of the Wallkill Valley Railroad (the ties and rails have been removed), from the southern boundary of the town of Gardiner to the northern boundary of the town of New Paltz. Those parts of the trail in the towns of Gardiner and New Paltz are managed and maintained by volunteers of the Wallkill Valley Rail Trail Association. The last section of rail-trail, in the town of Rosendale, is privately owned but at present is open to the public. It ends at the iron bridge that towers over Rondout Creek. The trail is mostly flat cinder and gravel based. It is ideal for walking, mountain biking, cross-country skiing, and horseback riding. All users should be respectful of private property just beyond the narrow boundaries of the trail. For more information, including a brochure with a map, contact the Wallkill Valley Trail Association. **Highlights:** This easy, very accessible trail, close to a number of communities, travels through lovely pastoral countryside and boasts fine views looking west of the Shawangunk Ridge. It makes a nearly perfect beginner's trail for practically anyone. Historical landmarks, mostly associated with the history of the railroad and the Huguenot settlement, are also plentiful. Using rural roads, a number of circuit loop trips may be fashioned. **Downside:** When you reach the end, you want it to go farther. Also, traffic noise can deter from the experience in a number of places. **Difficulties and hazards:** Beware traffic at road crossings. Poison ivy is plentiful along the way, as are mosquitoes in proximity to wetland areas. Bicyclists should beware some gravelly patches. Because this is a multiple-use trail, always be mindful of other users. Cross-country skiers should be aware that this trail is not groomed in wintertime, and there are numerous footprints of walkers as well as the unfortunate tracks of snowmobiles. Snowmobile use is illegal on the rail-trail.

The Wallkill Valley Railway ran between the village of Montgomery in Orange County and the city of Kingston. The Wallkill Valley Railway Company was organized in 1866. Touted as an economic boon to a depressed agricultural area that was in decline, the railroad was largely funded by local towns, which issued bonds. In 1868, construction commenced. Large numbers of Irish immigrants were employed in the project. By 1869, the railroad reached as far north as Gardiner; by 1870, New Paltz. Between 1870 and 1872, a 150-foot-high iron bridge was constructed over Rondout Creek in Rosendale, and by April 1872 the entire length was complete from Montgomery to Kingston. The Wallkill Valley Railway hauled fresh produce and vegetables from the farmlands of Ulster County to New York City. It also carried coal, cement, and passengers, including those bound for the resorts of Mohonk and Minnewaska. By carrying coal and cement, the Wallkill was in effect competing with the D&H Canal and likely was a factor in the demise of that human-made waterway.

While the railroad was indeed an economic boon for some of the communities along its route, it struggled to be profitable. In 1877, it went bankrupt and was reorganized as the Wallkill Valley Railroad by Kingston businessman Thomas Cornell, owner of Ulster Delaware Railroad and a large steamship company. This was the first of many changes in ownership. In 1881, it became part of the West Shore Railroad, and in 1885 part of the New York Central. Due to competition from the automobile and other rail lines, as well as the decline in agriculture in the region, traffic gradually dwindled; by 1937, passenger service was discontinued. In 1968, it became part of Penn Central Railroad, and when that railroad went bankrupt in 1976, it became part of Conrail.

In December 1977, Conrail ceased the Wallkill's freight operation and the rail line closed for good. By 1983, Conrail had removed all ties and rails. Six towns formed a committee to consider buying the abandoned railbed. The Wallkill Valley Land Trust, a local private nonprofit group dedicated to preserving open land, with the help of the Trust for Public Land, a national group, and the town and village of New Paltz, purchased 12.2 miles of railbed in the towns of New Paltz and Gardiner. The town and village of New Paltz purchased their sections. The section in the town of Gardiner is still owned by the Land Trust. Volunteers formed the Wallkill Valley Rail Trail Association, Inc., and helped clear the trail. Sections in the towns of New Paltz and Gardiner were informally opened in 1991, and officially dedicated in 1993, the 17th rail-trail in New York

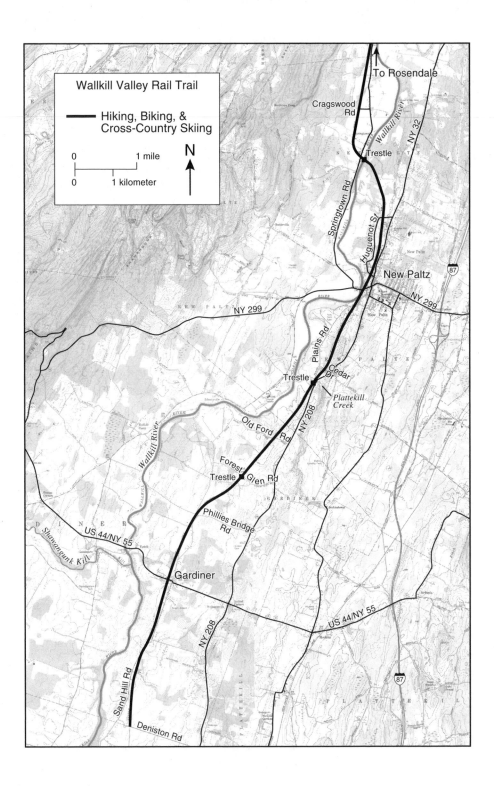

Wallkill Valley Rail Trail

Hiking, Biking, &
Cross-Country Skiing

0   1 mile

0   1 kilometer

N

To Rosendale

Cragswood Rd

Wallkill River

NY 32

Trestle

Springtown Rd

Huguenot St

New Paltz

87

NY 299

New Paltz

NY 299

Plains Rd

Cedar Dr

Trestle

Plattekill Creek

Old Ford Rd

NY 208

Wallkill River

Forest Glen Rd

Trestle

Phillies Bridge Rd

Shawangunk Kill

US 44/NY 55

Gardiner

NY 208

US 44/NY 55

87

Sand Hill Rd

Deniston Rd

State. The last 3 miles of the trail in the town of Rosendale are privately owned by John E. Rahl, who purchased the entire 11-mile section from the New Paltz boundary to the city of Kingston for just $1, hoping to someday restore rail service. Since 1991, this section of trail has been open to the public, including half of the long rail bridge that spans the Rondout Valley.

The southern terminus of the trail is on the north side of rural Deniston Road in the town of Gardiner, marked by a simple sign. There is off-road parking available for two or three cars; a bed & breakfast is nearby. To get to Deniston Road, go south from New Paltz on Route 208 for 8.5 miles. Go right onto Deniston and continue 1.2 miles to where the rail-trail appears on the right. Follow the trail north between open fields. Sand Hill Road appears to the west, paralleling the trail. There are views of the Shawangunks across the fields and through openings in the trees. After less than 1.5 miles, Sand Hill Road crosses the trail. It continues to run parallel to the trail for just over 1 mile, the rest of the way into Gardiner.

In the small village of Gardiner, the Wallkill Valley Rail Trail crosses Route 44/55. You'll find parking here, along with nearby restaurants, a deli, and some antiques shops. The Shawangunk Cycle & Sport/Gunks to Go, a bicycle shop/café, is located in the old 1869 rail station next to the trail. It sells, repairs, and rents bikes; call 845-255-3999. The town of Gardiner was entirely rural

A view of Sky Top from the Wallkill Valley Rail Trail

before the Wallkill Valley Railroad arrived. Practically overnight, a town sprang up, with a sawmill, gristmill, blacksmith shop, wagon-making shop, creamery, and hay storage. There was also a furniture store, drugstore, shoe-making shop, lumber- and coal yard, and large general store. The McKinstry House next to the depot was a first-class hotel later renamed the Gardiner Hotel. Floyd Mc-Kinstry was the Gardiner town supervisor and a farmer who owned much of the land that the town was built on. Dairy products and hay were the town's primary exports. By 1902, the population reached 200. In 1925, a major fire destroyed many of the buildings in the center of the town.

At 1.6 miles west of the rail crossing (follow Route 44/55 across the river to a flashing yellow light, then turn left and follow the signs) is the Tuthilltown Grist Mill. It was built in 1788 by Selah Tuthill and is the oldest continuously operating water-powered mill left in the Hudson Valley. In 1972, it was designated a National Historic Landmark. From the mill there are views overlooking the Shawangunk Kill. The mill contains a country store that specializes in natural foods and ground meal and flour produced on-site. It is open Friday and Saturday 10 AM–6 PM and Sunday until 4. For more information, call 845-255-5695.

When hiking or biking through Gardiner, you may be treated to a show of sky divers descending from above. If you want to try it yourself, visit Skydive The Ranch at 45 Sandhill Road, call 845-255-4033, or visit www.ranchskydive.com.

The trail continues through fields and woods. One mile north of Gardiner, it crosses Phillies Bridge Road and Old Ford Road. Just beyond, the trail enters woodlands, crossing a trestle over Forest Glen Road at just over 1.75 miles north of Gardiner. Forest Glen was the site of a small community. There was a station here. It is also the site where both the Catskill and Delaware Aqueducts cross under the rail line, though neither is visible. Less than 0.25 mile beyond, the trail crosses Bridge Creek Road and then continues another 0.75 mile through the woods to Old Ford Road.

Just beyond, the rail-trail enters the town of New Paltz. For the next mile, it offers its best vistas. A beautiful orchard is soon crossed, with a wonderful expansive view looking west across fields and rows of young apple trees to the Shawangunk Ridge from Sam's Point up to Bonticou Crag. Cross a gravel driveway and continue north. There are more partial views of the ridge and fields on the left, and finally another dramatic open view with Skytop as the centerpiece. There's a bench for sitting and admiring this scene. Just beyond, the trail crosses an elevated trestle over Plattekill Creek, which means "flat creek" in Dutch. There's another gorgeous vista from here of the lovely stream bisecting picturesque fields, with the Shawangunk Ridge forming an imposing backdrop. The Trapps cliffs make up the centerpiece of this view. There's another bench for resting and admiring.

Continue a short distance, crossing a driveway and passing the end of Plains Road on the left, with parking available for a few cars. Continue another 0.3 mile, close to Route 208 on the right, and cross Cedar Drive. Continue another 1.2 miles through a more tranquil section. Toward the north end of this section, pass a pond and wetland to the left (west) of the trail where wildlife may be observed.

Just beyond, cross Plains Road and enter the village of New Paltz. Sojourner Truth Park overlooking the Wallkill—which has a boat launch and views of the Shawangunk Ridge—is on the left. The trail continues north, passing a lovely area of floodplain forest below on the left with views of the Wallkill River. It is accessed via a short trail that descends from the rail-trail to the river's edge and then rejoins the trail a short distance to the north. (Note that this area may not be accessible due to seasonal flooding.) A short distance beyond, the trail crosses Water Street. On the right is the Water Street Market, a restored area of boutiques, galleries, and cafés in old railroad warehouses. There are three parking spaces available for trail users on the right in the private lot for Studley Real Estate. The trail then crosses Route 299 (Main Street). You've now come 8.5 miles from the beginning. Be careful crossing Main Street. There tends to be a lot of traffic on weekends, especially in the warmer months.

Continue north, passing the old New Paltz train station on the left, now a restaurant. It was built in 1907, replacing the original 1870 station, which was destroyed by fire. The Smileys used to park dozens of horse-drawn carriages here, ready to pick up guests arriving by train and carry them up to the resorts on the ridge. Continue north for a short distance and cross North Front Street. If you detour left here for half a block, you can visit historic Huguenot Street with its 17th- and 18th-century Stone Houses. Off to the right of the trail, the New Paltz League operated a large creamery from 1883 to 1931. Continue north, passing a 0.25-mile marker on the right. Just beyond, cross Broadhead Avenue. A detour left here will also bring you to Huguenot Street, where there's parking and more historic homes. Continue another block, crossing Mulberry Street and passing the 0.5-mile marker on the right.

Departing the village, some views looking west of the Shawangunk Ridge appear on the left. Cross a drainage on a small bridge and pass a 1-mile marker on the right. Then cross Huguenot Street and continue north, bending to the left and passing serene woodlands with shallow pools, lovely reflections, and a gun club on the right. One mile from Huguenot Street, cross the Wallkill River on a 413-foot-long railroad trestle. Just beyond the bridge, the trail crosses Springtown Road, with parking available for three to four cars. The trail passes through a horse farm with a nice view of Bonticou Crag to the west. Bend to the right and continue north, entering a woodland and then reaching Cragswood

Road about 1.5 miles beyond the bridge. The trail continues another 0.3 mile to the New Paltz–Rosendale boundary.

From here on, the trail is the private property of John E. Rahl, but as of this writing, access is permitted. Continue another 3 miles to the intersection with Mountain Road in the village of Rosendale and, just beyond, the spectacular 988-foot-long, 150-foot-high trestle over Rondout Creek. It was completed in 1872 and took two years to construct. The *Kingston Freeman* called it "the iron wonder!" John Rahl tried to use it for commercial bungee jumping, but the town objected. By 1991, the southern half was planked to be used as a pedestrian walkway. There's a sweeping view of the creek and the main part of the village far below to the right. The bluff to the right of the north end of the trestle is composed of dolomite of the Rondout Formation.

Wallkill Valley Rail Trail (Town of Shawangunk)

For many, the Wallkill Rail Trail appears to end at the town of Shawangunk. The truth is, there are two more segments of the rail-trail in the town of Shawangunk (Ulster County), one north and one south of the hamlet of Wallkill, located 12 miles south of New Paltz on Route 208, and a segment in the town of Montgomery (Orange County). For those who enjoy an easy walking trail, lovely rural scenery, and exceptional views of the distant Shawangunk Ridge, these trails are quite fulfilling. They're also little publicized, so you're unlikely to run into crowds here except for the occasional solitary jogger or individual out with his or her dog. The northern part begins at the corner of Railroad Avenue and C. E. Penney Drive, goes north for 1.5 miles, and ends at Birch Road. The southern part begins on Route 208 and continues south for 0.8 mile to the boundary with the town of Montgomery. Then it continues another 2.2 miles into the village of Walden. The northern part is unmarked and has no signs. However, it appears to be well maintained except for a few bumpy spots; these may challenge bicyclists, but hikers won't have any difficulty with them. This northern section is arguably one of the most scenic sections—if not the most scenic—of the entire Wallkill Valley Rail Trail. It passes through very rural countryside with a number of splendid west-facing views of the Shawangunks. Bicyclists may wish to do it in combination with some of the charming rural back roads in the area.

To get to the northern part, depart from Route 208 in the hamlet of Wallkill onto Park Avenue, which goes north and passes the library. After 0.1 mile, turn right on Main Street and make an immediate left onto Railroad Avenue. Continue north for another 0.3 mile to where Railroad Avenue bends right and turns into C. E. Penney Drive, which leads into a newer subdivision. At this juncture, there is a small parking area; the rail-trail departs on the left and continues north. After a short while, it passes a field on the left with an open view that includes the Shawangunk Ridge in the background. Right about here is a bumpy part that bicyclists may find challenging. Embankments appear on both sides of the trail, overgrown with shrubs, vines, and young trees. About two-thirds of the way along, arrive at a junction where an unpaved farm road crosses the trail. The embankment slowly recedes, exposing views of fields on both sides. These fields are part of a private hunting reserve. Please use caution and be sure to stay on the trail. Finally arrive at Birch Road, with the Wallkill Corrections Facility property across the road. Due to security concerns, no parking is allowed on the road here. Security personnel patrol this area. A right turn onto Birch Road (a dirt road) will lead 1 mile to Route 208.

The southern part of the rail-trail is referred to as the Jesse McHugh Trail. It was dedicated on June 5, 1993, and is maintained by the town of Shawangunk's Environmental Management Council. It is a multiple-use trail, although parts of it—especially after you cross into the town of Montgomery—are rough for bicyclists; the trail surface is rugged in places. You'll also find occasional downed trees and overgrown vegetation. However, these shouldn't present much of a problem for hikers. Please note that beyond the beginning, there are no markings or signs along this trail.

From the east side of Route 208, 0.1 mile north of its intersection with County Road 18 and across from the town of Shawangunk's police station, the trail heads south. There is a sign at the trailhead. Follow it as it passes a bus parking lot on the right. There are steep embankments on both sides of the trail. Pass agricultural fields on the left. Cross a dirt road. Vegetation now blocks views of nearby Route 208, but traffic noise can still be heard. After 0.75 mile, the trail crosses into the town of Montgomery and continues another 1.25 miles, past more agricultural fields and areas of shrubs and young or pioneer trees, to Lake Osiris Road, where you have to climb steep embankments on both sides. From there, it continues south for another mile into the village of Walden, finally ending at a bridge abutment near the corner of Highland Avenue and East Main Street (Route 52).

MOONBEAMS SANCTUARY

Once a dairy farm, this 150-acre nature preserve near Bloomingberg lies at an elevation of 500 to 650 feet. Its west side borders the Shawangunk Kill (the boundary between Orange and Sullivan Counties). The sanctuary provides an excellent opportunity to experience a variety of habitats typical of the valleys that lie next to the Shawangunk Ridge. The property includes eight meadows totaling 35 acres; a "cathedral" stand of mature hemlock and white pine; mixed deciduous and successional forests of black oak, American elm, hornbeam, American beech, white ash, aspen, red cedar, gray birch, sugar maple, and shagbark hickory; a pond; and a "bear" swamp with native rhododendron, wild azalea, mountain laurel, red maple, black gum, and 20 species of wildflowers. Hummingbirds and woodpeckers are often seen in the vicinity of the swamp. Partridgeberry, wintergreen, pink lady's slipper, and a variety of ferns can also be found on the property. There are west-facing views of the Shawangunk Ridge. The fields serve as nesting sites for red-winged blackbirds, meadowlarks, and bobolinks. Bluebirds nest along the edges. The meadows are feeding areas for hawks, swallows, and flycatchers. The property is managed by the Orange County Land Trust. It is open to the public for hiking, cross-country skiing, and snowshoeing, and is used as a study area by classes from Orange County Community College and by local bird-watching clubs. The site is listed in *Where to Find Birds in New York State*.

The land that is now Moonbeams Sanctuary originally consisted of four parcels. The largest was the Eliphalet Warner Farm. In 1796, Thaddeus Lockwood bought one of the other parcels from Nathaniel Tuthill. In 1855, Allan Lockwood purchased the largest parcel, and by 1871 had consolidated the four parcels into one holding. The Lockwood family sold it in 1908. The residence was used as a boardinghouse. In 1930, Raymond Dolfini bought it. Truman and Lena Moon acquired the land from the Dolfinis in 1961. Their daughter Peg Moon donated it in 1971 to The Nature Conservancy as a memorial to her parents. In 2001, The Nature Conservancy transferred ownership to the Orange County Land Trust.

To reach the sanctuary from the intersection of Routes 17K and 17, go west on Route 17K for a very short distance and make a left onto County Road 76. Follow this road south for 1.3 miles. Turn left on Prosperous Valley Road and go 0.9 mile to a T-intersection. Turn right and continue another 1.5 miles. There's a small wooden sign on the left before the pond. Just before the sign, you'll find off-road parking on the right. Moonbeans Sanctuary is located on both sides of Prosperous Valley Road.

The small trail network here is unsigned and unmarked. From the parking area, a trail diagonally crosses a field, then heads through a patch of forest. It turns right, following the boundary between field and forest. Then it bends right and returns to the parking area, again following the boundary between field and forest.

On the opposite side of the road, across from the parking area and opposite a private residence, a short spur trail descends to the shore of a 1½-acre pond that boasts a large amphibian and insect population. Herons, ducks, and migrating shorebirds can also be seen there. Another trail follows an old tree-lined farm road, climbs briefly, then turns left into an open field. The trail crosses the field and climbs to a vantage point where you have a west-

EPILOGUE:
PRESERVING THE LAND

Open space protection makes a lot of sense in the Shawangunks for a number of reasons:

1. Watershed protection has historically been a major impetus behind land preservation efforts. The large area of undeveloped land on the ridge and the fractured bedrock aquifer is an excellent source of high-quality groundwater and surface-water flow that can supply growing populations in the neighboring valleys. Streams on the ridge flow into larger streams and rivers in the neighboring valleys. The Shawangunk Ridge is part of both the Hudson and Delaware watersheds. However, the complex faulting and jointing of the bedrock creates a topography that is highly vulnerable to ground- and surface-water pollution. Land that is naturally forested retains water better, reducing runoff, which prevents soil erosion and flooding, which in turn ensures better water quality as well as an adequate supply.

Awosting Lake from Castle Point in Minnewaska State Park Preserve

2. Preservation of land on the ridge promotes biodiversity. Many species of plants and animals require huge areas of protected land to maintain viable populations. Setting aside extensive natural areas that are representative of different ecological regions, and protecting these preserves from alteration or development, will help retain the variety of communities and species of animals and plants native to the Northeast.

Pine barrens, dwarf pine plains, and ice caves are examples of rare and unique habitats deserving of special protection. Plants and animal species such as the broom crowberry and peregrine falcon, recognized as endangered or threatened at the state level, are crucial to protect in the Shawangunks. In a diverse landscape such as this, the advantage of protecting the entire region would be the preservation of a variety of habitats that a number of species of animals and plants depend on.

Land preservation in the neighboring valleys is also of great importance. These areas provide a necessary buffer without which the Shawangunk Ridge might become an island in a suburban sea. Loss of these buffer lands to development would seriously confine and degrade the Shawangunk Ridge as a habitat. It would remove lowland habitats that many upland species depend on. It would increase pollution problems, and the aesthetic impact would be severe.

3. In addition to biological resources, archaeological and historical resources may be protected through land preservation. As you've read throughout this book, the area abounds in remnants from Native American as well as pioneer, colonial, and Revolutionary War histories. It also bears the legacy of our agricultural and Industrial Age past. Preservation of these resources maintains a storehouse of data for historical and scientific research. It also provides a historical perspective that expands and deepens our awareness and appreciation of the past and the transformations that have occurred.

4. Land preservation on the ridge creates recreational opportunities. Many feel that the presence of open space is necessary for our mental, spiritual, and even physical health by providing a refuge from urban crowding and the stresses of modern life. Open space provides opportunities for privacy, solitude, and contemplation outside the confinement of our abodes. The importance of the Shawangunk Ridge for recreational purposes cannot be overstated. It is one of only three wilderness areas that lie within 100 miles of New York City and are accessible to the 20 million residents of the greater New York area. Rock climbing, hiking, mountain biking, cross-country skiing, swimming, sunbathing, horseback riding, scuba diving, bird-watching,

and other forms of nature study are just some of the reasons visitors flock to the Shawangunks.

5. Preservation of land on the ridge is good for local economies. The financial impact of tourism is considerable. Many local communities depend on it. Tourism is the primary industry in Ulster County, where the most visited portion of the ridge lies.

   Open space provides a buffer from development while preserving an area's scenic character. This ensures a higher quality of life outside the buffer, and this may in turn encourage new residents to areas that border the ridge, as well as new businesses, services, and jobs. It also forces developers to make more efficient use of land that is available. Preservation of the ridge may actually improve the economic, social, and environmental health of communities that border it.

Most open space land on the Shawangunk Ridge and in the neighboring valleys is privately owned. It remains open space for agricultural purposes, or as a privacy buffer, or for speculation, or for recreation, or for aesthetic reasons. It may belong to a resort, a sporting club, or a private individual or family. Hikers can sometimes use this property if the owner has made arrangement with a hiking club or land preservation organization. The primary issue is that maintaining the land as private open space and permitting access for low-impact recreation depend on the prerogative of the landowner(s). Landowners can and often do change their minds. They may sell the land or develop it themselves. In many cases, then, private ownership does not provide sufficient long-term protection for property whose value lies in its maintenance as open space.

PUBLIC AGENCIES

Historically, one of the primary ways that land is preserved is through direct acquisition by the state. However, lack of funds and political will has restricted these purchases. Today, the state often acquires land through indirect means. Private organizations such as The Nature Conservancy and the Open Space Institute may make the initial purchase and then sell or donate the land to the state. The New York State Department of Environmental Conservation and the Palisades Interstate Park Commission are two public agencies involved in managing these acquired lands. For public agencies, land resource management means balancing recreational and other uses with the needs for preservation.

The Department of Environmental Conservation

The New York State Department of Environmental Conservation (DEC) was created July 1, 1970, to bring together in a single agency all of the state programs directed toward protecting and enhancing the environment. From Section 1-0101 of the New York State Environmental Conservation Law, the DEC's mission is "to conserve, improve, and protect the state's natural resources and environment, and control water, land, and air pollution in order to enhance the health, safety, and welfare of the people of the state and their overall economic and social well being." The DEC is involved in regulating, dispersing, and treating toxic waste, recycling, protecting wetlands, conducting sound forestry practices on state lands, fish and wildlife management and research, public education, and managing the Adirondack and Catskill Forest Preserves. The Shawangunks are located in DEC Region 3, which includes Dutchess, Orange, Putnam, Rockland, Sullivan, Ulster, and Westchester Counties. The regional office is located in New Paltz.

The DEC manages 4 million acres of state land. Lands managed by the DEC in the Shawangunks include the 88-acre Shawangunk Multiple Use Area below the Trapps, the 2,300-acre Wurtsboro Ridge State Forest, the 1,300-acre Lands and Forest Tract south of Route 52, the 2,225-acre Basha Kill Wildlife Management Area, and 451 acres of the Witch's Hole property east of Ellenville, recently acquired from the Open Space Institute. Though the DEC plays a large role in land management in the Shawangunks, it isn't a dominant role—unlike the Catskills, for example, where the DEC manages more than 300,000 acres. This is largely because other agencies and private organizations have played such a huge role in land preservation and management in the Shawangunks.

Palisades Interstate Park Commission

The Palisades Interstate Park Commission (PIPC) was created in 1900 in an effort to save from quarry operations the Palisades cliffs overlooking the Hudson opposite New York. The New Jersey Federation of Women's Clubs was instrumental in raising awareness of this threat and gaining the necessary political support for preservation of the Palisades. This new park was administered by 10 commissioners, 5 appointed by the governor of New York and 5 by the governor of New Jersey. The park eventually expanded northward. Today, more than 100,000 acres of land on the west side of the Hudson—including Bear Mountain Harriman State Park and a number of Revolutionary War historical sites—are managed by the PIPC. This includes Minnewaska State Park Preserve and the section of the Wallkill Rail Trail that lies within the town of Gardiner.

Other Government Bodies

Counties, towns, and villages are also involved in land preservation in the valleys that flank the Shawangunk Ridge, either purchasing land or maintaining it. The National Park Service through its River, Trails, and Conservation Assistance Program is involved in the D&H Canal Heritage Corridor. This 35-mile-long corridor, located north and west of the Shawangunk Ridge, follows the historical route of the D&H Canal and the Ontario & Western Railroad. The D&H Canal was designated a National Historic Landmark in 1968. In 1988, the D&H Steering Committee was formed with help from the Rivers, Trails, and Conservation Assistance Program and the New York Parks and Conservation Association. The Rivers, Trails, and Conservation Assistance Program has acted as a catalyst and facilitator, providing expertise, coordination, and planning help. It has produced brochures, maps, newsletters, and helped fund and develop two sections of linear park—between Kingston and High Falls, and between Accord and Kerhonkson. The goals of the program are to protect historical landmarks; create trails, linear parks, and bike and canoe routes; establish educational programs; and foster a strong sense of community within the corridor.

PRIVATE NONPROFIT ORGANIZATIONS

In addition to the state, private organizations have played a huge role preserving open space in the Shawangunks. These efforts date back to the revolutionary efforts of the Smileys, who acquired nearly 20,000 acres of Shawangunk property, largely protecting it from harmful development.

Mohonk Preserve

The Mohonk Preserve is the largest private nature preserve in New York State. It began in 1963 as the Mohonk Trust. Between 1966 and 1982, 5,293 acres of land were donated or sold by the Mohonk Mountain House at a nominal fee to the preserve. Another 1,140 acres have been purchased from neighbors and organizations other than the Mountain House. Acquired lands must share a common boundary with the preserve, occupy a significant part of its viewshed, or have realistic potential for future unification with existing preserve lands. The preserve has a land acquisition fund augmented by special contributions from preserve members, grants, and help from other organizations such as the Open Space Institute and the Friends of the Shawangunks. The education programs of the preserve promote awareness of preservation issues and environmental sensitivity.

It takes a lot of knowledge to provide optimum management of this resource. To accomplish this, the Daniel Smiley Research Center, a part of the Mohonk Preserve, was built by Dan Smiley (1907–89) in 1980. Its purpose is to carry on the research of its founder and catalog environmental change over time. Dan Smiley was an avid and meticulous collector of ecological data, which he first began gathering in 1925 and continued to collect throughout his life. The other purpose of the center is to apply this information to the management of the Mohonk Preserve and other major Shawangunk properties. The center is located in the Elms, Dan Smiley's former residence. It has archives of rare books, observations, historical photographs, as well as archaeological artifacts and natural history specimens, the largest collection of ecological data on the Shawangunk Ridge and one of the largest collections of data about any one single place.

The Nature Conservancy

The Nature Conservancy is an international membership organization dedicated to the preservation of biological diversity through habitat conservation. The organization was founded in 1951. The Eastern New York Chapter was founded in 1954, the first local chapter of The Nature Conservancy. To date, the Conservancy and its members have been responsible for protecting more than 8 million acres of land in 50 states and around the world. The Eastern New York Chapter first became involved in the Shawangunk Ridge in 1969 with the purchase of the Virginia Smiley Preserve, which lies just north of the northeastern boundary of the Mohonk Preserve. The Virginia Smiley Preserve eventually grew to 408 acres and in 1993 was deeded to the Mohonk Preserve to manage and protect.

In 1970 and 1987, the Eastern Chapter assisted New York State and the Palisades Interstate Park Commission in acquiring Minnewaska State Park Preserve. In 1993, The Nature Conservancy declared the Shawangunk Ridge one of the world's 75 "Last Great Places." In 1997, working with the Open Space Institute, it was able to foster an agreement with the village of Ellenville to create Sam's Point Dwarf Pine Ridge Preserve. Today, The Nature Conservancy manages this land for the Open Space Institute. The Eastern Chapter of the Nature Conservancy maintains a local office in New Paltz. The Nature Conservancy has also been involved in land preservation in the valleys that flank the ridge. In 1971, it acquired the Moonbeams Sanctuary in the town of Wallkill, which it transferred to the Orange County Land Trust in 2001. In addition, The Nature Conservancy's Neversink Program is dedicated to protecting the Neversink River watershed, another "Last Great Place." In partnership with the Mohonk Preserve, The Nature Conservancy funds and staffs the Shawangunk Biodiversity Partnership.

Open Space Institute

OSI is a New York–based not-for-profit public charity that has operated since 1974 protecting land in New York State from development, creating parkland, preserves, and wildlife refuges and creating opportunities for low-impact recreation. Often OSI will purchase undeveloped properties and then sell or donate the land to the state or federal government. It works cooperatively with state and local governments and will join with other land trusts, conservation organizations, private clubs, or individuals. In addition to buying land, OSI helps sponsor efforts to preserve open space, enforce environmental laws, upgrade zoning, oppose unsound development, and educate the public on conservation issues. OSI also sponsors studies and provides consultation on conservation and land preservation issues.

So far, OSI has protected 130,000 acres in New York State, including nearly 17,000 on the Shawangunk Ridge. It began in 1985 with the purchase of 2,300 acres of the Wurtsboro Ridge. This land was transferred to New York State in 1989 and is now managed by the DEC. In 1993, OSI—with the help of The Nature Conservancy—acquired from the village of Ellenville what eventually became the 4,600-acre Sam's Point Dwarf Pine Ridge Preserve. In 2000—with the help of the Trust for Public Lands, a national land preservation group, and the New York–New Jersey Trail Conference—OSI acquired the 1,300-acre Lands and Forest Tract. That property was recently sold to New York State and is currently managed by the DEC. In 2000 and 2001, OSI purchased the 2,000-acre Witch's Hole property southeast of Ellenville. It includes Napanoch Point and parts of Old Smiley Road. Some of this property has already been transferred to the DEC, though most will eventually be transferred to the Palisades Interstate Park Commission and become part of Minnewaska State Park Preserve.

There have been a number of smaller purchases, as well. Some were done with the help and cooperation of the Mohonk Preserve, including the 160-acre Trapps Gateway where the new Mohonk Visitors Center is located and other purchases of land contiguous to the preserve. In 2000, OSI—with the help of the New York–New Jersey Trail Conference—acquired 90 acres at the foot of Stony Kill Falls, which will eventually become part of neighboring Minnewaska State Park Preserve. The goals of OSI are threefold: protecting 13,000 acres of wilderness that lie south of Minnewaska (this includes Sam's Point, the Witch's Hole, and Lands and Forest Tract), protecting and buffering Mohonk and Minnewaska, and creating linkages along the entire length of the ridge down to the New Jersey border and northwest, connecting the Shawangunks with the Catskills.

Conservation Easements

With limited funds, organizations are likely to use conservation easements as a means of protecting land. An easement is a legal agreement a property owner makes voluntarily to restrict some or all of the development rights on a piece of property he or she owns. The land remains in his or her possession, but the future development of the property is restricted by the terms of the easement. Easements may be purchased. Also, the donation of an easement for conservation purposes to a qualified conservation organization or public agency may be considered a tax-deductible charitable gift.

Small private nonprofit organizations like the Wallkill Valley Land Trust and the Orange County Land Trust use conservation easements to protect land. Larger organizations also use easements, often as the preferred way to protect property, especially agricultural land. The Mohonk Preserve has negotiated protective easements with 12 of its neighbors whose land borders the preserve, limiting development on these properties. These agreements help buffer the preserve, protecting viewsheds and ecosystems. The Open Space Institute has also used easements to protect agricultural lands in the Wallkill and Rondout Valleys, and the Friends of the Shawangunks has used easements to preserve land on the Shawangunk Ridge.

Friends of the Shawangunks

The Friends of the Shawangunks is a private advocacy organization whose focus is land protection in the northern Shawangunks. The organization got its start in 1963 when there was a proposal before Congress to extend Skyline Drive north from Virginia through the Shawangunks. Keith Smiley, then owner of the Mohonk Mountain House, used the 30,000 names on the Mohonk guest mailing list to contact enough influential friends to quell the idea. Thus the Friends of the Shawangunks was created. In the early days, it was a small, loosely organized club. Between 1979 and 1987, the Friends became embroiled in efforts to prevent the Marriott Corporation from developing Minnewaska Lake. Since then, the organization has grown in size and membership. In 1985, it was involved in efforts that prevented the development of a 1,200-acre wind energy farm near Sam's Point. Today, it is actively promoting land preservation and fighting development. In recent years, it has become more involved in preservation efforts in the southern Shawangunks. It is a member of the Shawangunk Biodiversity Project.

The Shawangunk Conservancy, a sister organization of the Friends, was formed in 1988 at a time when no other environmental organization was purchasing land in the northern Shawangunks. Its primary purpose is to protect lands along the Shawangunk Ridge through either acquisition or conservation easements. Most of its purchases have been of small but critically important tracts adjacent to the Mohonk Preserve.

The Friends of the Shawangunks currently has 600 members. It offers a great newsletter with wonderful articles about Shawangunk issues.

Other advocacy groups include te New York–New Jersey Trail Conference and the Basha Kill Area Association.

Low-Impact Development

Considering the kind of development pressures now affecting the Shawangunk Ridge, it is inevitable that more development will take place in those areas that have not been protected. However, new development need not be as destructive as past development has been. *The Shawangunk Ridge Conservation and Design Guidebook,* written by David Church and John Myers for the Catskill Center for Conservation and Development (1993), provides guidelines to ensure that future developments on the ridge are more sensitive to the environment.

The authors provide a number of examples of hypothetical good and bad development. They recommend that on large properties, residential development be clustered on one side or in one corner of the property, preferably on sites of lower elevation closer to existing roads. This preserves the majority of the property, especially the higher, more sensitive and unique parts, for trail corridors and recreation, water resource protection, and habitat for plants and animals.

They recommend design guidelines for new homes and structures that encourage blending in with the landscape and siting to avoid obstructing or degrading public views. Cutting forest for construction and access should be limited as much as possible. New homes and structures should be buffered by native vegetation. Where such vegetation is absent, new native vegetation may be planted as a screen. They prefer the use of stone or natural wood siding and the use of earth-toned colors for roofing. They also advocate restrictions on exterior lighting and the prohibition of billboards and other signs beyond business sites. They recommend the use of underground wires for all communication lines servicing new developments, and discourage the construction of new telecommunication towers while encouraging the shared use of current towers.

The Biodiversity Partnership

The Shawangunk Ridge lies within three counties and 11 towns, all of which have different rules and for the most part act independently of one another when it comes to land use. What one community does in the sector may impact others. Seeing the Shawangunk Ridge as a single entity and treating it as such is a challenge many groups and organizations face as they work on preservation issues. The Biodiversity Partnership is a consortium of 10 not-for-profit organizations and government agencies working together to assure protection and appropriate stewardship for the land. Members of the Shawangunk Ridge Biodiversity Partnership share resources and ideas to guide protective actions by individual partners for the lands they own or manage. The partnership has developed management plans to assure the continued viability and sustainability of rare species and natural communities and to encourage human uses of the ridge that are compatible with maintaining the ecological resources of the Shawangunks.

A clear understanding of the natural communities of the Shawangunks and how they are maintained is critical to making informed resource management decisions. The partnership launched a coordinated research program to inventory and study the natural communities, and now uses this information as a foundation for planning protection for the region's most unique and fragile areas.

Members of the Biodiversity Partnership include the Friends of the Shawangunks, the Mohonk Preserve, Inc., The Nature Conservancy, the Open Space Institute, the New York Natural Heritage Program, the New York State Department of Environmental Conservation's Division of Fish and Wildlife, the New York State Museum, the Palisades Interstate Park Commission, and the New York State Office of Parks, Recreation and Historic Preservation.

RESOURCES

Name	Address	Phone	Web Site
Adirondack Mountain Club	814 Goggins Road Lake George, NY 12845 Mid-Hudson Chapter P.O. Box 3674 Poughkeepsie, NY 12603	1-518-668-4447 1-800-395-8080	www.adk.org
Basha Kill Area Association, Inc.	P.O. Box 1121 Wurtsboro, NY 12790		
Cragsmoor Historical Society	Cragsmoor Road Cragsmoor, NY 12566	845-647-2362	
Delaware & Hudson Canal Museum	P.O. Box 23 High Falls, NY 12440	845-687-9311	www.canalmuseum.org
Ellenville/Wawarsing Chamber of Commerce	5 Berme Road Ellenville, NY 12428	845-647-4620	
Friends of the Shawangunks	P.O. Box 270 Accord, NY 12404	845-687-4759	
Highland Flings Footloose Holidays	P.O. Box 1034 Kingston, NY 12402	1-800-453-6665	www.highlandflings.com
Huguenot Historical Society	18 Broadhead Avenue New Paltz, NY 12561-1403	845-255-1660	www.hhs-newpaltz.org
International Mountain Bike Association (IMBA)	P.O. Box 7578 Boulder, CO 80306	303-545-9011	www.imba.com
Minisink Valley Historical Society	127 West Main Street Port Jervis, NY 12771	845-856-2375	www.minisink.org
Minnewaska State Park Preserve	P.O. Box 893 Route 44/55 New Paltz, NY 12561	845-255-0752	
Mohonk Mountain House	New Paltz, NY 12561	1-800-772-6646	www.mohonk.com
Mohonk Preserve	P.O. Box 715 New Paltz, NY 12561	845-255-0919	www.mohonkpreserve.org
Nature Conservancy, The	Eastern Chapter North Moger Avenue Mount Kisco, NY 10549 Shawangunks Office 108 Main Street New Paltz, NY 12561	914-244-3271 845-255-9051	http://nature.org

Name	Address	Phone	Website
New Paltz Chamber of Commerce	124 Main Street New Paltz, NY 12561	845-255-0243	www.newpaltz chamber.org
Neversink Valley Area Museum	26 Hoag Road Cuddebackville, NY 12729	845-754-8870	
New York–New Jersey Trail Conference	156 Ramapo Valley Road Route 202 Mahwah, NJ 07430	201-512-9348	www.nynjtc.org
New York State Department of Environmental Conservation Region 3	21 South Putt Corners Road New Paltz, NY 12561-1696	845-256-3000	www.dec.state.ny.us
Open Space Institute	1350 Broadway, #201 New York, NY 10018	212-629-3981	www.osiny.org
Orange County Land Trust	P.O. Box 2442 Middletown, NY 10940	845-343-0840	
Orange County Tourism	30 Mathews Street, Suite 111 Goshen, NY 10924	845-291-2136 1-800-762-8687	www.orangetourism.org
Sam's Point Dwarf Pine Ridge Preserve	Sam's Point Road Cragsmoor, NY 12566	845-647-7989	
State University of New York at New Paltz	75 South Manhein Boulevard New Paltz, NY 12561	845-257-2121	
Sullivan County Parks and Recreation Department	100 North Street Monticello, NY 12701	845-794-3000 ext. 5002	http://co.sullivan.ny.us
Sullivan County Visitors Association	100 North Street Monticello, NY 12701	845-794-3000 ext. 5010	www.scva.net
Table Rock Tours and Bicycles	292 Main Street Rosendale, NY 12472	845-658-7832	www.tablerocktours.com
Tri-State Chamber of Commerce	P.O. Box 121 Port Jervis, NY 12771	845-856-6694	www.tristatechamber.org
Ulster County Traveler's Information	10 Westbrook Lane Kingston, NY 12401 Mailing address: P.O. Box 1800 Kingston, NY 12402	1-800-DIAL-U-CO	www.co.ulster.ny.us
Wallkill Valley Land Trust	P.O. Box 208 New Paltz, NY 12561	845-255-2761	
Wallkill Valley Rail Trail	P.O. Box 1048 New Paltz, NY 12561		www.gorailtrail.org